AF905509

This is an outstanding collection of papers that address deeply contested questions about the nature and foundations of human rights, and in particular, consider to what extent an institutional, contextual, and 'functional' approach can bypass philosophical enquiries aimed at establishing moral truths. All readers, whether they are new to these debates or already well acquainted with them, will be richly rewarded.

Jeffrey Goldsworthy, Monash University

Political and Legal Approaches to Human Rights

This collection of essays explores and illustrates issues arising from 'political' approaches to human rights in contrast to the more traditional 'moral' and 'legal' approaches. The book contributes to the understanding and analysis of 'political approaches', including consideration of their diversity, and discussion of their strengths and weaknesses. The contributors present a balance between those who favour some version of the political approach and those who are dubious about the perceived advantages. The chapters are grouped together in parts which constitute the distinctive issues addressed in the book.

At a time when there is considerable uncertainty concerning their conceptual clarity, operation, feasibility, and their normative justifications, this volume will be of interest to those involved with the theory and practice of human rights, within law schools, and in politics and philosophy departments. It will also provide a useful resource for human rights practitioners and policy makers.

Tom Campbell is an Adjunct Research Associate at Charles Sturt University, Australia, formerly Professorial Fellow in the Centre for Applied Philosophy and Public Ethics (CAPPE), previously Professor of Law at The Australian National University and prior to that Professor of Jurisprudence at the University of Glasgow, UK. He has published extensively on Legal Theory and Political Philosophy.

Dr Kylie Bourne is Senior Research Assistant at the Regional Australia Institute. She was formerly Research Assistant at Charles Sturt University and prior to that, Research Management Coordinator in the College of Law at the Australian National University.

Political and Legal Approaches to Human Rights

Edited by
Tom Campbell and
Kylie Bourne

Routledge
Taylor & Francis Group
LONDON AND NEW YORK

First published 2018
by Routledge

2 Park Square, Milton Park, Abingdon, Oxfordshire OX14 4RN
52 Vanderbilt Avenue, New York, NY 10017

Routledge is an imprint of the Taylor & Francis Group, an informa business

First issued in paperback 2019

Copyright © 2018 selection and editorial matter, Tom Campbell and Kylie Bourne; individual chapters, the contributors

The right of Tom Campbell and Kylie Bourne to be identified as the authors of the editorial material, and of the authors for their individual chapters, has been asserted in accordance with sections 77 and 78 of the Copyright, Designs and Patents Act 1988.

All rights reserved. No part of this book may be reprinted or reproduced or utilised in any form or by any electronic, mechanical, or other means, now known or hereafter invented, including photocopying and recording, or in any information storage or retrieval system, without permission in writing from the publishers.

Notice:
Product or corporate names may be trademarks or registered trademarks, and are used only for identification and explanation without intent to infringe.

British Library Cataloguing-in-Publication Data
A catalogue record for this book is available from the British Library

Library of Congress Cataloging-in-Publication Data
Names: Campbell, Tom (Law professor), author. | Bourne, Kylie, author.
Title: Political and legal approaches to human rights / Tom Campbell, Kylie Bourne.
Description: Abingdon, Oxon [UK] ; New York : Routledge, 2017. | Includes bibliographical references and index.
Identifiers: LCCN 2017028353 | ISBN 9781138744585 (hardback) | ISBN 9781351717182 (adobe reader) | ISBN 9781351717175 (epub) | ISBN 9781351717168 (mobipocket)
Subjects: LCSH: Human rights. | Human rights—Philosophy. | Human rights—Political aspects. | Human rights—Social aspects. | Human rights—Economic aspects.
Classification: LCC K3240 .C3625 2017 | DDC 342.08/5—dc23
LC record available at https://lccn.loc.gov/2017028353

ISBN: 978-1-138-74458-5 (hbk)
ISBN: 978-0-367-88698-1 (pbk)

Typeset in Galliard
by Apex CoVantage, LLC

Contents

Contributors

James Allan, Professor of Law, University of Queensland

Sonu Bedi, Associate Professor, Dartmouth College

Kylie Bourne, Research Associate, Charles Sturt University

Tom Campbell, Adjunct Research Associate, Charles Sturt University

Jovana Davidovic, Assistant Professor, University of Ohio

Octavio Luiz Motta Ferraz, Reader in Transnational Law, King's College London

Duncan Ivison, Professor of Philosophy, University of Sydney

Suzy Killmister, Assistant Professor, Human Rights Institute, University of Connecticut

David Kinley, Professor of Human Rights Law, University of Sydney

Denise Meyerson, Professor of Law, Macquarie University

Seumas Miller, Professorial Fellow, Chares Sturt University

Rhiannon Neilsen, Research Associate, Charles Sturt University

John Tasioulas, Director, Centre for Politics, Philosophy and Law, King's College London

Laura Valentini, Associate Professor of Political Science, London School of Economics

Caroline West, Senior Lecturer in Philosophy, University of Sydney

Introduction

Tom Campbell and Kylie Bourne

Political and Legal Approaches to Human Rights explores and illustrates issues arising from recent attention given to 'political' (or 'practical') approaches to human rights, in contrast to 'orthodox moral' approaches, which are said to conceptualize and justify human rights in terms of specific priority rights which are both universal and morally overriding. Political approaches focus on those human rights practices involved in the development and operation of human rights institutions, including human rights laws and political procedures, in relative independence from their alleged moral foundations. Our aim is to contribute to the understanding, analysis and critique of political approaches to human rights, including consideration of their diversity, and discussion of their strengths and weaknesses. We explore this recent and relatively novel perspective on human rights, generated at a time when there is considerable uncertainty concerning the conceptual clarity, the efficacy, and the normative justifications of human rights.

What we are identifying as 'political approaches' to human rights were pioneered by John Rawls in *The Law of Peoples* (1999),[1] developed by Joseph Raz in 'Human Rights without Foundations' (2010)[2] and manifest in the recent work of political philosophers, such as Charles Beitz, *The Idea of Human Rights* (2009),[3] and Allen Buchanan, *The Heart of Human Rights* (2014),[4] along with a recent extensive collection of essays, *Philosophical Foundations of Human Rights* (2015), edited by Rowan Cruft, S. Matthew Liao, and Massimo Renzo,[5] which devotes considerable attention to, and offers some support for, political approaches. This literature challenges the contemporary relevance of orthodox moral approaches to human rights, which are said to be unhelpfully abstract and timeless and divert attention from the understanding and improvement of contemporary human rights practice, in both political and legal domains.

The persistent lack of theoretical agreement regarding the meaning, application, and justification of human rights, together with a degree of scepticism regarding their foundations, has prompted philosophical focus to move away from the pursuit of theoretical or cultural unanimity as to the content and moral justification of human rights, and attend instead to obtaining more cross-cultural agreement on the standards and mechanisms with which states could actually hold each other to account with respect to how they mistreat their own citizens and how they violate the human rights of persons within other states. This sets up a more practical approach which involves critique of, or intervention in, the domestic affairs of those states that are considered to be violating 'human rights' standards. It is claimed that this can be done without reaching agreement as to the content and justification of universal and absolute moral rights founded on a common human nature.

Consequently, abstract moral analyses of human rights, such as those which focus on what are claimed to be overriding universal moral rights which human beings have in virtue of their humanity, are challenged by the broadening scope of publically identified human rights, social and economic as well as civil and political, as they develop within both national and international contexts. Although not often implemented, external state interventions are associated with contemporary human rights practice. In these circumstances, philosophical pragmatists consider it is better to think of human rights, not as abstract moral formulae, but in real political and legal norms.

In this vein, Beitz suggests that philosophers should pay more attention to 'the emerging practice of human rights' which he sees as 'a public political project with its own distinctive forms of action, and culture'.[6] In his view, pre-political conceptualizations of human rights, such as universal priority rights which defend the dignity or equality of all human beings on the basis of their humanity, neither describe human rights as they operate today nor suffice to determine the scope and content that human rights institutions ought to promote.

In contrast, more orthodox moral theorists reject this scenario, claiming that political approaches rob human rights of their distinctive moral basis and with it their implicit political priority, pointing out that traditional human rights theory is in fact concerned with implementation as well as definition, and noting that political approaches do have a place for a variety of moral justifications, which are normally grounded in a plurality of moral values. Orthodox moral theorists therefore see no difficulty in reconciling political with orthodox moral approaches in ways which retain strong normative foundations for human rights, together with realistic approaches as to their practical implementation.

Most of the contributors to this collection of essays explore the possibilities of such harmonized political and orthodox viewpoints, at least in relation to the key defining features of both current political and orthodox moral approaches. In the process, they expose a number of misrepresentations and misunderstandings as to what each approach embodies, factors that tend to exaggerate the differences between the various approaches. Other contributors explore what they see as major underlying disagreements that highlight significant differences of opinion as to the preferred content and political role of human rights. Together, the essays cover a wide range of substantive discussions concerning the advantages and disadvantages of adopting political or orthodox moral approaches, particularly when it comes to finding practical solutions to the problems that arise in the definition and implementation of human rights in a range of specific contexts.

Part I: Identifying Political Approaches

Part I has five chapters, each of which articulates a particular conception of a political approach to human rights, together with an exploration of its explanatory potential as well as its practical benefits. This serves the purpose of presenting and commenting on the variety of contentions to be found within political approaches.

In Chapter 1, 'Human Rights Morality and Human Rights Practice: An Interactive Approach', Tom Campbell presents political approaches as attempting to engage in political debate about desirable human rights developments, drawing on a broad range of practitioner moral values, and joining in the interaction between morally charged political debate and the feasibility of achieving successful implementation. Developing this theme, Campbell outlines an 'interactive model' which considers the interplay of human rights principles and human rights practices. He notes that sceptical responses to the increasing variety of human rights claims have given rise to less 'moral' and more 'political' approaches within the philosophy of human rights, and sees political approaches as focusing on the current practice of human rights, while rejecting traditional moral theories which seek to conceptualize human rights on the basis of their universality and distinctive moral foundations, without sufficient reference to their current and potential political functions.

Drawing on the work of Joseph Raz, Charles Beitz, and Allen Buchanan, Campbell encourages taking into account existing human rights practices, including the mechanisms which feature in their institutionalization. He then explores ways of modifying political approaches to render them more inclusive of human rights morality and more interactive with respect to the relationship between abstract moral justifications and the objectives and mechanisms emerging within human rights practice.

In Chapter 2, 'Human Rights for Non-Believers', Caroline West takes a similar line with respect to normative perspectives within political approaches, presenting this in the ontological terminology of 'political constructivism', within which holds human rights are regarded as entities whose nature and existence constitutively depend on the existence of certain political institutions and practices. This results in a moderately sceptical version of a political approach which holds that human rights justifications do not need to be grounded in practice-independent values. West's analysis is deployed to support the currently influential political approach which holds that human rights are essentially political constructs: entities whose nature and existence constitutively depend on the operation of certain political institutions and practices.

The most common philosophical objection to political approaches is that they sever human rights from their customary normative underpinnings. The criticism is that, if human rights are simply the product of human rights practice, then human rights determinations are arbitrary, and may lack moral justification. The principal aim of West's chapter is to show that this line of criticism is misguided, for human rights do not need to be grounded in a set of practice-independent values in order to play the important roles they do in international political life. Moreover, she argues, the 'foundationalist' insistence on the necessity of providing such a moral grounding poses threats to the acceptance, and therefore the success, of human rights practice.

In Chapter 3, 'Traces of Recognition: Rights and Political Realism', Duncan Ivison presents a political approach in terms of 'realism', arguing that there is something important missing in the discourse of human rights if their existence conditions do not include an element of 'social recognition'.

The question he poses is whether or not a suitably realist account of the existence conditions of rights, as well as the social and political requirements for their implementation, helps us address the challenge of enduring injustices. One response is to say that the only rights that really exist are legal rights, and if not literally legal rights, then rights that are either actually, or in principle, enforceable. One function of human rights, for example, is to provide critical standards in conditions where the interests to which certain rights claims refer are not currently enforceable, and to help us create the conditions in which they could be enforced. However, Ivison notes that there is a range of urgent interests that are not immediately or universally enforceable as rights which we would hesitate to dismiss as human rights altogether. Nevertheless, a 'politically realist' account of rights must build some aspect of the social recognition thesis into the determination of the existence conditions of human rights.

In Chapter 4, 'A Practical Account of the Concept of Human Rights', Jovana Davidovic presents a conceptual version of a political approach which opens the way for the idea that human rights must be sensitive to human rights practice. She develops the thesis that political approaches to human rights have the purpose of conceptualizing, in morally neutral terms, what counts as a human right, a matter which precedes addressing normative issues as to what human rights we ought to adopt. In contemporary terms, this means viewing human rights in accordance with what is taken to be human rights practice. Davidovic therefor calls for a clear conception of human rights in terms of its current usage, prior to discussing both practical and normative questions, and holds to the view that this must be tied to what can be referred to as contemporary human rights institutionalization. However, this does not mean that this sort of practical approach does not also provide a measure of normative moral guidance.

Davidovic goes on to point out that analyses of human rights tend to be open, either to the criticism from the practitioner side that they are too idealistic and 'top-down', or to criticism from the philosopher's side, that they are too dependent on the way human rights practice is in fact, rather than how it ought to be. She argues that it is possible to ground the conceptual analysis of human rights in their practice without falling prey to worries about not being able to criticize such a practice. This is done by asking what counts as a conceptual analysis of human rights and what the purpose is, in having such an account. Being clear on that, we can then find a place for a concept of human rights that is sensitive to the practice of human rights. She suggests that one relatively successful attempt at providing just such an analysis, is to be found in Charles Beitz's 'practical' account of the nature of human rights.[7]

Rounding off Part One, in Chapter 5, 'Deriving Human Rights from Human Dignity: A Novel Political Approach', Suzy Killmister casts doubt on the assumption that orthodox human rights are individualistic while political approaches are more group-oriented, with respect to both the right-holders and the correlative duty-bearers. This enables her to identify a political approach in terms of a conception of dignity which features membership of the global community of human beings, thereby excluding individualist interpretations of human dignity in order to identify human rights.[8]

Developing this analysis of the concept of dignity, Killmister takes human rights to involve the articulation in the public morality of world politics of the idea that each person is a subject of global concern.[9] Putting aside foundationalist accounts, she then uses her conception of dignity as a status that persons attain through membership in a normative community. Dignity is violated, on this analysis, when individuals are prevented from upholding the standards applicable to them *qua* group members. Human rights enter the picture primarily as a mechanism for treating individuals in accordance with their standing *qua* membership in the global community of human beings. On this analysis, human rights violations are an affront to human dignity, an approach to human rights which fulfils three key desiderata, in that (1) it can account for the fact that human rights are borne by all human beings, (2) it allows for human rights to expand in scope and content, as global social and political conditions improve, and (3) it explains the normative weight human rights are expected to carry.

Part Two: Critiquing Political Approaches

Part Two has three chapters, each of which focuses on specific alleged shortcomings of political approaches to human rights. John Tasioulas critiques misrepresentation of the orthodox moral approach, while Denise Meyerson identifies inaccuracies with respect to alleged human rights practices, and James Allan points to the democratic deficit that arises in the implementation of orthodox moral approaches.

In Chapter 6, 'Exiting the Hall of Mirrors: Morality and Law in Human Rights', John Tasioulas examines the debate between the moral and political accounts of human rights from the perspective of international human rights law (IHRL). He rejects Allen Buchanan's claims[10] that all the orthodox moral approaches (1) fail to engage with important questions concerning the nature, and justifiability, of a system of IHRL, (2) hold to the mistaken view that IHRL should 'mirror' timeless universal moral human rights, and (3) cannot adequately respond to the contention that IHRL includes rights which protect the public good and not just the interests of individual rights-holders.

Tasioulas goes on to argue that Buchanan's own approach to explaining the nature of IHRL in terms of constraining state sovereignty, in order to protect the equal moral status of all persons and secure for them a minimal level of well-being, is parasitic on the orthodox moral approach which explains the functions of human rights in terms of universal moral rights, as Tasioulas himself agrees.

In Chapter 7, 'The Mismatch between Theory and Practice in Recent Theorizing about Human Rights', Denise Meyerson examines the views of Charles Beitz and Joseph Raz, that our philosophical understanding of human rights should be guided by the way in which human rights are understood in the international practice of human rights. Meyerson argues that the descriptive and normative aspects of their enterprise pull apart at this point. She suggests that the international practice of human rights imposes arbitrary constraints on their theorizing, by forcing them to reproduce elements of the practices that are irrelevant from the normative point of view, and that, in other ways, their normative views do not align with the international practice. This brings it about that there are respects in which the practice of human rights leads them astray and respects in which their normative theories are not relevant to the practice.

Three specific examples are explored by Meyerson. The first concerns using the international practice of human rights to set the agenda for philosophical reflection on human rights, which forces Beitz and Raz to focus exclusively on responses to violations of human rights that are warranted at the international level. Yet many of the responses they discuss may be warranted only at the domestic level, and from the moral perspective it is difficult to see how it can be appropriate to conceptualize human rights as rights whose violation necessarily deserves to be remedied only at one of the two possible levels. Second, Meyerson questions Raz's claim that reflection on the practice of human rights supports his view that human rights are rights that provide a morally sound justification for sovereignty-limiting measures. Third, Beitz and Raz take a strongly state-centric approach, one in which human rights are essentially moral standards applying only to states. Again they both claim that this is how human rights are conceptualized within the practice of human rights. However, international human rights law has resorted to increasingly technical understandings of the ways in which states can fail to fulfil their human rights responsibilities, making the requisite nexus with governmental misconduct difficult to discern.

In Chapter 8, 'Human Rights, Doubts and Democracy', James Allan develops a critique of the political approach, attributed to Charles Beitz, by outlining a largely sceptical position on foundational approaches to human rights, if these are taken to be moral rather than legal, on the grounds that there is no way of determining objectively what are the morally best democratic foundations. Similarly, no decisive justification of democracy can be given, so that there is no rational basis for subjecting decisions about the content and interpretation of human rights to democratic procedures. There is therefore no non-debatable, non-contentious answer as to the source or genealogy of these non-legal human rights.

Given these doubts, Allan contends that Beitz cannot be faulted for remaining agnostic about foundational moral justifications of human rights and the desirability of the democratic procedures when these conflict with human rights practice. However, Beitz can still be criticized, on consequentialist grounds, drawn from what he often mistakenly takes to be facts about human rights practice. Doubts therefore remain about the political approaches attempts to circumnavigate the shortcomings of political approaches by focusing on the currently accepted human rights practice.

Part Three: Accommodating Economic Rights

Part Three consists of three chapters, which discuss how far political approaches can accommodate economic human rights. It is to be expected that orthodox moral approaches have difficulties in this regard, given the feasibility issue arising from their idealistic liberal assumptions. However, political approaches have their own difficulties with respect to locating the correlative duties on which a system of rights depends. As a result, the analysis of economic rights brings to the fore controversies concerning the practicality and questionable determinacy of socio-economic human rights, such as rights to health care, education, housing, and social security.

In Chapter 9, Octavio Ferraz in 'Two Conceptions of Social and Economic Rights: Basic Needs versus Equality' deals with problems arising from the indeterminacy of the correlative duties to social and economic rights to such matters as health, education, housing, and other socio-economic interests. Ferraz suggests that this indeterminacy can be overcome by relying rather more on equality of opportunity, and rather less on basic needs, when determining the allocation of content and quantity within the feasible scope of available resources within a society. This, he considers, could receive 'a reasonable degree of consensus around both why these socio-economic interests ought to be regarded as rights (justification) and what concrete duties these rights give rise to (content).'[11] This reads, very much like a political approach backed by a justice framework.

In Chapter 10, 'The Politics of Human Rights and Finance', David Kinley also is concerned with the issue of open-endedness and indeterminacy regarding the nature and quantum of the correlative duties to economic human rights, adding to his analysis that strong self-interest is an exacerbating factor. His solutions may be said to call for more engagement with financial mechanisms and investigating ways of overcoming the practical limitations of human nature though appropriate political orders.

Kinley points out that the task of financing human rights objectives sufficiently and sustainably is exhausting and never-ending. This is so because of financial greed, selfishness, and systemic complexity. Indeed, the uphill task is made even harder by the lack of effective engagement with financial considerations in both public and private sectors, by human rights scholars, advocates and institutions. To gain traction on these issues, the human rights community desperately needs to improve its understanding of the motivations, limitations and complexities of financial systems, while at the same time explaining precisely what it is that human rights organizations can expect from financial institutions, and how that can be achieved.

In Chapter 11, 'Human Rights, the Political View, and Transnational Corporations: An Exploration', Laura Valentini considers the economic role of transnational corporations.

She examines the popular view within political theory which holds that only political agents – typically states – can be primary bearers of human-rights duties, in which case the political view cannot account for the human-rights responsibilities of powerful non-state actors, such as transnational corporations. Valentini responds to this challenge by suggesting a more plausible understanding of what counts as a political agent, holding that a corporation qualifies as political agent if it exhibits what she calls an 'authority-plus-sovereignty package' together with the capacity to discharge such duties. Since some existing transnationals meet these two conditions, Valentini concludes that they count as bearers of primary human rights responsibilities even from a recognizably political perspective, thus articulating a strong case for recognizing the human rights responsibilities of powerful and affluent corporations, especially within the borders of states which are organizational failures or controlled by recalcitrant governments.

Part Four: Beyond the Nation State?

While political approaches have the apparent advantage that, with respect to those duties which are correlative to human rights, they are concerned largely with the functions of nation states, in both domestic and international settings. Nevertheless, there appear to be many examples of individuals and non-state institutions having correlative human rights duties, both to refrain from human rights violations and acting to counter them. Similarly, in Chapter 12, 'The Absence of Horizontal Effect in Human Rights Law: Domestic Violence and the Intimate Sphere', Sonu Bedi presents a powerful example of this with respect to domestic violence, extreme cases of which are readily considered to be violations of human rights, despite the fact that they are perpetuated by family members rather than by states. Again, in Chapter 13: 'The 'Human' Right to Self-Defence: Natural, Institutional or Political Right?', Seumas Miller mounts an examination of the role of self-defence with respect to protecting human rights, and, in Chapter 14: 'Beitz's Two-Level Modelof Human Rights and Statelessness', Kylie Bourne emphasizes the need to remedy the gap in human rights implementation that arises because of the lack of protection for stateless persons within nation states.

Removing the monopoly of states with respect to both the violation and the protection of human rights can be viewed as providing a harmonizing compromise, either between the political and the orthodox moral approaches, or broadening the range of what counts as a political agent with respect to human rights. Certainly most political approaches have no difficulty in incorporating non-governmental institutional sources as human rights violators and/or as responsible for undertaking remedial arrangements. Alternatively, they could follow Allen Buchanan's example by including only international human rights law as the locus of human rights practice. However, the structural differences still remain, in that the orthodox moral approach tends to abstract from the contemporary context of human rights institutions, while political approaches take these for granted.

In Chapter 12, Sonu Bedi presents domestic violence as a problem of global dimensions and notes that feminists make clear that the claimed private or intimate sphere makes it difficult to deal with the perpetration of domestic violence. Human rights law and, in particular, the Convention to End Discrimination Against Women (CEDAW) represent extant efforts to bring the language of human rights to bear on the problem of domestic violence. This invites us to consider these efforts in light of the distinction between the political and moral conception of human rights. Although this distinction is a familiar one in current philosophy of human rights, its relationship to domestic violence and the intimate sphere has gone largely unnoticed. Bedi points out that human rights law tries to deal with the problem of domestic violence by contemplating only states, not individuals, as the relevant duty bearers. In this case, the political approach to human rights fits in with this feature of human rights law, while its orthodox moral counterpart challenges this perspective, contemplating both individuals and states as the relevant duty bearers. As a result, the orthodox moral conception goes further than its political counterpart in authorizing human rights protection against domestic violence.

In Chapter 13: 'The 'Human' Right to Self-Defence: Natural, Institutional or Political Right?', Seumas Miller draws on the insights of the political approach to human rights, arguing that the right of an individual human being to defend him/herself against an aggressor is, or should be, a human right. Some theorists hold that the individualistic and the collectivist rights of self-defence are entirely different, but Miller contends that they are closely related, as both rights are ultimately grounded in natural, universal properties as well as in contingent, institutional (notably, political) considerations.

Finally, in Chapter 14, Kylie Bourne, presents 'Beitz's Two-Level Model of Human Rights and Statelessness' in order to reflect on human rights for stateless individuals or groups. She points out that observed practice shows that human rights are primarily linked to citizenship. Without access to this citizenship, a stateless person is not assured that her claims will be fulfilled. For this reason, the international community, rather than acting as a direct guarantor for human rights claims of stateless persons *per se*, is primarily concerned with obtaining citizenship for them so that such claims can then be made. Thus, on Beitz's two-level model, citizenship acts as a quasi-foundation for human rights claims by stateless persons, who, by definition, are unable to effectively ground their demands.

Bourne holds that this model does not adequately address the status of human rights claims that remain unfulfilled due to an implementation deficit in current international practice. In failing to consider this deficit in the functioning of the international community as a guarantor for human rights claims, the model suggests that unfulfilled claims may not be associated with human rights generally in the first instance. However, statelessness is a complex international problem, the solution to which requires sustained cooperation between states, regions, and other non-government organizations. It is particularly vulnerable to the non-cooperation of state actors, complicated diplomatic relationships, and regional politics that characterize the implementation deficit.

Yet it does not necessarily follow that an unfulfilled human rights claim of a stateless person asserts the existence of a mere interest rather than a genuine human right. This means that sharp focus on states as primary duty bearers of human rights does not allow adequate scope for the kinds of dynamic regional solutions that are emerging in response to current instances of statelessness and irregular migration. The competent participants in the present international practice extend beyond states and Beitz's model does not adequately reflect this. Nevertheless, this mode may be seen as an improvement on orthodox moral conceptions of human statelessness as predictable threats to human rights in the modern world. This could lead to the consideration of extending the scope and role of primary duty-bearers beyond states, so that stateless persons may be better placed to make effective human rights claims.

Political Approaches: Democratic or Judicial?

This introduction, together with the chapters that follow, seek to avoid head-on challenges directed at those who see the vital aspect of human rights institutionalization to be the empowerment of courts to override democratic political decision-making, as when they judge ordinary legislation to be invalid because it is contrary to existing charters or bills of rights, either domestic or international. This may be regarded as an exercise of 'judicial' rather than 'political' power, or as a political mode of judicial power.

Much depends here on a complex of ambiguous terminology, often drawn upon to critique court administered bills of rights for being 'political' instead of 'judicial', inferring that there is a clear distinction between political and judicial action, while others take the view that there is at the very least a substantial overlap between legislation and adjudication, so that lawmaking cannot be confined to legislatures. It may still be said that normally legislatures legislate while courts interpret what is legislated, and yet in effect make laws in so doing. Such disagreements around and within the terminology of 'political' are familiar in the ongoing debate between the jurisprudential factions representing or opposing 'legal positivism', either with respect to empirical questions as to how legal systems can or do operate in practice, or as commending how legal systems ought to operate, based on their normative moral judgments as to what laws ought to be made and by whom.

The development of legal theories around the terminology of political approaches to human rights may be seen as combining scepticism as to the possibility of strict division of labour between legislatures as law makers and courts as law appliers, the first requiring moral debate and investigation of practicalities, and the second ideally applying clear and comprehensive enacted rules to, often complex, factual situations. For most legal theorists, the latter is an idealistic goal which has a limited feasibility but there remains some commitment to a limited division of legitimate power between legislatures and courts, especially if the former involves dominant democratic procedures, and the latter have independence in judicial interpretation and enforcement.

On this basis, within these parameters, it may seem appropriate to locate human rights implementation primarily within the confines of democratic process, together with a dominant degree of judicial deference to legislatures so far as this is feasible. Inevitably this accepts an element of the 'political', within the scope of substantive human rights decision-making in courts, for this often involves determining the outcomes of value laden disagreements about the meaning and implication of the human rights in question. However, this does not require that institutionalized human rights procedures are controlled primarily by courts rather than democratic legislatures.

What it does mean is that, however we understand what is 'political' about political approaches to human rights, it is best to exclude those approaches which are 'moral' in the orthodox sense that they rest on abstract intuitive truths that can be determined independently of democratic political considerations and contingent circumstances. This is not to say that moral considerations are not relevant to determining what ought to be adopted as human rights or how they should be conceptualized and administered, but it does mean that we should not make the mistake of assuming that we can identify human rights as morally overriding truths independently of a measure of political realism and contingent political circumstances.

This scenario need not be read as an effort to involve an extensive variety of approaches to human rights, but it is designed to encourage seeking an acceptable combination of realistic political approaches to human rights in democratic states and in relation to less stringent requirements with respect to the sort of political approaches to human rights which can illuminate and contribute to international as well as domestic domains.

Notes

1 John Rawls, *The Law of Peoples* (Cambridge: Harvard University Press, 1999).
2 Joseph Raz, 'Human Rights without Foundations', in *The Philosophy of International Law,* edited by Samantha Besson and John Tasioulas (Oxford: Oxford University Press, 2010).
3 Charles Beitz, *The Idea of Human Rights* (Oxford: Oxford University Press, 2009).
4 Allen Buchanan, *The Heart of Human Rights*, (Oxford: Oxford University Press, 2014).
5 Rowan Cruft, S. Matthew Liao and Massimo Renzo, *Philosophical Foundations of Human Rights* (Oxford: Oxford University Press, 2015).

6 Charles Beitz, *The Idea of Human Rights*, p.12.
7 Jovana Davidovic, Chapter 4, this volume, pp. 42–45.
8 Suzy Killmister, Chapter 5, this volume, Section 5.
9 Suzy Killmister, Chapter 5, this volume, Section 6.
10 John Tasioulas, Chapter 6, this volume, pp. 73–80.
11 Octavio Ferraz, Chapter 9, this volume, p. 135.

Part I

Identifying political approaches

1 Human rights morality and human rights practice

An interactive approach

Tom Campbell

Sceptical responses to the increasing variety of human rights claims have given rise to less 'moral' and more 'political' approaches to the philosophy of human rights. These political approaches focus on the current practice of human rights, and reject traditional moral theories which seek to conceptualize human rights on the basis of their universality, importance and moral foundations without sufficient reference to their current political functions. Drawing on the work of Charles Beitz and Joseph Raz, this chapter endorses taking into account the existing political functions of human rights practice, including the mechanisms, which feature in their institutionalization. It then explores ways of modifying the political approach to render it more inclusive of human rights morality and more interactive with respect to the relationship between moral justifications for human rights and the objectives and mechanisms current within human rights practice.

Since the early 1970s, the discourse of human rights has achieved a remarkable prominence in the domain of politics and law.[1] At the same time, how that discourse is best understood and how it might be improved upon, have become increasingly controversial questions. In particular, the proliferation of human rights claims and the diversity of their practical uses have generated a measure of scepticism as to their meaning, purpose, content, practical implications and moral justification.[2] While there is considerable cross cultural agreement on abstract statements of human rights, this agreement does not extend to their specific content, their practical implications, or how they ought to be institutionalized and implemented.[3] In consequence, while there is widespread goodwill towards human rights, there is considerable doubt about how they should be conceptualized and how to settle moral disagreements as to their content and scope, the political purposes they serve, and the legal and other mechanisms appropriate to their implementation.[4]

A comparatively recent response to such human rights scepticism is the emergence of what has become known as 'political'[5] or 'practical'[6] or 'functional',[7] as opposed to 'moral'[8] or 'traditional'[9] or 'orthodox'[10] or 'natural law',[11] approaches to identifying the distinctive characteristics and roles of human rights. A common factor within 'political' approaches is their critique of the orthodox 'moral' view that human rights are morally important 'pre-political' rights that belong to all human beings in virtue of their humanity. In contrast, the political approach contends that human rights are better understood as socio-political constructs characterized primarily by their functions in various political arena. The orthodox moral view, it is argued, neither explains nor adequately evaluates the contemporary political and legal practice associated with the Universal Declaration of Human Rights (1948) (UDHR) and the subsequent human rights institutionalizations associated with the various human rights conventions and treaties adopted since 1948.[12]

Overtly 'without foundations' and firmly 'practice-oriented', the political approach renounces free-standing moral debate as to what human rights are, and eschews abstract philosophical reflection on the issues which trouble human rights sceptics. Instead, the political approach concentrates on the human rights doctrines which operate within the political practice of human rights, particularly the functional roles which human rights norms play in the sphere of global politics and constitutional law. The normative programme of the political approach commends empirically informed moral reflection directed at understanding and developing the existing functions of human rights, principally from the perspective of those involved in these processes. This requires examination of the working assumptions concerning the meanings and purposes of human rights that feature in the discourse of those who are knowledgeable about or involved in, what Beitz calls the emergent 'public political project' of human rights.[13]

The discourse embedded in this project, at the international level, is held to have a certain authority deriving from its historical connection with the post-Second World War origins of human rights and the generally beneficial outcomes of current human rights practice. More particularly, human rights are conceived of as rights the violation of which merits international concern, and may legitimate some degree and type of external intervention in the internal affairs of a state, something which would otherwise be regarded as an infringement of the sovereignty of that state. This human rights-based intervention is related, in a variety of ways, to the special responsibility of states to protect and promote the interests of their citizens as identified in human rights declarations, conventions and treaties.[14] Domestically the discourse principally concerns the constitutionalization of human rights in order to limit or extend the activities of governments with respect to their citizens.

This chapter explores the advantages and the limitations of the political approach to human rights. Its perceived advantages are, first, that it provides a clear empirical paradigm for identifying human rights, thus assuring the practical relevance of philosophizing about human rights. Second, political approaches highlight the contexts in which it is possible to formulate the content and scope of human rights at a level of specificity that is appropriate for their operationalization in legal and political decision-making. Third, political approaches by-pass some intractable philosophical disagreements concerning the conceptualization and distinctive moral justification of human rights. On the other hand, the perceived limitations of political approaches relate, first, to the gap they open up between the practice of human rights and the moral imperatives underpinning their political salience, and, second, the lack of critical engagement with the practices, particularly the functions and mechanisms, that have come to be associated with the implementation of human rights.

Following this analysis, the chapter examines ways in which the moral and the political approaches might work, as it were 'in tandem' as one commentator puts it, and in an interactive way in which not only do human rights values, such as equality, liberty and dignity, influence human rights practice but human rights practice impinges on the selection and interpretation of human rights values. The relatively easy part is to demonstrate the need for the fundamental values that critique and direct our practice, but difficulties are encountered in demonstrating how human rights practice can legitimately impact on the understanding of human rights values.

By taking articulation and interpretation together, a case is made for a modified, more 'interactive', political approach which, while keeping in focus the political purposes and institutional mechanisms involved in current and emerging human rights practice, retains significant continuity with those aspects of traditional human rights philosophy that involve the elucidation and application of the universal values, such as life and liberty, which serve as the moral foundations of human rights discourse. The proposed interactive approach endorses the contention that the specific content, scope and form of human rights cannot be determined outside of a particular social context, and without taking into account the actual processes and concrete mechanisms that are available and likely to be involved in their application. These mechanisms include human rights-based judicial review of legislation and United Nations Security Council endorsed foreign intervention, as well as the less dramatic institutional processes of monitoring, public condemnation and the deployment of diplomatic pressure. However, the interactive model retains a place for characteristic human rights values, both in the conceptualization of human rights in general and in the justification of particular human rights. In this process, neither the characteristic moral justifications nor the existing mechanisms are fixed givens. Thus, it is suggested that conceptual analysis and normative reflection concerning content and functions of human rights should involve matching characteristic human rights values and human rights mechanism, without giving unconditional conceptual or normative priority to either.

1 Political critiques of moral approaches to human rights

Political approaches to the philosophy of human rights are, in part, responses to growing scepticism about human rights. Now the preferred moral discourse of politics, the human rights brand attracts an ever-widening variety of adherents and gives rise to an increasingly broad range of claimed human rights and their associated methods of implementation. This, in turn, makes it difficult to develop an overarching conceptualization of human rights which has sufficient precision to provide adequate practical guidance as to what human rights are, what they are for and how they should be developed.[15]

The scepticism that prompts political critiques of moral approaches to human rights concentrates on several suspect strands, which are attributed to the orthodox philosophy of human rights. This includes what may be called (a) 'moral monism', (b) 'descriptive naturalism', and (c) 'acontextual conceptualism'. Moral monists attempt to trace a normative thread that leads back to a single moral basis for all human rights, usually drawing on the natural rights tradition with its emphasis on individual autonomy and the associated idea of 'respect for persons', as derived from enlightenment philosophers, such as Immanuel Kant.[16] Descriptive naturalists seek to provide a basis for human rights in a secularized version of the sort of natural law theory which seeks to identify a number of authentic human characteristics, capacities or needs derived from our knowledge and understanding of human nature and human circumstances.[17] Acontextual conceptualists, in their concern with the universal meaning of rights discourse and the categorization of human rights within a formal analytical scheme, seek to identify what they claim to be the content-independent and contextually-neutral characteristics of human rights, such as their human universality, and their peremptory moral prescriptivity.[18]

Advocates of the political approach, such as Beitz, point out that all these endeavours run into serious difficulties. Moral monists come up against the evident connection between many generally accepted human rights and a broad conception of human well-being which cannot be reduced to one single value, such as autonomy or dignity, to the exclusion of other values, such as justice, equality and freedom from suffering. Descriptive naturalists, in their approach to the empirical realities of human nature and human needs, inevitably pick and choose between what is 'natural' in the sense of what is normal in human societies and what is 'natural' in the sense of what is wholesome, fulfilling or uncorrupted. The first interpretation of 'natural' lacks normative force and the second interpretation raises moral questions that cannot themselves be settled by an appeal to 'nature'. Acontextual conceptualists, in their attempts to define human rights in a content-independent and context-neutral way, are unable to persuade others of the conceptual necessities to which they are committed, such as the alleged universality and prescriptive overridingness of all human rights. They cannot demonstrate, for instance, that 'universality' distinguishes human rights from all other rights, if only because universality does not in itself imply moral importance, and moral importance is not dependent on universality.[19]

These thumb-nail sketches provide some indication why theoretically minded persons engaged with the practice of contemporary politics are keen to distance themselves from what they see as the philosophical morass of contemporary human rights philosophy, and place on hold the search for a distinctive moral theory of human rights. This enables them to focus on human rights as a contemporary phenomenon, in contrast to what they see as the now outdated concept of natural rights, and to look, instead, at current opportunities for articulating, implementing and developing the current practical discourse of human rights.

However, while rejection of seemingly intractable abstract philosophizing in relation to human rights is understandable, fastening purely on the historically distinctive current human rights practice has both intellectual and moral downsides. Intellectually the political approach appears rather ad hoc and piecemeal. Morally it lacks a clear basis for the critique of existing practice, and tends to fracture the moral integrity of human rights into a plurality of diverse political arrangements based on a range of ill-defined values such as justice (legal and social), equality (formal and substantive), autonomy (individual and collective) and well-being (negative and positive). As a result, the political approach calls into question the distinctiveness of the human rights as a basis for justifications of the development and deployment of mechanisms relating to international intervention, constitutionalized democracy and mandatory humanitarianism.

The more modest ambitions of political approaches may turn out to be precisely what is required to rescue the philosophy of human rights from the theoretical impasse reached within traditional approaches. In particular, it may help us to avoid embracing human rights 'fundamentalisms', which put forward ultimately untestable claimed moral insights to legitimate the exercise of global power, or limit democratic institutions in questionable ways. A measure of epistemological humility regarding the moral foundations of human rights and some political suspicions arising from the selective enforcement of those human rights that are socially recognized may be seen as healthy consequences of attending to the issues at stake in the contemporary practice of human rights. On the other hand it may be unduly cautious to withdraw from systematic reflection on the moral foundations, which sustain the powerful political significance of human rights discourse.

The challenge here is to develop readily understandable and practically applicable philosophical approaches to human rights which are inclusive of the diverse and developing functional roles of human rights in the political arena, as well as the associated mechanisms used for their institutionalized implementation, without relying on abstract affirmations as to which rights are 'natural' or 'universal' or 'peremptory'.

2 Political approaches to human rights

In a recent article, Laura Valentini asks 'In what sense are human rights political?' and identifies three possible answers: (a) they are *institutional*, in that 'human rights are meant to evaluate political institutions . . . rather than personal conduct', (b) they are *public*, in that human rights appeal to 'reasons that are or can be publicly endorsed' in that they can be justified from within a variety of different ethical and moral outlooks, and (c) they are *feasible*, in that the content of a human right 'depends on what is reasonably feasible in current political circumstances.'[20]

Together these three senses of 'political' neatly characterize the 'pragmatic conceptualization' commended by Beitz when he criticizes the sort of foundationalism which seeks to ground human rights in a moral philosophy that is detached from current human rights practices. Beitz presents what Valentini calls a 'narrow' version of the first (institutional) way in which human rights may be 'political'. He takes the distinctive political function of human rights to be setting the threshold for legitimating the intervention of foreign powers in the internal affairs of a human rights violating state. In more general terms, human rights are thus 'standards for domestic institutions whose satisfaction is a matter of international concern.'[21]

Beitz's pragmatic conceptualism also fits Valentini's second 'political' criterion, according to which the determination of whether such intervention is legitimate depends on whether this is 'capable of being endorsed from within a variety of different overall ethical and moral outlooks' and therefore can be viewed as part of 'public discourse.'[22] For Beitz, satisfying the public criterion requires understanding the political nature of human rights through knowing the 'practice' of human rights as it arises in a common effort to develop standards that apply to all nations on a global scale. This excludes, for instance appeal to particular religious traditions or to narrow self-interest. With respect to public discourse, he looks to the emergence of a progressive consensus between those participants in human rights practice who are 'reasonable', 'competent', and 'fair minded',[23] requirements which are typical of, although rather more selective than, the normally accepted bounds of public discourse.

Valentini's third sense in which human rights can be 'political' (the feasibility requirement) is central to Beitz's practical model[24] in which the factors to be considered include not only 'the feasibility of implementing the protection in typical circumstances' but also 'the likely cost of making the protection effective'.[25] Thus, if intervention in the circumstances in question would not, for instance, typically assist the citizens whose interests are involved, then they cannot be said to have a human right to such an intervention. The limits that this requirement of efficiency places on the circumstances required for recognizing a human right provides Beitz with his main reason for holding that contemporary human rights are neither universal nor indefeasible.

Yet, even if Beitz's conceptualization of human rights is 'political' in all three senses of the term identified by Valentini, this does not adequately distinguish his position from orthodox moral approaches. As Beitz notes, Enlightenment theories of natural rights were developed and deployed for political purposes, particularly legitimating opposition to oppressive governments, although, of course, these political functions are not identical with, and not so specifically institutionalized as, those of contemporary international human rights practitioners.[26] This is true of Hobbes as much as of Locke, Rousseau and Kant, all of whom were concerned with political rather than individual morality. Indeed, while proponents of the contemporary political approaches are right to indicate that there are some very different political issues which arise in a more globalized world, some of these, such as the legitimacy of political rebellion against rights violating governments, remain important ingredients of contemporary human rights politics, as is demonstrated by the role of human rights discourse in the 2011 'Arab Spring'.[27]

Further, there is a great deal in common between the public discourse criterion adopted by contemporary political approaches and the work of classical social contract theorists, all of whom sought to provide a mainly secular basis for natural rights in order to address the problem of religious conflict. Hobbesian subservience to sovereigns, Lockean affirmations of toleration and Rousseau's articulation of the 'general will' are all attempts at reasoned public discourse which reaches beyond cultural and religious differences in a search for a common interest in political cohesion and the common good. Indeed, the development of public discourse is in many respects a defining feature of the Enlightenment. And so, while social contract theorists are all to some extent 'pre-political' in that their reflections start from the hypothesis of social circumstances prior to political institutionalization, these reflections are all ultimately directed towards the determination of what constitutes morally legitimate political authority.[28]

As to feasibility, the entire Hobbesian enterprise can be viewed as a rather exaggerated realism in which moral or natural rights established by the social contract reflect a powerful awareness of the practical limitations as to what can and what cannot be done to curb tyrannical government. Further, the Enlightenment focus on the importance of property can be seen as a recognition of the political pre-requisites of personal and collective material security. Overall, therefore, granting that the historical contexts of Enlightenment natural rights and contemporary human rights are significantly different, they both share the characteristics of being political, in all of the three senses of 'politics' to which Valentini draws our attention.

However, Beitz's distinction between human rights and natural rights philosophies is aimed less at the classical Enlightenment theorists and more at contemporary philosophers, such as James Griffin and Martha Nussbaum. Yet, his critique of these authors relates to specific ***ad hominem*** matters, such as the moral monism which is manifest in fact that they seek to found all human rights on a particular single value: 'personhood' in the case of Griffin[29] and 'human capabilities' in the case of Nussbaum'.[30] Also, while Griffin includes 'practicality' as a necessary feature of human rights, it is not a topic to which he actually devotes much attention.

These points are well made and have some basis in relation to their chosen targets, but they cannot be said to apply to all morally focused theories of human rights, many of which embrace both moral pluralism with respect to their human rights justifications and do not purport to derive the content of human rights from the formal acontextual characteristics ascribed to them. Beitz does not, therefore, provide a decisive critique of orthodox human rights philosophies, since their 'political' credentials are more evident than he allows.

3 Moral foundations of human rights

Knowing the currently accepted institutional implications of acknowledging the existence of a human right is clearly crucial for determining the specific content and scope of a human right. We need to know whether what we are talking about is aimed, for instance, at the protection of minorities through the mechanism of judicial review, or at the elimination of poverty through requiring adherence to human rights standards in international trade agreements, or at the limitation of corporate power through expanding corporate legal liability.[31] It makes little sense to try and answer whether or not a right qualifies as a human right unless we know what sort of mechanisms are to be deployed to secure its implementation as a result of its adoption as a human right. Will it feature in human rights-based judicial review? Might it legitimate the invasion of another country? Is it to be used as a basis for providing international aid? Will it form the basis of a new type of international criminal law? Such questions support the contention that the substantive content and scope of human rights cannot be determined in sufficient detail without recourse to knowledge of the relevant practice of human rights.

However, knowledge of the context-relative functions of human rights does not in itself do away with the need for politically oriented moral reasoning to specify the human rights objectives and evaluate the overall impact of deploying different practical mechanisms. A complex process of moral argumentation is required in order to determine the content, scope and the rights that are, or ought to be, human rights however well the contingencies of human rights practice is taken into account. This is not denied by either Beitz or Raz. Both insist on the significance of the morally legitimating public arguments that are involved in determining the content, scope and mechanisms of particular human rights.

Thus, Raz outlines how human rights are 'derived from three layers of argument' first by identifying an individual interest or other 'rock-bottom' consideration that 'establishes an individual moral right'; second, holding that 'under some conditions states are to be held duty bound to respect or promote the interest'; and third, showing 'that they do not enjoy immunity from interference regarding these matters.'[32] Despite the title of Raz's essay, he is not arguing that human rights cannot or do not have moral foundations in the sense of moral justifications. Beitz takes a similar line, insisting that the moral argument about the proper content of human rights is indeed part of the contemporary practice of human rights, and adding that there is reason to hold that this practice is on the whole a good thing,[33] a view Raz shares despite a measure of cynicism as to some of its operations.[34] Accordingly, Beitz presents 'a schema for justifying claims about the content of human rights doctrine with three parts': first, '[t]hat the interest that would be protected by the right is sufficiently important when reasonably regarded from the perspective of those protected that it would be reasonable to consider its protection to be a political priority'; second, '[t]hat it would be advantageous to protect the underlying interest by means of legal or policy instruments available to the state'; and third, '[t]hat in the central range of cases in which a state might fail to provide the protection, the failure would be a suitable object of international concern'.[35]

If there are such moral justifications for human rights, what is at stake in this debate about the foundations of human rights? Beitz holds to the view that moral reasons are required to justify human rights practice and accepts that his position is, in this sense, 'foundationalist'.[36] Raz accepts the substance but not the terminology of this position when he agrees that 'vindicating any evaluative position relies, among other facts, on universal evaluative truths'.[37] His point is not, therefore, that human rights lack foundations but rather that human rights (or some other sort of moral rights) are not, or at least are not always, themselves those foundations. He points out that there can be sound moral reasons which justify and to an extent constitute the existence of human rights, but he insists that these moral reasons are not always moral rights, human or otherwise. The principal reason Raz has for holding that human rights are 'without foundations' is that the reasons which explain where human rights 'come from' are contingent on the realities of international relations: 'they [human rights] lack foundations in not being grounded in a fundamental moral concern but depending on the contingencies of the current systems of international relations.'[38] Raz is not arguing here, against the positions adopted by Nussbaum and Griffin, that there is only one type of moral concern involved in the justification of human rights. Rather, he is pointing out that the justification of most human rights requires reference to instrumental factors, such as the contingencies of international relations, as well as appeals to intrinsic values. Similarly, Beitz argues that there is a sense in which human rights are not 'foundational', since '[f]or any particular human right it is always possible to ask why this right should be part of a global normative doctrine and to expect a reply that brings forward further moral (and other) considerations'.[39]

Raz and Beitz thus agree that the justification of human rights, both in general and in particular, involve a measure of complex contextual and consequentialist reasoning. It follows that the justification of a human right is never purely 'foundational'. Nevertheless, all instrumental moral reasoning eventually terminates in an affirmation of the desirability of the outcomes of the instrumentality. And so, while seeing human rights as a type of political practice may undermine the view that human rights or their distinctive justifications are acontextually self-evident or 'pre-political', it does not establish that human rights are without moral foundations – at least in the sense of the non-derivative values in which all moral justifications ultimately terminate.

In this case, the previous analysis, the political approach to human rights is not entirely detachable from the sort of reasoning associated with the traditional philosophies of human rights. These feature, for instance, in the first level of justification in Raz's justificatory model, that is, in the selection of important interests that are deemed to generate correlative political obligations. Further, Beitz does frequently emphasize the evident variety of moral reasons current in the human rights community as a basis for not conceptualizing human rights in terms of their moral justifications. However, the issue of whether human rights are in some sense with or without foundations cannot be reduced to the question of whether or not human rights justifications are ultimately multiple or monist, for both positions have a place for moral foundations in the justification of human rights. The most that can be conceded, therefore, is that some moral theorists have over-simplified the moral reasoning involved in providing an adequate justification for adopting a human right and underemphasized the misunderstandings and complexities involved in using human rights as moral foundations for normative political conclusions.

4 Interactive approaches to human rights

The main advantages of the political approach to human rights are that it encourages bringing moral considerations to bear on clearly identifiable and immediately significant political issues and practicalities, and casts reasonable doubts as to the practical utility and plausibility of abstract and acontextual analyses of human rights. Traditional moral philosophies of human rights do tend to make questionable factual claims about human nature and about their normative implications. They also often make unwarranted conceptual stipulations which oversimplify both the justification and the practice of human rights by neglecting the plurality of human rights values and failing to take account of the political functions of human rights practice.

Nevertheless, given the limitations of the political approach outlined previously, there may be both conceptual and practical advantages in retaining core human rights values within human rights philosophy. In this case, human rights discourse might be seen as the coming together of characteristic moral considerations and characteristic political practice on, as it were, a more equal footing. The moral considerations, which may be identified as characteristic human rights values, include autonomy, freedom from suffering and non-discrimination. These are values that are routinely adopted and deployed for the purpose of establishing human rights for the protection and furtherance of the basic interests of human beings. The political considerations are the practicalities of creating and sustaining the institutions and mechanisms for articulating and implementing human rights values in specific social, economic and political contexts as these are embedded in the shared activities of the participants in human rights practices.

Doing justice to the political approach requires that this reciprocity has to be something more than simply requiring that human rights must be practicable. If the interactive approach is to go beyond current moral philosophies of human rights it has to contend that the existing practice of human rights rightly affects the selection and interpretation of human rights values within that practice. This sees human rights practice as containing its own inner morality which brings an independent authority to the determination of the specific content and scope of human rights. The main challenge is to identify the justifiable moral impact of human rights practice. Merely taking into consideration the availability and effectiveness of mechanisms (such as domestic judicial review by courts or international trade sanctions through the World Trade Organization) does not go beyond paying heed to the sort of implementation practicalities acknowledged by moral philosophers such as Griffin. A genuinely interactive model has to involve something more substantive than taking into account the current feasibility of implementation through contemporary mechanisms.

In this regard there are two contemporary lines of thought which may help to identify a truly interactive approach to the philosophy of human rights. The first of these is the idea of 'intermediacy' derived from the work of Richard Arneson; the second is the idea of 'practice-dependence', discussed by Andrea Sangiovanni.

The first line of thought, which gives more than an instrumental interpretation of the interactive approach, relates to the variability of the interplay between the abstract morality of human rights and the functions and contingencies of their political and legal institutionalization. Arneson points out, and Beitz echoes, the view that human rights occupy a position between political values and their concrete applications, there being differing levels of abstraction and various degrees of concretization within human rights discourse. Human rights are thus said to have an 'intermediate' place between value affirmation and concrete institutionalization. This is a characteristic of declarations and conventions of human rights.

On this model, human rights come in a variety of modes, ranging from abstract statements of value (such as life and liberty) to very specific norms stating precise and authoritative obligations (such as prohibitions on state inflicted capital punishment). However, even the abstract human rights value statements, such as bills of rights, are characteristically presented in practice-oriented contexts, and even the more specific articulations of human rights retain their powerful moral force. In this way human rights play mediating roles between value affirmations and specific rule-governed implementations.[40]

One such role is the adoption of certain basic values and the desirable political institutions associated with them, all in broad and unqualified terms. Thus human rights declarations, bills or conventions simply affirm fundamental moral and political values on the basis of which, it is held, political institutions, policies and methods should be developed. These abstract and indeterminate statements of human rights have the function of affirming the political values of particular communities or regional international associations. Such human rights affirmations are characteristically lacking in precision and in the attribution of specific correlative obligations and methods implementation that would make them appropriate for use in policy formation and implementation through the mechanisms of human rights law.

At the other end of the spectrum, other statements of human rights take the shape of rights which have the characteristics of good legal rules, namely, clarity and specificity with respect to both form and content. In this mode highly practice-oriented interactive human rights discourse features in both the political implementation and the legal adjudication of human rights charters and conventions. Yet it is part of their characterization as human rights that these specific affirmations not only carry with them the backing of powerful human rights values, but help to make clear more precisely and concretely what these values are.

From the intermediacy perspective, indeterminate affirmations of human rights in the form of human rights values are important for political debate. Moreover, indeterminate affirmations of human rights provide a basis for education, for persuasion, for legislative scrutiny of existing and proposed laws by legislative assemblies, and for the development of political culture generally. This is so, even if they are 'rights' only in the sense that they are important moral values, such as autonomy, non-discrimination and the absence of suffering, which call for institutional recognition. 'Manifesto rights' of this sort[41] are amenable to being developed into a more precise set of norms that can reasonably serve within a range of different mechanisms. At this level, issues of feasibility, and the political significance of the sort of intervention involved, become unavoidably relevant, but this does not exclude the important functions of less specific manifesto human rights in which issues of feasibility play a less prominent role.

The intermediacy model illuminates the role of human rights as affirmations of intermediate values, which influence the formulation of more specific human rights. However, the intermediacy model is not particularly helpful with respect to the ways in which the specific, more concrete form of human rights might reasonably affect how we understand the more abstract affirmations, although there may be heuristic value in reflecting on specific statements of human rights to help us appreciate what it means to live a life which respects such human rights values as autonomy, dignity, and equality.

Here we may turn to advocates of 'practice-dependence',[42] who argue that, very properly, human rights practice is not simply about devising mechanisms for the implementation of previously identified moral goals, but includes consideration of how the existing practices bear on the justification of human rights, including their associated moral values or foundations. Central to our understanding of this position is precisely what is meant by 'practice' in this context.

One idea of 'practice' is Beitz's view of a 'practical conception' of human rights as being the conception of those who are involved in the practice of human rights, namely those practitioners who are engaged in international political life which he regards as 'a collective political enterprise – a practice – with distinctive purposes and modes of action'.[43] In Beitz's case, the normative work here derives from the thoughts and actions of practitioners as embedded in the enterprise in which they are routinely involved. These intentions have a normative authority which derives from the overall benefits of human rights practice which entitles them to an independent moral place in the determination of which human rights values are germane to a case in hand and how these values should be understood. This seems to give too much weight to the status quo in human rights political practice which is, in any case, internally very variable.

'Practice-dependence' theorists, such as Sangiovanni, point to the nature of the social and political systems which human rights are intended to regulate rather than the conduct of human rights practitioners to illustrate what constitutes 'practice' in this context. True, he notes that, '[t]he reasons we might have for rejecting or endorsing a certain understanding of human dignity or human needs as a part of a justification of a particular conception of human rights will be fundamentally shaped by the role human rights are intended to play in current international practice',[44] but, as he expounds his views, the emphasis is on the variable and political nature of the practices that human rights are intended to regulate. For Sangiovanni, the emphasis is on the specific political institutions for whose regulation human rights are designed and adopted. Practice in this sense is an institutional social and political given at which human rights are directed by those who are the focus of Beitz's conception of human rights practice. Here what affects the choice and interpretation of relevant moral principles is not so much the routine conduct of practitioners, but the social and political situations to which human rights are directed, so that '[t]he content, scope and justification of a conception of justice depends on the structure and form of the practices that the conception is intended to govern'.[45]

5 Conclusion

Bringing foundational moral values back in to the picture may be seen as a setback to the political approach's strategy of diminishing human rights scepticism through side-lining the analytical and moral debates which are part of traditional moral philosophies of human rights. Yet, the most helpful way forward may be to endorse those aspects of human rights scepticism that call for more careful analysis of human rights practice and avoid simplistic forms of moral reasoning unrelated to the practical institutionalization of human rights goals. This can be done without giving up on the ongoing task of matching human rights morality and human rights mechanisms, in an interactive manner.

This modified political approach does not contest the sort of scepticism that is directed toward a human rights 'fundamentalism' which holds to the self-evident, absolute and literally universal model of human rights, often derived from one core human rights value, such as autonomy or respect. Rather, it seeks to provide a framework for an orderly and very practical way of conducting democratic debate as to interpretation and application of human rights values in contemporary circumstances.

Notes

1 Samuel Moyn, *The Last Utopia: Human Rights in History* (Cambridge, MA: Harvard University Press, 2010), p. 3: 'The drama of human rights . . . is that they emerged in the 1970s seemingly from nowhere.' See also N. Bobbio, *The Age of Rights* (Cambridge: Polity, 1996).

2 For instance, Mary Ann Glendon, *Rights Talk: The Impoverishment of Political Discourse* (New York: Free Press 2001); Richard J. Arneson, 'Against Rights', *Philosophical Issues* 11 (2001): p. 172; Tom Campbell, K. D. Ewing and Adam Tomkins, eds., *Sceptical Essays on Human Rights* (Oxford: Oxford University Press, 2000); Raymond Geuss, *History and Illusion in Politics* (Cambridge: Cambridge University Press, 2001); Costas Douzinas, *Human Rights and Empire: The Political Philosophy of Cosmopolitanism* (London: Routledge-Cavendish, 2007).

3 Examples include the debate over human rights-based judicial review of legislation within democratic polities (see Jeremy Waldron, 'The Core Case Against Judicial Review', *Yale Law Journal* 115 (2006): p. 1346 and Richard Bellamy, *Political Constitutionalism: A Republican Defence of the Constitution of Democracy* (Cambridge: Cambridge University Press, 2007), and the human rights rationale for humanitarian intervention (see Ned Dobos, *Insurrection and Intervention: The Two Faces of Sovereignty* (Cambridge: Cambridge University Press, 2012).

4 Jeremy Waldron, *Law and Disagreement* (Oxford: Oxford University Press, 1999); Michael Ignatieff, *Human Rights as Politics and Idolatry* (Princeton: Princeton University Press, 2001); Conor Gearty, *Can Human Rights Survive?* (Cambridge: Cambridge University Press, 2006); and Tom Campbell, K. D. Ewing and Adam Tomkins, eds., *The Legal Protection of Human Rights: Sceptical Essays* (Oxford: Oxford University Press, 2011).

5 Joseph Raz, 'Human Rights Without Foundations', in *The Philosophy of International Law*, edited by Samantha Besson and John Tasioulas (Oxford: Oxford University Press, 2010), p. 327: 'The task of a theory of human rights is (a) to establish the essential features which contemporary human rights practice attributes to the rights it acknowledges to be human

rights; and (b) to identify the moral standards which qualify anything to be so acknowledged. I will say that accounts which understand their task in that way manifest a political conception of human rights'. See also Andrew Vincent, *The Politics of Human Rights* (Oxford: Oxford University Press, 2010).

6 Charles R. Beitz, *The Idea of Human Rights* (Oxford: Oxford University Press, 2009), p. 8: 'I want to explore a different approach, one we might describe as practical. It aims to exploit the observation that the human rights enterprise is a global practice. The practice is both discursive and political. As a first approximation, we might say that it consists of a set of norms for the regulation of the behaviour of states together with a set of modes or strategies of action for which violations of norms may count as reasons.'

7 Beitz, *The Idea of Human Rights*, p. 6: 'the functions that the idea of a human right is meant to play, and actually does play, in the practice'. See James Griffin, *On Human Rights* (Oxford: Oxford University Press, 2008), p. 27.

8 James W. Nickel, *Making Sense of Human Rights*, 2nd ed. (Oxford: Blackwell 2007), p. 62: 'I propose that we take as basic the idea that people have secure, but abstract, moral claims in four areas'.

9 Raz, 'Human Rights Without Foundations', pp. 322–327.

10 John Tasioulas, 'Taking Rights Out of Human Rights', *Ethics* 120, no. 4 (2010): p. 673.

11 Beitz, The Idea of Human Rights, ch. 3.

12 Moyn, The Last Utopia, ch. 1; Beitz, The Idea of Human Rights, ch. 2; Vincent, The Politics of Human Rights, ch. 4.

13 Beitz, *The Idea of Human Rights*, p. 13: 'It is essential for what follows to see that human rights as we find them in contemporary world politics constitute a public political project with its own distinctive purposes, forms of action, and culture'.

14 Beitz, *The Idea of Human Rights*, p. 13: 'The central idea of international human rights is that states are responsible for satisfying certain conditions in their treatment of their own people and that failures or prospective failures to do so may justify some form of remedial or preventative action by the world community or those acting as its agents.' Similarly, Raz, 'Human Rights Without Foundations', p. 328: 'Following Rawls I will take human rights to be rights which set limits to the sovereignty of states, in that their actual or anticipated violation is a (defeasible) reasons for taking action against the violator in the international arena.'

15 Raz goes as far as to assert that 'There is not enough discipline underpinning the use of the term 'human rights' to make it a useful analytical tool. The elucidation of its meaning does not illuminate significant ethical or political issues.' Raz, 'Human Rights Without Foundations', p. 336f.

16 Examples include Alan Gewirth, *Human Rights* (Chicago: University of Chicago Press, 1982), and Griffin, *On Human Rights.*

17 Examples include John Finnis, *Natural Law and Natural Rights* (Oxford: Oxford University Press, 1980), and Martha C. Nussbaum, 'Human Rights Theory: Capabilities and Human Rights', *Fordham Law Review* 66 (1997): pp. 273–300.

18 Examples abound in definitions of human rights in terms of their universality and overriding moral importance. Thus Jack Donnelly, *Universal Human Right in Theory and Practice*, 2nd ed. (Ithaca: Cornell University Press, 2003), p. 10: 'Human rights are, literally, the rights one has simply because one is a human being.' Donnelly himself adopts a more inclusive view.

19 Upendra Baxi, *The Future of Human Rights* (New Delhi: Oxford University Press, 2008), p. 44; Tom Campbell, *Rights* (London: Routledge, 2006), pp. 34–39.

20 Laura Valentini, 'In What Sense Are Human Rights Political? A Preliminary Exploration', *Political Studies* 60, no. 1 (2012): pp. 1980–1994. Valentini, making the assumption that these senses are all to be regarded as preconditions for inclusion as a human right, expresses some doubts about the second and further doubts about the third answer. My thanks to Laura Valentini for her comments on this article.

21 Beitz, *The Idea of Human Rights*, p. 128. While Beitz includes in his account of the political role of human rights that they set standards which limit the activities of all governments domestically, he regards the special role of human rights as pertaining to intervention when a state fails to provide protection of human rights. See Beitz, *The Idea of Human Rights*, p. 137 and Charles R. Beitz, 'Human Rights as a Common Concern', *American Political Science Review* 92 (2001): p. 277.

22 Valentini, 'In What Sense Are Human Rights Political?'. This also derives from Rawls. Compare Beitz, *The Idea of Human Rights*, p. 21: 'This conception of international human rights as a public doctrine open to a variety of justifications is indispensable to a proper appreciation of its historical uniqueness'.
23 Beitz, *The Idea of Human Rights*, p. 106ff. Thus, Beitz, *The Idea of Human Rights*, p. 106: 'It would make explicit the kinds of linguistic commitments one would undertake if one were to participate in good faith in the discursive practice'; and Beitz, *The Idea of Human Rights*, p. 107: 'First, in identifying the central elements of the practice, the model should seek to represent a consensus among competent participants.'
24 As indeed it has for some time in most 'traditional' analyses of human rights from Maurice Cranston, *What Are Human Rights* (London: Bodley Head, 1973), p. 43 to Griffin, *On Human Rights*, p. 44: 'I propose, therefore, only two grounds for human rights: personhood and practicalities'.
25 Beitz, The Idea of Human Rights, p. 110.
26 Beitz, *The Idea of Human Rights*, p. 57: 'Natural rights theories, at least in modern variants such as Locke's, were primarily attempts to formulate constraints on the use of a government's coercive power in circumstances of religious and moral diversity.'
27 For a different view, see Moyn, *The Last Utopia*, p. 1f: 'The eternal rights of man were declared in the era of Enlightenment, but they were so profoundly different in their practical outcomes – up to and including bloody revolution – as to constitute another conception altogether'. Also Vincent, *The Politics of Human Rights*, ch. 4.
28 My thanks to Ben Saunders for drawing my attention to these points. It is worth noting that the acknowledge initiator of the contemporary political approach, John Rawls, is a social contract theorist.
29 Griffin, *On Human Rights*, p. 33: 'In what should we say human rights are grounded? Well, primarily in personhood. Out of the notion of personhood we can generate most of the conventional list of human rights.' Compare Alan Gewirth on 'agency' in Gewirth, *Human Rights.*
30 Martha Nussbaum, *Women and Human Development: The Capabilities Approach* (Cambridge: Cambridge University Press, 2001).
31 John Ruggie, *Promotion and Protection of All Human Rights: A Framework for Business and Human Rights* (UN Doc. A/HRC/8/5, 2008); Tom Campbell, 'The Normative Grounding of Corporate Social Responsibility: A Human Rights Approach', in *The New Corporate Accountability*, edited by Doreen McBarnet, Aurora Voiculescu and Tom Campbell (Cambridge: Cambridge University Press, 2007).
32 Raz, 'Human Rights Without Foundations', p. 336.
33 Beitz, *The Idea of Human Rights*, p. 11: 'we have a prima facie reason to regard the practice of human rights as valuable. On the face of it, its norms seek to protect important human interests against threat of state-sponsored neglect or oppression which we know from historical experience are real and can be devastating when realized'.
34 Raz, 'Human Rights Without Foundations', p. 322.
35 Beitz, The Idea of Human Rights, p. 137.
36 Beitz, The Idea of Human Rights, p. 103. Compare Beitz, The Idea of Human Rights, p. 137.
37 Raz, 'Human Rights Without Foundations', p. 335.
38 Raz, 'Human Rights Without Foundations', p. 336.
39 Beitz, The Idea of Human Rights, p. 127.
40 R. J. Arneson, 'Against Rights', *Philosophical Issues* 11 (2001): pp. 12–21, and Beitz, *The Idea of Human Rights,* p. 170: 'Within the practice, human rights operate in the same way as middle-level principles operate in other branches of political discourse.'
41 The term comes from Joel Feinberg, *Social Philosophy* (Englewood Cliffs: Prentice Hall, 1978). It can be understood as referring to the rights that ought to exist, or moral values which are candidates for being the basis for 'real' rights which have correlative specific and located correlative duties.
42 Andrea Sangiovanni, 'Justice and the Priority of Politics to Morality', *Journal of Political Philosophy* 16 (2008): pp. 137–164. See Aaron James, 'Constructing Justice for Existing Practice: Rawls and the Status Quo', *Philosophy and Public Affairs* 33 (2005): pp. 281–316,

and 'Global Economic Fairness: Internal Principles', in *Global Justice and International Economic Law: Opportunities and Challenges,* edited by Chi C. Carmody, Frank J. Garica and John Linarelli (Cambridge: Cambridge University Press, 2012). I am indebted to Andrea Sangiovanni and Oisin Suttle for their comments on an earlier version of this paper.

43 Beitz, The Idea of Human Rights, p. 102

44 Sangiovanni, 'Justice and the Priority of Politics to Morality', p. 151.

45 Sangiovanni, 'Justice and the Priority of Politics to Morality', p. 138.

2 Human rights for non-believers

Caroline West

In contemporary politics, the concept of human rights plays a prominent role. The idea that every person anywhere, regardless of citizenship or territorial legislation, has some basic rights that others must respect carries tremendous moral appeal and authority. Appeals to human rights have been used for many different purposes, from resisting torture and various forms of discrimination, to mobilizing and justifying large-scale political reform, revolution, succession, economic sanctions and even military intervention.

However, despite its practical import, the theoretical foundations of human rights are murky and contested. The traditional view – that human rights are 'natural' rights that all human beings have unconditionally, simply in virtue of being human – faces well-known objections. These objections have in part motivated an increasingly popular alternative: the so-called 'practical' approach, which has been prominently developed and defended by Charles Beitz, among others.[1] On this approach, human rights are not to be understood as grounded in some independent, pre-institutional moral order; rather, they are the norms of a highly beneficial political practice that humans have constructed or evolved.[2]

Whether a 'natural' or a 'practical' approach, so understood, provides the best account of the nature of human rights is a hotly contested theoretical issue that I shall not venture into directly here. The main objective of this chapter is to draw attention to an important pragmatic dilemma that threatens to arise for advocates of a practical approach, and then to determine how proponents of this approach should respond to this dilemma, if – or when – it arises.

In Section 1, I outline the practical approach in more detail, using Beitz's account as an exemplar of the approach. In Section 2, I outline the pragmatic dilemma. Briefly and roughly, the dilemma is that promoting the truth of the practical account risks undermining the value of the practice it is intended to vindicate. For, as a matter of fact, achieving the ends that are commonly thought to justify the practice of human rights – broadly, the protection of an important class of human interests from particular sorts of threats – may depend crucially on widespread belief in the practice-independent nature of human rights norms. If so, then publicly recommending or advocating the practical approach will be dangerously subversive.

How should proponents of the practical approach respond to this possibility? Should the practical account be held, at best, as an 'esoteric' theory of human rights: a closely guarded secret to be believed, if at all, only by an enlightened few?[3] In Section 3, I address this question, and consider the costs.

1 The practical approach

The basic idea behind the practical approach is that human rights are best understood as the objects of an evolving international political practice that humans have developed in order to secure certain important benefits. This evolving political practice helps to determine the concept of a human right. As Beitz puts it, the practical approach 'tries to grasp the concept of a human right by understanding the role this concept plays within the practice.'[4] Consequently, theoretical

> [q]uestions like What are human rights?, What human rights do we have?, and [w]ho has duties to act when human rights are violated? are understood to refer to objects of the sort called "human rights" in contemporary international life, however these are best understood.[5]

To be an object of the sort called a 'human right' is to play a certain 'functional role' in the 'emerging global practice' of human rights.[6] This functional role can be understood by attending 'to the practical inferences that would be drawn by competent participants in the practice from what they regard as valid claims of human rights.'[7] This functional role then plays a crucial subject setting role in determining the extension of the concept of a human right; it helps to fix the reference of the term 'human rights.' As Beitz puts it, 'we take the functional role of human rights in international discourse and practice as basic; it constrains our conception of human rights from the outset.'[8]

According to Beitz, the functional role that helps to determine the concept of human rights has three aspects. First, human rights 'protect urgent individual interests against certain predictable dangers ("standard threats") to which they are vulnerable under typical circumstances of life in a modern world order composed of states'.[9] This protective function, Beitz claims, explains the importance of the institution of human rights. Second, they 'apply in the first instance to the political institutions of states'.[10] Third, they 'are matters of international concern. A government's failure to carry out its first-level responsibilities with respect to human rights may be a reason for action for appropriately placed and capable "second-level" agents outside the state.'[11] According to Beitz, forms of foreign intervention that may be licensed by a government's failure to carry out its first-level human rights responsibilities range from non-coercive or weakly coercive mechanisms of assistance or persuasion (such as 'naming and shaming,' cajoling in official speeches and diplomatic relations; public criticism by non-governmental organizations or private parties; demands for justification, or requests for accountability; policy adjustment within international organizations, e.g., as regards lending or aid), all the way to military intervention. This particular characterization of the functional role of human rights helps to distinguish Beitz's view from other so-called 'practical' or 'political' accounts which construe the defining function(s) of the practice somewhat differently.[12]

Human rights, on Beitz's view, are just those rights that are well suited to fulfilling these three aspects of the functional role of the objects called 'human rights' within global human rights practice. Importantly, this account does not imply that all and only those things called 'human rights' within the practice satisfy this standard, for something may be well suited to the role without currently being recognized as a 'human right' – in which case, the account implies that it ought to come to be called a 'human right.' Conversely, some of the things presently called 'human rights' might, on closer inspection, turn out to be ill suited to the practice; if so, they should no longer be recognized as human rights.

The approach just described has a number of distinctive – and distinct – features. First, it is what we might call a *practice-dependent* account of human rights: something (e.g. freedom from arbitrary state arrest) counts as a human right in part just because there exists a particular practice that, *inter alia*, licenses certain sorts public responses to acts of this kind (moral outrage, verbal condemnation, 'naming and shaming'), and constitutes a *pro tanto* reason for foreign intervention designed to discourage or prevent acts of this kind from occurring, etc.[13]

We can contrast this kind of practice-dependent approach with the more traditional understanding of human rights, which we might call the *practice-independent* approach. As Beitz describes it:

> Some philosophers have conceived of human rights as if they had an existence in the moral order that can be grasped independently of their embodiment in international doctrine and practice – for example, as "natural rights" or their secular successors, as fundamental rights possessed by human beings "as such" or "solely in virtue of their humanity," or as conditions for social institutions about which all the world's social moral codes agree . . . The usual view is that international human rights – that is, the objects referred to as "human rights" in international doctrine and practice – express and derive their authority from some deeper order of values.[14]

As Beitz suggests, the practice-independent approach views human rights as existing prior to, and independently of, their institutionalization in global human rights practice: it is because something (e.g. freedom from arbitrary detention) is, independently, a human right that it should be institutionalized in human rights practice – for instance, by being included in international declarations of human rights. The practical or practice-dependent approach, by contrast, insists that the direction of explanation goes the other way around: arbitrary detention counts as a human rights violation in part just because there exists a certain kind of political practice that licenses the kinds of practical responses previously enumerated to acts of this kind.[15] It is thus an implication of practice-dependence – but not of practice-independence – that while there may be other sorts of moral and legal rights against torture, in the absence of (enough of) the relevant practice, there exists no *human* right not to be tortured. If practice-dependence is right, it is a contingent – and, to some degree, arbitrary and accidental – matter just what human rights there are; indeed, it is contingent that there are any human rights *at all*.[16]

A second distinctive feature of Beitz's account is that it is 'political,' in the sense of holding that human rights impose duties 'in the first instance' on a political entity – i.e. *states* – as opposed to private individuals.[17] Torture, for example, violates its victims' human rights when it is performed or sanctioned by a political authority, but not when perpetrated by private parties, such as a lone sadist. This 'political' aspect of Beitz's view is, in an important way, logically independent of its practice-dependence. The difference between practice-dependent and practice-independent approaches to human rights concerns the *grounds* of human rights, whereas the 'political' aspect of the view concerns who are the primary *duty bearers* of human rights claims. It would therefore be a perfectly consistent position to agree with Beitz about the distinctively political nature of human rights (i.e. to hold that the primary duty bearers of human rights are states, or state-like organized political authorities), whilst rejecting his thoroughgoing practice-dependence; or vice versa.[18]

This distinction between the political and practical dimensions of accounts like Beitz's is important to note for present purposes because the pragmatic concerns that are my focus in this chapter are generated by the practice-dependent, rather than political, aspect of accounts like Beitz's. These concerns arise from taking seriously the idea that human rights norms are merely artefacts of contemporary political practice (as opposed to institutionalized embodiments of a practice-independent moral order), not from claims about *who* bears primary responsibility for human rights claims. They are thus worries that arise for all practice-dependent accounts of human rights, but not necessarily for all political accounts of human rights (when these are paired with a practice-independent account of the grounds of human rights).

2 The pragmatic dilemma

Practice-dependent theorists of human rights tend to take a broadly consequentialist view of the importance of the institution of human rights: human rights practice is justified, insofar as it is, because it helps to make the world a better place by promoting certain important ends.[19]

Of course, just what the relevant ends are, why they matter, and what list of human rights they support, are highly contested theoretical questions. Fortunately, however, for present purposes, we can set these disputed matters aside – important though they obviously are for a substantive account of human rights. For, *whatever* particular end(s) human rights practice is (or should be) in the business of promoting, there arise a separate cluster of *pragmatic* questions about what is the best way to achieve these ends in the real world – i.e. under prevailing economic, social, environmental and political conditions; given facts about human psychology, etc.

Pragmatic questions about how best to realize, in the real world, the ends that justify human rights practice are distinct from theoretical questions about the nature of human rights, but equally important – insofar as we care, as most of us rightly do, about the real-world implications of our theories. Consequently, apart from considering which account of the nature of human rights is *correct*, we need also to attend to pragmatic questions such as which account of human rights it would be best for us to *internalize* in order to promote the ends – whatever they are – that human rights practice is designed to achieve.

In this context, we should give consideration to what are the likely psychological effects of internalizing a practice-dependent understanding of human rights. Suppose that advocates of the practical approach were to succeed in converting many of us to the truth of the practical conception of human rights. As a result, we come explicitly to conceive of human rights as objects that originate in, and derive their normative status and authority from, a particular sort of contemporary political practice (as opposed, say, to being a set of absolute, unconditionally-binding normative requirements imposed by nature, reason and/or God). What effects will adopting this conception have on our patterns of thought and behaviour? In particular, will adopting this practical conception serve to promote, or to undermine, the ends that we wish to achieve through human rights practice?

Consider that to achieve the sorts of beneficial outcomes that are generally thought to justify human rights practice, human rights norms must exert a considerable degree of normative and motivational authority over the attitudes of individuals and authorities. People must feel strong normative pressure to comply with these norms (often in the face of considerable contrary temptation), and also to expect and encourage others to comply, and also to punish in some way anyone who fails to comply, and also to punish those who fail to punish those who fail to comply, and so forth. (For brevity, in future 'compliance' should be read as including all of the above.) These attitudes and expectations are partially constitutive of human rights practice.

But to what extent does motivation to comply with human rights norms depend on their being assumed – rightly or wrongly – to possess practice-independent normative authority? Would the recognition that human rights norms are practice-dependent weaken normative pressure to comply with these norms – especially in situations where powerful reasons of self- or national interest favour non-compliance? Would thinking of human rights as mere institutional constructs help to mobilize public outrage and organized resistance to various forms of political oppression, or would it undermine these efforts? Would widespread belief in the conventional nature of human rights norms make ordinary citizens more willing to give governments and other political authorities leeway to depart from the norms, thus decreasing public pressure on authorities to comply, and hence the likelihood that they will actually comply? Would it make us more or less willing to sacrifice income or lives to safeguard human rights beyond our own borders? Will political agents and authorities be more, or less, likely to refrain from violating human rights, if they see human rights norms as conventional in original – akin to norms of custom, such as those of etiquette?

Let us call the prospect that widespread belief in the practice-dependent nature of human rights norms will undermine the general tendency to comply with these norms the *undermining hypothesis.* The undermining hypothesis, so stated, is an empirical hypothesis. It should be distinguished from the question of whether recognition of the conventional nature of human rights norms *rationally ought* to undermine our confidence in human rights norms, or weaken our motivation to comply with them. This rationality question has been the focus of much attention in the debunking literature in ethics. But the factual question is just as important as the rationality question, if not more so. Perhaps the 'discovery' that human rights norms are at bottom merely conventional, by itself, gives us no good reason for being less motivated to comply with them; this does not mean, however, that it won't have this effect. We do not always think and act rationally – even when we try.

Undermining is of particularly great concern in the less-than-ideal world in which we presently find ourselves, where institutional respect for the human rights practice and the international order is in decline. In such a context, we can no longer rely so confidently on institutional supports and incentives to comply with human rights norms; motivation to comply with the norms will *have* to be of a first-order kind, driven directly by a belief that there are individual human rights that must be respected precisely because they are human rights.

The practical conception implies that as the practice crumbles, so too do human rights. In these troubled times, when the human rights practice is increasingly under threat, we need more than ever to rely on a conception of human rights that does not make their existence hostage to a practice that is itself somewhat under siege.

The force of the undermining worry is well appreciated in discussions of practice-dependent accounts of moral norms, such as moral relativism and universal subjectivism. An influential objection to accepting ethical relativism is the feeling that accepting it will somehow weaken our confidence in, or undermine our adherence to, our own values.[20] As Michael Ruse writes, 'we think [morality is] binding upon us *because we think it has an objective status*' (his emphasis).[21] Morality, we feel, has a special kind of importance attaching to it, an importance incompatible with its being merely a matter of contingent social custom or convention. Similar feelings surround human rights norms, perhaps because they are often regarded as a subset of basic moral norms. When we condemn the Holocaust, or ethnic cleansing in the former Yugoslavia, as gross human rights abuses, for example, we generally do not *merely* take ourselves to be claiming that acting in this manner is contrary to law or established international political practice. We mean that it is wrong, absolutely and objectively; and the feeling that it is categorically and objectively wrong plausibly strengthens and sustains the widespread desire not to do it (and often also to go to considerable lengths to stop or punish others who try to do it, and also to punish those who fail to punish those who do it, etc.).[22] As even moral relativists themselves admit, 'people who condemn torture . . . as an offence against the moral fabric of the world may possess a certitude not available to relativists and may find it easier to make the personal sacrifices that morality requires.'[23]

Yet if a practice-dependent account of human rights is correct, then human rights norms are not absolute and objective, but rather subjective and contingent; in an important sense, they are like norms about which side of the road to drive on, where it doesn't matter exactly how we settle the matter, just so long as we do settle it one way or another. It happens that we have settled things so that there are human rights against discrimination on the basis of race and sex; however, practice-dependence seems to imply that, had the practice evolved somewhat differently (or were it to do so in the future), then these would not be human rights.

This example is by no means far-fetched. The original instigators of the Universal Declaration of Human Rights (UDHR) had two aims, one of which was to curtail state aggression and facilitate international peace.[24] As history actually transpired, this aim of curbing the propensity to war became of secondary importance to a second aim of protecting individuals from the threat of grave harms permitted or perpetrated against them by their own government. But history could quite easily have taken a different turn and the aim of facilitating peace might have taken precedence instead. Had it done so, freedom from racial or sexual discrimination (along with other currently recognized 'human rights,' such as rights to political participation) would probably not have counted as human rights, since these interests are not obviously well suited to promoting the end of curtailing state aggression and facilitating peace.[25] Widespread acceptance of the conventional and contingent nature of norms against discrimination may lessen the general tendency to adhere to, and comply with, these norms – with the result that interference with important human interests that are supposed to be safeguarded by human rights practice becomes more common.

Undermining can obviously come in degrees. In the absence of reliable empirical evidence, we should be wary of making dogmatic armchair predictions about complex matters of fact. It may seem *a priori* unlikely that recognition of the practice-dependent nature of human rights would instantaneously entirely erode respect for human rights, transforming decent states and peoples into despotic ones overnight (although recent global political events should perhaps give us pause for thought on this score). It may seem more likely that the process of transformation, if it occurs, would be more subtle and gradual, and perhaps vary somewhat from individual to individual, and community to community. Even so, its total impact may be significant. If belief in practice-dependence made on average even just a small difference to the rate of compliance with human rights norms on any given occasion, it is a reasonable bet that many more human rights-violations would occur than at present.

While such armchair observations in support of the undermining hypothesis are common in ethics, more empirical research is needed before we are in a position confidently to affirm (or deny) its truth. This means that, at present, both the undermining hypothesis and its negation remain on the table as live possibilities. However, it is worth noting some suggestive preliminary research findings that appear to lend some support to the undermining hypothesis. Research has found a positive correlation between relativistic moral beliefs and an increase in (reported) non-compliance with moral norms.[26] For instance, Indonesian consumers scoring high on relativism report being more likely to engage in questionable but legal activities, and being more likely to initiate an illegal activity from which they would benefit.[27] While discussing the issue of whether 'moral relativism leads to a weakened adherence to moral principles', Katinka Quintelier and Daniel Fessler offer the following summary of current empirical research:

> More relativistic adult U.S. consumers are less likely to find a range of consumer practices wrong. (Vitell and Paolillo 2003). Practices examined concerned illegal behaviour such as changing prince tags as a consumer on consumer products, lying about a child's age in order to get a lower price, not telling the truth when negotiating about the price of a car, and illegally copying computer software. Among marketing managers, those who score high on relativism have been found to think that ethics is less important for a firm's long term plans (Vitell et al. 2003). Chinese manages are reportedly more favourable towards bribery and kickbacks if they score higher on relativism (Tian 2008). In another study, relativists are shown to be more accepting of violating property rights (Winter et al. 2004). Business undergraduates at a U.S. university who score higher on relativism score lower on corporate social responsibility, the extent to which they take the wider social impact of their business into account instead of just caring about profits and stockholders
>
> (Kolodinsky et al., 2010).[28]

The authors conclude that these and other findings suggest 'a negative relationship between relativism and confidence'; but caution, 'more research on this topic is clearly necessary.'[29]

We cannot, then, rule out the undermining hypothesis – that is, we cannot rule out the possibility that widespread internalization of the practical conception of human rights will undermine motivation to comply with human rights norms. If human rights norms are valuable because they serve to safeguard and promote a class of important human interests, then widespread belief in the practical conception will help to defeat, rather than to achieve, the ends that justify human rights practice.

None of this, of course, provides any reason to think that the practical account of human rights is not *true* – perhaps the objects we call 'human rights' really are, unbeknownst to many of us, merely conventional political artefacts. Just as, for some time, most of us were mistaken about the nature of the person(s) who left us presents labelled 'from Santa' under the tree on Christmas Eve, so too it may be that we have a mistaken conception of the true nature of human rights norms. That fact, in itself, would not have any tendency to weaken our motivation to comply with human rights norms, unless it became widely known. There is thus a pragmatic question about the extent to which it is desirable to advocate the practical account of human rights, given that publicizing it risks undermining the utility of the practice.

3 An 'esoteric' theory of human rights?

How should advocates of the practical conception respond if it turns out that widespread acceptance of this view would be counter-productive – i.e. likely to undermine, instead of promoting, the benefits that justify human rights practice in the first place?

This closely resembles a question that arises for consequentialist accounts of ethics. Consequentialists about first-order individual choices believe that the morally right action for a person to perform is that which, of all those available, will lead to the best overall consequences. This is commonly known as the consequentialist 'criterion of rightness.' However, as consequentialists themselves often note, there is a further important pragmatic question as to whether (some, any, many?) individuals should internalize this consequentialist standard and use it as a 'decision-procedure' or method of choice; for doing so may have very bad consequences, and thus contravene the consequentialist standard of rightness.

Henry Sidgwick famously noted the possibility that internalizing the consequentialist standard of rightness as a method of choice may, in the wrong hands, have bad consequences. In response, he proposed that society should be divided into 'enlightened utilitarians' who may be able to live by 'refined and complicated' rules that admit of exceptions, and the rest of the community to whom such sophisticated rules 'would be dangerous.'[30] As a result, he endorsed what has come to be known as esoteric morality. A tenet of Sidgwick's esoteric morality is that although the consequentialist believes that consequentialism is the right moral theory, the consequentialist may need to discourage others from embracing consequentialism.

Should proponents of the practical conception of human rights follow Sidgwick's lead? If widespread internalization of a practical conception would itself pose a threat to the interests that human rights practice has evolved to safeguard and promote, should those who believe it defend it as an esoteric philosophy of human rights: a theory best believed, if at all, only by an enlightened few?

There are different kinds of esoteric philosophy and different degrees of secrecy that might be justified or required. The kind of esoteric morality that Sidgwick recommends is *partially* esoteric.[31] Sidgwick thinks that some people ('enlightened utilitarians') can safely believe utilitarianism without this leading to the bad effects that would be likely to result if this belief were more widely held. Consequently, these enlightened few are free to employ the utilitarian standard of rightness in private moral deliberation and discussion amongst themselves, but should keep this a tight-lipped secret. Keeping the doctrine alive among an enlightened few may be consequentially preferable to the alternative of *no one* believing it because it guards against the danger that members of society will blindly keep following rules that, due to changing circumstances, are no longer beneficial.

Should the practical conception likewise be a partially esoteric theory of human rights? Ultimately, this demands a fuller analysis of the costs and benefits of this and alternative policies than I can undertake here. In the previous section, I focused primarily on potential costs to compliance should the practical conception become general public knowledge. (The 'general public' here includes state officials and human rights activists, as well as ordinary citizens.) However, there may be advantages to restricted deployment of the practical conception among an enlightened few human rights theorists and international policy makers.

One context in which employing the practical conception, rather than a natural rights conception, may be advantageous is in situations where there is disagreement about whether or not something is a human right. Debates about what human rights there are are notoriously difficult rationally to resolve when we think of human rights as natural rights – not least because it is unclear where natural rights come from, and how we acquire knowledge of them, supposing that they exist. Disputes over whether something is, or is not, a (natural) human right often appeal to 'educated' intuitions about their nature and grounds; but, as intuitions differ, this methodology often leads to impasse. By contrast, debates about whether or not it would be net beneficial to grant a certain sort of politico-legal status to interests of a particular kind in order to achieve this or that desired aim seem less mysterious, and more amenable to rational resolution – at least in principle. We may not all agree on *why* certain interests are important, but perhaps we can reach some agreement on what interests are important and on practical matters about how best to safeguard or promote them. Thus, a partially (as opposed to fully) esoteric practical philosophy of human rights may be desirable in order to help settle first-order human rights disputes.

Against this, however, we need to balance the risk that a practice-dependent conception will undermine morality in general by giving badly-intentioned individuals and groups just the sort of justification they need to rationalize illiberal interference with important human interests. For, one significant difference between consequentialism and the practice-dependent theory of human rights is that consequentialism is a *moral* theory. It is part of this theory that you should promote human rights, insofar as it is beneficial to do so. Thus, those in the inner circle who accept this theory have an internal reason, in virtue of accepting this theory, to do what will have the best consequences. If those in the inner circle are truly enlightened, they will not promote consequentialism as a theory of choice, even in themselves – and certainly not in others.

The practice-dependent theory of human rights, however, is different: it is a purely *descriptive* theory. So, for example, if a charismatic national leader comes to power who has scant respect for human rights, the practice-dependent account of human rights might provide her with just the ammunition she needs to ignore the objects of this (to her mind) pernicious liberal political practice, and do exactly as she pleases. Human right are, after all, simply the product of a particular sort of liberal political arrangement; there is no prior independent normative requirement to respect the things called 'human rights' within this practice. Consequently, while it may be fine for consequentialists or other antecedently well-motivated people to believe the practice-dependent theory, in the wrong hands this theory may be dangerous. Given recent developments in international politics – the rise of populist ethnocentrist national leaders, religious intolerance, growing disdain for liberal institutions and international order – we should not be too sanguine about these dangers.[32]

4 Conclusion: counting the cost

One question we can ask about the practical conception is whether it is true, or the best theory of human rights. In this chapter, I have focused on a different, but equally important, pragmatic question: true or not, would it be desirable for the practical conception to be generally believed? I argued that widespread acceptance of the practical conception runs the risk of undermining the ends that justify human rights practice. This is an empirical hypothesis; we do not yet know exactly how significant this risk is. However, if the risk is real (and there is some reason to think that it is), then advocates of the practical conception may be forced to defend the practical account as an esoteric philosophy of human rights.

Does this constitute a damaging objection to a practical approach to human rights? Some may think so. Esoteric philosophy strikes many people as paternalistic, duplicitous and objectionably elitist.[33] There are, of course, good reasons to feel uncomfortable about an esoteric political philosophy: keeping things secret is risky (word may get out), elites cannot entirely be trusted, and no one likes the idea of deceiving or being deceived. Having to be esoteric is undeniably costly, even if you believe – as Sidgwick did – that these costs are ultimately worth paying. This may not provide a good reason to doubt the truth of the practical account; but it is, perhaps, a reason to hope that it never becomes too popular.

Notes

1 Charles Beitz, *The Idea of Human Rights* (Oxford: Oxford University Press, 2009). The 'practical approach' is Beitz's label. Other scholars apparently sympathetic to a practical approach include John Rawls, *The Law of Peoples* (Cambridge: Harvard University Press, 1999), Joseph Raz, 'Human Rights Without Foundations', in *The Philosophy of International Law*, edited by

Samantha Besson and John Tasioulas (Oxford: Oxford University Press, 2010), and Aaron James, 'Constructing Justice for Existing Practice: Rawls and the Status Quo', *Philosophy & Public Affairs* 33, no. 3 (2005), pp. 281–316.

2 James Nickel, 'Human Rights', in *The Stanford Encyclopedia of Philosophy,* edited by Edward N Zalta (Winter 2014 ed.), URL=<https://plato.stanford.edu./archives/win2014/entries/rights-human/>

3 I borrow this description from Henry Sidgwick's famous discussion of 'esoteric morality' in Henry Sidgwick, *The Methods of Ethics,* 7th ed. (London: Palgrave Macmillan, 1907), book 4, ch. 5.

4 Beitz, The Idea of Human Rights, p. 8.

5 Charles Beitz, 'Human Rights and the Law of Peoples', in *The Ethics of Assistance: Morality and the Distant Needy,* edited by Deen Chatterjee (Cambridge: Cambridge University Press, 2004), p. 197.

6 Beitz, *The Idea of Human Rights*, pp. 103, 136.

7 Beitz, The Idea of Human Rights, p. 102.

8 Beitz, The Idea of Human Rights, p. 103.

9 Beitz, The Idea of Human Rights, p. 109.

10 Beitz, The Idea of Human Rights, p. 109.

11 Beitz, The Idea of Human Rights, p. 109.

12 Rawls, *The Law of Peoples*, for instance, offers a narrower characterization of the function of human rights than Beitz. Rawls identifies human rights with the 'special class of urgent rights' whose violation licenses *coercive* foreign intervention in a society's internal affairs, intervention which would otherwise be impermissibly disrespectful or intolerant. Since this burden of justification is more difficult to meet, the list of genuine human rights that Rawls proposes is considerably shorter than that endorsed by Beitz.

13 This feature is sometimes described as 'anti-foundationalism,' by contrast with 'foundationalist' approaches, which try to derive and justify human rights norms from some independent ultimate value, or set of ultimate values. See Suzy Killmister, this volume.

14 Beitz, The Idea of Human Rights, p. 7.

15 There is some dispute in the human rights literature about exactly how to characterize the difference between naturalistic and practical accounts; some authors even question whether these accounts are mutually exclusive. (See S. Matthew Liao and Adam Etinson, 'Political and Naturalistic Conceptions of Human Rights: A False Polemic?', *Journal of Moral Philosophy* 9, no. 3 (2012): pp. 327–352. The practice-dependent/practice-independent distinction provides one axis along which theories of human rights may usefully be distinguished.

16 The sense in which it is arbitrary what human rights there are is that, had the aims of the practice been (somewhat) different, (somewhat) different things would have been human rights. This result might be avoided by tying the idea of human rights to *current* human rights practice (e.g. defining human rights as objects that *actually* play the relevant roles in political life, here and now). But this does not sit well with Beitz's desire to allow for conceptual evolution without subject change.

17 For a helpful discussion of various senses of 'political' in the human rights literature, see Laura Valentini, 'In What Sense Are Human Rights Political? A Preliminary Exploration', *Political Studies*, 60, no. 1 (2012): pp. 180–194.

18 For an outline of an approach that is both political and practice-independent see Christian Barry and Nicholas Southwood, 'What Is Special About Human Rights?', *Ethics & International Affairs* 25, no. 3 (2011): pp. 369–383. Of course, there is a sense in which a political account makes human rights dependent on a practice: since political accounts by definition hold that the duty bearers for human rights are political entities of some kind, a political conception implies that a world without *any* political entities would be a world without human rights.

19 For further discussion of how consequentialism can accommodate the idea of rights see e.g., Richard Arneson, 'Against Rights', *Philosophical Issues*, 11, no.1 (2001): pp. 12–21, and Katarzyna de Lazari-Radek and Peter Singer, *The Point of View of the Universe: Sidgwick and Contemporary Ethics* (Oxford: Oxford University Press, 2014). We should note, however, that consequentialist justifications of human rights practice are independent of consequentialist views in ethics. Those who reject consequentialist approaches to first-order ethical

questions can consistently endorse a consequentialist account of human rights, which can be seen as concerned with how to structure public policies and social institutions, rather than first-order individual choices. Indeed, one possible consequentialist justification of human rights is that they help to create the background social and political conditions that enable individuals everywhere to thrive, where 'thriving' involves living in a way that satisfies a deontological ethical standard. Thus ethical deontologists, as well as ethical consequentialists, can be consequentialists about human rights.

20 For further discussion see e.g., Neil Levy, *Moral Relativism: A Short Introduction* (London: Oneworld Publications, 2002).

21 Michael Ruse, 'Evolutionary Ethics: A Phoenix Arisen', in *Issues in Evolutionary Ethics*, edited by Paul Thompson (Albany: SUNY Press, 1995), p. 235.

22 Here I am disagreeing with Beitz's claim that the practical account accurately captures 'what an ordinary competent participant in the discourse would understand herself to be committed to if she were to acknowledge that a human right to such and such exists' – i.e. that it is a descriptively adequate account of 'human rights in the sense in which they occur in contemporary public discourse', see Beitz, *The Idea of Human Rights*, p. 11. The practical account has too many counter-intuitive implications to be plausibly viewed as a descriptively adequate account of the content of the folk concept of human rights. Perhaps, unbeknownst to many of us, the objects that we call 'human rights' really are conventional in nature; however, if so, this would be a surprising social scientific discovery about the nature of human rights – akin to the once-surprising biological discovery that whales are mammals, not fish.

23 David Wong, 'Relativism and Moral Confidence', in Moral Relativism (Routledge Encyclopedia of Philosophy, 1998), https:www.rep.routledge.com/articles/thematic/moral-relativism/v-1/sections/relativism-and-moral-confience.

24 Beitz, The Idea of Human Rights.

25 Barry and Southwood, 'What Is Special About Human Rights?', p. 378.

26 For a summary of existing research findings see Katinka J.P. Quintelier and Daniel M.T. Fessler, 'Varying Versions of Moral Relativism: The Philosophy and Psychology of Normative Relativism', *Biol Philos* 27, no. 1 (2012): pp. 95–113.

27 L.C. Lu and C.J. Lu, 'Moral Philosophy, Materialism, and Consumer Ethics: An Exploratory Study in Indonesia', *Journal of Business Ethics* 94, no. 2 (2010): pp. 193–210, cited in Quintelier and Fessler, 'Varying Versions of Moral Relativism', pp. 95–113.

28 Quintelier and Fessler, 'Varying Versions of Moral Relativism,' pp. 106–107.

29 Quintelier and Fessler, 'Varying Versions of Moral Relativism', p. 110.

30 Sidgwick, *The Methods of Ethics*, book 4, ch. 5. ß3, paragraphs I,8.

31 For further discussion of the idea of a partially esoteric morality, see Derek Parfit, *Reasons and Persons* (Oxford: Oxford University Press, 1984).

32 I am grateful to David Braddon-Mitchell for emphasizing this point.

33 Brad Hooker objects to Sidgwick's account of esoteric morality on these grounds. See Brad Hooker, *Ideal Code, Real World*, p. 94. See also Bernard Williams, who famously disparagingly labels Sidgwick's view 'government house utilitarianism' in Bernard Williams, 'Social Choice', in *Utilitarianism For and Against*, edited by J.J.C. Smart and Bernard Williams (Cambridge: Cambridge University Press, 1973), p. 139. For an important recent defence of Sidgwick's esoteric morality see Katarzyna de Lazari-Radek and Peter Singer, 'Secrecy in Consequentialism: A Defence of Esoteric Morality', *Ratio* 23, no. 1 (2010): pp. 34–58.

3 Traces of recognition

Rights and political realism

Duncan Ivison

1 Introduction

The motivation for this chapter lies in a question about how the legacy of historical injustice continues to structure contemporary politics, domestic and global. In particular, how do enduring injustices shape our structures of justification, whether linked to practices of democratic legitimation, or to the way we address and justify important normative claims, including the justification of rights?[1] I am particularly interested in the situation of indigenous peoples and liberal democratic states, as well their place within the international order more generally.[2] And I am interested in the way their claims are (or are not) translated into the discourse of rights, which has been both a powerful feature of indigenous peoples' domestic and global activism, as well as a source of deep critique.[3] These arguments touch on both the existence conditions of rights, as well as their institutionalization.

In this chapter, my main question is: how, in the context of deep, persistent, structural injustices, do our discourses and practices of rights either help to reify those very injustices, or serve as a genuine source of critique of them? How is it that rights protection can come apart from the realization of justice? To put it another way: John Rawls argued that we do not have an obligation to submit to unjust institutions – to institutions that 'exceed the limits of tolerable injustice'.[4] But how do we ascertain where to draw the line beyond which injustice becomes intolerable?[5] And can the language of rights help us do this? Or are rights, more often than not, insufficiently attuned to the structural features of 'real politics'?

These are large (and no doubt ill-posed) questions. But I want to consider at least one aspect of this issue from the perspective of the theme of this volume, focused as it is on 'political approaches' to human rights. Would a more suitably 'realistic' account of both the existence conditions of rights, as well as the social and political requirements for their realization, help us address the challenge of enduring injustices? One argument would be to say that the only rights that really exist are essentially legal rights, and if not literally legal rights, then rights that are either actually, or in principle, enforceable. But one function of human rights, for example, is precisely to serve as a critical standard for politics in conditions where the crucial interests to which rights claims refer are *not* currently enforceable, and to help us create the conditions in which they could be. Moreover, there is a range of important human interests that are not immediately or universally enforceable as rights claims, but that we would hesitate to dismiss as rights altogether. For example, there is a robust debate occurring now around the idea of a human right to 'health' that turns, in part, on whether anything like such a claim could be enforceable.[6] However, regardless of where one stands on this particular question, it would be hard to dismiss that access to healthcare (or education) is not in some way linked to the kinds of interests that our language of rights aspires to claim. So whatever 'realism' means it can't mean a simplistic dismal of all rights claims that aren't already legal claims.

In this chapter I want to explore what a suitably 'realistic' account of rights might be. And I shall argue, tentatively, that a realistic account of rights must build *some* aspect of a social recognition thesis into the existence condition of rights. However, the forms of recognition required are not reducible to recognition by the extant *state*, nor does it explain everything that is important about the nature of rights. So it is intended as a modest defence of a recognition thesis concerning rights, not a claim that explains everything about them. The main aim is to reflect on how our language and practice of rights (and especially human rights) can be shaped by historical injustice, and what the consequences might be for how we justify and argue about rights. In short, I shall argue that in taking both rights and 'realism' seriously in these contexts, we should embrace a more pluralistic approach to the grounds of human rights, and as a result accept a more constrained universality for their claims and a more dynamic account of their development.

2 Realism about rights

What would it mean to have a suitably politically realistic account of rights? It depends, of course, on what we mean by realism, and what we mean by 'politics'. One uninteresting version would be that our theories of rights should simply mirror the way the world is now. Taking a broadly 'interest based' approach,[7] this approach would mean that rights are those claims, grounded in the most important interests that individuals (and potentially groups) have, which they have managed to get institutionalized and enforced in some way. Rights, including human rights, would not set normative standards against which reality can be judged, but rather would simply *reflect* that reality, and whatever normativity could be elicited from it.

This seems a deeply impoverished conception of rights and a far too strong conception of political realism – one in which the very possibility of normativity (other than that sustained through force) is cast into doubt.

On the other hand, there is clearly also something dissatisfying about the proliferation of claims about the moral reality of rights (and especially human rights) today in a world that is so depressingly resistant to that reality. There is clearly no philosophical consensus on even the plural grounds of human rights. And the acceptance and enforcement of the terms of our most important international human rights instruments is inconsistent and patchy at best – a gross charade of moralism at worst. One quick response to this thought is to say that it is one thing to assert the reality of a right – and a human right at that – and another to make good on that assertion. We shouldn't confuse the existence conditions of a right with their institutional realization and enforcement. Philosophers should focus on developing arguments for the former, not the latter. A division of labour is required between the work of philosophy, on the one hand, and that of institutional design and implementation, on the other. I shall return to this point later, but like the quick submission to the way the world is now, this quick dismissal of the conditions required for the realization of rights seems equally unsatisfactory.

In recent political theory, a conception of 'political realism' has emerged in opposition to 'utopian' political theory and, in particular, to what we might call the 'high Kantianism' of Rawlsian normative political theory that has been so dominant in the Anglo-American world since the 1980s. Raymond Geuss has developed a particularly robust version of this critique, and has targeted not only Rawlsian political theory as a whole, but also the philosophy of human rights. It is a bracing argument, but also an overly general one.[8] His argument hinges on two controversial claims: first, on the rejection of the possibility for objectivity and normativity in moral and political theorizing altogether; and second, on the assumption that a justification of human rights must satisfy a standard akin to the justification of classical natural rights. In both cases, the argument overreaches. Rejecting moral realism does not entail rejecting the possibility of appealing to non-arbitrary standards of justification for our most important normative claims, including human rights claims.

Is there a more plausible version of political realism? Consider a spectrum that runs from 'complacent realism' at one end, to what we might call 'extravagant utopianism' at the other.[9] A political theory is extravagantly utopian when it involves asking people to do something they literally can't do, or what would be unreasonably burdensome or costly for them to do. It's important to note two points here. First, we need to distinguish between something that is literally impossible, and something that is unlikely to happen. Probability is not the same thing as actual ability.[10] It might be highly unlikely, for example, that the wealthy, without coercion, would be willing to forego a large part of their income to help the worse off. But it's not impossible. No doubt ending the slave trade seemed impossible to imagine in the early part of the 18th century, but it wasn't literally impossible. On the other hand, there might be extremely demanding aspects of a moral theory that are genuinely hard to imagine being realized in politics. But we shouldn't confuse people's moral imperfections or weaknesses with the requirements of morality itself. The fact that people just aren't very good doesn't necessarily impugn the demands of morality. So as long as we pay attention to something like 'ought implies can', the objection might go, the distinction between so-called 'realist' approaches and 'utopian' ones is not really significant. More seriously, it risks undermining the very possibility of acting morally in politics at all.

A political realist might respond to the objection in this way: the point isn't that politics is a morality-free zone, but that it has certain important features that distinguish it from other domains – in particular, a focus on questions of authority, legitimacy and power. Political philosophy, in this sense at least, is not simply applied meta-ethics, or a discourse focused mainly on principles. For Geuss, it means that we should start with not how people ought ideally or rationally to act, desire or value, but with the way 'social, economic [and political] institutions actually operate in society at some given time, and what really does move human beings to act in given circumstances'.[11] Geuss assumes that it follows from this that principles or normative claims are therefore irrelevant to politics. But this isn't the case. After all, people involved in all kinds of practical struggles appeal to notions of justice, equality and freedom to help explain and justify their actions to themselves and to others. That doesn't make them Kantians either, but it does mean the contrast between the 'real' and the 'normative' is more complex then he assumes.

I want to recast realism in a slightly different way. A suitably realist approach for political theory should understand politics as a distinctive mode of human activity, not always reducible to modes of scientific (or meta-ethical) explanation. It should place power, political disagreement and plurality at the heart of politics, and thus see conflict as ubiquitous and ineradicable. It should take seriously the role of institutions as relevant not only to the implementation and application of concepts or theories, but also, in complex ways, to their justification. This entails a broader sense of 'institutions': they are not only the products of desires, beliefs and human actions over time, but also shape and help produce the very beliefs, motivations and conduct of the people subject to them. This raises considerable challenges for self-consciously liberal conceptions of political legitimacy.[12]

Bernard Williams, for example, distinguishes between the 'enactment' and 'structural' models of political theory. According to the first, the whole *point* of political philosophy is to formulate principles, concepts, ideals and values which are then expressed in political action through the use of (legitimate) power, persuasion etc. According to the second, political theory lays down the moral conditions of co-existence under power, conditions in which power can be exercised. Utilitarianism is an example of the first, Rawlsian liberalism of the second. Both represent the priority of the moral over the political: politics is either the instrument of the moral, or the moral is meant to constrain politics.

For Geuss, political realism entails a rejection of both of these approaches. Williams, however, has a more subtle view. Realism does not mean that there is not anything to say about either evaluating political regimes, or distinguishing between mere coercion and legitimate authority. In fact, legitimacy is one of *the* key normative concepts for political theory, along with its close relation, power. But how then to distinguish legitimate from illegitimate rule? For Williams, those who claim political authority over a group must have something to say to each member about the basis of that authority. A legitimate political order can't literally be *any* kind of political order; it must at least solve the basic problem for which it is the proposed solution. This means a legitimate state, as opposed to an illegitimate one, must meet the 'Basic Legitimation Demand' (BLD). At a minimum, meeting the BLD entails a political order in which legitimacy does not simply mean 'might makes right', and Williams connects this idea with the protection of the most basic human rights. In fact, a political order consisting of one group of people terrorizing another is not yet a genuine *political* relation – it describes a situation to which the 'first political question' is addressed and for which an account of legitimate political authority is required.[13]

The BLD might still be a kind of moral conception then, but not one that originates prior to politics; as Williams puts it, 'It is a claim that is inherent in there *being* such a thing as politics.'[14] What I take Williams to mean here is that genuine political relations presuppose freedom: To paraphrase Michel Foucault, power presupposes free agents over and through whom power is exercised, and who in turn are capable of questioning and resisting it. Power without freedom is mere domination.

So what counts as an adequate response to the BLD? For Williams this is partly a historical and contextual question (the onset of modernity renders some legitimation stories literally nonsense), but he also introduces the 'critical theory principle': 'The acceptance of a justification does not count if the acceptance itself is produced by the coercive power which is supposedly being justified'.[15] Of course, the difficulty now is identifying what counts as having been '*produced by*' the coercive power in the relevant sense. Liberalism will set more stringent conditions for what counts as being disadvantaged under a political scheme and thus the standard of justification required (including one with reference to rights). For the realist, however, the path to understanding and grasping these standards of justification is essentially a historical one: they will start with the various practices and institutions within which agents find themselves enmeshed and try to identify the various justifications and rationales for the coercive powers being exercised over them.

Yet lying at the base of this approach – however practical and however political – is an appeal to the force of justification, to the demand that those who exercise power over others provide a justification for their purported authority. There remains, in other words, an appeal here to a fundamental moral demand for justification, albeit one, as Williams suggests, which is at the same time, distinctly political, and which can only ever be grounded in a free exchange of reasons between historically constituted individuals. The appeal then, is to a fundamental notion of freedom, one that accompanies or undergirds the appeal to justification at the heart of modern legitimation stories in particular. If legitimacy is a close normative relation to power – and thus to political order and control (the Hobbesian 'first question of politics') – then so too is freedom.

Of course, Williams' distinction mirrors, to some extent, a more familiar priority between ideal and non-ideal theory. Non-ideal theory is said to proceed by reference to the content of an ideal theory – or as Rawls puts it, 'how this long term goal might be achieved, or worked toward, usually in gradual steps'.[16] What Williams is suggesting is essentially an inversion of the priority assumption between ideal and non-ideal theory. In other words, how 'non-ideal theory' – or what we might call a political or 'practice-based' approach – functions as a kind of anticipation of a new (ideal) theory; a provisional, defeasible formulation of a set of norms of recognition and distribution.[17]

3 A political conception of rights

Is there, then, a suitably 'political' conception of rights that doesn't entail a submission to the way the world is, but also doesn't simply ignore the social and political conditions required for rights to be effective instruments against domination? One motivation underlying this chapter – not fully justified here – is that in taking seriously the context in which the conception of 'Aboriginal rights' emerged, for example, we see the extent to which the existence of certain rights does, in fact, seem to depend on socially recognized ways of acting and being acted upon. It is often argued that one reason why we should reject any form of social recognition thesis is that it makes fundamental moral rights – and thus human rights – susceptible to social and political contingency. Surely the *existence* conditions of the right not to be tortured, or the rights of slaves in 19th century America, or the property and self-determination claims of Aboriginal peoples, are not contingent on the social and political recognition of those rights? Whether or not we have the institutional means to fully prevent torture, or whether American society lacked the will to end slavery in the 1830s (or Australian society to recognize Aboriginal peoples' property rights), surely you and I have a right against being tortured, just as African Americans in the Antebellum south had a right not to be enslaved, and indigenous peoples have always had genuine property rights?

Of course, rights discourse – including natural rights discourse – is not the only way of protesting against the wrongness of slavery or torture. So it doesn't follow that if you hold a sceptical view about the justification of human rights, you are therefore incapable of *any* form of moral or social criticism. Nor does it follow that even if you want to hold onto the idea that a slave, for example, has a right not to be enslaved that stands independently of the likelihood of it being enforced by existing legal and social arrangements, you are committed to a natural rights view. There are different meta-ethical approaches to justifying the nature of rights claims. However, if the justification of the existence of our most important human rights, for example, can be said to be *entirely* independent of any form of social recognition, then we run into problems with regard to their putative universality. Either the general interests to which they refer are so abstract as to be highly indeterminate (and thus difficult to reconcile with our most important human rights instruments), or they are not in fact genuinely universal and instead describe a particular liberal form of life. I shall return to this point later.

Let me return for a moment to the issue of the rights of indigenous peoples. According to one account, the whole notion of 'indigenous' or 'aboriginal' rights is tainted by their continuing submission to what is essentially the continuation of a colonial and racial order put in place during the period of global imperial expansion from the 16th century onwards.

Taiaiake Alfred, for example, has argued that 'Aboriginal rights' are, in fact, 'the benefits accrued by indigenous peoples who have agreed to abandon their autonomy in order to enter the legal and political framework of the state . . . indigenous rights get defined not with respect to what exists in the minds and cultures of Native people, but in relation to the demands, interests and opinions of the millions of other peoples'.[18] Here liberal rights seem not so much protection *against* the arbitrary exercise of power, but rather a manifestation of the very relations of power against which they were supposed to protect indigenous peoples.

And yet, other indigenous theorists have sought to reconstruct the potential of liberal rights on very different grounds. John Borrows, for example, in the course of a discussion of the impact of the *Canadian Charter of Rights and Freedoms* on Aboriginal self-government, argues that the underlying principles of the *Charter* could potentially help realize indigenous peoples' claims. More specifically, Borrows argues that the *Charter* can help create a 'conversation' between the forms of equality embodied in the European languages of rights, and those within Indigenous traditions and political theories.[19] What is striking in Borrows' argument is the alignment of three distinct modalities of politics that are often kept apart: conversation, tradition, and rights. Borrows suggests that by exploiting the conjunction of the wide acceptance of rights language in the broader Canadian community, along with the conceptual and justificatory indeterminacy of rights claims themselves, they can be put to work in contributing to the emancipation, as opposed to the domination, of indigenous peoples.[20] It is no easy task however, 'retranslated and transposed by [indigenous peoples]', Borrows argues, the language of rights can be used to 'convey our meanings'.[21] The specific example he is discussing is the debate over sexual equality both within Aboriginal communities and between them and the state, but the general point is this: the language of rights, just like other normative languages, can be translated through mutual conversation between different traditions – one that itself has certain prior conditions – and a living tradition can be re-invigorated, and some of its more vulnerable elements even gain strength from, a transformed discourse of rights and citizenship.[22] Borrows calls this a form of 'critical pragmatism'.

Debates over the history and use of the 'doctrine of aboriginal rights' exemplify the kind of genealogical conceptual analysis practised by Foucault and others, where the purposes that governed the emergence of a concept (or institution or social practice) may be quite different from those it might come to serve in the present. These rights came into existence in the context of colonial rule and the imposition of imperial constitutional law between the 17th and 18th centuries in Canada, Australia and elsewhere.[23] So it's clear that the doctrine was formed within the context of deeply unequal relations of power between colonizers and colonized, and helped entrench unjust relations between indigenous and settler populations. And yet today, in different contexts – including, among other things, different beliefs about race, anti-discrimination and amidst a resurgence of indigenous activism – this very doctrine has offered one avenue through which indigenous peoples have been able to contest the actions the state and other powerful actors inflict on them. Although pursuing contestation through the language of rights has been required precisely because of the persistence of the legal and political doctrines and institutions that were imposed on them, Borrows (and others) still claim they can play a role in aboriginal struggles for and of freedom. How can this be?

One straightforward argument, as we've seen, is that the sheer ubiquity of rights in our public discourse offers a tool for indigenous peoples to exploit. Insofar as the ascription of rights entails the ascription of some form of equal worth and agency to individuals (and sometimes groups), this can be used by the more vulnerable in society to promote their claims for equal consideration and entitlement. In Australia, for example, Larissa Behrendt has argued that, for all its faults, the language of rights enables the principle of non-discrimination to become publicly manifest in various ways – connecting the harms suffered by indigenous people to a moral (and legal) register accessible to the vast majority of citizens.[24] Rights offer one way of articulating social and political harms and signal the significance of those harms. Note that this means the appeal to the pragmatism of rights cannot be a purely strategic play. There is an explicit appeal to the equal moral worth of individuals underlying these arguments. So it is value-infused pragmatism, and pragmatic or practical in the sense that it focuses on the *actions* or activities of individuals (or groups) as rights claimants.

But as attractive as this critical pragmatism might be, it is vulnerable to a powerful objection that has its origins in variations of Marx's critique of liberal rights in *On the Jewish Question*.[25] Marx argued that liberal rights were a product of the relations of power constitutive of bourgeois society, and are thus unable to provide the grounds for an effective critique of the inequality and alienation in that society. This is one of the foundations for Williams's 'critical theory principle' outlined previously: the normative justification we offer for the institutions and practices to which we are subject cannot be a product of those very institutions.

This critique has been extended in interesting ways that touches on the issue of the relation between the existence condition of a right and its instantiation in juridical and political regimes. Moral philosophers tend to want to keep a very strict delineation between these two domains. But I think political philosophy needs to pay attention to the way they can become entwined.

The concept of a right has both intensional and extensional dimensions. The crucial question is the *relation* between these dimensions – between the claim that 'X is a right' and the claim that 'P has a right to X', where P represents a particular agent at a particular point and place in time. Wendy Brown has argued that the fundamental paradox of rights is 'the paradox between the universal idiom and the local effect of rights'.[26] That is, the interplay between the apparent freedom to act in a certain way, and the regulatory, discursive and normative context within which that 'free action' takes place.[27] Thus rights can end up doing two different things at the same time. First, rights can work so as to align individual conduct with various kinds of particular social, political, economic and cultural norms. Rights under-determine action in a myriad of ways (they can be waived, withheld, alienated or suspended), but also structure a range of possible actions. A right to sue for defamation or invasion of privacy ensures that the law will enforce culturally specific standards of civility.[28] A right to be immunized from certain kinds of interference might embody various assumptions about the proper scope of governmental 'interference' in society or the economy. Of course, rights are also used to challenge prevalent social norms as well. However a crucial issue is often not only the absence or presence of a legally enforceable right, but of the social and political conditions surrounding it: to which interests, reasons, norms or capacities do rights refer? How and in what context is the right exercised and by whom? Will it be an individual, a group? Will it be exercised by the agent herself, or by a representative? And how will it be enforced, and by whom? In other words, what are the social, historical and norm-based 'surrounds' of the claim? What conventions and norms govern both the justification and the *uptake* of a rights claim? Although rights are often invoked against social practices and to criticize them, they are also a kind of social practice themselves. They simultaneously presuppose various kinds of social arrangements and patterns of interaction, as well as reinforce and help bring various institutions and ways of acting into being.

To summarize: rights empower different individuals and groups unevenly, depending on their capacity to exercise the powers, capacities or immunities to which the rights refer. The danger of rights-talk is that in some instances, it can end up entrenching various relations of power if rights are ascribed but the effective means for exercising them are not. And (or) it can end up de-politicizing those relations of power; that is, by abstracting or obscuring those relations of power constitutive of a particular identity or subject relevant to the ascription of rights. The designation 'women's rights', for example, according to Brown, 'may entail some protection from the most immobilizing features of that designation' but 're-inscribes as it protects us, and thus enables our further regulation through that designation'.[29] Standard liberal rights protecting bodily integrity or freedom from violence, for example, can fail to protect women from harms perpetrated elsewhere when combined with other claims to do with religious freedom or property rights. Rights are not the only means of protecting individuals from harm. But they are a particularly powerful discourse in liberal democratic societies.

Is the language and practice of rights suitably commodious to accommodate such re-inscriptions and re-translations, especially as envisaged by advocates of 'Aboriginal rights'? Is there a conception of rights which can contribute to promoting the conditions for effective contestation by the most vulnerable in domestic and global politics – including contesting the way conceptions of rights themselves function to entrench or de-politicize discrimination? I think there is, but my suggestion is that it must be suitably 'realist' in the sense I am trying to develop here.

4 Conclusion: taking rights and recognition seriously

To conclude, I want to suggest there are four elements to what it might mean to take political realism seriously for our theories of rights. Harking back to the first section, we need to embrace a *pluralistic* approach to the grounds of rights; a *constrained* universality with regard to their scope; a dynamic conception of the underlying interests to which they refer; and the need for some kind of *social recognition* as a constitutive feature of the existence conditions of rights. Let me say a bit more about each of these in turn.

First of all, we should embrace pluralism with regard to the grounds of rights. Although a number of recent important arguments about rights, and especially human rights, have been concerned to limit the grounds of rights claims to a narrow band of values and interests, this runs into considerable difficulty.[30] Limiting the justification of the grounds of human rights, for example, to the crucial interests humans have in liberty and autonomy makes it difficult to redeem many of the important other rights enumerated in our human rights instruments (and especially social and political rights). Although no doubt the profligacy of rights claims should motivate a desire to impose greater conceptual and justificatory discipline on the field, the danger is that the narrowing of the grounds can appear arbitrary. James Griffin, for example, struggles to see how a human right to work can be reconciled with his account of the fundamental grounds of human rights resting on our crucial interests in autonomy and liberty.[31] However, as John Tasioulas points out, there is no obvious reason why we shouldn't seek out other goods and prudential values to help justify our current, most paradigmatic human rights that extend beyond our interests in protecting and promoting our autonomy and liberty (including the right to work).[32]

Second, we should embrace a more constrained universality concerning our most important rights, including human rights. Many of our paradigmatic human rights, for example, are clearly related to interests that we have as members of particular kinds of societies, with historically specific social, legal, political and cultural structures in place. The fact that an inhabitant of a Lockean or Hobbesian state of nature would have no obvious claim to rights of free speech, employment, nationality or to collective self-determination is sometimes taken to expose the blatant improbability of universal human rights, or the fact that they consist only in what are extremely abstract (to the point of meaninglessness) rights to liberty or autonomy. On the other hand, if it is then admitted that the interests to which our most important rights refer are limited to historically specific interests, then does it follow that there really are no genuinely universal rights? It is a short step from there to the claim that human rights, for example, are essentially parochial, and that their justification entails the imposition of a particular form of life on those who hold very different conceptions of the good and the right.

But we should not be tempted by either of these moves. Instead, we should embrace a constrained universality for our most important rights, including human rights. The interests to which they refer are unavoidably connected to particular historical contexts and the development and presence of specific social, cultural, political, economic and legal practices and institutions. But here the aforementioned pluralist approach to the grounds of rights can help illuminate justificatory pathways to our most important rights claims, which can then help to create the conditions for productive conversations between different traditions about the most important interests deserving of rights protection. It does open the grounds of the existence conditions of our most important rights to contestation and thus to the potential expansion of the grounds for rights claims – but that is an unavoidable consequence of embracing the pluralist position. Public reasoning about rights, whether in domestic or global contexts, requires acceptance of what Rawls called the 'fact of reasonable pluralism' regarding the ultimate grounds of their justification.

Third, we should embrace a dynamic conception of the interests underlying our most important rights. This follows from the pluralism and constrained universality arguments outlined previously. But it also follows from the indeterminacy of a right's normative implications more generally. The duties generated by a right, for example, can vary dramatically depending on the nature of the agents, institutions and social contexts in which they are claimed. This is because, as Tasioulas has put it, what drives the interest-based theory of rights 'are the interests a right protects rather than any *specific* set of normative implications they generate'.[33] Rights will have different consequences in varying historical, social and cultural contexts, depending on existing practices and institutions and what is required to protect or promote the underlying interests to which they refer. But I believe that it also follows (as perhaps Tasioulas does not) that as our understanding of the underlying interests changes, so too do the rights to which they refer. The dynamism goes both ways – not simply in the direction of the varying normative implications of rights claims, but also with regard to the existence conditions of the rights themselves. In fact, the kind of interests to which indigenous peoples have referred with reference to their own normative and social orders might well generate new kinds of rights hitherto unnoticed or unrecognized in liberal democratic social and political orders. There is an inherent dynamism to our rights discourse that can only be captured by taking an appropriate historical view of our practices of rights.

Finally, I think a politically realist account of rights should embrace a modest version of the recognition thesis as an element of the existence condition of rights, including our most important rights. By this, I mean the view that what it means to possess a right – including a moral right – involves some form of genuinely mutual recognition by others. Why is this important? Taking the perspective of those who often struggle most to realize their rights, the claim that the existence condition of a right has nothing *whatsoever* to do with whether or not it can be made effective is deeply implausible. In fact, one of the persistent effects of historical injustice is the way in which the promise and realization of rights becomes a kind of mirage that dissolves precisely at the moment when it is needed most.

The standard objection to this argument, as we've seen, is that building a social recognition thesis into the existence condition of our most important rights seems to rob the rights discourse of its vital critical force, and hold the content of rights (and not just their putative enforceability) hostage to extant social practices and conventions. But according to what I am calling the modest version of the social recognition thesis, it does not follow that such recognition must always come from the *state*, or even from the majority of one's fellow citizens. A slave, for example, may be denied recognition as an equal by the state, but not necessarily by the communities of which she is a member and who do indeed treat her as an equal.[34] Similarly, many Indigenous political theorists in Australia and Canada are now arguing for eschewing the recognition game with the state and instead asserting the validity of their rights claims as also inhering in their own normative and social orders, and thus a more complex set of practices of mutual recognition and legitimation.[35]

Of course, this in turn generates the need for reconciling these plural sources of normativity, and thus different modes of cross-cultural mutual justification. We are always members of more than one community. And it is precisely when the claims we make in these different communities generate conflict, such that recognition afforded in one is denied in another, that social and political change ensues – including our understanding of our most important rights, as well as what it takes to realize them in practice.[36]

Notes

1 For further discussion on historical injustice see Duncan Ivison, 'Historical Injustice', in *The Oxford Handbook of Political Theory*, edited by Jon Dryzek, et al. (Oxford: Oxford University Press, 2006), pp. 507–525, and Jeff Spinner-Halve, *Enduring Injustice* (Cambridge: Cambridge University Press, 2012).

2 Duncan Ivison, *Postcolonial Liberalism* (Cambridge: Cambridge University Press, 2002).

3 Duncan Ivison, 'The Logic of Aboriginal Rights', *Ethnicities* 3, no. 3 (2003): p. 321.

4 John Rawls, *A Theory of Justice: Revised Edition* (Cambridge: Harvard University Press, 1999), p. 96.

5 See Tommie Shelby, 'Justice, Deviance and the Dark Ghetto', *Philosophy and Public Affairs* 35 (2007), p. 145.

6 See, for example, Gopal Sreenivasan, 'A Right to Health? Some Inconclusive Scepticism', *Proceedings of the Aristotelian Society*, Supplemental Volume 86 (2012): p. 239; John Tasioulas, 'The Place of Human Rights and Common Good in Global Health Policy', *Theoretical Medicine and Bioethics*, 37, no. 4 (2016): p. 365.

7 For an overview of rights theory see Duncan Ivison, *Rights* (Stocksfield: Acumen, 2008).

8 Raymond Geuss, *Philosophy and Real Politics* (Princeton: Princeton University Press, 2008); also Raymond Geuss, *History and Illusion in Politics* (Cambridge: Cambridge University Press, 2001). For further discussion see Ivison, *Rights*, pp. 89–91.

9 I have discussed the dangers of moralism in Duncan Ivison, 'Multiculturalism and Resentment', in *Political Theory and Australian Multiculturalism*, edited by Geoffrey Brahm Levey (New York: Berghahn Books, 2008), pp. 129–148.

10 David Estlund, 'Utopophobia', *Philosophy and Public Affairs* 42, no. 2 (2014): p. 113.

11 Geuss, *Philosophy and Real Politics*, p. 9. Importantly, taking a realist approach in this sense doesn't mean reducing everything in politics to 'self-interest', which is simply the mirror image of moralism. Rather, it is to take a broader view of the nature of political activity, whilst at the same time taking a more realistic approach to the powers and limitations of political actors. See Bernard Williams, *In the Beginning Was the Deed: Realism and Moralism in Political Argument* (Princeton: Princeton University Press, 2005), pp. 12–14.

12 This might seem to entail that a political realist approach is necessarily state-focused and non-universalist. If institutions matter in this way, so this argument goes, then we have special obligations to those with whom we share subjection to a common regime of coercion and not to others. We certainly do have special obligations to others, but it doesn't follow that all forms of political realism are necessarily state-centred to the exclusion of other non-state based and transnational institutions. There might well be certain 'general' special obligations that all of us share in light of the development of transnational practices and institutions that form part of a 'global basic structure'.

13 Interestingly, this is a fundamental insight shared by both Hobbes and Rousseau: 'The social contract is a sacred right, which provides the basis for all others. Yet this right does not come from nature, it is therefore founded on conventions. The problem is to know what those conventions are'. See Jean-Jacques Rousseau, *The Social Contract*, ed. Victor Gourevitch (Cambridge: Cambridge University Press, 1997), p. 41.

14 Williams, In the Beginning Was the Deed, p. 8.

15 Williams, In the Beginning Was the Deed, p. 7.

16 John Rawls, *The Law of Peoples: With the 'Idea of Public Reason revisited'* (Cambridge Mass.: Harvard University Press, 2001), p. 89.

17 This distinction and the focus on a practice-based approach to theorizing is a key feature of the work of James Tully. See James Tully, 'Wittgenstein and Political Philosophy: Understanding Practices of Critical Reflection', *Political Theory* 17, no. 2 (1989): p. 172.

18 Taiaike Alfred, *Peace, Power, Righteousness: An Indigenous Manifesto* (Toronto: Oxford University Press, 1999), p. 140. This section draws on material first explored in Duncan Ivison, 'Consent or Contestation?', in *Between Consenting Peoples: Political Community and the Meaning of Consent*, edited by Jeremy Webber and Colin M Macleod (Vancouver: University of British Colombia Press, 2010), pp. 188–206.

19 John Borrows, 'Contemporary Traditional Equality: The Effect of the Charter on First Nation Politics', *University of New Brunswick Law Journal* 43, no. 1 (1994): p. 21.

20 For a related but different approach to putting rights to work for indigenous peoples, see Larissa Behrendt, *Achieving Social Justice: Indigenous Rights and Australia's Future* (Sydney: Federation Press, 2003).

21 Borrows, 'Contemporary Traditional Equality', p. 23.

22 See John Borrows, 'Landed Citizenship: Narratives of Aboriginal Political Participation', in *Citizenship in Diverse Societies, edited by* Will Kymlicka and Wayne Norman (Oxford: Oxford University Press, 2000), especially at pp. 329–330. The idea, roughly speaking, is that Aboriginal self-government also means bringing to bear Aboriginal political philosophies and values on the wider community and its decision-making processes. Without the recognition of both separateness and interdependency, Aboriginal people lack the means to effectively contest those norms and institutions acting on their most important interests.

23 See Brian Slattery, 'Understanding Aboriginal Rights', *Canadian Bar Review* 66, no. 2 (1987): p. 727; Brian Slattery, 'Aboriginal Sovereignty and Imperial Claims', *Osgoode Hall Law Journal* 29 (1991): p. 681; Cole Harris, *Making Native Space: Colonialism, Resistance, and Reserves in British Columbia* (Vancouver: University of British Colombia, 2002); Paul Kael, *European Conquest and the Rights of Indigenous Peoples* (Cambridge: Cambridge University Press, 2002).

24 Behrendt, Achieving Social Justice.

25 See David McLelland, ed., *Karl Marx: Selected Writings* (Oxford: Oxford University Press, 2001).

26 Wendy Brown, 'Suffering Rights as Paradoxes', *Constellations* 7, no. 2 (2000): p. 233.

27 For further discussion of this point in relation to conceptions of freedom see Duncan Ivison, *The Self at Liberty: Political Argument and the Arts of Government* (Cornell: Cambridge University Press, 1997).

28 This example was suggested to me by Robert Post.

29 Brown, 'Suffering Rights as Paradoxes', p. 232.

30 The most powerful recent case for limiting human rights claims is made by James Griffin, *On Human Rights* (Oxford: Oxford University Press, 2008).

31 Griffin, *On Human Rights*, p. 207.

32 John Tasioulas, 'Human Rights, Universality and the Values of Personhood: Retracing Griffin's Steps', *European Journal of Philosophy* 10, no. 1 (2002): p. 89.

33 John Tasioulas, 'The Moral Reality of Human Rights', in *Freedom From Poverty as a Human Right: Who Owes What to The Very Poor?* edited by Thomas Pogge (Oxford: Oxford University Press, 2007), p. 22.

34 See the excellent discussion in Derrick Darby, *Rights, Race and Recognition* (Cambridge: Cambridge University Press, 2009), p. 156 ff.

35 See especially Glen Coulthard, *Red Skin, White Masks: Rejecting the Colonial Politics of Recognition* (Minneapolis: Minnesota University Press, 2014); Duncan Ivison, 'Justification, Not Recognition', *Indigenous Law Bulletin* 8, no. 24 (2016): p. 12.

36 My thanks to Tom Campbell for the invitation to participate in this project, as well as his comments on a draft of this chapter, and to the participants of the workshop in which an earlier version was discussed, especially John Tasioulas, David Kinley and Wojciech Sadurski (who suggested the title).

4 A practical account of the concept of human rights

Jovana Davidovic

Conceptual analyses of human rights tend to be open to either the criticism from the practitioner's side that they are too idealistic and 'top-down' or from the philosopher's side that they are too dependent on the human rights practice. In this chapter, I defend a view that it is possible to ground the conceptual analysis of human rights in their practice without falling prey to worries about not being able to criticize such a practice. I do this by first showing that most of the conceptual analyses to date have ignored the two, properly speaking, prior question: (a) what exactly would count as a conceptual account of human rights and (b) what is the purpose of such a conceptual account? I argue that once we make clear that purpose, we will make space for a concept of human rights that is sensitive to practice.

In Section 1, I start by clarifying my main aim of carving out a space for a practice-sensitive conceptual analysis of human rights. In particular, I try to explain why we ought to care about answering the question 'what are human rights?' In Section 2, I look at one relatively successful attempt at a concept of human rights, namely Charles Beitz's practical account of human rights, which he develops in *The Idea of Human Rights.*[1] In Section 3, I turn to the criticisms, which his and other practical accounts have faced. In particular, I examine Christian Barry's and Nicholas Southwood's criticism of Beitz's approach as well as their alternative – the substantive, pluralist account of human rights.[2] I also address John Tasioulas's rejection of, what he calls, the functional approach.[3] Finally, in Section 4, I defend attempts to ground the concept of human rights in practice. I argue that most, if not all, scholars who have asked the question 'what are human rights?' have gone on at some length without making clear the purpose of their inquiry. I argue that we first have to clarify whether we are seeking a concept of human rights, or the nature of the object that such concept picks out; second, we need to ask what the purpose of our conceptual analysis is. Only after we have established answers to these two questions should we attempt to make sense of the debates about the nature of human rights. I will ague that once we have asked these questions we will have further reason to embrace the practical account of human rights.

Ultimately, my aim is to articulate an account of human rights that respects the distinction between the metaphysical, conceptual and normative projects and that can describe the concept of human rights as it exists today, rather than try to conform it to some practice-independent notion of natural rights or their kin. I defend such an account by (a) suggesting various ways one can understand the projects which have tried to answer 'what are human rights?' and arguing that (b) if these projects are seen as conceptual then the practical approach does better with respect to a number of possible aims of such conceptual inquiry. In trying to defend (b), I will argue that the practical approach to human rights can provide meaningful normative guidance that is critical of the current human rights practice.

1 The concept of human rights

What exactly does it mean to engage in a theoretical analysis of human rights? Is it to ask: (a) what are human rights, or (b) what is the nature of human rights, or (c) what is the meaning of 'human rights,' or (d) what is the concept of human rights, or something altogether different?[4] To ask questions (a) or (b) is to assume that there are some objects/human rights whose nature one can describe. But trying to describe the nature of the object is a different project from trying to describe the concept of human rights. The concept of human rights, if we take one popular view 'lies between words and meanings on one hand, and the object(s) the concepts pick out on the other.'[5] If that is what a concept is, then the conceptual analysis of human rights, at a minimum, seeks to provide grounds on which one can make meaningful assertions about human rights.[6] A conceptual analysis of human rights is then an attempt to describe an idea that is widely used by people to make sense of their condition and the social institutions that surround them. Such an analysis is also meant to inform the normative questions about what human rights require of us and why, but it is not meant to exhaustively answer them. Both of these projects (the conceptual and the normative) are incredibly important and not fully independent; the conceptual project limits answers to interesting normative questions. But it should be clear that the conceptual project ought to (at least in this case) come first.[7] In fact, it is hard to imagine what it would mean to ask why human rights are reason-giving and to whom they are reason-giving without knowing what human rights are. Unfortunately, all too often normative and practical proposals with respect to human rights seem insensitive to the relevance of a coherent concept of human rights. It often seems that practitioners assume that what human rights are is either clear or irrelevant to the practical debates. But this is obviously wrong.

For example, one often hears calls for taking the cultural, economic and social rights seriously and on a par with civil and political rights. The reasons usually given in support of such proposals either take the form of suggesting that the cultural, economic and social rights are as important to the human life as political and civil rights or that these cultural, economic and social rights are necessary to put political and civil rights into practice. Providing either one of those two arguments in support of the effort to promote the cultural, social and economic rights assumes not only a particular understanding of what human rights are, but also a particular understanding of why we ought to care about them. But it is enough to look at the breadth of philosophical literature to understand that each proposed understanding of human rights and their grounding comes with a variety of problems. The different understandings of the concept of human rights and the unique problems that come with each such understanding put different limits on what one is entitled to appeal to in calls for a change in the human rights practice. Even more importantly for the practitioner, they put limits on the mechanisms one can coherently propose for putting their proposal into practice. For example, one's reasons for suggesting we ought to focus more on the cultural, economic and social rights limit the type of solution one can give when satisfying those rights and directly conflicts with satisfying civil and political rights. Simply put, conceptual analyses of human rights must be prior to answers about the practice of human rights. It is exactly this last assertion and the common misinterpretation of this assertion that leads so many practitioners to reject conceptual analyses of human rights as irrelevant for what they do. The suggestion that we can understand human rights, like some do, by looking at, for example, what features humans all necessarily share and without referring to the facts about the current legal and political state of affairs with respect to the human rights practice seems outrageous to many practitioners, and rightly so.

But a call for a clear concept of human rights and one that is prior to practical questions and normative claims need not be a call for a concept that is isolated from such practice. The misunderstanding probably arises around the notion of a concept being *prior* to practice. Clearly, for one to coherently assert that the concept is *prior* to practice *and that* the practice can inform the concept requires that the elements of the practice one appeals to in making sense of the concept be *in principle* different from those that such a concept is meant to inform.[8]

The claim that we may glean the concept of human rights from its practice is not new and several attempts at practical accounts have been given, most recently and I believe most successfully by Beitz in his book *The Idea of Human Rights.*

2 Beitz's practical approach to human rights

A number of scholars have attempted to argue in favour of what is commonly called the practical or functionalist or political approach to the concept of human rights. While these accounts vary greatly they nonetheless share at least the belief that human rights have political/institutional functions that in part define them. For example, Beitz argues that we can develop an understanding of the concept of human rights from the role that this concept plays in our discursive practice. In particular he suggests that we can learn quite a bit about the concept from asking what the participants in the practice see themselves as committed to (linguistically and conceptually) once they assert there is a human right to X. This then requires that we describe the practice of human rights so as to define the role the concept plays in that practice. Describing such a practice in turn requires we choose elements of our global relations that properly fit within it and those that do not. This seems like a difficult task. In fact often it seems that nowadays our discursive practice of human rights is so overly broad that any non-evaluative attempts to delineate such practice are bound to fail. Scholars in nearly all fields seem all too often to discuss issues of social and global justice through the lens of human rights without at the same time explaining or justifying their reasons for doing so. Obviously, not every issue of social and global justice is an issue of human rights. In a weak sense, what this means is that there are at least some reasons (which might be pragmatic or theoretical) to suggest that some social justice questions are better addressed via the language of human rights and others are not. But that in itself is a judgement that cannot be used to exclude such instances of appeal to human rights in literature, at least not without some further justifications. How can one then assert, as Beitz does, that the best way to understand the concept of human rights is through the role it plays in our discourse and practice, and also develop an account of human rights that can ground criticism of such practice?

Beitz is keenly aware of this worry which is why his proposal is not that we simply collect every assertion about human rights people make and attempt to 'read off' the concept of human rights from there. Instead he proposes that we take the 'doctrine and practice of human rights as we find them in international political life as the *source materials* for constructing a conception of human rights.'[9] In the source materials Beitz includes not only legal texts and enforcement mechanisms, but also observations of critical public discourse, political action and others.[10] He then suggests that we can use various sifting tools to move from these source materials gathered from the current state of the practice to the model that is meant to capture the concept of human rights. These sifting tools assume that: (a) the model should seek to represent a consensus regarding the pattern of usage (not normative content), (b) the 'model should rely on a conception of the practice's aim or purpose in order to adjudicate among conflicting beliefs about the practical significance of its central terms,' (c) the model should allow for disagreements to be endemic to the practice, and that it should (d) distinguish between disagreements about the practice and within the practice.[11] These sifting tools allow us to move from the 'raw data' about the practice and its current state of affairs to a model of its concept. The sifting tools allow us to isolate from the practice the shared understanding of the role that the concept of human rights plays in the practice of human rights. In other words, even though we do not agree on what gets on the list or what human rights require, we nonetheless seem to have a certain level of shared understanding of the times when it is appropriate to invoke human rights, i.e. we agree on the function that the concept of human rights plays in our discursive global practice. The two-step model of the concept of human rights according to Beitz has three elements.[12] On his view human rights are

> 'requirements whose object is to protect urgent individual interests against certain predictable threats [and they] apply in the first instance to the political institutions of states, [but are nonetheless] matters of international concern [when a government fails] to carry out its first-level responsibilities.'[13]

The tools we use to sift through the 'raw data' then allow us to assert that we are not just describing the practice as it is, but are developing a concept that can inform the normative and practical questions regarding human rights. And given that there are these three conditions on something properly being called a human right, one can imagine that not everything that is in the international legal documents necessarily fits this concept. In other words, these sifting tools allow us to differentiate between those things that are properly called human rights and those that are not and at least in that way they allow for criticism of the practice.

In the rest of the chapter, I elaborate on the common criticism, which Beitz's practical approach has encountered regarding its reliance on the current state of affairs. In light of those criticisms, I provide a defence of a generic practical/political account of human rights. There, I retain, what I take to be Beitz's great contribution – the attempt to make clear to practitioners that to do conceptual analysis of human rights, which we must, we need not take the top-down approach.[14]

3 Common criticisms of practical approaches

The most common criticism of Beitz's approach is that it supports the status quo. After all the concept of human rights is for Beitz directly dependent on the way participants in the practice see human rights. And even though it is by no means new or shocking to assert that a social practice can only be understood properly from the perspective of a genuine participant in that practice, nonetheless these sorts of approaches (common to social sciences) often face the worry that they are unable to meaningfully criticize the practice if they depend too much on the participants' perspective. Christian Barry and Nicholas Southwood offer a criticism of Beitz that builds on this worry.[15]

Barry and Southwood worry that grounding the concept of human rights in the role it plays in our discourse necessarily ties it to an assumption of a plurality of nation states which in turn results in some highly worrisome consequences. For example, Barry and Southwood argue that if in a world of no nation states genocide occurred we would, they argue, still want to say that that genocide is a violation of human rights. They worry that given Beitz's second element of the model of the concept of human rights – namely that human rights must be in the first instance addressed to a state's institutions – Beitz has no tools to explain why genocide in a world of no nation states would nonetheless be a violation of human rights.[16]

Another related worry for Barry and Southwood is that accounts like Beitz's leave us 'hostage to historical fortune,' so that if human rights practices end up being construed as primarily aimed at peace (as opposed to justice and protection of urgent interests) we might end up with a very different set of human rights.[17]

Barry and Southwood further worry that Beitz is confusing the question about the concept of human rights with the proper institutionalization of human rights. They think we should only pay attention to contingent facts about the global order when we ask questions about how to institutionalize human rights, and not when we ask what human rights are. I will argue later on that they are right with respect to this but only to a certain extent. Namely, they are wrong in their assumption that all the institutional features of the global order are simply contingent.

In light of these worries, Barry and Southwood propose, what they call, a structural pluralist account which is meant to remedy the problems of Beitz's account (as well as some naturalist accounts).[18] They propose an account that would be independent of the current practice and substantive in the sense that it would protect a multiplicity of urgent interests. Their account is pluralist and substantive in that it would (unlike some naturalist accounts) include protections among human rights of a broad range of core human interests. Their account is nonetheless not committed to the view that the protection of a core human interest is alone sufficient to classify a right as a human right; instead, Barry and Southwood agree with Beitz that human rights are (protections which are) primarily aimed at political institutions, just not that they are primarily aimed at states.

Barry and Southwood are not alone in their rejection of Beitz's approach. John Tasioulas for example also argues against, what he calls, the functional approach and he too offers a substantive account of human rights.[19] He defines functionalist accounts as those that believe that 'it belongs to the essence of human rights that they play a certain political role or combination of such roles, e.g. operating as benchmarks for the legitimacy of states or triggers for intervention against states that violate them.'[20] He argues against such views by suggesting that human rights are a subset of natural rights. He argues human rights are primarily moral standards and that they are moral rights held by all in virtue of their humanity (much like most naturalists argue). He argues that the functionalist/political approach is wrong in asserting that the very nature of human rights is partly determined by certain institutional roles they play. He worries that by committing to functionalism we 'abandon the characterization of human rights as moral rights possessed by all human beings simply in virtue of their humanity.'[21] Tasioulas further argues that while human rights do clearly impose duties on other people as well as institutions and while they clearly can and do play an institutional role, it is 'not written into the concept of a human right that they perform these other functions.'[22] What Tasioulas ultimately wants us to accept is that we can understand what human rights are without understanding their political role. An additional worry that Tasioulas has with respect to the functionalist approach is that it requires that we call cosmopolitan theorists and anarchists 'incoherent,' given that on a functionalist view what it means to say that there is a human right to X is, in part, that the state has an obligation to fulfil the right to X.

Scholars like Tasioulas, Barry and Southwood ultimately think that human rights are not primarily political, and that the concept of human rights should not be too closely tied to its practice. Instead they argue that it is an essential element of human rights that they are held by all human brings in virtue of their humanity. And while they are critical of some implications of the traditional naturalist view of human rights, like the one offered by James Griffin, they nonetheless think that failing to understand human rights as protecting core human interests is failing to describe the concept well.[23]

What these naturalist and substantive accounts share is the view that human rights are pre-institutional, that they are held by humans even in the absence of human rights mechanisms and that their content is not determined by moral conventions or legal rules, but that they are prior to those. They argue that the content of human rights can be known independently of knowing anything about the practice. Usually, for naturalist scholars we ought to turn to some feature of us as humans to make sense of what gets on the list and why. For Griffin, for example, what makes us essentially human is our normative agency, i.e. our ability to have a conception of a good life and act on it. On his view, then, human rights are protections of personhood (normative agency).[24] Normative agency requires protections of our autonomy, liberty and welfare rights. So the sorts of interests that ground human rights on Griffin's account can be picked out by asking whether or not the protection of that interest is necessary for protection of our normative agency. For Barry and Southwood, there is a broad range of interests that have different substantive grounds that in turn ground human rights. And for Tasioulas it is the interests we have in virtue of our humanity jointly with our human dignity that ground human rights. It is important to know that for all of these scholars, these grounds are not just meant to answer the conceptual questions, but also the normative ones as well. In other words, for naturalists (whether they be of normative agency, pluralist interests, dignity or pluralist interests and dignity kind) that which grounds answers to the conceptual question also grounds and often exhausts the normative questions like why human rights are reason-giving to others and what should be on the list of human rights. Practical scholars (like Beitz) instead commonly separate the two questions. For Beitz, the concept of human rights informs the normative questions, but it does not do that exhaustively or on its own.[25]

The main differences between the practical and naturalist approaches are in the answers to the following two questions: (a) is the appeal to some features of personhood necessary for grounding the concept and (b) is the appeal to human rights institutions necessary? The naturalist scholars answer in the affirmative with respect to (a) and in the negative with respect to (b), whereas practical approach scholars take the exact opposite stance.[26]

4 Practical approach and the conceptual analysis

A practical approach to the concept of human rights has a lot to offer. In part this is because we ought to be sympathetic to any approach that has a clear answer to give to practitioners regarding its relevance to practice. In fact, it is not clear why scholars think that ignoring institutional features in the first level of analysis of a concept is obviously good (as they often seem to). It seems that there are some concepts that cannot be separated from the notion of institutionalization, like for example the concept of law. And given the history of human rights it seems that the concept of human rights might very well be just such a concept. If that is the case then Barry's, Southwood's and Tasioulas's suggestions are akin to saying that we ought to separate the concept of law from the institution of law.[27] None of this is meant to deny the importance of or the existence of natural rights. Whether or not there are natural rights and whether some of the drafters of, for example, the Universal Declaration of Human Rights (UDHR) had them in mind when they were drafting the human right documents, today human rights are an institutional concept, and such a concept plays a very different role in our society from the role that the concept of natural rights plays.

These are some starting intuitions that lead me to try to answer the main criticisms against the practical approach. But these reflections aside, to start we must first ask what exactly are we searching for in our conceptual analysis of human rights? Only after we answer that question (at least provisionally) should we endeavour to actually start filling out the concept of human rights. I believe most of these scholars fail to state what the purpose of their inquiry is exactly. Failing to clearly state what the purposes of various analyses are makes it difficult to compare different claims about human rights.[28] That is why it is so important that we start by asking what is the purpose and aim of a 'conceptual' investigation of human rights? Are we after a concept, or the nature of the object the concept picks out? If we are after the concept, are we after it to 'maintain a structure within which meaningful discussion can occur,' or so as to provide normative standards for using the term?[29] In the rest of this chapter I answer these questions about how best to understand the naturalist and practical projects. I ask what it would mean to suggest these are conceptual projects and then what such conceptual projects aim at? One of the possible aims of a conceptual analysis, I will suggest, is imposing moral standards for using the term human rights.[30] In discussing that aim I will finally address some of the main criticisms of the practical approach and argue that the practical approach can play a significant role in making sense of interesting normative questions.

a. *Types of conceptual analyses*

Naturalist theorists have a different idea of what a conceptual analysis of human rights is supposed to yield than the practical scholars. At a minimum, and on the surface, the differences become obvious when one acknowledges that the naturalist accounts are at the same time conceptual as well as normative projects. For naturalists, the sorts of answers that tell us what human rights are also tell us what gets on the list of human rights and why, as well as what sorts of reasons human rights give rise to. That is not necessarily the case with practical approaches. In fact, as we saw, Beitz is committed to separating the conceptual and normative analyses and considers the fact that this is possible on his account to be one advantage of it. In addition, the differences also seem obvious when we consider the scholar's primary audience. While the practical scholars are significantly more interested in providing an account that is bottom-up and relevant for the practitioners, the naturalist scholars primarily address other philosophers.[31] These two reasons (separation of conceptual and normative projects and the intended audience of the account) should at least on the first pass make us wonder whether these theories are best understood as actually aiming at the same type of analysis, or whether they might be to some extent talking past one another.

There are at least two ways to explain the sense in which these theories seem to be addressing different questions: on one interpretation while the practical approach is a theory about *the concept* of human rights, the naturalist accounts are attempts to describe *the object* that the concept picks out.[32] On another interpretation of the difference between the practical approach and the naturalist approach both are conceptual, but while the practical approach is describing the concept of human rights within the practice, the naturalist accounts seek the concept of human rights devoid of its practical aspects.[33]

Consider the first interpretation of the differences in the types of project in which naturalist scholars and practical scholars are engaging. On this interpretation, practical approach scholars are interested in describing *a concept* or *the concept* of human rights. Naturalist scholars, on this interpretation of their differences, seem to be after something else: when they ask 'what are human rights?' they seem to assume that there is some object or category that the concept of human rights picks out and that this object can be described. To help make this distinction clear consider the distinction, mentioned earlier, that Raz makes between the concepts and the objects they pick out. For Raz 'concepts lie between words and meanings on one hand, and the object(s) the concepts pick out on the other hand. One can 'have a concept' without having detailed knowledge of the thing it is a concept of.'[34] On this view, it is not necessarily the case that naturalist scholars are not at all interested in the conceptual question, but they are either primarily interested in the nature of the object that the concept picks out or are committed to the view that human rights are the type of an object such that to do conceptual analysis we essentially need to describe the nature of the object, rather than tend to words and meanings.[35] So there are genuine questions about whether the practical theories and naturalist theories are in fact about the same things.

Thinking of the differences between the two approaches in this way can make sense of a number of features of the theories. For example, it explains why it should not be shocking that in attempting to capture the *concept* of human rights, we might, as Beitz does, refer to the way people use that concept to make sense of their world and its social institutions.[36] This interpretation of the differences between the approaches might also explain why it seems, at times, that practical approach theorists and naturalist scholars are actually describing different things: one group is describing the social institutions and the others are describing the abstract object that they think justify those social institution and exist independent of them. In spite of the partial clarity we might gain from interpreting their differences in this way I nonetheless think a better way of making sense of the divergences in these projects is not to assert that one of the projects is conceptual while the other is not, but to assume that they are both conceptual projects (albeit maybe focused on different concepts). In other words, it is worth comparing the two projects as if they were both engaging in conceptual analysis, for a number of reasons.

One reason in favour of thinking of both projects as conceptual is that it will allow us to compare and contrast their claims and take them at their word when they claim to explicitly disagree. Another reason for suggesting that both sets of projects are conceptual is the fact that even if naturalist scholars are after the nature of the object, they still might be after it for the same reasons of gaining clarity regarding the concept – after all the concept in that case would be filled out or closely connected to the nature of the object. With that in mind I now turn to trying to understand these projects as conceptual and trying to understand their differences via differing aims of their conceptual analyses.

As mentioned, conceptual analyses can have a number of purposes. In general, conceptual theories of human rights try to separate the world in such a way so that we can appropriately term certain things human rights while others not. The value of a conceptual account of human rights can only be decided once we know what the purpose of the conceptual project is, since different conceptual claims can very often have different aims.[37] One possible purpose of a conceptual project is to maintain a space within which meaningful discussion about the concept and its content can be achieved. This seems to be obviously what is on the mind of practical theorists in asserting that we ought to start from a set of inferences about what people see themselves as committed to (linguistically and conceptually) when they assert that there is a human right to X. Beitz explicitly states that we are searching for a concept that can capture the way we use the notion of human rights, but allow for disagreements about the content of that right. Naturalist approaches on the other hand seem to be primarily focused on an alternative aim for their conceptual analysis: coming up with a human rights concept that yields morally most appropriate consequences.

It is obvious that no conceptual analysis (especially in cases like this where its aim and purpose are not explicitly stated) is ever only aimed at one thing, but whether we are primarily focused on '(1) tracking and explaining linguistic usage or [alternatively trying] to (2) discover the 'significance' of a concept, hidden in our practices and intuitions regarding usage or (3) [trying] to impose moral . . . criteria which must be met before the label should be applied,' affects both (a) whether the theorists are talking past one another as well as (b) which standards we should use to evaluate their conceptual analysis.[38] While both naturalist and practical scholars seem to test their theory against (1), there are good reasons to think that Beitz is primarily focused on (2) and that naturalists scholars are primarily aiming at (3).[39] Beitz's theory, we might argue, is primarily focused on capturing the political and institutional aspects of human rights, stressing the feature that distinguishes human rights from ordinary moral rights – namely, that they primarily impose requirements on states and domestic institutions and, secondarily, when states fail that they give *pro tanto* reasons to the international community to interfere in the affairs of that state. Naturalist scholars seem to be more focused on (3): they are (and often see themselves as) simultaneously providing a conceptual as well as a normative account suggesting that it is impossible to separate the two. They argue that we ought not to put institutional, political elements of the human rights practice before the individual, moral elements. Many of them, like Griffin, worry about the indeterminateness of the sense of the term 'human rights' exactly because the term seems to carry a lot of moral weight.

Even though these theories seem to be primarily focused on different aims it nonetheless seems that they do all at times make appeals to all of these aims. This is just one reason why it might be useful to see how well they each do with respect to all of these possible aims.

First, regarding (1), consider how well their projects do with respect to tracking linguistic usage. Beitz and practical accounts in general argue that when we speak of human rights we are speaking of violations that give rise to claims against states and institutions and when they do not, it is not clear whether appealing to a human right really makes sense. This sort of analysis seems to fit squarely with the legalistic notion of human rights. On the other hand, and possibly in favour of naturalist accounts, we have seen a shift in everyday use of the term 'human rights,' referring simply to something like 'really important rights.' Consider for example the fact that recently there have been many cases of claiming that bullying is a human rights violation and in fact many human rights educators spend their careers suggesting that the best way to understand bullying is as a human rights violation.[40] The fact that the language of human rights is infiltrating everyday language and thus shifting to mean 'really important rights' might be one reason to think that naturalists are actually closer to the way the term is used today. But it is not clear that this shift ought to count in their favour since clearly they think that individual use of the concept of human rights ought not to inform what human right actually are. I disagree.

I believe that in as much as one is after the *concept* of human rights, there are good reasons to focus on what competent participants in the practice see themselves as being committed to when they assert that there is a human right to X. Beitz is right in asserting that the competent participants in the practice use the notion of human rights if and when there is a social justice issue that needs to be or could be addressed by state and is such that it can give rise to reasons for action for international institutions when state fails. The alternative, naturalist concept of human rights instead insists on the claim that there is continuity between the notions of natural and human rights. However, we cannot, without begging the question, assert that the notion of human rights is continuous with the notion of natural rights. Although this is controversial, I think we have good reasons to think that the term 'human rights' meaning what it means today emerged sometime between the 1950s and 1970s and in parallel with and within the legal framework, and that if we accept the Razian picture of a concept laying between the object and the words and their meanings, then the historical facts about the emergence of the term matter.[41] Now, I do not mean to argue that therefore the legalistic notion of human rights is the appropriate one. But it does seem obvious that the evaluation of the institutional aspects of human rights is a necessary step in trying to track the linguistic usage of the term. If that's the case then it follows that practical approaches are better at both capturing the historically correct understanding of the term human rights as well as better at pointing to one significant aspect of human rights practice and human rights in general and that is that they are the sorts of rights that impose claims on state's institutions. In other words, we have reasons to think that practical approaches do better not only with respect to (1), but also with respect to (2).

Before I turn, in more detail, to how well the theories do with respect to (2), I want to mention one final reason to think some practical approaches, namely those that use a method like Beitz's do better with respect to (1). Remember, Beitz develops the concept of human rights by tending to the inferences people make regarding human rights. His sifting tools are meant to hold on to as many disagreements with the practice, as long as they weed out the disagreements about the usage of the term. It seems to me that a method that as its source for the concept leans towards to what people actually say and do when they assert a human right to X will do a better job of tracking linguistic usage than any of the alternatives.

I now turn to how well the theories do with respect to (2). One reason to think that the practical approach is better at uncovering something significant about the concept of human rights is that it allows us to point to unique problems of injustice and evaluate social justice issues in unique terms. The fact that human rights are on this view primarily directed at state's institutions and secondarily at international institutions is what separates them from other legal rights or other moral rights. In fact if this was not an essential and a necessary feature of human rights, it is not exactly clear what the concept of human rights would really add to our debates about social justice issues that arguing that certain interests are exceptionally important for one reason or another and therefore certain rights are important in some sense, could not. The practical approach to the concept of human rights puts that which is unique about them and differentiates them from other rights at the heart of the argument – namely it puts front and center the answer to the question: who are the primary and secondary duty holders with respect to human rights as well as what types of duties do they have? What is significant in the mind of practical scholars is *the unique role that human rights play – not that they protect a subset of interests that are uniquely important.* Ultimately what is at stake here is which feature of human rights is more significant and why? It is certainly the case that practical scholars think that some interests are urgent. They just don't particularly care why that is the case. Instead they are interested in the way that protecting those interests *as* human rights requires a different set of responses than protecting them as ordinary rights. For naturalist scholars what is significant about human rights is that they pick out a subset of interests that are in kind different and more important than other human interests that ground ordinary moral rights. With all of this in mind, I believe practical scholars do better with respect to (2), in part because I think we should evaluate conceptual analyses based on what we can do with them.[42] Practical accounts allow us to argue that what's different in analyzing a particular problem in terms of human rights rather than ordinary rights or social justice or equality is that we can point to the appropriate mechanisms that ought to respond to that problem – namely, state's institutions and international institutions when states fail. This however commonly leads critics to argue that if we accept the practical account we are left without an answer to why exactly should the states worry about these rights and the underlying interests? Critics also further ask whether the practical approach can say anything interesting and critical of the practice, as it exists today?

b. The practical approach and normative questions

Can the practical approach actually criticize the human rights practice or does it commit us to the status quo? Does the practical approach commit us to reading off the concept from whatever states actually do? After all, critics might argue that the key aspect of human rights is that they are tools by which to evaluate the human rights practice (legal practice especially). If what human rights are is directly read human rights practice and its role in international law, then it is unclear how exactly we might use such a concept to then criticize and recommend reform for such a practice. And it is clearly the case that whether or not we see conceptual practice as primarily aiming at (3), the motivation behind any conceptual analysis of a concept like that of human rights is always at least in part driven by caring about moral and normative implications. In addition to the worry about the practical approach promoting the status quo, there is a worry about whether the practical approach can explain why states should see X, but not Y as a human right. In other words, does the practical approach have tools to explain why, for example, a right not to be tortured is a human right.

The key worry seems to be that the institutional element of human rights comes second, and that we should not be injecting any elements of human rights institutions into the concept. I think this is mistaken and that worries about the status quo can be assuaged by distinguishing between elements of the human rights institutions and practices that are necessary and those that are contingent. This distinction I think is well tracked by the distinction about disagreements over the content of a human right and the role the concept plays in our practice. In other words, it doesn't seem to me that by tending to people's claims and trying to understand the way in which they use the concept requires that we import their normative commitments about human rights.

On this analysis and contrary to people like Barry and Southwood the existence of a set of states and international community are necessary features of the human rights practice. Trying to describe a concept of human rights without the role that it plays in the international community and for states seems extremely odd. This is because human rights are not first and foremost moral rights; instead as I have argued they are first and foremost tools (or a shorthand) for making sense of a particular type of problem, namely those problems that a state's institutions can remedy and that are urgent enough that the international community would care if states fail to do so. Were it not the case that the type of problem is such that the state or its institutions or possibly international institutions were the types of structures that can and ought to respond to them, I argue framing the issues in the language of human rights would not be useful. And that is ultimately what is at stake here. I believe that we ought to evaluate the competing concepts of human rights by what they allow us to do with them. The practical concept of human rights has a consequence that it separates a particular type of problem that have to do with groups of people and institutional responses, and the naturalist concept of human rights does not. The naturalist concept of human rights proudly insists on the claim that we want to say that genocide in a world with no individual states would still be a violation of human rights. But I am not sure why exactly we would want to say that. Clearly we have a number of ways, from speaking about rights in general, to speaking in terms of natural rights, to speaking in terms of harm and lesser evil to explain why genocide would be wrong. If we are so keen on being able to say that genocide is a human rights violation (even in that situation) it would be because we would think that the world government (in the case of no states) would have an obligation to respond (notice that in this case, the concept of human rights would shift – as it has and as it ought to). In other words, in a world of no states, the practical approach is committed to saying either that the genocide would not be a human rights violation (because the concept of human rights would not play a role in analyzing the issue in such a society) or that it is a human rights violation, but that what it means to be a human rights violation is to some extent different than what it means to be a human rights violation today (in the sense that it imposes duties on the world state government). In other words, if we still wanted to say that genocide is a human rights violation in a world state, it would be because the concept of a human rights violation would change because the role that the concept of human rights plays would shift and so would the concept itself.

It is not obvious why we should think that the commitment to the possibility of a shifting concept is detrimental to a theory. After all, a large part of the linguistic tracking argument for the particular understanding of human rights comes exactly from the fact that people have started using it in a number of ways. This concept after all was not a part of the everyday vernacular a century ago. The fact that the notion of human rights is the tool that people around the world are using to evaluate crises is in part because that language transcends cultural differences and because that language provokes the claim that others should respond. The concept of human rights, I argue, does not point primarily to human universalities, but structural, institutional ones.

Returning to the status quo worry – if the concept can shift with the shift in the world order it seems difficult to understand how such a concept can ground a normative analysis that could be critical of the practice. This is where making a distinction between necessary and contingent features of the human rights practice (whose concept we are describing) becomes relevant. It is essential to the approach I argue for here that there be states and that they be organized in some way in an international community with some tools that enable them to address human rights violations. It is not necessary that there be the same international institutions we have today, nor that we be committed to the same set of human rights. And it is the case that human rights account is not going to be able on this account to criticize the existence of states, but it is not clear why one would want to say that the best way to make sense of what is wrong with a state system is via the language of human rights. The practical concept of human rights will be nonetheless able to criticize all other aspects of the human rights practice – the human rights law and humanitarian laws, additions of rights to the list that are not properly speaking human rights, and vice versa.[43]

Furthermore, on this account it is possible to assert that human rights are natural rights that meet the conditions (most interestingly) I described previously, but I think that this account need not be committed to that. It is sufficient to focus on a state's institutional response and international community's response to be able to identify what gets on the list of human rights. What gets on the list are the sorts of (moral, but not necessarily natural) rights for which domestic institutional response is appropriate for, in other words those rights that come under standard threats. These threats need to be the sorts of threats that could give rise to *pro tanto* reasons for another culture to interfere, and strong reasons to hold others accountable; in other words they need to be the types of threats that people outside of one's culture would also see as relevant. So what sorts of threats are those? What makes something an urgent interest of the kind the international community will see as important enough to interfere? Threat against interests that we see as important in our culture will obviously be good candidates, but not because we see these interests as grounded in some particular understanding of what a flourishing human life is about. As Jacques Maritain famously said 'we agree about the rights, but on the condition that no one asks us why.'[44] Clearly that can't be enough, after all we might not have an international agreement on what interests are important. This is exactly why naturalist scholars are particularly interested in identifying the subset of interests that are uniquely important, that can act as reasons for action by others. But the tools which naturalist scholars use to identify this subset often seem too abstract, as Beitz argues, to settle disputes about the content of human rights. And as I have argued and at least some critics of practical approach agree (like Barry and Southwood) it is not clear why we have to have a single ground for human rights. For Beitz what makes something an urgent interest is that 'those who might be called upon to protect it could reasonably recognize' it as such.[45] Many see this answer as unsatisfying and as one that ignores the original worry. While I do not hope to settle the dispute here it seems to me that both sets of theories have a worry with respect to identifying interests that ground human rights, but practical accounts rely only minimally on the urgency of the interest, whereas naturalist accounts rely on it almost exclusively – thus making this concern much more significant for naturalist scholars.

Finally, one might worry that in giving this answer, the practical account misses out on the answer to the question: why should I care about human rights? I believe that it captures why one should care about a protection of certain rights *as human rights* as opposed to other types of rights. It is because when one cares about a protection of an interest via a human right one cares about and suggests that this is a sort of an interest that can come under a standard threat, but is amenable to state intervention and foreign intervention when the state fails. Notice that on this view one might care about a violation of a right to an education both in the sense that it is a human rights violation and a violation of a natural right or a legal right or an ordinary right. I argue that unless one thinks of a violation of a *human* right to an education as one amenable to state response it is not clear why one should care about human right to an education at all in addition to caring about it as an ordinary moral right.

In this chapter I have argued that the concept of human rights has the features outlined previously and that it is not clear why the alternative naturalist concept ought to drive what human rights practitioners do. Naturalist scholars can not have it both ways: developing a concept of human rights independent of the practice and developing a concept of human rights that ought to inform the practice. If there are reasons why natural rights ought to put limits on our human rights institutions, those reasons should be grounded in something other than a claim that the human rights our institutions are protecting *just are* natural rights. This is the case, if for no other reason than because the domestic and international institutions we have developed to protect human rights were not developed around a singular notion of natural rights, but in spite of it.[46]

Notes

1 Charles Beitz, *The Idea of Human Rights* (Oxford: Oxford University Press, 2009).
2 Christian Barry and Nicholas Southwood, 'What Is Special About Human Rights', *Ethics and International Affairs* 25, no. 3 (2011): pp. 369–383.
3 John Tasioulas, 'Toward a Philosophy of Human Rights', *Current Legal Problems* 65 (2012): pp. 1–30.
4 Coleman and Simchen ask a similar question and identify eight types of questions scholars working in the philosophy of law ask. See Jules Coleman and Ori Simchen, 'Law,' *Legal Theory* 9 (2003): pp. 1–41.

5 Brian Bix, 'Joseph Raz and Conceptual Analysis', *Philosophy and Law APA Newsletter* 6, no. 2 (2007): p. 2. Joseph Raz, 'Can There Be a Theory of Law?', in *Blackwell Guide to the Philosophy of Law and Legal Theory*, edited by Martin Golding and William A. Edmundson (Oxford: Blackwell Publishing, 2005): p 325.

6 Nonetheless, this does not mean that the conceptual analysis of human rights need to exhaustively answer the interesting normative questions about human rights and their application.

7 I acknowledge that there are some interesting worries about some normative questions and their conceptual counterparts in terms of the order in which they are taken up. For example, the concept of legitimacy of a state (or terrorism or torture) might be such a concept that requires a parallel analysis between the concept and the justification, but it seems to me also that human rights analyses don't (without argument for such an approach) stray from the obvious motto: concept first, justification later.

8 I provide one such account in Section 4.

9 Beitz, *The Idea of Human Rights*, p. 102. My emphasis.

10 Beitz, The Idea of Human Rights, p. 107.

11 Beitz, The Idea of Human Rights, pp. 107–108.

12 It's called a two-step model because it argues for a two-level duty bearer picture but it has three elements: first one addresses interests and threats, second the first level of duty bearers and the third the second level of duty bearing.

13 Beitz, The Idea of Human Rights, p. 109.

14 I should note that Beitz is by no means the first person to offer a bottom-up approach. Even some natural rights scholars like James Griffin have attempted to provide, what they consider to be, bottom-up approaches, although I believe less successfully. James Griffin, *On Human Rights* (Oxford: Oxford University Press, 2008).

15 Barry and Southwood, 'What Is Special About Human Rights?'.

16 Properly speaking, it is the relationship between the first level and second level of the two-level model that gives rise to their worry.

17 What would get on the list if we used human rights for peace rather than justice is clearly different – think of cases of torturing a terrorist or political participation.

18 Barry and Southwood are also critical of certain types of naturalist accounts like for example that of James Griffin.

19 Although what he means by 'pluralist' is different.

20 Tasioulas, 'Towards a Philosophy of Human Rights.'

21 Tasioluas, 'Toward a Philosophy of Human Rights,' pp. 7, 18.

22 Tasioluas, 'Toward a Philosophy of Human Rights,' p. 18.

23 James Griffin, *On Human Rights.*

24 Griffin, *On Human Rights*, pp. 31–33. On this understanding we need rights that provide autonomy, some minimal provisions and liberty rights.

25 Beitz provides a schema for answering normative questions that depends on the two-level model of human rights together with the purpose of the practice (from the point of view of the individual).

26 In the rest of this paper I use the term 'naturalist' to mean both pluralist scholars of naturalist persuasion (like Barry, Southwood and Tasioulas) as well as naturalist scholars (like Griffin). I use the term 'practical accounts' or 'practical approaches,' much as I have been using it: to denote not only Beitz's practical approach, but also other functionalist and political accounts of human rights that share the feature of thinking that institutional element of human rights is necessary for its concept.

27 Their argument for this rests on looking at what the drafters of human rights texts had in mind when they were writing the human rights documents – they assert that 'they [were] trying to institutionalize pre-existing rights.' But surely they say, there was 'something to institutionalize.' But why think that this therefore means there were human rights prior to institutionalization. One might, I think more appropriately, describe human rights by suggesting that there were certain interests that people deemed important to protect from common threats and that once they were institutionalized in some way they became what we know as human rights. In fact, the history of the modern human right practice doesn't seem to support Barry's and Southwood's claims. Were the founders have been speaking of 'finding' human rights this would have had a detrimental effect on the ability of all to agree. Beitz

for example suggests that 'there was, for example, no agreement that human rights should be regarded as the expression in law of a more fundamental order of rights possessed by human beings "by nature" or by the gift of the creator.' This was because drafters were after a human rights doctrine that was acceptable from various points of view. As Jacques Maritain suggests 'we agree about the right but on the condition that no one asks us why.'

28 Brian Bix, *Jurisprudence: Theory and Context*, 6th ed. (Durham: Carolina Academic Press, 2012), p. 15. 'The merit of a conceptual claim can only be evaluated once it is clear what the purpose of the claim is, and descriptively and historically speaking, different conceptual claims often have different purposes.'

29 Bix, Jurisprudence, p. 18.

30 Here I follow Brian Bix's analysis of conceptual projects in general and the concept of the law in particular.

31 That being said, Griffin does think he is providing a bottom-up approach as well since for his it is not just the normative agency but also some practicalities that answer the question of what gets on the list. That being said, for Griffin, the practicalities are far from contingent or current facts about the world, they are instead necessary facts about human understanding and motivation. In fact, it is unclear to me why exactly then his account is considered bottom-up, but I put this worry aside here. I am grateful to my Human Rights seminar students for impressing this point on me.

32 There is so much to be said about whether or not we can really understand any projects in theory of human rights as about the object and what exactly would that mean if one was not a metaphysical realist (as I am assuming most naturalist are not). Unfortunately and because I will not embrace this understanding of the difference between naturalist and practical approaches I set this question aside here. I am grateful to the audience at a colloquium at University of Iowa and Greg Landini in particular for impressing on me the need to answer this question.

33 This is in part because naturalist scholars think that human rights are pre-institutional and would exist independent of the role state and its institutions play in implementing them.

34 Bix, 'Joseph Raz and Conceptual Analysis.'

35 Brian Bix does an excellent job of clarifying this point in his 'Joseph Raz and Conceptual Analysis,' arguing that while such claims about the tight relationship between the concept and object might work for concepts like gold and water, but are less obviously fruitful and right for human institutions.

36 In Bix, 'Joseph Raz and Conceptual Analysis,' Bix cites and discusses Raz.

37 Bix, *Jurisprudence*, p. 15.

38 Bix, *Jurisprudence*, p. 20.

39 We can and I think should think of Beitz's account very much like trying to accomplish the same thing H.L.A. Hart was trying to do with the concept of law in his *A Concept of Law* (Oxford: Oxford University Press, 1961).

40 I am grateful to Andrea Cohen, a human rights educator working on these issues for teaching me about the field of human rights education (especially in high schools) and the push to understand bullying in schools via the lens of human rights violations.

41 Many philosophers do seem to put some weight on the intellectual history of the concept in their arguments, but they seem to disagree exactly how to pick out the concepts that comprise the intellectual history of the notion of human rights. Some want to go as far as Roman Empire suggesting that the concept of ius latently held the concept of human rights, others go back to Enlightment (like Griffin) and yet others think that human rights in this sense as a concept do not emerge until after the WWI (like Beitz) or even until mid 1970s (like Samuel Moyn). Moyn has example relies on the use of the concept in a number of languages and argues that the term was not at all widely used or had by people around the world until the 70s. Samuel Moyn, *The Last Utopia: Human Rights in History* (Cambridge: Belknap Press, 2012).

42 This claim is controversial. For example Joseph Raz thinks there is no space for practical evaluations in conceptual analysis. Jules Coleman disagrees and instead argues that there is space for practical considerations in conceptual analysis. Jules Coleman, *The Practice of Principle: In Defence of a Pragmatist Approach to Legal Theory* (Oxford: Oxford University Press, 2001). For more on Raz's view on this see Bix, 'Joseph Raz and Conceptual Analysis'.

43 Practical account of human rights can further make sense of why it makes sense, for example, to talk of women's rights – even though they are grounded in the same set of urgent interests as rights had by men. Practical account by focusing on the aspect of standard threats and states as primary duty holders can point to the difference in the standard threats to men's and women's rights (for example consider the case of slavery – for men the most common enslaver/unjust imprisoner is the state, for women it is the family).

44 Jacques Maritain, 'Introduction', *UNESCO, Human Rights: Comments and Interpretations* (New York Columbia University Press, 1949), pp. 9–10.

45 Beitz, The Idea of Human Rights, p. 137.

46 I want to stress that I had two aims in this paper: one of which was to argue that practical approaches do better with respect to various aims of conceptual analysis. My other aim was to stress the importance of making clear what one means when they ask 'what is a human right?' One need not be conclusively persuaded by my argument for the practical approach to be persuaded of the relevance of making clear (a) whether one is engaging in a conceptual or normative or metaphysical analysis of human rights and (b) if one is engaging in conceptual analysis of human rights what the aim of that analysis should be.

5 Deriving human rights from human dignity

A novel political approach

Suzy Killmister

Much of the recent philosophical debate over human rights has focused on the question of whether or not human rights are primarily derived from philosophical foundations. I will be arguing that they are not, but via a route that might at first blush appear slightly counterintuitive: I will be arguing that human rights can and should be derived from human dignity. Why this seems counterintuitive is that it strongly suggests adherence to the foundationalist side of the debate, given that dignity is one of the moral concepts frequently pointed to by both philosophers and practitioners as grounding human rights. Why it nonetheless sits closer to the anti-foundationalist side of the human rights debate is that dignity, insofar as it connects to human rights, itself turns out to be a social construct. Or so I shall argue.

The structure of this chapter is as follows. In Section 1 I identify the relevant aspects of the debate, and extract three desiderata that I take a theory of human rights to have an obligation to meet. In Section 2 I sketch a novel conception of dignity, which is then unpacked in Sections 3 and 4 into two strands, which I call personal and social dignity. In Section 5 I argue in favour of one particular instance of social dignity – namely, human dignity – as grounding human rights. I conclude in Section 6 by showing how this leads to a hybrid foundational/political position that can fulfil the three desiderata identified in Section 1.

1 The debate

As the debate is commonly construed there is a rift between, on the one hand, the philosophical traditionalists who seek to derive human rights primarily from moral philosophical foundations,[1] and on the other hand the revisionists, who reject the necessity of philosophical foundations and instead construe human rights in terms of the practice as it is found in the world today.[2] Naturally, the waters are much murkier than this simplification suggests. Each side involves subtleties and distinctions that are lost through this categorization, and there is a growing body of literature seeking to find a middle ground between the two poles – a body of literature to which I hope to contribute.[3] For my purposes here, I will be largely sidestepping expository questions about the details of any particular view. Instead, I will focus on general features of each side that are pertinent to my argument.

There are three interrelated features that those on the foundationalist side commonly exhibit. These are: first, that human rights are those rights we have in virtue of being human; second, that these rights are derived from some universal and inherent feature of personhood; and third, that these rights are pre-institutional, in the sense that they do not depend for their existence on the recognition or enforcement of any political institution or practice.

The anti-foundationalist, or political, view is more eclectic. Laura Valentini has usefully provided a taxonomy specifying three distinct ways in which a theory might be considered political: a theory might construe the principles laid out by human rights as evaluating political institutions, rather than individuals (what she calls human rights' 'iudicandum'); a theory might identify human rights with the results of a political process of justification; or a theory might restrict the content of human rights to those ends that are politically feasible.[4] While there are undoubtedly political views that exhibit one or more of these features, the form of anti-foundationalist view that I will be advancing here rests on a different claim: that human rights are constituted by political institutions and practices.[5]

Each side of the debate is vulnerable to pointed objections, and I will now use these objections to generate three desiderata that any theory of human rights should meet. On the foundationalist side, philosophers have commonly encountered the objection that their theories do not accord with a *prima facie* constitutive feature of human rights, namely that they are borne by all human beings. This objection arises because of a constraint foundationalist theories face, in having to identify a feature of human beings that is sufficiently normatively weighty such that human rights can plausibly be derived from it. The problem is that features that are sufficiently weighty are also restricted in their extension. James Griffin, for instance, identifies the relevant feature as normative agency, arguing that such agency is central to our personhood, and is thus a viable candidate as the foundation of human rights; however, he acknowledges that this has the implication that human rights don't extend to all human beings, but instead are only borne by those with the appropriate rational capacities.[6] While Griffin is willing to bite this bullet, doing so seriously restricts the moral work that human rights can be asked to do.

The second objection to foundationalist theories is less commonly expressed. Insofar as foundationalist theories take the content of human rights to be derived from one or more features typical of human beings, such as rationality or agency, they also take the content of human rights to be relatively fixed. This leads to an undesirable conservatism, in that it doesn't sufficiently allow for the practice of human rights to evolve and expand in its ambition, as conditions for human advancement improve.

To be fair, foundationalist theories can allow for new human rights to emerge, insofar as these rights are derived from a more general right. For instance, assuming a foundationalist theory includes a human right to physical security, it can allow that a new *specific* right – to borrow a phrase from Pablo Gilabert[7] – can be derived from the *abstract* right to physical security, as new threats emerge. What the foundationalist approach has more difficulty with is the idea either that new *sui generis* rights might emerge, or that the content of a particular right might alter as our capacity to fulfil it increases. Of the *sui generis* type, we might consider something like the sometimes proposed right to the internet.[8] While there is perhaps some story we can tell whereby access to the internet is necessary for free speech, or for sharing in scientific advancements, this overlooks the possibility that such a right might be justified on the basis that the internet is a new form of good, of sufficient importance to human flourishing in the 21st century that we can claim access as a human right. In terms of altering content, consider rights such as subsistence, or education. On a foundationalist model we have such rights because they are necessary to protect or preserve some feature of persons. As such, the level of, i.e., subsistence or education that the right entitles us to is set by those features, rather than by the level of economic and social advancement of global society.[9]

There are, however, good reasons to encourage flexibility in the content of human rights. First, as more voices are drawn into international political discourse, new values can be articulated and a place found for them in the moral framework of human rights. The recent recognition of indigenous rights as human rights is a prime example. To presuppose that all human rights are derived from a single – or even a plurality of – pre-identified features of personhood closes down the epistemic humility that should be ***de rigour*** as we strive to understand the human condition in a deeply pluralistic world.[10] And second, insofar as human rights occupy a privileged place in the discourse of international relations, they are an effective rhetorical tool in pursuing global justice. As new possibilities for addressing global poverty develop alongside increases in global wealth, allowing for more demanding human rights to emerge is one way to work towards a more just world.

The core objection to political approaches, by contrast, focuses on their anti-foundationalism. If there is no theoretical check on the content of human rights, it raises the worry that human rights are too arbitrary and contingent to bear the normative weight they are typically expected to carry. If the practice of human rights is our only guide to the content of human rights, then it looks like we have no normative grounds from which to critique or defend those rights as morally important.

Taken together, these objections suggest three desiderata for a theory of human rights.[11] First, it should have the resources to justify extending human rights to all human beings; second, it should allow for the content of human rights to evolve and expand; and finally, it should explain how the content of human rights has normative weight. In the remainder of this chapter I will propose a theory of human rights that I take to fulfil all three desiderata. This theory hinges on a connection between human rights and a particular conception of dignity.

The resulting theory is primarily political, in that it takes human rights to be the result of a political process rather than an inherent feature of humanity. Nonetheless, I take it to be part of the reconciliatory project that is currently emerging in the cracks between the foundationalist and anti-foundationalist views. While I agree with the anti-foundationalist side that human rights are a political construct, the theory I am proposing leaves space for moral foundations to play some role in that construct.

2 Dignity as standards

The conception of dignity that I am advancing here construes dignity in terms of normative standards.[12] What it means to ***have dignity***, in the sense of being an agent who possesses dignity, is to be subject to some or other normative standard. This is to be distinguished from ***being dignified***, which signifies a status that is achieved when an agent successfully upholds the relevant normative standards.[13] On this account, an agent can become less dignified by failing to uphold the relevant standards, though in doing so she continues to have the status of an agent with dignity; likewise, preventing an agent from upholding the relevant standards can leave her less dignified, while nonetheless leaving her ***possession*** of dignity unscathed. While we may accurately describe egregious indignities as violations of dignity, or even as stripping the agent of her dignity, what is being taken away in such cases is the condition of ***being dignified***, rather than the status of ***having dignity***.[14]

One of the most significant implications of this conception of dignity is that even the basic status of having dignity does not refer to some inherent feature of persons, but is instead a status that is gained. Dignity is gained, on this view, if and when an agent comes to be subject to normative standards. As I will go on to explain, an agent can confer dignity upon herself, through the recognition of some or other normative standard as being relevant for her; or it can be conferred by others, when they are committed to viewing her as a member of their community, for whom some or other normative standards apply. In other words, dignity is conferred through the practice of holding ourselves or others to normative standards.

Typical normative standards that confer dignity include standards of dress, such as a norm against public nudity; standards of bodily function, such as a norm of private toileting; and standards of interpersonal interaction, such as a norm of being addressed by one's title. As these examples should also make clear, the standards relevant to dignity are highly varied and deeply relative. What is involved in having dignity, then, will depend on the context: to have the dignity of a judge will require being subject to the normative standards of dress, bearing, and address of being a judge; and this will differ from having the dignity of a queen, or the dignity of a democratic citizen.[15] Likewise, to have one's dignity violated as a judge means being prevented from upholding the normative standards of dress, bearing, or address relevant to being a judge, and this involves very different acts from having one's dignity violated as a democratic citizen – for instance, refusing to stand when a citizen enters a courtroom is not an indignity to her; refusing to stand when a judge does so is.

3 Personal dignity

I alluded earlier to the claim that the standards relevant to dignity have two potential sources: they can either be recognized by the agent herself, or they can be recognized by the community of which she's taken to be a member. That claim now needs to be unpacked, as it has significant implications for how I am suggesting we understand human rights.

Let's start, then, with the subjective source of normative standards. For this form of dignity, an agent comes to be endowed with dignity if and when she recognizes some normative standard as holding for her. It is important to be clear what this recognition amounts to. What it takes to recognize a standard is simply that the agent has a sufficient understanding of what is required to uphold that standard (where this can be demonstrated through practical competence, and not necessarily the ability to articulate the content of the standard on demand), combined with an acceptance of the normative force of the standard (where again this acceptance can be demonstrated through her patterns of reactive attitudes rather than necessarily requiring the ability to articulate that acceptance).

Importantly, not just any normative standard will do – I would not become less personally dignified in virtue of running a red light, though I would become less personally dignified if I did drunken burnouts in my departmental carpark. The distinction lies in the fact that in the latter case, but not in the former, I would take the latter but not the former to be shameful. More precisely, I would take performance of the latter but not the former act to render me less worthy of self-respect. The standards relevant to personal dignity, then, are standards that we take ourselves to be required to uphold in order to warrant our current levels of self-respect.

The standards relevant to personal dignity can cover such morally trifling issues as how we dress, or how we are addressed by others, meaning that dignity can be reduced – or even lost – when an agent wears the wrong thing, or is addressed by the wrong title. If this is the case, why should we think that personal dignity matters at all? How can we reconcile this picture with the centrality given to personal dignity in moral discourse?

The first thing to note is that, while the standards relevant to personal dignity can extend to matters such as dress, they also commonly cover moral behaviour. Indeed, for most people the central normative standards they recognize will tend towards the moral end of the spectrum, insofar as violations of these norms are more tightly connected to loss of self-respect. Second, though, it is important not to dismiss the importance of issues such as dress and address too quickly. Consider for a moment the role that religious dress might play in a devout person's life; failure to meet those standards can be experienced as a failure of religious duty. Actively preventing such an agent from being able to uphold their standards of dress is widely recognized as imposing a significant burden upon them, because the inability to do that which we take ourselves to be obligated to do is deeply damaging to our well-being.

To make this claim particularly vivid, consider the distinct wrong of torture.[16] As David Luban has forcefully argued, the wrong of torture is closely related to the wrong of humiliation.[17] Torture is ***designed*** to humiliate, in part by forcing people to betray their most central commitments. While this will often involve betraying commitments to loved ones or causes, it can also involve betraying standards of comportment or bearing. The horrors of Abu Ghraib illustrate this point all too clearly: the practices were tailored to the particular normative standards that the victims held, including norms of religious dress, and sexual comportment. Whatever we think about those standards taken in abstraction, it should not detract from our condemnation of the trauma inflicted by forcing people to betray those standards.

While obviously not all indignities amount to torture – to argue otherwise would be to trivialize torture beyond all recognition – I am claiming that indignities inflict the same *type* of harm (though of course torture inflicts additional harms as well). To force an individual to violate a standard that she takes to have normative authority for her is to force her to undermine her own agency.[18] She is failing to uphold standards that she takes to have authority over her, and it is thus unsurprising that both torture and other forms of humiliation typically lead to feelings of shame and loss of self-respect. This conception of personal dignity is thus well placed to explain many of the moral harms associated with violating someone's dignity.

I have suggested that this conception of personal dignity has significant resources for understanding the moral importance of dignity, especially in relation to wrongs such as torture. Should we then consider personal dignity as a potential moral foundation for human rights, on the grounds that all and only severe violations of personal dignity constitute human rights violations? No. The primary reason for this is that this conception of personal dignity fails to fulfil the first desideratum laid out previously: it cannot justify extending human rights to all human beings. Individuals have personal dignity insofar as they recognize normative standards for themselves. While the capacities required for this are fairly minimal – arguably more minimal than Griffin's normative agency – they are nonetheless not universally held. Individuals with severe mental disabilities, for instance, may not recognize any standards at all.

In addition, personal dignity would leave the content of human rights implausibly vague. Which acts constitute violations of personal dignity, on this account, depends on the subjective standards of the individual in question. A given act may violate the dignity of one individual, but not of another. Consider the act of forcefully shaving a man's beard: while for any agent this would presumably involve a violation of physical integrity, on the conception of dignity presented here it would only constitute a severe violation of personal dignity – and thus a violation of human rights – for an agent who conceived the wearing of a beard to be a strong normative requirement, the violation of which rendered them less respect-worthy. What this would mean in practice is that which acts constitute human rights violations would depend on the identity of the victim. While there could be some scope to accommodate this subjectivism within an account of human rights – consider how the definition of torture can make reference to the beliefs of the victims – there are limits to the practicality of this. So unless we assume an implausible degree of overlap in the normative standards that individuals share across religions and cultures, the content of human rights would either have to be impractically vague, or else include acts that are only indignities for some individuals, while failing to include acts that are indignities for others.

4 Social dignity

Let's turn, then, to social dignity. An individual has social dignity, I suggest, insofar as she is a member of a community that holds its members to some set of normative standards.[19] An individual fails to be socially dignified insofar as she is in transgression of a normative standard that applies to that community. Just as for personal dignity, not just any old normative standard will be relevant here. There may be a communal norm of having milk in one's tea, for instance, where failure to do so is seen as misguided or idiosyncratic, but not undignified. We need to pinpoint the kinds of normative standards that affect an agent's social dignity.

As for personal dignity, the necessary feature we are looking for relates to respect. Unlike for personal dignity, though, there are two distinct ways in which a person can be less socially dignified. On the one hand, and paralleling personal dignity, we can point to standards the violation of which render the agent *less respect-worthy* within the community. So if a particular community deems it to be a necessary condition for continued respect that members only eat food with their right hand, then anyone who eats food with their left hand will be socially undignified (in that community). On the other hand, and departing from personal dignity, we can point to standards the violation of which render the agent *less respected* within the community. At first blush these may seem synonymous. The difference lies in the potential passivity of the socially undignified agent in the latter case. Consider a community with established norms concerning the kind of respect each member is owed – perhaps, in this community, it is generally accepted that to show appropriate respect to another member one must doff one's hat at them. Now imagine that one member refuses to doff her hat at another member. This refusal constitutes a denial of respect for the target, and thus renders her less respected (however slightly) within that community. Such refusals to accord someone the respect owed her *qua* group member, on my account, is a violation of that person's social dignity.

At first glance, social dignity may seem even less well-placed to underpin or justify human rights than personal dignity. This is because an individual's possession of social dignity is hostage to whether or not others take her to be a member of the community, and thus worthy of respect.

Before addressing this concern, it is important to stress that the conception of dignity being developed here – whether individual or social – is not supposed to be the core of morality. I am suggesting that social dignity can be thought of as grounding the practice of human rights, but it does not follow from this that either personal or social dignity is a good that must be pursued under all circumstances, or that outweighs all other moral goods. The moral value of dignity – whether the personal or social form – will vary with the moral value of the standards that it invokes.

That said, social dignity has significant resources to respond to the concern about inclusion. In this regard, social dignity is in fact better placed than personal dignity. Unlike personal dignity, the possession of social dignity does not depend on the individual having any capacities whatsoever. All that is required is that she is taken to be a member of a community that applies normative standards to itself. Consider an individual with Alzheimer's who is a member of a family whose normative standards include going to dinner clean and clothed, but whose illness has advanced to the point where she no longer recognizes such standards for herself. Such an individual would not have personal dignity. Moreover, were she to be neglected to the point where she was never washed, or was left to wander the hallways naked, there would be no grounds to say this neglect *violated* her personal dignity. When we consider her *social* dignity, by contrast, the family's standards continue to apply: neglecting her in these ways would constitute violations of her social dignity. The idea of social dignity thus enables us to makes sense of the claim that even the very young or the very mentally disabled can have their dignity violated.

This response still leaves something to be desired. While it shows that there are advantages to social dignity, in terms of who is included, it does not actually respond to the worry as stated, which is that whether or not an individual has social dignity is contingent on the recognition afforded her by others. More precisely, it is contingent on which – if any – communities the individual is taken to be a part of. To return to the previous example, the worry could be restated as follows: if the family in question disowned the Alzheimer's patient as a member of the family, it looks like the neglect would no longer constitute a social indignity.

While this worry cannot be fully blocked, it can be diminished. What it means to take someone to be a member of a community does not turn on whether or not the community explicitly acknowledges that person to be a member of the community. Membership, on this understanding, is a social norm, and like social norms more generally is established through practice, rather than declaration. So just as declaring that *x* is a social norm is insufficient to make it so – it depends on whether or not *x* is in fact respected, even if only in the breach – so, too, declaring that a particular person is not a member of the community is not necessarily sufficient to make it so. The kind of membership that matters for social dignity turns on whether the individual is being held to the normative standards of the community. If the community does in fact hold the individual to those standards, where this can be assessed by consideration of the reactive attitudes of other community members (i.e. reacting with indignation or empathetic shame to a breach of standards), then this indicates that she is a member.

What this means in practice is that perpetrators of dignity violations cannot simply decide that their victim is not a member of the relevant community, and so change the moral status of their act. Moreover, and perhaps surprisingly, the very act of publicly humiliating an individual serves to confirm her membership in the group.[20] This is because the success of the humiliation relies on the public seeing the individual as having violated a norm that is relevant for her.[21] Consider what would happen if someone tried to humiliate a rock; it cannot work, at least in part because there is no recognition of normative standards applying to a rock. Humiliating a person works because the viewers recognize that she is falling short of standards that apply to her. Ironically, then, public humiliation actually works to *reaffirm* the dignity of the victim, even while it strips her of her dignity: by confirming that the normative standards of the community apply to her, the humiliation confirms that she *has* dignity; by forcing her to violate those standards, the humiliation prevents her from *being dignified*.

While personal and social dignity can come into conflict, it is important not to assume that they are necessarily in tension. In fact, in most cases they will be mutually supportive. This is because the norms associated with social dignity are commonly internalized, thus becoming standards the violation of which damage personal dignity. Consider the example of eating with one's right hand, given previously: while this injunction is recognized for all members of the community, and thus constitutes part of their social dignity, it will also typically be recognized as having normative authority by the individual members, thus constituting part of their personal dignity. Were such a person to be forced to eat with their left hand, then, it would be a violation of both their personal and their social dignity.[22]

The distinction between personal and social dignity is important nonetheless, because of the ways in which they can come apart. On the one hand, an individual can hold normative standards that are distinct from those of the broader community around her. In such cases, it is important to be alive to the ways in which her dignity can be violated even if she is treated according to common standards. On the other hand, as we've seen, an individual can fail to have the capacities necessary to recognize normative standards of her own. To ensure that such a person is able to meet the standards of the community is not necessarily an act of oppression, but can rather be a morally valuable affirmation of her belonging.

5 Social dignity and human rights

The core suggestion of this paper is that human rights can be understood in terms of social dignity. To reiterate, an individual has social dignity insofar as she is a member of a community; and she is socially dignified insofar as she upholds the normative standards of that community. Conversely, she is socially undignified if she either violates a standard the upholding of which is taken to be necessary to maintain the respect of the community, or she finds herself subject to behaviour that constitutes lessened respect within the community. To extend the concept of social dignity to human rights is to see human rights as part of the articulation of a new set of normative standards, which apply to a newly constituted global community.

For those of us living in the 'human rights culture',[23] the idea that all human beings are worthy of concern is something of a platitude. Nonetheless, it constitutes a significant achievement. While it doesn't necessarily replace, or even outweigh, the importance of smaller communities such as nations, the recognition that all other persons matter morally and deserve to be treated with respect is increasingly accepted.[24] In the terms of my account, this idea of a global community is the first step towards constituting one another as agents with human dignity.

The second step involves the development of the relevant standards, which are to apply to all human beings. Here we need to tread carefully, and the distinction between the two different ways in which social dignity can be violated becomes crucial. The first way, to reiterate, is that an agent may fail to uphold a standard, the violation of which is taken by the community to render her less respect-worthy, *qua* community-member. Since the relevant community for human dignity is global, we would need to find a standard the violation of which was taken, by humanity at large, to render the transgressor less worthy of respect *qua* human. To put this in Darwallian terms, it would have to be a standard the upholding of which entitled the agent to recognition respect as a person.[25] It is questionable whether any standard fits this description. After all, it's part of the 'human rights culture' that all human beings are owed equal respect merely in virtue of their humanity. If that's right, then there is nothing an individual could do to undermine her human dignity, and thus render herself 'subhuman'.[26]

Here's where the second pathway to violations of social dignity become especially salient. Someone's social dignity can be violated if they are placed in a situation within which they are refused the respect owed to them, as a member of that community. When it comes to human dignity, then, we can say that someone's human dignity is violated if they are denied the respect owed to them, *qua* human.

The question then becomes: what manifestations of respect are human beings owed, *qua* members of the human community? I focus here on two such manifestations: first, to take one another to be objects of global concern;[27] and second, to treat one another as having the standing to demand that our human rights are respected. To uphold another's human dignity, then, requires attending to her suffering, and acknowledging the legitimacy of her human rights claims. Conversely, to deny the significance of another individual's suffering, or to deny the legitimacy of her human right claims, is to violate her human dignity. Importantly, the wrongs of human dignity violation are highly significant – over and above any material harm caused to the victim, to deny the importance of her suffering, or to deny her standing to make human rights claims, is to deny her the respect she is owed *qua* human. As such, it is to deny that she is fully human.

This account of human rights thus far leaves out any description of the content of human rights, i.e. which particular rights have the status of human rights. The short answer is: whichever ones we have accepted. More precisely, on this account the content of human rights is determined as part of the broader process of developing and refining the normative standards that we apply to the global community, and hence part of the process of constituting one another as bearers of human dignity. The core of these normative standards, I have suggested, is to take one another to be objects of global concern, who have the standing to demand that their rights be fulfilled. The first half of that standard requires that there be global institutions in place to attend to the suffering and injustices individuals face, irrespective of their location. The branches of the United Nations, alongside other international organizations dedicated to human rights, can thus be seen as a socially constituted response to the emerging fact of human dignity. As part of the process of constituting a normative standard which requires all individuals to be present as objects of global concern, we have established institutions that enable that global concern to be expressed.

The second half of that standard requires that a set of human rights be identified, which individuals have the standing to demand. On my account, the process of identifying those human rights is itself a process of emerging social norms – in other words, a claim has the status of a human right if and when the global community comes to accept that individuals have the standing to demand the fulfilment of that claim.

The precise boundaries of human rights so understood will necessarily involve some ambiguity. Human rights evolve out of a set of social norms, and like all social norms there will always be questions about when that status is achieved. Some heuristics we might consider include whether individuals reliably use the language of human rights to make a particular claim, and the extent to which their use of that language is contested; and whether the international community responds with moral condemnation when violations occur.[28] Plausibly, the rights laid out in the Universal Declaration of Human Rights have by and large achieved this status; however, since this status depends on the social norms supporting them, it can shift and change over time. More rights can come to be accepted as human rights, and doubt can be cast on others that had previously achieved this status (the much-maligned right to paid holidays may be a case in point here.)

To summarize the account so far, my claim is that the practice of human rights emerged in response to, and as a way of substantiating, human dignity. The content of human rights emerges as part of the process of articulating the details of the normative standard that confer human dignity. What this amounts to is the claim that we collectively constitute one another as bearers of human rights, at the same time and by the same process as we constitute one another as bearers of human dignity.

6 Satisfying the desiderata

With this account now on the table, it is time to consider the extent to which it can satisfy the three desiderata laid out in Section 1. To reiterate, these were: 1) to justify the extension of human rights to all human beings; 2) to allow for the content of human rights to evolve and expand; and 3) to explain how the content of human rights has normative weight. The first two desiderata will be relatively easy to satisfy, while the third poses the greatest challenge. Showing how the final desideratum can be satisfied, however, brings to light a feature of the theory that has thus far remained under the surface, namely the extent to which it brings together foundational and anti-foundational elements.

Let's start, though, with the first desideratum. Foundational theories of human rights typically search for some inherent feature of persons from which human rights can be derived. As we've seen, this approach runs into the problem that, for virtually all inherent features of persons, some human beings lack it. These theories thus face the dilemma of either declaring that such humans don't have human rights, or proposing a theoretically un-motivated extension of human rights to agents who do not have the features that supposedly generate those rights. By contrast, the social dignity approach to human rights has a different way of identifying the relevant community. All that is required, on this approach, is for the global community to take a given individual to be a member. Admittedly, this acceptance has an element of contingency built into it; it needn't be the case that all human beings are taken to be members of the global community.

Here is where the objection to foundationalist approaches actually works in the favour of the social dignity approach. The objection, to recall, was that restricting human rights to a subset of human beings was in tension with a *prima facie* constitutive feature of human rights, namely that they extend to all human beings. Insofar as the contemporary practice of human rights assumes their extension to all human beings, the social dignity approach will consider all human beings to have human rights. There need be no feature other than this social norm of inclusion to motivate the extension of human rights to all human beings, irrespective of what typical features of personhood they lack. This approach thus secures the universality of human rights, satisfying the first desideratum outlined in Section 1.

The second desideratum also plays to the strengths of the social dignity approach. As we've seen, on this approach the content of human rights is determined by global social norms. This builds flexibility into the very concept of human rights; as global social norms evolve, so too does the content of human rights. This approach thus allows that, say, a human right to the internet may emerge. All that would be required is that the global community come to see the right to the internet as something that all human beings have the standing to demand. Likewise, this approach allows that the content of rights to subsistence or education might become more demanding in response to increases in global wealth. Again, what matters is that the global community sees these more expansive rights as something that all individuals have the standing to demand. Admittedly, how progressive human rights become depends on the direction that these social norms take, and there is no guarantee that this will always be towards the recognition of stronger rather than weaker rights. Nonetheless, this account at least leaves open the possibility for such an expansion, in a way that foundationalist approaches struggle to do.

This strength of the social dignity approach is also its greatest vulnerability, and this brings us to the final desideratum. Can this account explain the normative weight of human rights? One reason to suspect it might not is that the content of human rights is determined through social norms. Since social norms don't necessarily have any moral weight, the worry is that the human rights that are constituted via social norms won't have any moral weight, either. This worry, though, overlooks the ways in which social norms can themselves appeal to morally significant values. Consider a social norm to avoid harming sentient beings: it doesn't have moral weight in virtue of being a social norm, instead it carries with it the moral weight that attaches to avoiding harming sentient beings. The same applies to particular human rights: they don't have what moral weight they do in virtue of being constituted through social norms. Rather, they have moral weight in virtue of the morally significant goods that they protect.

It is at this point that the foundationalist aspect of the theory can be brought into focus. I have claimed that human rights are constituted via their emergence as a social norm, whereby individuals are taken to have the standing to demand their fulfilment. This claim appears to place the theory firmly on the anti-foundationalist side of the debate, since the existence conditions of a human right make no reference to any pre-institutional moral claims. However, things start to look somewhat different if we turn our attention more closely to certain features of the relevant social norms. On this account, the existence conditions of human rights turn on whether or not there is a social norm to recognize them as such. But social norms can themselves be understood as dependent on foundational moral claims. In fact, it is plausible that the social norms surrounding human rights are of just this form. For instance, if there is a global social norm to recognize individuals' standing to claim pre-institutional – or natural – rights as human rights, then on my account all natural rights will qualify as human rights. My suggestion is that just such a global social norm does in fact exist: when asked about what human rights there are, people are quick to point to something along the lines of natural rights, even if they do not all articulate the same rights as falling within this category. The idea, then, is parallel to that made previously with reference to community membership conditions. Just as an individual can be a member of a community without the rest of the community realizing this fact, provided she meets membership conditions that they accept as sufficient, so too a right can achieve the status of a human right without the global community recognizing this fact, provided they recognize existence conditions that the right in fact meets. If this is correct, then being a natural right is sufficient but not necessary to achieve the status of a human right. It is sufficient insofar as it is built into the social norms that constitute human rights that natural rights always have that status. It is not necessary, though, because it is *not* part of the relevant global social norms that *only* natural rights achieve that status. I more tentatively suggest that there is an emerging global norm of recognizing the standing of all humans to claim the fulfilment of many so-called 'positive' rights – even where those rights are not considered 'natural'. If this is correct, then human rights include, but are not limited to, natural rights.

The social dignity account of human rights is thus a hybrid account. While it accepts the anti-foundationalist's claim that moral foundations are not necessary for the existence of human rights, it also allows that moral claims may be sufficient to prove the existence of certain human rights. What the account nonetheless leaves open is the possibility that human rights extend beyond pre-institutional rights, where this extension is achieved through the evolution of social norms. Human rights that emerge in this way will have whatever moral weight they do not in virtue of their genesis in a social norm, but in virtue of the values that they protect. While this allows for the possibility that a human right may have very little moral weight at all, the likelihood of a global social norm emerging to recognize a right that protected nothing of value is slim indeed.

To conclude, then, the social dignity account of human rights that I have sketched here threads a path between foundationalism and anti-foundationalism. It takes human rights to be constituted through social norms, and thus rejects the foundationalist claim that human rights are necessarily pre-institutional. Nonetheless, it recognizes the role that pre-institutional rights can – and probably do – play *within* those social norms, and thus provides significant room for the importance of moral foundations.

This hybridity allows the account to avoid some of the challenges faced by either side of the debate: it can explain how human rights extend to all human beings, in a way that foundationalist theories struggle to do; it leaves room for human rights to expand, recognizing their crucial role in shaping the priorities of international governance, again in ways that foundationalist theories struggle to accommodate; but it can nonetheless account for the moral weight of human rights, by recognizing the role that moral foundations play within the relevant global social norms.

Notes

1 See, e.g., James Griffin, *On Human Rights* (Oxford: Oxford University Press, 2008), pp. 39–44; Allen Gewirth, 'The Basis and Content of Human Rights', in *Human Rights*, edited by J. Roland Pennock and John W. Chapman, *Nomos* (New York: New York University Press, 1981):pp. 119–147; John Tasioulas, 'Are Human Rights Essentially Triggers for Intervention?', *Philosophy Compass* 4 (2009): p. 938. It should be noted that even the moral foundationalists will typically appeal to more than purely moral considerations. Griffin, for instance, supplements his personhood approach with what he calls 'practicalities'.

2 See., e.g., Charles Beitz, *The Idea of Human Rights* (Oxford: Oxford University Press, 2009); Joseph Raz, 'Human Rights Without Foundations', in *The Philosophy of International Law*, edited by Samantha Besson and John Tasioulas (Oxford: Oxford University Press, 2010): pp. 321–337; Allen Buchanan, *The Heart of Human Rights* (Oxford University Press, 2013); John Rawls, *The Law of Peoples* (Harvard University Press, 2001).

3 See, e.g., Laura Valentini, 'In What Sense Are Human Rights Political? A Preliminary Exploration', *Political Studies* 60 (2012): p. 180; S. Matthew Liao and Adam Etinson, 'Political and Naturalistic Conceptions of Human Rights: A False Polemic?', *Journal of Moral Philosophy* 9 (2012): p. 327; Pablo Gilabert, 'Humanist and Political Perspectives on Human Rights', *Political Theory* 39 (2011): p. 439.

4 Valentini, 'In What Sense Are Human Rights Political?'.

5 This is closest to Valentini's second category, though not identical with it. While both appeal to the dependence of human rights on political processes, Valentini's category of justification appeals to the availability of public reasons for human rights; the kind of view I am presenting, by contrast, has a more positivist flavour, in that it looks for convergence on social norms of recognizing human rights.

6 Griffin, *On Human Rights*, pp. 83–94.

7 Gilabert, 'Humanist and Political Perspectives on Human Rights.'

8 Michael L. Best, 'Can the Internet Be a Human Right', *Human Rights & Human Welfare* 4 (2004): p. 23.

9 This implication could be resisted if a foundationalist theory incorporated distributive equality as part of the grounds for human rights. As far as I know, no foundationalist approach does this. Griffin, in particular, is highly resistant to such a move. See Griffin, *On Human Rights*, pp. 39–44.

10 Duncan Ivison's chapter in this volume links in with this sentiment here, as Ivison advocates for a *constrained universality* and *plurality* in time, place, culture and practices.

11 c.f. Tasioulas, 'Are Human Rights Essentially Triggers for Intervention?'. Tasioulas likewise proposes three desiderata for a theory of human rights, though his depart somewhat from mine. While we agree on the importance of normative force, Tasioulas also includes fidelity to the so-called International Bill of Rights, and the ability to resist the charge of ethnocentrism. His requirement that a theory of human rights cohere with current practice is in tension with my third desideratum, whose import I defend above. His requirement that a theory of human rights be able to resist the charge of ethnocentrism signals a difference in how we are understanding the project of theorizing human rights. I follow those, like Beitz, who take the object of our study to be an existing political practice. I thus leave open whether that practice is, in fact, ethnocentric. This move may at first blush seem to be in tension with my rejection of Tasioulas' second desideratum. The tension is removed, however, if we acknowledge that the practice in question operates at a higher level of abstraction than the Treaties and

Covenants on which Tasioulas focuses. So while I am searching for a theory that accurately captures the normative work that human rights discourse does in contemporary global politics, I take that normative work to be relatively independent of the precise content of the International Bill of Rights.

12 For a more detailed exposition of this idea, see Suzy Killmister, 'Dignity: Personal, Social, Human', *Philosophical Studies* (2017) Volume 174, Issue 8, pp 2063–2082.

13 This idea of 'being dignified' seems to be closest to how Avishai Margalit understands dignity, when he says that: 'Dignity consists of the behavioral tendencies that attest to the fact that one's attitudes towards oneself is an attitude of self-respect. Dignity is the tendency to behave in a dignified manner which attests to one's self-respect.' See Avishai Margalit, *The Decent Society* (Cambridge: Harvard University Press, 2009), p. 51.

14 The possibility that someone can 'lose' their dignity, in this way, helps explain the common tendency to describe some people as more dignified than others. Such judgements could be tracking one of two things; either an agent is exceptionally good at upholding the standards that she has, even against extreme adversity (Nelson Mandela might come to mind for such an agent); alternatively, an agent may be seen to be trying to uphold particularly stringent or demanding standards. This in turn suggests that dignity is connected to respect in at least two ways: insofar as dignity is an achievement, as 'being dignified' clearly is, we recognise that achievement through what Darwall calls appraisal respect. Simply *having* dignity, by contrast, renders the agent an appropriate object of Darwall's recognition respect, insofar as it is a fact about persons that ought to be taken into consideration in one's deliberations. See Stephen Darwall, 'Two Kinds of Respect', *Ethics* 88 (1977): p. 36. In Darwall's more recent work, a more complex relationship is offered between dignity and respect (see Stephen Darwall, *The Second-Person Standpoint: Morality, Respect, and Accountability* (Cambridge: Harvard University Press, 2006) esp. ch. 10.) Space precludes a proper consideration of the connections between that work and the theory of dignity being proposed here.

15 c.f. Jeremy Waldron, *Dignity, Rank, and Rights* (Oxford: Oxford University Press, 2012).

16 The connection between torture and personal dignity is developed more fully in Suzy Killmister, 'Dignity, Torture, and Human Rights', *Ethical Theory and Moral Practice* 19 (2016): p. 1087.

17 David Luban, 'Human Dignity, Humiliation, and Torture', *Kennedy Institute of Ethics Journal* 19 (2009): p. 211.

18 Luban, 'Human Dignity, Humiliation, and Torture'.

19 As such, social dignity is conferred by others, rather than being either inherent or self-generated. For an excellent discussion of the idea of dignity as conferred, as opposed to inherent, see Colin Bird, 'Dignity as a Moral Concept', *Social Philosophy and Policy* 30 (2014): p. 150.

20 C.f. Killmister, 'Dignity: Personal, Social, Human.'

21 The only exceptions to this would be if the humiliation was aimed at forcing the individual to publicly violate her own standards, where these weren't recognized by the community at large. Such acts would be violations of personal dignity, but not violations of social dignity.

22 For a discussion of the comparative harms involved in both personal and social dignity violations, see Killmister, 'Dignity: Personal, Social, Human.'

23 Richard Rorty, 'Human Rights, Rationality, and Sentimentality', in *On Human Rights*, edited by Stephen Shute and Susan Hurley (New York: Basic Books, 1993): pp. 111–134. While Rorty seems to assume that all in the post-Holocaust world are part of this culture, I am less sure. It is worth being sensitive to the possibility that this culture is not just temporally, but also geographically and culturally, bounded.

24 Which is not to suggest that it is universally accepted. On the picture being drawn here, the global community, along with the normative standards to which all persons are taken to be subject, are constituted through social norms. Like all social norms, these do not require universal consent for their existence; moreover, those with greater social power will typically have more sway in the formation and direction of social norms than those on the margins. Building a theory of human rights upon the notion of social norms thus foregrounds the ambivalence some might feel about the role of human rights in global politics, and in particular the worry that human rights constitute a new form of colonial power.

25 C.f. Darwall, 'Two Kinds of Respect.'

26 An exception to this might be human rights violators – the proverbial 'moral monsters – who are sometimes taken to have removed themselves from the human community through their actions. While this is an idea I hope to pursue in future work, I leave it aside here in order to focus on what I take to be the more important issue for human rights, namely the kind of respect we owe one another, *qua* human being.

27 c.f. Beitz, The Idea of Human Rights, p. 1.

28 C.f. Rawls, *The Law of Peoples*; Raz, 'Human Rights without Foundations'. Both of these authors claim that human rights are those claims the violation of which justify intervention in the affairs of sovereign states. The condition articulated here is both weaker and more positivist, focusing as it does on condemnation rather than intervention, and on the actual response rather than the response that would be justified. (Though it should be noted that the relevant response is limited to *moral* condemnation – this is intended to rule out mere posturing, or condemnation that is simply masquerading as moral).

Part II

Critiquing political approaches

6 Exiting the hall of mirrors

Morality and law in human rights

*John Tasioulas**

This chapter explores, from the perspective of international human rights law (IHRL), the philosophical debate that has emerged in recent years between proponents of orthodox and political accounts of human rights. It treats IHRL as among the key phenomena which theories of human rights must help us to understand if they are to succeed in their aims. I take as my chief interlocutor in this endeavour Allen Buchanan's provocative book, *The Heart of Human Rights.*[1] Although himself a prolific contributor to the recent surge of philosophical interest in human rights, Buchanan's contention is that the leading theories in the area have systematically overlooked a vital topic: the nature, and justifiability, of a system of IHRL. And yet, according to Buchanan, any philosophical theory that hopes to engage with what he calls 'the practice of human rights' must have IHRL as its principal 'explanandum'. Anything less consigns a theory to irrelevance, an unhappy condition he believes afflicts both sides of the orthodox/political divide, including some of his own previous work in an orthodox vein. Rather than making yet another contribution to this evolving debate on the nature of human rights, Buchanan's 'plague on both your houses' verdict attacks its very terms. He thereby aims to shift the philosophy of human rights onto more fertile ground, stimulating nothing less than 'a radical transformation of the way philosophers have tended to think about human rights'.[2]

Buchanan's call to grapple with conceptual and normative questions raised by IHRL is entirely justified. For a long time, the philosophy of international law has languished as the poor relation of other, livelier provinces of legal philosophy, such as the philosophy of criminal law. Given international law's increasing role within global and domestic governance, this comparative neglect is unfortunate. Moreover, in light of the central significance within the international legal order that many accord to human rights norms, IHRL is in special need of philosophical scrutiny. In addition, many philosophers who have engaged with IHRL have done so at a very high level abstraction, one that displays a tenuous grasp of the institutional and doctrinal specificities of IHRL and that fails to address the work of theoretically-inclined international legal scholars. Changing this dismal status quo is no easy task. It is difficult to master the intricacies of customary international law, *jus cogens*, *erga omnes*, subsidiarity, horizontal effect, and other technical legal notions; it is yet more difficult to articulate their proper nature and role in a way that is truly philosophically informed. However, this is the work that philosophers must now undertake, just as philosophers from H.L.A Hart to Antony Duff have done so successfully for criminal law.

Yet despite this general point of agreement, I believe Buchanan's book exaggerates the place of IHLR in the explanandum of a theory of human rights. Partly as a result, it also seriously underestimates the extent to which leading accounts of human rights already do shed valuable light on IHRL. Therefore, his pessimistic thesis that recent philosophical work on human rights is a sustained exercise in missing the point is unconvincing. More positively, I argue that the orthodox view of human rights – according to which they are essentially universal moral rights – offers an account of human rights that makes good sense of the formative aim of IHRL. A measure of its power is that Buchanan needs to presuppose something like the orthodox account to make good on his own constructive efforts to theorize IHRL. Hence, his account is no real alternative to orthodoxy, let alone a 'radically transformative' one.

This chapter is organized as follows: (1) I begin by reprising how to interpret the controversy between orthodox and political accounts of human rights: as a conceptual debate within a larger explanatory philosophical enterprise in which making sense of IHRL has a role, but not quite the dominant role envisioned by Buchanan; (2) Buchanan's attack on the orthodox account, and some versions of its political rival, assumes that proponents of both approaches are committed to the crude and indefensible Mirroring View of the relation between human rights and IHRL. But this attack misfires: the latter view is not endorsed by leading orthodox theorists, nor are they logically committed to it. Still, (3) the orthodox view of human rights remains crucial for understanding the integrity of IHRL as a discrete body of law. This is because the formative aim of IHRL is to give effect to human rights morality to the extent that it is appropriate to do so by means of a uniform set of individual legal rights assigned to all human beings. Most importantly, Buchanan's argument that IHRL justifiably offers protections that far exceed anything that is demanded by human rights morality is shown to rest on a flawed interpretation of the latter; and (4) against orthodox and political accounts of human rights, Buchanan's rival proposal for understanding the nature of IHRL is as a set of legal constraints on state sovereignty intended to secure (a) the basic moral equality of all individuals or (b) the conditions of a minimal level of well-being for all. I contend that for any version of this proposal to succeed, it needs to draw on the orthodox account of human rights. In consequence, it is parasitic on that, the latter, rather than a serious rival to it.

1 Orthodox v. political views of human rights

The debate between proponents of 'orthodox' and 'political' views of human rights is fundamentally conceptual in character. It is about the nature of human rights, about what it is we grasp when we have mastery of the concept of a human right. Crucially, only if we are talking about a recognizably uniform subject-matter can we profitably discuss – and have disagreements about – a range of other vitally important topics, including: the grounds of human rights; the holders of human rights and the bearers of corresponding obligations; the content of human rights, i.e. the obligations associated with them; the justification for responding to violations of human rights in various ways, e.g. intervention, punishment, etc.; and the relationship of human rights to other elements of morality, such as common goods, charity, etc. Nonetheless, it may be that the very concept of a human right incorporates a stance on one or more of these matters. But there is good reason to keep the concept ecumenical and hence disentangled from commitments on any of these controversial matters, perhaps especially the vexed question of grounds.[3]

In recent years, two rival families of views as to the concept of a human right have emerged:

> *Orthodox view:* human rights are moral rights possessed by all human beings simply in virtue of their humanity (and discoverable through ordinary moral reasoning).[4]

Political view: human rights are moral standards of a certain type that involve some distinctive political function or combination of functions, e.g. triggers for intervention or benchmarks of political legitimacy.[5]

In making sense of this debate, it is vital to distinguish the question of whether the concept of human rights is political from whether it plays a political role. It is entirely open to adherents of orthodoxy to hold that human rights play various important political roles without thereby regarding the concept as inherently political. This is akin to the way in which nuclear energy has played an important geo-political role, even though the concept of nuclear energy is not geo-political, but rather physical, in character. Not everything important about human rights is already inscribed in the very concept of a human right. So, for example, one of the most important questions about human rights concerns their grounds. But, as I remarked previously, we should avoid building a comprehensive theory of grounds, such as a deontological or theistic account of their source, into the very concept of such rights. This is so even if we believe a given theory of grounds to be demonstrably correct. Of course, it is not impossible that the theory might eventually become part of the concept of a human right, assuming it came to be widely endorsed. But we are currently very far away from any such philosopher's panacea. So, for now, any attempt to build a comprehensive account of their grounds into the concept of such human rights can only be treated as a radical proposal in conceptual reform.

In previous work I have defended a version of the orthodox account as against a variety of political views.[6] This defence involves two broad lines of argument: positively, the attempt to give a compelling version of the orthodox view, and negatively, the identification of problems with the political view, both wholesale problems afflicting such views in general, and retail problems afflicting its specific variants. I believe a version of the orthodox view is on balance superior, especially in the context of a philosophical inquiry geared to understanding whether there is a distinctive and defensible ethical idea underlying the discourse of human rights in its post-Universal Declaration of Human Rights (UDHR) manifestations. However, it is worth noticing that the debate between adherents of orthodox and political views has become somewhat less polarized over time. In consequence, it is increasingly hard to distinguish between more sophisticated versions of such views, to determine what if anything turns on the choice between them, and so to adjudicate between them. All this is as it should be, since this convergence is often an indication of genuine dialogue and the intellectual progress to which it is a prelude. Let me offer some evidence for this claim.

An important early assault on the orthodox view of human rights, objecting to its poor fit with human rights as understood in the post-UDHR world, turned on the assumption that orthodoxy is committed to a fixed set of diachronically universal or timeless human rights.[7] In what sense, the objection goes, could a Stone Age caveman have a right to democratic political participation, a fair trial or a nationality when the relevant institutions are not feasibly accessible for many centuries to come? Although some orthodox theorists have embraced timelessness whilst seeking to retain the link with contemporary human rights discourse,[8] others have rejected the idea that timelessness is a feature of the very concept of a human right. Instead, on this latter approach, human rights can be specified in a way that is temporally-relative yet synchronically universal. For example, they can be indexed to the socio-economic conditions characteristic of modernity.[9] Versions of orthodoxy of the latter kind bring it closer to the political view in animating spirit.

Another way in which the orthodox view has been elaborated so as to address concerns that inspire the political view is by emphasizing the idea – traceable to John Stuart Mill, but stretching much further back in the history of ethics – that human rights are rights that should, in some broad sense of 'enforcement', be socially enforced, at least as a *pro tanto* matter. This view differs from standard political views in stopping short of conceptually privileging a specific mode of enforcement, such as legalization, or various forms of international intervention or concern.[10] Finally there is the observation, already noted, that an orthodox theorist can accept that the political uses of human rights constitutes an important topic of investigation, even if it lacks the kind of significance needed to make any specific political function part of the concept of a human right. In these three ways, at least, orthodoxy is responsive to concerns that motivate the family of political views without collapsing into a version of the latter.

Something similar can be said about the evolution of political views of human rights. Some versions are radically opposed to the orthodox view insofar as they regard the concept of human rights as sui generis, rather than a sub-species of the broader category of moral rights.[11] But other, more plausible versions treat human rights as not only a sub-species of moral rights, but of universal moral rights (as broadly understood on the orthodox view). This is true of Joseph Raz's influential conception of human rights as universal moral rights that disable the otherwise applicable protections against intervention afforded by the principle of state sovereignty.[12] A crucial first step in establishing the existence of a human right, for Raz, is that of justifying a background universal moral right. The question whether it is a human right proper then turns on whether it ought to be accorded the relevant sovereignty-limiting role. Raz is brought even closer to the orthodox view by his rather idiosyncratic interpretation of sovereignty. Since he apparently takes sovereignty ordinarily to disallow even the criticism of one state by another, the extension of his concept of a human right heavily overlaps with the orthodox account. Another sophisticated proponent of the political view is Jean Cohen, who begins by appealing to a broad class of 'human rights' that are political only in the rather thin sense that they constrain political power, something that does not radically differentiate them from universal moral rights. Within that broad category, she focuses on a very narrow set of human rights norms that can in principle justify military invasion in the event of their extensive violation.[13] Evidently, the versions of the political view that treat human rights as a subset of universal moral rights are hardly root and branch repudiations of orthodoxy. Instead, they presuppose, but build on, the orthodox view.

So, there is a moderately upbeat appraisal of the debate between proponents of the orthodox and political views of human rights that stresses considerable convergence. Differences remain, and the question arises as to the value of insisting on them. Beyond some point, as with most philosophical debates, diminishing marginal returns rapidly set in. Then mere scholasticism looms, and the philosophical caravan moves on. Contrary to this genial assessment, Buchanan's uncompromising 'plague on both your houses' response calls all the leading theories into question. The key reason for this is the supposedly fatal tendency of all parties to discount the crucial significance of IHRL in shaping a theory of human rights. I discuss this objection in the next section. But it is worth registering that Buchanan finds theorists of all stripes guilty of what he calls 'conceptual imperialism', i.e. making the undefended, and presumably indefensible, assumption that there is a *single* concept of human rights waiting to be uncovered.[14] But this objection seems to be a red herring. Of course, there are many concepts of human rights, in the sense that the phrase 'human rights' may legitimately be used in various senses – for example, universal moral rights, human rights law, what ought to be enshrined in human rights law, etc. Still, we can nonetheless ask whether there is a central or focal sense of the concept, one which has explanatory priority in relation to the others, at least within a theoretical enterprise aimed at a certain kind of understanding or evaluation of aspects of our world. This requires setting out more fully the nature of the explanatory enterprise, with the caveat that, of course, there may be other legitimate such enterprises.

Elsewhere, I have characterized the project I am engaged in as making sense of the post-1945 human rights culture, the culture of which the UDHR is a focal point. The question arises whether this culture may be appropriately interpreted as organized around a central concept of a human right, one in relation to which others are derivative or marginal, and which can potentially be mobilized in judgements that justify that practice and furnish a basis for its continuation or enlightened reform. Among the 'meta-theoretical' criteria of success for this project are: normative plausibility, ecumenism, and fidelity.[15] And it goes without saying that there is no guarantee in advance that we can helpfully see the human rights culture as anchored in a focal concept, or that any focal concept, once articulated, can perform any genuine justificatory or critical work.

2 International human rights law and the Mirroring View

Let us now consider two major strands in Buchanan's radical challenge to the orthodox view in *The Heart of Human Rights:*

(a) Central to the contemporary practice of human rights are the norms, institutions and practices of IHRL, but philosophers – especially those of an orthodox persuasion – have tended to ignore the question of how to understand and justify IHRL in fashioning their theories of human rights.

(b) Insofar as orthodox views, and some versions of political views, engage with IHRL, they embrace the 'Mirroring View' fallacy. On the Mirroring View, human rights are 'simply moral rights in legal dress'.[16] But, according to Buchanan, the reality of human rights practice is inconsistent with this mirroring picture: an antecedent moral human right is neither necessary nor sufficient to justify a corresponding IHRL; nor (in an extension I address later) is it strictly necessary for the latter to be a means of promoting fulfilment of antecedent moral human rights.

A certain tension between these two theses is evident. It is odd to suppose that any theorist of human rights who is inattentive to IHRL would endorse anything like the Mirroring View, with the simple – more accurately, simple-minded – connection it forges between the morality of human rights and IHRL. The Mirroring View hardly seems plausible as a mere by-product of an analysis of human rights motivated independently of any concern with IHRL. Instead, something like the Mirroring View is charitably attributable only to a theorist who is exercised by IHRL from the very outset. In other words, it seems most unlikely that all the theorists Buchanan accuses of dismissiveness towards IHRL should have miraculously converged upon the Mirroring View. The better view, I think, is that the obviously false formulations of the Mirroring View cannot, in general, be charitably attributed to these theorists, and this is partly because, although they regard IHRL as relevant in fashioning a theory of human rights, they rightly do not accord it anything like the dominant significance that Buchanan does. Hence the conjunction of (a) and (b) that Buchanan attributes to most philosophers of human rights is dubious. But there are problems with each thesis considered on its own.

Regarding criticism (a) – that of ignoring the centrality of IHRL to the contemporary practice of human rights – two points are salient. First, Buchanan seems to attack a straw man in accusing philosophers of neglecting the place of IHRL in the practice of human rights. Orthodox theorists like James Griffin and Sen, and political theorists like Beitz and Raz, make repeated references to IHRL, and in particular to the UDHR. This instrument, although not legally binding in itself, contains norms which have become binding as a matter of international law both through subsequent treaties (in particular, the 1966 International Covenants on Civil and Politics Rights and on Economic, Social and Cultural Rights) and incorporation into customary international law. These philosophers may quite simply disagree with Buchanan about the kind of significance to be accorded to this body of law within any worthwhile philosophical project that takes human rights as its subject-matter. I pursue this line of thought further (see Section 3) in giving an account of how the orthodox theorist can take IHRL seriously without succumbing to the clearly flawed Mirroring View.

The other point is that Buchanan himself exaggerates the centrality of IHRL to the practice of human rights. Telling here is his treatment of the UN Guiding Principles on Business and Human Rights (2011), one of the most significant recent developments in human rights governance. They seem to be a clear counter-example to the thesis that the human rights practice is essentially legalistic in character, i.e. principles that *pro tanto* ought to be embodied in international law. The Guiding Principles do not purport to impose legally-binding obligations on corporations. Instead, the architect of the principles, John Ruggie, explicitly appeals to the orthodox view of human rights, in the form elaborated by Sen, as their conceptual underpinning.[17] Legal enactment and enforcement, according to Ruggie, are better seen as 'precision instruments', applicable to some principles in some contexts, rather than a universally mandatory or desirable method of implementing the principles. In the background is the conceptual point upon which Sen has powerfully insisted: that we should not incarcerate human rights in a legalistic framework, conceiving of them either as the 'progeny' of law (as Bentham did) or as 'parents' of (international human rights) law (as the Mirroring View does).[18]

Now, Buchanan acknowledges that the Guiding Principles are not legally binding, yet persists in seeing them as exemplifying the explanatory centrality of IHRL. Admittedly, the principles can be interpreted as deriving their familiar names from IHRL. But this, by itself, is a fairly superficial feature. What matters is their content and, even more, their status. As to content, it is essential to Ruggie's scheme that while states have the responsibility to *protect* human rights (e.g. by ensuring compliance by third parties, including corporations), corporations only have a more limited duty to *respect* the principles in their own activities. But the more important observation concerns their status. The mere fact that the principles are in some sense derived from IHRL does not make them legal principles. Yet Buchanan seeks to stretch the point, risking incoherence by arguing that 'states – and non-state actors such as corporations – can sometimes be held accountable for violating ILHR norms even when the corresponding legal duties are not ascribable to them'.[19] But this statement tries to have it both ways. It's akin to saying that if the Australian law on murder is derived historically from English common law, then an Australian citizen who commits murder in Australia also thereby violates English law, even though the legal duties associated with it do not apply to them. The far less strained conclusion to draw is that the Guiding Principles testify to the fact that human rights are not conceptually wedded either to law in general or IHRL in particular.

The Guiding Principles are just one of many elements of contemporary human rights practice that cannot be shoe-horned within IHRL. This illustrates the more general point that the human rights culture post-1948 is not narrowly legal in character, but also more broadly a moral and political movement. Another illustration of this is the feminist critique of human rights violations in the private sphere. Many sexist practices, such as those related to the distribution of domestic labour or decision-making processes within the family, may appropriately be assessed on human rights grounds without there being any implication that the enforcement of these rights should, even pro tanto, be a matter for the law or the state. On the basis of such considerations, I have argued that the orthodox view, rather than harking back nostalgically to an outmoded natural rights tradition, turns out to be indispensable to understanding the most imaginative innovations within contemporary human rights practice.[20]

Let us turn now to objection (b), which is centred on the imputation of the Mirroring View to orthodox theorists. What this view amounts to is not exactly clear, so I shall quote at length Buchanan's key characterization of it:

> The Mirroring View holds that to justify an international legal human rights typically involves defending the claim that a corresponding moral human right exists. The qualifier 'typically' is designed to accommodate the fact that some who hold this view acknowledge that in some cases a justified international legal right does not mirror a moral human right, but rather is either (a) a specification of a moral human right (as the right to freedom of the press is a specification of the right to freedom of expression); or (b) something that is instrumentally valuable for realizing a moral human right (as some think that an international legal right to democratic government is instrumentally valuable for realizing some important moral human rights, even if there is no moral human right to democratic government).[21]

The problem here is in cashing out the kind of relationships between a moral human right and a right in IHRL that the Mirroring View has in mind. We get a clearer picture of the 'mirroring' relation in question by noting Buchanan's strategy for refuting it in chapter 2 of his book:

> I will show that appealing to an antecedently existing moral human right is not necessary for justifying international legal human rights and that, in the case of a number of important international legal human rights, appealing to a pre-existing moral human right is not sufficient to justify the legal right.[22]

So, what is primarily at issue in the Mirroring View is a conjunction of two claims: (1) for any given right in IHRL there is typically a counterpart right in human rights morality with the same or substantively equivalent content, and (2) that the latter right is typically either necessary or sufficient to justify the enactment of the former. The use of 'typically' here is meant to accommodate the two exceptions noted by Buchanan in the long passage quoted previously.

I have already indicated that the imputation of the Mirroring View to proponents of the orthodox view is questionable. Writers such as John Finnis, James Griffin, Onora O'Neill, Amartya Sen nowhere, to my knowledge, explicitly assert the Mirroring View. Some of them explicitly reject it, and the silence of others on the matter cannot charitably be taken to be self-incriminating.[23] For example, Sen has long insisted that we should not conceive of claims about human rights as even presumptively entailing a commitment to their enshrinement in law (let alone, therefore, to their enshrinement specifically in IHRL). There may be all sorts of obstacles standing in the way of such an entailment, some of which may be practical (e.g. laws would not be effective instruments for the implementation of the relevant rights) and some of which may be principled (e.g. the right pertains to a matter within the private sphere, such as the distribution of domestic labour, which does not fall within the scope of the state's legitimate law-making power).[24] Nor is there a compelling basis for pinning on orthodox theorists the thesis that enacting an international legal right requires, as a necessary condition, the existence of a background moral human right with broadly matching content. Perhaps the most seemingly plausible candidate for this view is Griffin, especially in his discussion of 'discrepancies' between international human rights law. But Griffin's overriding concern in engaging with IHRL is not to argue that a counterpart norm in human rights morality is a necessary (or sufficient) condition of including any right within IHRL. Instead, it is to oppose the tendency among many, especially human rights lawyers, to bypass the question of whether something really is a human right, in the moral sense, by treating the law as dispositive of the matter. Consistently with this objective, Griffin is willing to acknowledge that IHRL properly enjoys a certain 'autonomy' from human rights morality, which is partly manifested in the fact that it may permissibly include norms that lack any counterparts in human rights morality such as, in his opinion, the legal right to compensation for miscarriage of justice.[25]

In short: when Buchanan contends that 'many philosophers assume the Mirroring View and none argues for it',[26] we ought to take the lack of arguments for such a breathtakingly crude thesis as throwing doubt on the claim that these philosophers assume it. More specifically, we have seen that leading orthodox theorists have tended to embrace the anti-Mirroring thesis that Buchanan himself endorses, i.e. that 'the existence of corresponding moral rights is neither necessary nor sufficient for justifying international legal human rights'.[27] Foisting the Mirroring View on them, therefore, looks like the setting up of a straw man.[28] But this still begs the question: is not Buchanan right to insist, at a general methodological level, that an acceptable theory of the nature of human rights must shed light on IHRL? How can the orthodox view, in particular, do so if it does not build any reference to IHRL, international law, or even law into the very concept of a human right?

3 The Formative Aim Thesis

This is an important challenge which needs to be met. The starting point is to abandon the idea that the concept of human rights contains or implies some specific 'mirroring' prescription about the inclusion of norms of human rights morality into the body of IHRL. A better way to think of the issue is as addressing a question of legal integrity: what gives the domain of IHRL its coherence as a domain within public international law, distinguishing it in a principled way from other domains of law, such as humanitarian law, the law of the sea, and so on? My contention is that those persuaded by the orthodox view should accept the Formative Aim Thesis. This holds that IHRL's integrity as a department of international law consists in the fact that it is ***primarily concerned with giving effect to universal moral rights, insofar as it is appropriate for international law to do so through the technique of assigning a uniform set of individual rights to all human beings.*** The concept of a human right, then, is the formative idea or normative seed underlying IHRL, but this does not entail commitment to the Mirroring View. Or, to put it more precisely, the Formative Aim Thesis does not carry the implication that the norms of IHRL will typically simply reproduce ('mirror') in content prior norms of human rights morality. It is entirely possible, for example, that rather than being 'exceptions', the phenomena of specification and instrumentalization extensively characterize the proper relationship between these two bodies of norms. The only kind of 'mirroring' that the Formative Aim Thesis inherently involves is of a very limited, formal kind: the general form of human rights morality – *universal* (moral) *rights* possessed by *all* human beings – will itself be mirrored by the distinctive legal technique adopted by IHRL to realize those rights, i.e. *universal* (legal) *rights* possessed by *all* human beings.

Now, the Formative Aims Thesis needs elaboration. The idea is not the manifestly false one, which Buchanan seems to embrace, that IHRL is the only area of law concerned with giving effect to the morality of human rights.[29] If one were to ask which area of international law does most to safeguard human rights morality, one very plausible answer would be the laws on the use of force and intervention, since the conduct they prohibit often results in massive human rights violations. Hence, it is wrong to suppose that only human rights law advances the morality of human rights, or is even the most important department of law that does so. Instead, the claim is that IHRL has as its *primary goal* that of realizing human rights morality *through a distinctive legal technique*, i.e. assigning a uniform set of individual legal rights to all human beings, a technique that is not generally adopted by the law on the use of force and intervention. Moreover, it should pursue this aim only to the extent that it is *appropriate for it to do so*. This caveat allows for principled constraints (e.g. questions of human rights morality that should be left to the self-determination of individuals, families, communities, states, etc) and pragmatic constraints (e.g. the likelihood that enshrining certain moral human rights in IHRL will be counterproductive with respect to compliance with those rights or in some other way) on the legal implementation of human rights morality. None of this, of course, means that IHRL has as a matter of historical fact been suitably responsive to its formative aim. Indeed, it is arguable that it often has failed to maintain its integrity, which has presumably fuelled the well-rehearsed complaints about the uncontrolled 'proliferation' of international human rights norms. But it *is* to say that this is the guiding aspiration that characterizes the distinctive nature of IHRL.

To sharpen the point, consider some analogies from municipal law. We might ask what is the formative idea behind contract law, the notion that gives this body of law its identity and distinguishes it from other areas of law, such as restitution and tort? Now, one promising line of thought is that the root of contract law is the idea of a promise, a moral notion but one that is pregnant with legal implications.[30] It does not follow from this view that all promises should be 'mirrored' by legally enforceable contacts. This is so for a variety of reasons. Some promises may involve no intention to create legal relations; in some there is insufficient at stake (no 'consideration') to warrant the law's concern; while, for others, such as promises made in certain intimate contexts, it is beyond the proper jurisdiction of the law and the state to regulate such undertakings, no matter how gravely important they may be to the people involved. Nor is an advocate of the promise theory committed to the idea that all contracts must involve, as a necessary condition of their legal enforceability, a counterpart promise. Various agreements or understandings might be quite properly legally upheld as contracts even if they are not exactly promises, e,g. implied contracts. Such extensions of the idea of contract beyond the strict domain of promises may be driven by economic or public good considerations. Still, promises might nonetheless be the core organizing idea behind contract law, identifying its primary aim of recognizing and giving effect to certain promises that are apt for legal enforcement. Other types of agreements enforced by contract law are, in this sense, treated *as if* they were promises.

A similar account can be given of other areas of law. Criminal law, for example, may be understood as rooted in the idea of a special category of public wrong. More specifically, it is centred on the idea of certain moral wrongs that the community as a whole has an interest in prohibiting by means of law, and whose condemnation and, perhaps, whose punishment, is not to be left to the discretion of the immediate victim of the wrong-doing.[31] As before, there is no implication that any crime must have as its counterpart a wrong of this kind, since it may be useful, at the margins, to deploy the criminal law in realizing certain regulatory goals that do not straightforwardly involve independent moral wrongs. Why does this matter? The general formative idea shapes doctrine, preventing it from losing coherence through distortion by means of extraneous considerations, as could conceivably happen if contract law is treated simply as a mechanism of wealth-maximization, or criminal law as a means of social control that is inattentive to the question of the wrongfulness of the conduct it prohibits and punishes.

Analogously to these familiar areas of law, my contention is that IHRL is best conceived in line with the Formative Aim Thesis. Moreover, this interpretation finds a responsive echo in the contemporary human rights movement, including in the activities of the framers of the UDHR. One striking illustration is the history of Article 27 of the UDHR, whose second clause provides: 'Everyone has the right to the protection of the moral and material interests resulting from any scientific, literary or artistic production of which he is the author'. As Lea Shaver has highlighted in a fine study, Article 27(2) was virtually unique in provoking protracted debate among the framers as to whether it should be included at all, as opposed to merely generating disagreements regarding the precise formulation of the right to be incorporated into the text of the Declaration. Also atypical was the narrow majority on the basis of which the right was adopted, in contrast to the more usual procedure of unanimity one way or another, with occasional abstentions.[32] The debate in the drafting committee over the inclusion of this right testifies to IHRL's formative goal of giving effect to background universal moral rights through universal legal rights. Anglophone countries protested its inclusion on the basis that intellectual property rights should be conceived as generating economic incentives to spur creativity and innovation, rather than as realizing background human rights. Unlike human rights, such rights were alienable, could be held by artificial persons, such as corporations, and could expire over time. By contrast, the civil law tradition had long recognized inalienable moral rights of authors.[33] This debate powerfully illustrates the way in which a background conception of universal moral rights guided the construction of the UDHR and influences the human rights practice to which Buchanan aspires to be faithful. Yet we need not, in embracing this interpretation, saddle the framers with anything as crude as the Mirroring View.

Two responses to the line of thought developed so far can be excavated from Buchanan's work, one less interesting than the other. The first response is to specify a weaker version of the Mirroring View which may more plausibly be attributed to orthodox theorists. On this interpretation, IHRL will 'mirror' the morality of human rights if the point of the former is largely seen as 'instrumentally valuable for realizing' the latter. But this move confronts three problems. The first is that an 'instrumental' relation is poorly captured by the 'mirroring' metaphor, since it carries no necessary implication that the legal rights that best give effect to moral rights will be identical or even very similar to them in content. Part (1) of the initial Mirroring View claim – the part that gives the 'mirroring' metaphor its purchase – is abandoned. It is unsurprising therefore that this instrumental relation was originally introduced by Buchanan as an exception to the Mirroring View: it was one of the reasons, denoted in the long passage quoted previously as (b), why the Mirroring View held only typically, alongside (a), the exception concerning specification.[34] Second, even this instrumental view is too crude as it stands since, for example, it does not take on board the principled constraints that exist on giving effect to some duties associated with universal rights, such as a duty to give family members a say in major family decisions, by means of IHRL.

Finally, if the new interpretation is suitably adjusted in light of the second objection, then something like the Formative Aim Thesis may well emerge. Even if all orthodox theorists do not explicitly hold this thesis, I have argued they should embrace it as a view about the integrity of IHRL. At this point, however, the path to enlightenment involves abandoning talk of 'mirroring' as an unhelpful focus of discussion, and asking instead whether Buchanan has a compelling objection to the Formative Aim Thesis.

Here the second, and more interesting, response comes into play. It is to insist that we should be trying to make 'best sense' of human rights practice, and in this process we must be receptive to the need for significant revisions to long-established self-understandings, including the Formative Aim Thesis. These revisions may be dictated by the need to resolve tensions within the practice itself. Buchanan highlights a tension between two elements of the practice: (1) the existence of extensive legal entitlements under IHRL, and (2) the widespread assumption that these entitlements somehow reflect background universal moral rights (as in the Mirroring View or the Formative Aim Thesis). These two elements are in tension, according to Buchanan, because (1) flies in the face of (2). This is because universal moral rights entitle us to considerably less than we normally assume that they do and, in consequence, considerably less than the entitlements embodied in IHRL. This state of affairs calls for a 'radical transformation' in the way philosophers think about human rights, both moral rights and those embodied in IHRL.[35] The radical transformation would leave behind the Formative Aim Thesis in favour of Buchanan's dualist theory of the point of IHRL.

Buchanan helpfully summarizes this response in terms of a seven-stage argument.[36] For our purposes, it can be distilled to the following propositions: (i) many standard human rights in IHRL impose duties the fulfilment of which 'requires large-scale social investment and limitations on liberty';[37] (ii) these legal rights cannot be justified on the basis of a prior moral right, since no prior moral right generates anything like such extensive duties; (iii) nevertheless, these legal rights are justified, but their justification does not consist in giving effect to human rights morality in the way envisaged by the Formative Aim Thesis. The key premise here is (ii), and Buchanan develops it by setting the following condition on justifying a duty associated with a moral right, call it the 'individualist condition':

> In the case of moral rights, the corresponding duties must be justifiable by appeal solely to some morally important aspect of the individual to whom the right is ascribed, because the duties are supposed to be owed, morally speaking, to the individual to whom the right is ascribed.[38]

It this individualist condition, according to Buchanan, that cannot be fulfilled by any existing theory of moral rights in such a way as to underwrite existing IHRL. So, for example, on an interest-based account of human rights, it would be necessary to show that the duties ordinarily associated with the right to health in IHRL give effect to a background moral right to health. Buchanan's claim is that this project is doomed, since any given individual's interest is not sufficient, *considered in isolation from the interests of others*, to justify the large-scale 'social investment' and 'limitations on liberty' that the relevant duties involve, e.g. public health measures such as vaccination programmes against diphtheria. Hence, contrary to the Formative Aim Thesis, the justification of the right to health in IHRL must be sought elsewhere.[39]

This result, according to Buchanan, generalizes very widely across the array of rights in IHRL, including not only standard socio-economic rights, but also classic civil and political rights such as the right to democratic government and the freedom of expression. Indeed, it could well be argued on this basis that even the legal human right not to be tortured, as standardly understood, cannot be fully justified in terms of a universal moral right not to be tortured. After all, that right is interpreted as requiring states to devote vast resources to preventing, condemning, and punishing incidents of torture, as well as to compensating the victims. How can the massive material and moral costs involved in doing so be justified by any one individual's interests considered on their own, without those interests being aggregated along with others' interests in having these costly policies and institutions in place? It seems an unnervingly open question whether in fact they can be.

Yet it is precisely the radically sceptical implications of Buchanan's argument – the way that it results in issues in moral rights far less extensive than we might ordinarily assume that we possess – that should alert us to the fact something has gone seriously awry. We do not have to acquiesce in the austere, essentially libertarian, account of moral rights implied by Buchanan's argument. And this is because we do not have to accept his interpretation of the individualist condition that must be satisfied to establish the existence of a right on the basis of the interests of an individual right-holder. As with the Mirroring View, I think that Buchanan has again set up a straw man opponent. But even if some formulations given by leading theorists, such as Raz, can be read in the way suggested by Buchanan, the untoward implications of this interpretation suggest that we should seek an alternative before embracing it.

I have argued elsewhere that we should reject the thesis that on the interest-based account the individual right-holder's interest must suffice *on its own* to justify a duty to bear the *whole* costs of securing the right for all putative right-holders. The individual right-holder, after all, is only one among many who enjoy the benefits of rights-securing public policies and institutions, such as a vaccination programme intended to achieve herd immunity against diphtheria. His individual benefit does not need to justify incurring the entirety of the costs of a rights-securing policy or institution. Instead, what needs to be justified by the right-holder's interest is the right-holder's *proportionate share of the costs* of securing his right as one among many other right-holders who also benefit in the same way from the system. Given that we are dealing with human rights, and a standardized profile of interests that abstracts from certain variations among individuals, this share will be notionally the same for all. So, the test that putative duties must pass if they are to be justified as rights-based is an affirmative answer to the following question: does the notional benefit to any individual right-holder of securing the putative duties for all justify a proportionate share of the costs involved in doing so?

This is a notably less demanding test than Buchanan's, one that leads to a more extensive array of universal moral rights, and also one that restores confidence in the Formative Aim Thesis as an explanation of IHRL. Moreover, this interpretation of the individualist condition preserves the crucial idea that the duties associated with rights are 'directed' in character, i.e. that they are owed to some determinate individual who is personally wronged when the duties are violated. The directedness of rights-based duties arises from the fact that such duties are grounded in the interests of the individual right-holder in the manner explained previously. By contrast there will be other duties – so-called 'imperfect' duties of charity, mercy, and so on – which are not owed to anyone in particular, hence not claimable as a matter of individual rights, because the interest of any given individual does not suffice to justify incurring the cost of securing the putative duty.

We should conclude that, in pillorying the orthodox view, Buchanan is engaged in a struggle with a straw man of his own construction. Friends of the orthodox view are not committed to the Mirroring View, nor are they committed to his excessively demanding formulation of the individualist condition on rights-based duties. On the contrary, they have compelling reasons to reject both of the premises Buchanan foists on them. Hence, Buchanan's motivation to abandon the orthodox view of human rights is massively undercut.

4 Equality and well-being without moral rights?

In this final section, I will not scrutinize in detail the alternative conception of human rights Buchanan advances in place of the orthodox view, although I am broadly sympathetic to the important role that he assigns to considerations of basic moral equality and well-being in grounding IHRL.[40] Instead, I want to suggest that the very workability of his positive view *presupposes* the truth of the very thesis he intends it to supplant, i.e. that IHRL has as its primary aim giving effect to a background human rights morality as understood by the orthodox theorist. To this extent, it is not genuinely an alternative to the orthodox account, and its companion Formative Aim Thesis, but rather builds on them.

According to the positive thesis elaborated in *The Heart of Human Rights*, the point of IHRL is to 'constrain the exercise of sovereignty for the purposes of affirming and promoting the equal basic status of all people (the status egalitarian function) and helping to ensure that all have the opportunity to lead a minimally good or decent life by providing protections and resources that are generally needed for such a life (the well-being function).'[41] This dualist account is offered in place of conceptions of human rights such as those associated with both orthodox and political approaches; it is the promised 'radical transformation' of human rights theory, one that takes IHRL seriously. Now, two preliminary observations are worth making about this view.

First, it is not at all clear that this is a direct competitor to the orthodox or political views of the nature of human rights. Buchanan's thesis seems to be mostly a contribution to a different debate, that regarding the grounds of human rights. Of course, it is possible for reference to grounds to figure in the concept of a human right, but I have suggested that it is preferable to maintain a general ecumenism as to grounds at the conceptual level. However, Buchanan's reply may be that, like Griffin, he presents a grounds-based conceptual account of human rights as part of a project of conceptual reform, one aimed at resolving tensions in the existing practice of human rights and arriving at a more perspicuous interpretation of them. This may be so even if he does not go so far as Griffin's harsh verdict that the use of the phrase 'human rights' is 'virtually criterionless' in contemporary practice.[42]

The second observation is that Buchanan claims, without extensive elaboration, that the norms of IHRL are limitations on sovereignty. But this seems contestable. Does this follow from the fact that IHRL purports to be binding law and – in the specific case of customary international law and *jus cogens* – binding independently of the will of the states subject to it? If so, this implausibly construes the relationship between state sovereignty and international law as zero sum. States, and the scope of their freedom of action, are constituted by international law, rather than being simply constrained by it. Perhaps Buchanan has a more restricted notion of sovereignty in mind, such as freedom from intervention, e.g. attacks on territorial integrity. But if so, it is far from clear, as Brad Roth has argued, that the mere existence of a norm of IHRL represents any kind of limitation on state sovereignty.[43] After all, a human right can exist as a matter of international law without its violating generating any legal justification case for intervention. Buchanan at one stage asserts a connection between human rights and armed humanitarian intervention, but even here he observes that such a connection holds only in relation to a subset of violations of some 'basic' norms of IHRL, not of IHRL violations generally. In short, Buchanan's conception of human rights as constraints on sovereignty is questionable. But it is also hard to evaluate because, if human rights 'disable assertions of sovereignty',[44] it is important to know what those assertions are. Unfortunately, Buchanan does not give a positive account of the ordinary extent of state sovereignty that he is prepared to endorse.

Leaving these preliminary concerns aside, the more important point is that the workability of the two functions identified by Buchanan appears to *presuppose* the idea of human rights as universal moral rights. If so, Buchanan's complex of equality- and well-being advancing functions cannot be presented as a true alternative to the orthodox view, but is instead parasitic upon it. Consider the status egalitarian function. I believe that Buchanan is correct in claiming that something like this function plays an important role in IHRL. But then the question arises as to what it means to serve this function through *human rights.* There are many ways in which status egalitarianism may be transgressed or not served, without this constituting a human rights violation, in the sense of the one that should sound in IHRL. For example, a 'liberal racist' may behave impeccably towards blacks, yet harbour negative racist feelings towards them, feelings that are perhaps the product of a racist upbringing that he strenuously disowns, but which nonetheless has left its affective imprint on his psyche. Still, the liberal racist is not obviously committing a human rights violation in virtue of his discreditable feelings, partly because it may not be possible for him to reform or self-police these spontaneous racist responses, partly because doing so is too costly to be demanded as of right. In other words, the goal of furthering status egalitarianism does not automatically bring us into the province of IHRL. We must ask the question to what extent does this goal reflect a universal moral right that one's basic equal moral status should be protected in this way? Or take another example. An individual may be confronted with the opportunity to promote the equal moral status of gay people in his community by risking his life, e.g. by 'coming out' as gay himself in circumstances that make it extremely dangerous to do so. It may certainly be laudable, even heroic, for him to run this risk. But it would not automatically follow that this sacrifice in the name of status equality is the kind of thing that may appropriately be demanded by IHRL. The fundamental reason, again, is that IHRL gives effect to universal moral rights, so we need to ask whether the individual right-holder's interest in having their status equality furthered through such life-threatening sacrifices suffices to impose a duty on others to make such sacrifices. The answer may well be 'No', hence status equality and IHRL would come apart in these instances. In short, the status equality is an important ground of both universal moral rights and IHRL, but the extent to which it is a matter of human rights (in both senses) is importantly constrained by the prior question: is there a universal moral right to basic moral equality being promoted or respected in this or that way?

These concerns apply with perhaps even greater force to the well-being function of IHRL identified by Buchanan. This directs IHRL to secure for all the conditions for the opportunity to lead a minimally good or decent life. The doubts here centre on the slippery idea of 'minimalism'. That something is 'minimal' entails that we could imagine or realize even more of it than the level identified by the speaker as 'minimal'. But this notion is too indeterminate to do the work that Buchanan intends it to do. In order to avoid this debilitating indeterminacy, we need some guidance as to how to set the 'minimal' level for the purposes of IHRL. Are the lavish entitlements to health care listed in the UN Committee on Economic, Social and Cultural Rights' General Comment 14 on the human right to health part of that minimum, or do they stray well beyond it, as many have persuasively argued? What is the criterion for identifying what is needed for a minimally good life as opposed to one that is extra-minimally good? What counts as 'minimal' cannot be merely be determined by the fiat of the institutions of IHRL; they themselves will need to be guided by some independent criterion, one that can be appealed to in critically assessing their decisions.

Now, for the orthodox theorist, the idea of 'minimalism' will be cashed out in a way that makes ineliminable reference to background moral rights. The first question will be: to what extent does an individual's interest in certain conditions of a good life generate an obligation on the part of others to furnish them with those conditions? Of course, it will take a lot of practical reasoning, backed up often by empirical inquiry, to arrive at a satisfactory conclusion in any given case. But the point is that the concept of a universal moral right is doing important work in giving substance to a notion of 'minimalism' that may otherwise remain hopelessly indeterminate. None of this precludes the possibility of other ways of explicating 'minimalism', e.g. by reference to universal human needs. But anyone tempted to go down this route has to provide that explication and then assess it against that yielded by the orthodox account. Buchanan does not really provide that alternative explication, nor does he engage in the comparative exercise, deriving instead false comfort his mistaken belief that the body universal moral rights is too meagre to be the normative kernel of IHRL.

At one point, Buchanan asserts that a concern with the protection and promotion of equal moral status and minimal well-being is 'peculiar' to IHRL among the departments of international law.[45] Presumably, he means that IHRL gets its integrity as a discrete body of international law through its primary concern with them, since it is wrong that no other area of international law ever serves such functions. Again, this seems questionable, certainly for the 'minimal' well-being function, but possibly also for the status egalitarian function. Why not suppose that the law of non-intervention, international economic law, international environmental law, and the laws of war, for example, are also concerned with securing a minimal level of well-being? Now, of course, none of this is to claim that the different departments of law are hermetically sealed off from each other. On the contrary, there is considerable overlap and interpenetration among domains, as between IHRL and humanitarian law. Still, it makes sense to argue that IHRL is primarily concerned with minimal conditions of well-being insofar as we have a universal moral right to them that is properly embodied and given effect through individual international legal rights assigned to all. Alongside, there may be areas of law that are concerned with protecting and promoting well-being in ways that both undershoot and overshoot what we are fully entitled to as a matter of moral rights and through mechanisms other than that of individual legal rights. Even if these other areas of law also further human rights instrumentally in various ways, they will lack the intimate relationship with universal moral rights, described by the Formative Aim Thesis, that gives IHRL its distinctive identity.

In short, human rights morality (on the orthodox conception) and, therefore, IHRL (on the Formative Aim Thesis) are both importantly grounded in considerations of status equality and well-being. We cannot, as some theorists have argued, rely solely on considerations of status or well-being in grounding the morality or law of human rights. But neither of these considerations can adequately play their grounding role in IHRL unless we mobilize a conception of universal moral rights. Instead of displacing the idea of a universal moral right, the status egalitarian and well-being functions can only contribute to the justification of IHRL by relying on the indispensable conceptual structure provided by that idea.

Notes

* I am indebted to the audiences that discussed different incarnations of this paper at the University of New South Wales, the University of Oxford, and Meiji University, Tokyo. I am especially grateful to Professor Shun Kaku who was my commentator on the latter occasion.

1 Allen Buchanan, *The Heart of Human Rights* (Oxford: Oxford University Press, 2013).

2 Buchanan, The Heart of Human Rights, p. 64.
3 I say more about this conceptual endeavour in John Tasioulas, 'On the Nature of Human Rights', in *The Philosophy of Human Rights: Contemporary Controversies*, edited by Gerhard Ernst and Jan-Christoph Heilinger (Berlin: De Grutyer, 2012), pp. 17–59.
4 A view associated with writers such as J.M. Finnis, James Griffin, Onora O'Neill, Amartya Sen, as well as myself.
5 A view associated in the first instance with John Rawls, and pursued in different ways by writers such as Charles Beitz, R.M. Dworkin, and Joseph Raz.
6 See, especially, Tasioulas, 'On the Nature of Human Rights'; John Tasioulas, 'Towards a Philosophy of Human Rights', *Current Legal Problems* 65, no. 1 (2013): pp. 1–30.
7 Charles Beitz, 'What Human Rights Mean', *Daedalus* 132, no. 1 (2003): pp. 36–46.
8 James Griffin, *On Human Rights* (Oxford: Oxford University Press, 2008), p. 149.
9 From the orthodox perspective, Tasioulas, 'On the Nature of Human Rights', pp. 31–36; from the political perspective, Raz, 'Human Rights Without Foundations', in *The Philosophy of International Law*, edited by Samantha Besson and John Tasioulas (Oxford: Oxford University Press, 2010).
10 Tasioulas, 'On Human Rights', pp. 40–43.
11 Charles Beitz, *The Idea of Human Rights* (Oxford: Oxford University Press, 2011).
12 Raz, 'Human Rights Without Foundations'.
13 Jean Cohen, Globalization and Sovereignty: Rethinking Legality, Legitimacy, and Constitutionalism (Cambridge: Cambridge University Press, 2012), ch. 4.
14 Buchanan, The Heart of Human Rights, p. 10.
15 Tasioulas, 'On the Nature of Human Rights', pp. 17–20.
16 Buchanan, The Heart of Human Rights, p. 18.
17 John G. Ruggie, Just Business: Multinational Corporations and Human Rights (London: WW Norton & Co, 2013), p. 8.
18 Amartya Sen, 'Human Rights and the Limits of Law', *Cardozo Law Review* 27 (2006): pp. 2913–2927.
19 Buchanan, The Heart of Human Rights, pp. 120–121.
20 Tasioulas, 'On the Nature of Human Rights'.
21 Buchanan, *The Heart of Human Rights*, p. 17; see also p. 65.
22 Buchanan, The Heart of Human Rights, p. 21.
23 Insofar as Buchanan himself previously endorsed something like an orthodox view, I am happy to take at face value his own testimony that he also endorsed the Mirroring View (p. 14). In my own case, I can appeal to the following passage (among others) as a rejection of the Mirroring View: 'The relationship that should obtain at any given time between the morality and law of human rights will seldom if ever resolve into a simple, one-to-one isomorphism. Sometimes there are conclusive reasons for not incorporating into law a norm with matching content, as when doing so would be counter-productive. Conversely, there can be conclusive reasons for establishing a legal human right that does not correspond to an independent moral right. For example, perhaps there is no human right not to be subject to the death penalty under any circumstances however, given the susceptibility to grave error and abuse endemic to the institution of capital punishment, there may be a decisive case of creating such a right in law. The reasons for doing so will consist in the ways in which the legal right serves various other values, including moral human rights to life and against unjust punishment, that do not match it in content'. See John Tasioulas, 'Human Rights', in *The Routledge Companion to the Philosophy of Law*, edited by Andrei Marmor (New York: Routledge, 2012), p. 359. See also Tasioulas, 'On the Nature of Human Rights'. I think it would be fair to say that proponents of the Political View have also tended to eschew the Mirroring View, at least with respect to IHRL. Admittedly, Buchanan's accusation that Raz is committed to the Mirroring View (pp. 14–16) is much more plausible. But notice that for Raz it seems essential to the idea of a human right that it is apt for embodiment in IHRL, which suggests that he is already taking on board Buchanan's strictures about taking IHRL seriously. Still, Buchanan might object that Raz fails to do so, insofar as his starting point for establishing a norm in IHRL is a universal moral right, understood in accordance with the orthodox view. I provide a defence of reliance on an orthodox view of human rights in explaining IHRL in Section 3, below.
24 Sen, 'Human Rights and the Limits of Law'; for similar points, see James Griffin, 'Human Rights and the Autonomy of International Law', in *The Philosophy of International Law*,

edited by Samantha Besson and John Tasioulas (Oxford: Oxford University Press, 2010), pp. 354–355.

25 Regarding this, and other provisions of IHRL that are only 'debatable' cases of moral human rights, Griffin claims '[t]he sensible answer, I think, is this: accept them as human rights'. Griffin, *On Human Rights,* p. 210.

26 Buchanan, The Heart of Human Rights, p. 21.

27 Buchanan, The Heart of Human Rights, p. 43.

28 It might be objected that Buchanan formulates the Mirroring View as holding only 'typically', subject to his two exceptions. But it seems to me very doubtful, for example, that orthodox theorists are committed to the two exceptions being exceptional, rather than pervasive, features of an adequately justified IHRL. The better view is that they have tended not to address the question at the conceptual level – leaving it as a further question to be decided on the merits in each case.

29 Buchanan, The Heart of Human Rights, Intro.

30 See, e.g. Charles Fried, *Contract as Promise: A Theory of Contractual Obligation,* 2nd ed. (Oxford: Oxford University Press, 2015).

31 For a view of this broad kind, see Sandra Marshall and R.A. Duff, 'Sharing Wrongs', *Canadian Journal of Law and Jurisprudence* 11, no. 1 (1998): pp. 7–22.

32 Lea Shaver, 'The Right to Science and Culture', *Wisconsin Law Review*, no. 1 (2010): pp. 121–184, p. 146.

33 'The enduring controversy over the protection element reflects an underlying international disagreement about the underpinnings of copyright law. Within the common law tradition, the exclusive rights of authors to control publication of their works are considered solely in economic and utilitarian terms as providing incentives for creativity. Within the civil law tradition, the natural law concept of *droit d'auteur* recognizes additional, inalienable rights of authors grounded in the ethical conception of the creative product as an extension of the creator's personality. From the civil law perspective, then, authors' rights were grounded in the same basis as other human rights and should sensibly be included in the Declaration. From the common law perspective, a moral rights provision risked introducing a complex area of disagreement that more appropriately belonged to the realm of economic and trade law'. Shaver, 'The Right to Science and Culture', p. 147.

34 Buchanan, The Heart of Human Rights, p. 17.

35 Buchanan, The Heart of Human Rights, pp. 62–64.

36 See Buchanan, The Heart of Human Rights, pp. 62–63.

37 Buchanan, The Heart of Human Rights, p. 62.

38 Buchanan, The Heart of Human Rights, p. 62.

39 Buchanan endorses this general line of argument as developed in relation to the human rights to health in Gopal Sreenivasan, 'A Human Right to Health? Some Inconclusive Scepticism', *Proceedings of the Aristotelian Society* 82 (2012): pp. 239–265. For an extensive criticism of this argument, which the rest of this section draws on, see John Tasioulas and Effy Vayena, 'The Place of Human Rights and the Common Good in Global Health Policy', *Theoretical Medicine and Bioethics* 37, no.4 (2016): pp. 365–382.

40 For my way rather different way of understanding and mobilizing these values, see John Tasioulas, 'On the Foundations of Human Rights', in *Philosophical Foundations of Human Rights,* edited by Rowan Cruft, Matthew Liao and Massimo Renzo (Oxford: Oxford University Press, 2015).

41 Buchanan, The Heart of Human Rights, p. 68.

42 Griffin, *On Human Rights,* ch. 1.

43 Roth criticizes the Razian idea, which Buchanan endorses (p. 94), that mere formal criticism of a state, whether by another state or by an international organization, is an invasion of state sovereignty, see Brad Roth, *Sovereign Equality and Moral Disagreement: Premises of a Pluralist International Legal Order* (Oxford: Oxford University Press, 2011), pp. 91–94.

44 Buchanan, The Heart of Human Rights, p. 94.

45 Buchanan, The Heart of Human Rights, p. 93.

7 The mismatch between theory and practice in recent theorizing about human rights

Denise Meyerson[1]

1 Introduction

What distinguishes human rights from other rights and interests? The traditional answer to this question – that human rights are moral rights possessed by all human beings by virtue of distinctively human capacities such as personhood and agency – has been challenged by theorists who argue for the superiority of a 'practical' or 'political' conception of human rights, according to which we need to understand the distinctive political functions of human rights in order to understand what they are. This chapter will be concerned with Charles Beitz's and Joseph Raz's practice-based versions of the political approach, in terms of which the international legal and political practice of human rights should set the agenda for philosophical reflection on human rights. Beitz's and Raz's understanding of this practice leads them to argue that human rights are those rights whose violation provides reasons in favour of external 'interference', broadly understood, in the internal affairs of rights-violating states.

This chapter argues that Beitz's and Raz's accounts are flawed. Although there are differences between their views, my arguments are mostly concerned with their shared features, and their differences are mentioned only where relevant. I argue that Beitz's and Raz's focus on the international practice of human rights imposes arbitrary constraints on their theorizing, by forcing them to narrow their theories in a way that is normatively implausible. I also argue that there are respects in which Beitz's and Raz's normative views do not align with the practice. Possibly this is because they are attempting to get normative beliefs they find independently attractive to mesh with a recalcitrant practice, the result being to distort both their normative accounts of human rights and their descriptive claims about the practice. I conclude that their claim to be grounding their theories in reality is shaky. There may be other reasons to accept their accounts, but they have not yet been explained.

2 Beitz's and Raz's accounts of human rights

Beitz and Raz believe that a philosophical understanding of human rights should be guided by the way in which human rights are currently understood in what Beitz calls 'the global human rights enterprise'[2] and Raz calls 'legal and political practice and advocacy'.[3] Raz says that a theory of human rights must begin by establishing 'the essential features which contemporary human rights practice attributes to the rights it acknowledges to be human rights',[4] and he explains that this practice comprises 'ratifying conventions, enacting legislation and adopting other measures in the name of human rights; litigating, implementing, applying and so on, those so-called human rights measures; advocating observance and incorporation into law of other so-called human rights, and more'.[5] Beitz writes: '[a] practical conception takes the doctrine and practice of human rights as we find them in international political life as the source materials for constructing a conception of human rights'.[6]

Taking his cue in this way from the practice, Raz goes on to argue that human rights are a subset of individual moral rights, namely, individual moral rights that states are under a duty to respect or promote,[7] while Beitz describes human rights as sui generis norms, which protect against standard threats to urgent individual interests and for which states have responsibility in the first instance.[8] Furthermore, both believe that human rights necessarily provide reasons in favour of international action when they are violated by states. For Beitz, human rights are necessarily a matter of international concern, in the sense that a state's failure to comply with its human rights responsibilities, whether by action or omission, provides 'pro tanto reason'[9] for 'outside agents to do something'.[10] In Raz's view, a moral right is not a human right unless its violation or prospective violation by a state (from now on, 'violation' for short) provides a 'defeasible reason' to 'take action' against the violator in the international arena.[11]

In so far as the kind of international response justified by infringements of human rights is concerned, Beitz understands 'doing something' very expansively. For him, it includes all of the following: coercive measures, such as military intervention and the imposition of diplomatic and economic sanctions; inducements, such as human rights conditions imposed on the provision of aid; the imposition of obligations to report on human rights compliance to international bodies; the provision of assistance, for instance, by assisting with elections in societies with undeveloped electoral institutions; various forms of human rights activism within societies with poor human rights records; and reform of global rules and structures, such as intellectual property rules enforced in international law that increase the cost of essential medicines.[12]

Raz is less informative on this matter. For him, human rights are 'rights whose violation can justify any international action against violators, provided that they are actions which normally would be impermissible being violations of state sovereignty'.[13] Raz explains that the principle of state sovereignty is the principle that states are entitled to freedom from external interference in their domestic affairs, even though they may be acting wrongly. Such immunity ceases, according to him, when states violate human rights.[14] Raz does not, however, spell out the concept of a violation of state sovereignty,[15] apart from saying that it is broader than armed intervention and includes the obligation on states to account for their compliance with human rights to international bodies.[16] As I will suggest in Part 5, this suggests a loose understanding of a sovereignty-violating measure, but even on a loose understanding it would be difficult to bring some of the measures mentioned by Beitz under this heading. Examples are the provision of assistance and reform of global rules in response to violations of human rights. It is hard to see why measures such as this would normally (ie, in the absence of a human rights violation) be precluded by respect for state sovereignty. Beitz himself is more circumspect than Raz in so far as the relation of the purpose of the practice of human rights to the norm of state sovereignty is concerned.[17]

In looking to the practice of human rights to grasp the idea of human rights, Beitz's and Raz's ultimate aim is to elucidate the moral principles governing the way in which the practice should operate. Raz describes his theory as an 'ethical doctrine of human rights',[18] and makes clear that his theory is a normative theory of human rights practice. He explains that his view is 'about the practice' only in the sense that it seeks to establish the criteria for judging the practice, an undertaking that might conceivably lead to abandoning the practice.[19] He is in search of the 'moral standards that qualify anything to be acknowledged'[20] as a human right and therefore regarding which 'sovereignty-limiting measures are justified'.[21] Thus his political conception of human rights does not identify human rights with the rights regarded as human rights in international law or with the rights whose violation is believed by members of the international community to justify action against a state. Raz writes: '[i]nternational law is at fault when it recognizes as a human right something which, morally speaking, is not a right or not one whose violation might justify international action against a state, as well as when it fails to recognize the legitimacy of sovereignty-limiting measures when the violation of rights morally justifies them'.[22]

Beitz's ambitions are also normative. In his view, the practice is the key that unlocks the concept of human rights but it does not tell us which norms deserve the status of human rights or what kind of response to their violation is appropriate. In order to answer these normative questions, Beitz states that we need to attend to other matters relating to the responsibility of states in the first instance and the international community in a secondary, back-up role. Is the interest sufficiently important that it is reasonable to regard its protection as a political priority? Would it be advantageous to protect the interest by means of legal or policy instruments available to the state? Would a state's failure to protect the interest be a suitable object of international concern? Would it, for instance, be feasible for outside agents to remedy the failure? Would such actions be permissible? Are there outside agents who are in a position to carry out these actions? Are the actions unreasonably burdensome?[23] As with Raz, the issues raised by Beitz are clearly issues of political morality, not political practice, even if some of them go to contingent considerations and arguably make human rights excessively hostage to fortune.

In summary, Beitz and Raz look to the practice of international human rights to grasp the idea of human rights but then turn a normative lens on the subject matter by directing us to the moral questions that present themselves once we think of human rights in this way. The trouble, though, is in getting the sociological/descriptive and normative aspects of Beitz's and Raz's enterprise to align. I will begin with a brief summary of my arguments.

3 Three difficulties

Beitz and Raz believe that human rights are moral rights/urgent interests that states have a duty/responsibility to protect and whose violation necessarily warrants a response at the international level. However, they also take an expansive approach to the kinds of responses that are justified in response to state failures to protect the relevant moral rights/urgent interests. This creates the possibility, discussed in Part 4, that some of the responses they contemplate might be available at the domestic level and warranted only at the domestic level. It seems that in such circumstances Beitz and Raz would have to say that the moral rights/urgent interests in question are not human rights. I will argue that this is a morally arbitrary restriction on the concept of human rights. Even if we accept the fundamental assumption of the political approach – namely, that human rights are norms that justify the taking of action against states that violate moral rights/urgent interests they are under a duty/responsibility to protect – it is difficult to see what is morally significant about the location of the secondary duty bearers for whom such violations provide pro tanto reasons to act (whether they are inside or outside the borders of the state). Necessarily, the international practice of human rights concerns itself only with the role played by outside bodies and actors in disciplining delinquent states. But this is merely an artefact of international human rights law. It is difficult to see why a normative theory of human rights should mirror the way in which the law carves up the subject-matter.

In Part 5, I will call attention to a second problem, which has to do with the connection Raz discerns between normative questions about state sovereignty and the practice of human rights. As noted previously, Raz views human rights as rights regarding which sovereignty-limiting measures are morally justified. This conceptualization of human rights does not, however, emerge from abstract philosophical reasoning. Raz does not argue, for instance, that we should understand human rights in this way because confining human rights to those that are sufficiently important to justify external interference cuts down on the proliferation of human rights claims or speaks to the need to respect other cultures and tolerate some degree of diversity at the global level. In line with his methodological approach, on which a theory of human rights should be relevant to the practice of human rights, Raz's view is supposed to emerge from reflection on how human rights are understood by participants in the practice of human rights. He claims that '[o]bservation of human rights practice shows that [human rights] are taken to be rights which, whatever else they are, set limits to the sovereignty of states'.[24] It is this 'observation' that leads him to claim that human rights are rights whose violation defeasibly justifies external interference.

I will suggest, however, that the relation between normative questions about state sovereignty and the practice of human rights is remote. Even supposing for the sake of argument that human rights are rights whose violation by states justifies actions that would normally be precluded by the moral value of state sovereignty, Raz's claim that the 'predominant mark of human rights in human rights practice' is to set limits to state sovereignty[25] is overstated. When violations of human rights give rise to 'action', this is generally because the violating state has voluntarily signed up to a human rights treaty, which makes it difficult to see the action as outside interference with sovereignty. Furthermore, the capacity to compel compliance with the rights regarded as human rights in the practice is limited. Mostly it is a matter of public criticism, which states are free to ignore. It is not even true to say that the label of 'human rights' in the practice is reserved for rights whose violation is believed to justify restrictions on state sovereignty, since many in the practice view such restrictions with suspicion. It follows that the task of determining which rights provide a morally sound justification for dislodging the moral value of state sovereignty would be only marginally relevant to the practice.

In Part 6, I will argue that there is another way in which there is a mismatch between Beitz's and Raz's conceptions of human rights and the practice they are supposed to be about. Beitz and Raz argue that human rights are moral standards that apply to state conduct and provide reasons for other states to remedy breaches of these standards. They adopt this state-centric view because they believe this is how human rights are conceptualized in the practice of human rights. Some critics reject Beitz's and Raz's conception of human rights on the ground that human rights are not inextricably bound up with the existence of states. I will make a different point. I will argue that the practice does not support a state-centric conception of human rights.[26] Although it is true that as a formal matter only states can be sued for breaches of international human rights, international human rights law has resorted to increasingly technical understandings of the ways in which states can fail to discharge their human rights duties, with a view to subjecting private individuals, not states, to international human rights norms.

Finally, in Part 7, I will draw the threads together by arguing that the weaknesses in Beitz's and Raz's approaches result from trying to accommodate conflicting desiderata and I will conclude that human rights as Beitz and Raz understand them are not the human rights of human rights practice. This casts doubt on their central claim that their accounts illuminate the practice of human rights and provide a basis for its moral assessment.

4 Why must there be a pro tanto case for international action before we can talk of human rights?

This section will be concerned with a difficulty that arises out of three claims made by Beitz and Raz. First, there is their central claim that a distinctive characteristic of human rights is that their violation by states provides pro tanto reasons for international concern (Beitz) or defeasible reasons for international interference (Raz). This claim is indebted to John Rawls's view of human rights. For Rawls, human rights should not be confused with natural rights. Instead, they play a role in a theory of international justice or justice between peoples. They guide just foreign policy by marking the limits where toleration of other peoples' domestic practices ends. Peoples that respect human rights (and are also non-aggressive) enjoy legitimacy and are entitled to tolerance. On the other hand, peoples that fail to respect human rights lose their right to respect for their autonomy, and other peoples become morally entitled to forcefully intervene in their domestic affairs. This may take the form of the imposition of economic and diplomatic sanctions or even military force.[27] Rawls's idea that human rights should be understood in terms of their international political role is the starting-point for Beitz's and Raz's theories.

Secondly, both Beitz and Raz argue that certain conditions pertaining to the international environment need to be satisfied before a state's failure to respect or protect a certain moral right/urgent interest gives rise to pro tanto concern or renders external interference permissible, and, therefore, before a human right can be said to exist. Raz says that since the contemporary practice of human rights views human rights as rights that should be enforced by law, in order to establish that a human right exists one must show that it is possible to set up impartial, efficient and reliable international institutions for protecting it. If it is impossible to establish such institutions, then the right in question cannot be a human right.[28] Beitz says that a state's failure to protect a certain urgent interest will be a matter of international concern only if (a) the state's failure can be corrected by actions that could be carried out by outside agents; (b) the actions are morally permissible; (c) there are outside agents that are in a position to carry out these actions by virtue of their location, capacity and resources; and (d) these agents have reason to bear the burdens involved.[29] These conditions consist in a mix of pragmatic and moral considerations, which, when satisfied, establish reasons for outside agents to act – albeit only pro tanto reasons, since, as Beitz makes clear, 'we cannot rule out that eligible agents will face even stronger reasons to act on some other front'.[30] Conversely, when these conditions are not met, there is not even a pro tanto reason for outside agents to act, and the interest in question cannot count as a human right.

Thirdly, Beitz and Raz depart from Rawls in expanding the responses that violations of human rights can merit. Since Rawls believes that only rights whose violation provides a ground for forceful intervention should be regarded as human rights, and since few rights will be sufficiently important to justify such extreme measures, this leads Rawls to a pared-down list of human rights. He maintains, for instance, that there is no human right to full liberty of conscience or to equal participation in political decision-making processes. Nor is there a human right not to be discriminated against on ground of gender. Many regard this as an arbitrarily narrow theory of human rights.[31]

Beitz and Raz seek to deal with this problem by providing a more complex view of the political role played by human rights, one on which the application of military and economic force does not exhaust the kinds of external 'interference' justified by infringements of human rights, and which is therefore able to support a more generous list of human rights. They find this more complex account in the international practice of human rights, since a right does not have to be capable of justifying forceful intervention (even as a pro tanto matter) in order to be regarded as a human right in the practice.[32] For instance, Beitz mentions the use of international courts to enforce human rights as well as bodies empowered to monitor and report on rights violations.[33] Raz likewise mentions the obligation on states to account for their conduct to outside bodies and the existence of institutions that are able to settle disputes about rights authoritatively and enforce respect for them.[34] In this way, Beitz and Raz seek to disentangle the political approach from Rawls's narrow view of the political role of human rights, which, in Beitz's words, 'is so much more limited than what we observe in present practice'.[35] This approach appears to hold out the promise of offering an account of the political functions served by human rights that is both sufficiently nuanced and also 'relevant' to practice, thereby satisfying Beitz's and Raz's methodological commitment that a theory of human rights should be about the practice of human rights.

I will argue, however, that this set of claims creates a problem. In particular, some of the responses in Beitz's and Raz's expanded suite of 'actions' are not intrinsically international – they can also be used at the domestic level – and I will argue that they might be warranted only at the domestic level. This would be the case if interference would not be feasible, effective or morally legitimate at the hands of outsiders, but would be feasible, effective and morally legitimate at the hands of insiders. The combination of the three claims I have described seems to imply that in such circumstances we cannot talk of human rights. I will argue that this substitutes one kind of arbitrary narrowness for another, since even if we assume for the sake of argument that human rights necessarily provide reasons for action when they are violated by states, there is no reason to think that a moral right/urgent interest that a state has a duty/responsibility to protect is not a human right just because the only agents who have pro tanto reasons to take action when it is violated are inside the borders of the state. I will now elaborate on this argument.

A more generous conception of the measures justified in response to human rights violations, which includes investigating human rights complaints, supervising human rights compliance, and making binding judicial determinations in respect of disputes about human rights, is obviously helpful in defusing the objections made to Rawls's approach. The international practice of human rights serves Beitz and Raz well in this respect. However, it serves them badly in another, in forcing them to tie the concept of human rights to the justifiability of these measures at the international level, when they can also be used at the domestic level and might only be justifiable at that level.

Consider, for instance, the power to make binding judicial determinations. An international body enjoying this power is the European Court of Human Rights (ECtHR), which is able under the European Convention on Human Rights (ECHR) to adjudicate human rights complaints made by individuals against member states and to make binding orders requiring states to change their laws and policies and pay damages to victims of human rights violations. Suppose we assume for the sake of argument that the rights contained in the ECHR are human rights in terms of Beitz's and Raz's criteria. This means that they are moral rights/urgent interests that states are under a duty/responsibility to protect and that the ECtHR has reasons to 'take action' if, say, UK legislation infringes these rights/interests. Raz himself suggests as much, because he gives Europe as an example of a region where there may well be the adequate institutions and procedures for the fair, efficient and reliable enforcement of human rights whose possibility is, in his view, the precondition for saying that human rights exist.[36] In this case, the interference in internal affairs would involve the ECtHR making a judgment that binds the UK government and that it is obliged to implement. Since the UK has enacted a statutory bill of rights, the Human Rights Act, which makes the rights and freedoms guaranteed by the ECHR directly enforceable in domestic law, the UK courts also have the power to 'take action' against the UK government when it fails to protect the ECHR rights, and presumably Beitz and Raz would say that the UK courts are also warranted in taking such action in such circumstances.

What, though, would Beitz and Raz say if a state's failure to respect or protect a moral right/urgent interest justifies a particular measure at the domestic but not at the international level, even as a pro tanto matter? This might be the case if the feasibility, effectiveness or legitimacy of the measure varies as between the two levels. It is, for instance, plausible to think that international courts should be more deferential than domestic courts when it comes to adjudicating human rights disputes. This is the moral idea underpinning the margin of appreciation doctrine adopted by the ECtHR, in terms of which the ECHR is seen as imposing fairly minimal, 'lowest common denominator' standards, and the ECtHR regards itself as obliged in certain circumstances to exercise restraint when considering whether national authorities have violated human rights.

There are a number of reasons to think that the margin of appreciation doctrine is morally sound. First, there is the fact that it is appropriate to impose the primary responsibility for securing human rights at the domestic level. The international system of protection is justifiably seen as merely subsidiary and consequently less exacting. Secondly, it can be argued that in 'sensitive' areas, such as public morals and religion, there are legitimate national variations, and that national courts are better placed to understand local practices and understandings and assess their weight in competition with other interests. Thirdly, national courts have superior fact-finding capacities when compared to their international counterparts. Fourthly, international bodies sitting in judgement on the conduct of national public authorities have more reason to worry about perceptions of illegitimacy, politicization and lack of accountability than national bodies charged with the same task. This means that the latter can afford to engage in a more independent and more intensive form of scrutiny.[37] As Martin Scheinin observes, '[a]s long as the European Court rests on a margin of appreciation, domestic courts should conduct an independent scrutiny in order to prove themselves worthy of the discretion left to them'.[38] Putting this in Raz's terms, we can say that external bodies are less likely to have defeasible reasons to take action against a delinquent state than internal bodies such as domestic courts adjudicating human rights disputes under constitutional or statutory bills of rights.

I have argued that domestic agents but not international agents might have defeasible reasons to take action against states that have failed to protect moral rights/urgent interests they have a duty/responsibility to protect, since such action might be feasible, effective and morally legitimate for the former but not the latter. Should this be the case, it seems that Beitz and Raz would have to say that the moral rights/urgent interests in question are not human rights. This would seem to be an arbitrary restriction on a political account of human rights. It is one thing to say that the concept of human rights implies a division of labour, such that if the primary duty bearers (states, according to Beitz and Raz) renege on their duties, this generates a pro tanto reason for secondary duty bearers to take action in a range of ways. One might disagree with the claim that this is an essential characteristic of human rights but it is not incoherent. However, it is quite another thing to say that specifically external agents must be justified in taking action before we can talk of human rights. There would seem to be no good reason for this restriction. Rawls's account does not face this problem, since the distinctive function of human rights, as he sees it, is to justify the use of force against states, and forcible intervention is by definition a measure available only to the international community. By contrast, there is nothing intrinsically international about some of the measures mentioned by Beitz and Raz, and it is hard to see why it matters morally where the agents who are capable of using them effectively and permissibly are located.

To be clear, I am not claiming that Beitz and Raz overlook the fact that there are domestic versions of the measures to which they refer. Instead, the problem comes from their claim that such measures must also be justified at the international level before we can talk of human rights. Of course, in the international practice of human rights it is necessarily external agents who take action against offending states. This in turn explains why Beitz and Raz are forced to tie their theories of human rights to measures warranted at the international level, since the virtue of their theories is supposed to be their relevance to international practice. However, their insistence on the international dimension is hard to combine with their particular version of the political approach, since once one expands the possible measures for remedying human rights violations, one opens the door to the possibility that a defeasible reason to use these measures might arise only at the domestic level.

Does this criticism perhaps miss something morally distinctive or important about *outsiders* having a reason to prevent or remedy human rights violations by states? Some points Raz makes in a recent article might appear to suggest that this is the case. In this article he attempts to justify his focus on international relations by arguing, first, that international human rights represent a radical development. They are radical, in his view, because the recognition that human rights should be internationally recognized and enforced departs from the previous orthodoxy that states have the unqualified right to order their internal affairs as they please. Secondly, Raz argues that international human rights are a special kind of right, quite different from the rights protected by domestic constitutions. This is because, in his view, constitutional rights 'emerged through improved understanding of the role and function and limits of government, . . . largely independently of ideas about human rights'. Relatedly, in Raz's view, loss of confidence in human rights ideas would not and should not shake one's confidence in constitutional rights, because there are other ways of arguing for them.[39] If Raz is correct, this would undermine my argument that it is arbitrary to confer or withhold the label of 'human rights' depending on whether a state's violation of a moral right that it is under a duty to protect warrants action at the hands of outsiders or only at the hands of insiders (for instance, under a constitutional bill of rights).

However, Raz's claims encounter a number of obstacles. First, his sharp distinction between international human rights and national constitutional rights is artificial. Although it is true that there are constitutional mechanisms for limiting government that are not based on human rights – two examples are the separation of powers and federalism – the improved understanding of the role, functions and limits of government that constitutional *rights* reflect is necessarily tied to the belief that there are certain interests of individuals that governments should be restrained from infringing or obliged to protect, and this is the same idea that animates international human rights. Both constitutional rights and international human rights give priority to certain interests of individuals at the expense of the achievement of governmental goals.

Furthermore, just as the rights contained in the UK's statutory bill of rights (the Human Rights Act) replicate the rights contained in the ECHR, the substantive requirements on governmental conduct that constitutional rights impose are generally similar to the requirements found in international human rights instruments. Some constitutional bills of rights virtually mirror the international human rights regime (for instance, the South African Constitution of 1996), and international human rights law is frequently cited by national courts dealing with comparable issues arising under national constitutions. Domestic constitutional systems have in turn influenced international law.

Of course, there are also differences between the international human rights regime and constitutional regimes. For instance, although some constitutions contain socio-economic rights, many do not, and some constitutional rights are the product of local circumstances. Furthermore, while there are some countries where the rights protected by constitutional law are like international human rights in applying to everyone, regardless of nationality – subject to the usual exceptions in both domestic and international instruments in so far as rights such as the right to vote and to run for elective office are concerned – in other countries, constitutional protection is limited, and constitutional rights or some constitutional rights are extended only to citizens, rather than to everyone within the jurisdiction.[40] So the picture is complex. It is nevertheless clear that there are sufficient similarities in function and content between constitutional rights and international human rights to justify the claim that they are, in Stephen Gardbaum's words, 'two systems for protecting the same thing: "the fundamental rights of individuals"'.[41] As Louis Henkin likewise observes:

> [i]nternational human rights derive from national constitutional rights. The international law of human rights and national constitutional law inspire and influence each other and become increasingly similar. National and international rights systems govern the same persons and the same activities and interests, serve the same purposes, serve the same values.[42]

Secondly, to the extent that international human rights are radical in limiting the internal autonomy of states to conduct their internal affairs in whatever way they please, the same is historically true of constitutional rights. Sovereignty was originally a domestic concept, not an international concept connoting the equality of states and their immunity from interference by other states. As first articulated by thinkers such as Jean Bodin and Thomas Hobbes, the concept referred to a ruler's supreme authority over the persons within a territory, such authority being entirely immune from *internal* interference by other actors and bodies in society. Bodin's concept of sovereignty is encapsulated in the Latin slogan: *Summa in cives ac subditos legibusque soluta potest* ('sovereignty is the supreme power over citizens and subordinates and which [supreme power] is not subject to the law').[43] When constitutional rights were first introduced, via instruments such as the US Bill of Rights, they represented a radical challenge to the idea of unlimited or absolute legislative power in the form of parliamentary sovereignty. They achieved this by imposing domestic legal constraints on the ability of governments to violate the rights of citizens.

I conclude that the emergence of international human rights as external constraints on how states can treat the inhabitants of their territories might be a relatively recent phenomenon but it is not a radically discontinuous phenomenon, as suggested by Raz. If anything, it represents an extension of the values of liberal constitutionalism from the domestic sphere into the international sphere. As Gardbaum observes, international human rights perform an inherently constitutional function.[44] They provide an extra layer of protection against governments – in this case, by giving external bodies and actors the right to interfere in the domestic affairs of rights-violating states. Raz might be right that a loss of confidence in international human rights would not shake confidence in constitutional rights but, if so, that would be because there is less scepticism about the effectiveness of constitutional rights in protecting the fundamental interests of individuals by comparison with international human rights. It is not because international human rights are a special kind of right. On the other hand, loss of confidence in the values of liberal constitutionalism would certainly shake one's confidence in international human rights.

I have argued that although the international practice of human rights serves Beitz and Raz well in providing a route out of Rawls's difficulty, there is a way in which it distorts their normative theories. In supporting a more expansive approach to the measures justified by violations of human rights, it allows them to avoid Rawls's arbitrary focus on forcible intervention. However, it also forces them to say that we cannot talk of human rights unless outside bodies and actors have reasons to use the relevant measures. If, due to the nature of the international environment, such measures are merited only at the domestic level, Beitz's and Raz's accounts seem to imply that the rights they are used to protect are not human rights. Yet, as argued previously, there is nothing morally distinctive about the use of these measures at the international level.

In my view, a theory that seeks to understand human rights via their political role, while rejecting Rawls's view that the distinguishing characteristic of human rights is their ability to warrant forceful intervention, should look for its concept of human rights in the larger practice of disciplining and monitoring the exercise of governmental power, whether via international or domestic norms. This would in turn support the normative view that the morally distinctive characteristic of human rights is that they are rights whose violation by states is a pro tanto ground for action, whether at the hands of internal or external actors. A theory of this kind would be able to retain the central political orientation of Beitz's and Raz's approach – namely, that human rights are distinctive in that their violation provides reasons for 'concern' or for 'interfering' in the internal autonomy of states – while jettisoning the claim that creates problems for them when combined with other aspects of their theory, namely, that human rights are rights whose violation necessarily justifies action at the hands of the international community. One might not agree with this modified political theory but at least the characteristic singled out would be suited to play a role in a normative theory of human rights.

So far I have suggested that once one has rejected the idea that human rights should be identified with rights that are capable of justifying forceful intervention, it is hard to see why a normative theory of human rights should identify human rights with rights whose violation necessarily provides reasons for an international response. I will argue next that there are two respects in which Beitz's and Raz's accounts are an inexact match with the practice of human rights.

5 Does the practice identify human rights with rights that either limit or should limit state sovereignty?

Raz states that use of the term 'human rights' in legal and political practice 'either relies on the legal recognition of human rights as limiting state sovereignty, or claims that they should be so recognized'.[45] So he seems to be committed to two descriptive or sociological claims about the way in which the term 'human rights' is used in the practice. According to him, the label is attached to (a) rights whose violation is in fact met by interferences with state sovereignty or (b) rights whose violation is thought to justify interferences with state sovereignty. Although (b) is a claim about people's moral judgements, it is still a descriptive claim. These claims provide the foundation for Raz's normative view (c), which is the view that human rights are those rights that provide a morally sound justification for sovereignty-limiting measures, and for his conclusion that the task for a normative theory of human rights is to determine which individual rights warrant recognition as limiting state sovereignty and to establish the precise limits that they impose.[46] I will begin by discussing (a), before saying something briefly about (b).

Raz's description of the legal situation, contained in claim (a), is problematic. Although attitudes towards sovereignty have changed, and it is no longer the case that how a state treats its own citizens is regarded as purely its own concern, when the rights regarded as human rights in the practice are violated, the remedy does not for the most part consist in limiting the sovereignty of the violating state, at least if the notion of a restriction on sovereignty is understood in the ordinary sense, as being non-consensual and coercive. There are two main reasons for thinking that claim (a) exaggerates the extent to which the rights regarded as human rights in the practice are used to set limits to state sovereignty.[47]

First, international human rights law, like all international law, is founded primarily on the idea of voluntarism: states are normally not bound by legal obligations in the absence of their consent. Conversely, when states are bound, this normally comes about as the direct result of the exercise of their sovereignty, rather than as a restriction on their sovereignty. Raz presumably does not believe that it is necessary for delinquent states to consent to international action being taken against them before such action can be morally justified. However, when it comes to the legal justification for international action, it is a different matter. International human rights law is primarily sourced to human rights treaties, which are covenants between sovereigns, imposing obligations only on the states that have opted in to them. Even the primary treaties, the Civil and Political Covenant and the Covenant on Economic, Social and Cultural Rights, have been widely but not universally ratified. The treaty bodies that monitor state compliance with human rights treaties exercise their powers in respect only of parties that have ratified the treaty. Furthermore, even states that have consented to be bound by a treaty can attach reservations to their ratification, excluding or varying their obligations under the treaty, unless reservation is prohibited or incompatible with the object and purpose of the treaty. The entering of reservations is a very common practice. Finally, states have the capacity in certain circumstances not only to limit their human rights obligations but also to derogate from or suspend them, which gives states a significant degree of flexibility in meeting any obligations they have voluntarily undertaken. As Henkin observes:

> [s]overeign states accept international human rights standards, if they wish to, when they wish to, to the extent they wish to. They consent to monitoring, to judgment by international human rights courts and commissions, if they wish, to the extent that they wish.[48]

It is true that there are some exceptions to the principle of voluntarism but they are too limited to support Raz's claim (a). There may, for instance, be a non-consensual element to treaties, relating to whether states can withdraw from or 'denounce' a treaty they have ratified. If denunciation is not expressly permitted by the treaty, this may not be possible.[49] Furthermore, there are two sources of international human rights law that are less consensual than treaties: customary international law and peremptory or *ius cogens* norms. The former results from a general and consistent practice of states followed out of a sense of legal obligation. For most states, their customary law obligations arise out of implied consent. However, since a general practice need not be universal, the existence of customary rules creates the potential for a small minority of states to have obligations imposed on them against their wishes – although, even so, persistent protests dating back to the emergence of the rule will block this effect. Peremptory norms are norms accepted and recognized by the international community of states as a whole, from which no derogation is permitted. Consequently, states cannot avoid the operation of these norms by persistently objecting to them. Although very few norms enjoy intransgressible status of this kind, it is correct to say that states do not enjoy sovereignty regarding these matters. Examples are the prohibitions against genocide, torture and racial discrimination. These limited exceptions to the principle of voluntarism are, however, insufficient to support Raz's claim that the 'predominant' mark of human rights in the practice of human rights is to set limits to state sovereignty.

The second reason to doubt Raz's claim is the fact that the mechanisms for achieving compliance with international human rights are relatively weak and rarely coercive. It is true that there are regional human rights courts, such as the ECtHR, with the power to adjudicate human rights complaints brought by individuals, and make binding orders requiring states to change their laws and policies and pay damages to victims of human rights violations. However, there is no global court of human rights with comparable powers. It is also true that the Security Council has the legal power to impose sanctions and authorize military interventions to deal with human rights atrocities, such as genocide, mass murder and ethnic cleansing. The use of force is nevertheless very much the exception, not the rule. Military intervention remains legally available only as a matter of last resort to deal with massive human rights violations that also threaten international peace and security. Outside of such truly exceptional situations, where human rights are internationally enforced by foreign intervention, most of the measures used to deal with violations of human rights at the global level are soft. The primary means for encouraging compliance is via monitoring, exposing and publicly criticizing states that have failed to respect human rights.

Thus, in so far as the implementation of treaty obligations is concerned, participating states are usually required to report regularly to treaty bodies regarding the measures they have taken to give effect to the treaty provisions. The treaty bodies then publicly discuss the reports with representatives of the states and provide concluding observations on the extent to which the reporting state has complied with its human rights obligations. Any recommendations are not, however, legally binding. Most of the treaty bodies also issue general comments on the interpretation of treaty provisions. Once again, this interpretative advice does not have to be followed. Some of the treaty bodies can initiate inquiry procedures, but only if the state in question has recognized their competence to do so and is willing to co-operate. In some cases, some of the treaty bodies can consider complaints from individuals that a state party has violated their rights. However, use of this mechanism once again requires the consent of states and, furthermore, any recommendations as to remedies are non-binding and cannot be enforced.[50] It seems, indeed, that states are willing to ratify treaties precisely because they have so few tangible consequences.[51] Outside of the treaty-based system, the Human Rights Council, which is a UN body, plays a similar role to the treaty bodies. All UN member states have to submit periodic reports on their human rights compliance to the Human Rights Council, regardless of whether they have ratified human rights treaties. The aim is the same: to exert pressure by 'naming and shaming' states with poor human rights records.[52]

Raz puts these reporting obligations front and centre of his account of human rights – as indeed he must, given his aim of constructing a theory of human rights around the practice. Thus he says that when countries acknowledge a human right to something – he gives the example of the right to health – they concede the right of international institutions to judge their health policies, and he specifically mentions the UN Human Rights Council and the human rights treaty bodies.[53] At the same time, his claim that the predominant mark of human rights practice is to set limits to state sovereignty obliges him to view these oversight activities as external interference. Thus in explaining why he thinks that human rights function in the world order to limit state sovereignty, Raz says: '[s]tates have to account for their compliance with human rights to international tribunals where the jurisdictional conditions are in place, and to responsibly acting people and organizations outside the state'.[54] This is an implausibly broad concept of external interference in a state's internal affairs, given that states mostly acquire their reporting obligations voluntarily, and are also free to ignore the condemnation of international bodies, retaining the final authority to decide whether their human rights practices are satisfactory.[55] It would be even less plausible to regard some of the other international measures used to encourage compliance with human rights as interferences with a state's autonomy – for instance, incentivizing reform by imposing conditions on economic aid or loans, and building institutional capacity in societies where institutions such as the courts, the police and the public administration are weak.

Can Raz perhaps fall back on claim (b), that the term 'human rights' in used in the practice to pick out rights that are believed to justify sovereignty-limiting measures, whether or not violations of human rights are in fact remedied by such measures? The problem with this claim is that even in the case of serious violations of human rights, many in the practice do not regard restrictions on sovereignty as an appropriate response, fearing that external interference does not promote human rights but opens the door instead to the pursuit of self-interested agendas by powerful states. Yet these practitioners do not say that the violations in question are not violations of human rights. Nor are practitioners' concerns about invading state sovereignty confined to sanctions and the use of military force. It is striking that there is not even wide support in the practice for the creation of a global court of human rights with the capacity to enforce international human rights.[56] Once again, those who think that a global court is undesirable do not withhold the label 'human rights' from the rights they think should not be enforced by such a court. Raz might respond that practitioners who describe a right as a 'human right' must see some reason, however slight, in favour of restricting sovereignty to protect it. However, I see no reason to accept this claim. It makes his theory true by definition and it implies that practitioners who disagree as to whether there are defeasible reasons to intervene in particular circumstances are having a conceptual disagreement, not a moral disagreement – they disagree as to whether the right in question is a human right. It is doubtful that practitioners would accept this analysis.

In short, Raz's normative claim that human rights are rights that provide a morally sound justification for interferences with state sovereignty, even if true, is at some remove from the way in which the term 'human rights' is used in the international practice of human rights, both in so far as the law is concerned and in so far as these matters are thought of normatively within the practice. Although the protection of state sovereignty is not unqualified, the practice does not license or advocate interferences with state sovereignty to any great extent. Suspending respect for state sovereignty on the basis of violations of the rights regarded as human rights in the practice is an outlier phenomenon, not the heart of the practice or a predominant feature. Indeed, to the extent that human rights function to license interference in the internal domestic affairs of states, this function is much more apparent at the domestic level, where domestic bills of rights really do play a constraining role via the activities of the courts charged with applying them. As a result, the moral issue highlighted by Raz, that of determining which moral rights justify restrictions on state sovereignty, does not emerge out of observing the international practice of human rights and would not be of great assistance in morally assessing the practice, however important it may be for other purposes.

6 Is the practice of human rights exclusively directed at regulating the conduct of states?

Beitz and Raz see human rights as a special class of moral standards applying to the relations between states and the individuals within their jurisdictions, by contrast with traditional views on which human rights are not inextricably tied to the existence of political institutions. Beitz and Raz do not deny that private individuals are under a duty not to harm the interests protected by human rights. They argue, however, that we cannot talk of a breach of human rights unless there is state wrongdoing in the background, in the form of a failure to fulfill the duty to prevent such harmful conduct or hold the individuals in question accountable. Raz writes: human rights are 'rights which are morally valid against states'.[57]

The claim is also central to Rawls's account. However, Rawls's state-centric conception of human rights is embedded in a theory of international justice. Human rights are standards for judging the conduct of regimes because free and equal peoples in a global version of the original position would choose respect for human rights as a moral principle to govern the terms of their co-operation. By contrast, Beitz and Raz believe that a state-centric conception of human rights emerges from observation of the practice of human rights.

I argue that Beitz's and Raz's understanding of the practice misses an important difference, that between (a) the weakly state-centric idea that complaints about breaches of human rights are addressed to the state and (b) the strongly state-centric idea that human rights are norms exclusively concerned with regulating relationships between states and the individuals within their jurisdiction. Although it was necessary to assign the task of implementing international human rights to states, this was for practical reasons, not for reasons to do with the special moral responsibility of states. On the contrary, from the start, human rights were thought of as a system of values for whose realization everyone bears responsibility.[58] Thus the UDHR declares that it is

> a common standard of achievement for all peoples and all nations, to the end that every individual and every organ of society, . . ., shall strive . . . to promote respect for these rights and freedoms, and . . . to secure their universal and effective recognition and observance.

With this in mind, international human rights law has come to be used to regulate private actors as well as states. The practice has managed this extension by greatly expanding the circumstances in which states can be held responsible or accountable for violations of human rights. As a result, the sense in which the state is the wrongdoer is in some circumstances quite artificial, as I will shortly explain. I argue that Beitz's and Raz's understanding of the practice of human rights is not sufficiently sensitive to these complexities, undermining their claim that their theories of human rights are about the practice.

Although Beitz and Raz do not elaborate on their understanding of the practice, they are presumably influenced by the fact that only states have legal obligations under international human rights law, and hence that only states can violate international human rights law. Putting this the other way around, international human rights law does not directly impose duties to respect human rights on private actors. The consequence is that private individuals or entities cannot bring a human rights claim against other private individuals or entities. In the terminology usually used to describe this situation, international human rights law does not have 'direct horizontal effect': one private party cannot sue another private party by directly invoking a protected human right.

It seems, however, that Beitz and Raz too readily infer from the absence of direct horizontality in the practice of human rights to the conclusion that human rights do not burden private individuals. In fact, international human rights law also regulates private actors so as to protect human rights in private relationships, albeit indirectly rather than directly. This phenomenon is known as 'indirect horizontal effect'[59] or the 'privatization' of human rights.[60] I will explain how private actors can be indirectly affected by international human rights by reference to three cases decided under the ECHR by the ECtHR. I have chosen the ECHR because the ECtHR's jurisprudence on this matter is highly developed. However, the UN bodies that monitor respect for the global human rights treaties take the same approach.[61]

Article 1 of the EHCR states that 'the High Contracting Parties shall secure to everyone within their jurisdiction the rights and freedoms defined in section 1 of this Convention'. The ECtHR has relied on this language to find that states can be responsible for breaching human rights when private individuals cause harm to the interests that human rights protect. One way in which such responsibility can attach is if officials have failed to exercise 'due diligence' to protect individuals whose rights are likely to be violated by other individuals. One such case is *Kontrová v Slovakia*.[62] Kontrová's husband had beaten her on a number of occasions and threatened to shoot himself and their two children. Although she had complained to the police several times, they had not taken any action. Shortly after her last complaint, her husband carried out his threat. Kontrová complained that the state had violated Article 2 of the ECHR, which states that 'Everyone's right to life shall be protected by law'. Clearly, the direct perpetrator of harm was the husband, not the state. Furthermore, his conduct could not be imputed to the state, since he was not, for instance, acting under the instruction of the police or encouraged by the police. The ECtHR nevertheless found that the Slovak Republic had breached human rights, on the ground that the police had failed to carry out appropriate criminal investigations, and the Court ordered it to pay compensation to the applicant for the damage she had suffered.

There is also a second way in which states can be held responsible for private rights-violating conduct under Article 1 of the ECHR, namely, if national legislatures fail to enact laws prohibiting or providing a remedy for such conduct. For instance, in *X and Y v Netherlands*,[63] the ECtHR found that the Dutch government had failed to provide an adequate remedy for interference with the right to privacy, respect for which is guaranteed under Article 8 of the ECHR. In terms of Dutch law at the time, investigation of a sex crime required a formal complaint. A parent could make the complaint for a child under 16 but the victim had to make the complaint if over the age of 16. A man had raped a resident of a privately-run home for mentally handicapped children in the Netherlands. She was over the age of 16 but incapable of making a formal complaint because of her mental condition. Her father complained to the police but the public prosecutor decided not to institute criminal proceedings, a decision that was upheld by the Court of Appeal on the ground that no one was legally empowered to file a complaint.

The victim and her father alleged that her human rights had been violated. Again, the direct perpetrator of the harm was the rapist. However, since he was a private actor, he could not be the subject of complaint under international law. Nor was the Dutch government complicit in his conduct. The ECtHR nevertheless found that the Dutch government had violated the victim's human right to privacy, saying that states have positive Convention duties under Article 8, which 'may involve the adoption of measures designed to secure respect for private life even in the sphere of the relations of individuals between themselves'.[64] Since the Dutch government had failed to put into place laws that secured respect for the right to privacy, the ECtHR ordered it to pay damages to the victim to compensate her for her emotional suffering.

Once the category of 'violations of human rights' is expanded to encompass legislative and executive 'bungling', states come under a positive obligation to regulate private actors so that their conduct conforms to human rights norms. This is one respect in which the

ECHR does not exclusively regulate the relations between individuals and the state.[65] There is also a second respect in which Article 1 has been used to facilitate the reach of international human rights law into the private sphere. If human rights regulated only the relations between individuals and the state, international human rights would apply solely to public law, such as criminal law and administrative law.[66] The truth, though, is that international human rights law has also come to apply to private law, where private law is the law that governs the rights and obligations of private parties *inter se*, such as the law of contract or the law of succession. This has been achieved by using the positive obligation approach to review the decisions of national *courts* in disputes between private parties,[67] with the ECtHR taking the view that Article 1 places duties on states via their courts to prevent private individuals from violating the human rights of other private individuals when they seek to exercise legal rights conferred by ordinary private law rules. In this way as well, then, international human rights law has an indirect impact on private actors – by subjecting the private laws that they invoke in their interpersonal disputes to human rights norms.[68]

This development can be illustrated by the case of *Khurshid Mustafa and Tarzibachi v Sweden*,[69] which involved a human rights challenge to the enforcement of a contract between two private parties. The applicants were Swedish nationals of Iraqi origin who were using a satellite dish mounted on the façade of their rented flat to receive television programmes in Arabic and Farsi from their home country. The tenancy agreement prohibited the erection of outdoor aerials. The landlord, a real-estate company, demanded that the dish be removed. When the applicants refused, the company notified them that it was terminating the tenancy agreement and instituted proceedings to enforce the termination notice. The matter eventually came before the Swedish Court of Appeal, which found that the applicants were in breach of contract and that the landlord was entitled to terminate the agreement. Although the landlord offered the applicants the option of staying in the flat if they removed the satellite dish, they refused and moved to another flat, as a result of which they incurred expense. They then complained before the ECtHR that their human right to freedom of information under Article 10 of the ECHR had been violated.

On the face of it, it was hard to see how this argument could succeed, since the case concerned a dispute over contractual obligations between two private parties, and private parties are not legally obliged to respect the Convention rights of other parties. Even if we assume that the landlord company wronged the tenants, only states can be sued for breach of human rights under the ECHR. The ECtHR nevertheless found that the ECHR applied, on the ground that the Swedish court's action was an action of the state. The ECtHR then went on to find that Sweden had violated the right to freedom of information, since its court had failed to protect the right of the tenants to receive information against the interference of a private party when it enforced the contractual agreement in terms of ordinary law.

The reality of the situation was that the ECtHR wished to subject the interpersonal dispute between the landlord and the tenants to human rights norms but it came up against the obstacle that the legal obligation to respect international human rights rests with states, not private individuals. Its solution to this problem involved two steps. First, it took the view that enforcement of the law by national courts is necessarily governmental conduct. In a sense, this is truistic: to the extent that the law permits certain conduct, the state is implicated in that permission. But secondly, and more controversially, the ECtHR took the view that when national courts apply and enforce national laws they are under a duty to make decisions that are compatible with the ECHR. The implication is that international human rights law applies to the conduct of national courts in applying and enforcing national laws, even if the laws are private laws, even if they are non-statutory laws, even if it is a private individual, not the state, who relies on private law rules to vindicate his or her conduct, and even if the rules are not on their face incompatible with human rights. Hence, despite the fact that the background private law rule the Swedish court enforced (freedom of contract) was not in itself objectionable from the human rights points of view, the ECtHR found that it was objectionable for the court to apply the rule in favour of one private individual against other private individuals who wished to exercise their human right to freedom of information. Enforcement of the landlord's rights under the contract therefore amounted to state misconduct and Sweden was ordered to compensate the tenants. It will be evident that this reasoning dissolves the distinction between (a) an act in breach of human rights authorized by legislation and committed by a public official and (b) an objectionable act committed by a private individual that is permitted in terms of a framework of background law not in itself incompatible with human rights. In both cases, the injury is attributed to the state.[70]

The upshot is that when a private party seeks the assistance of a national court in a private law matter, such as a dispute over a contract or a will, as the landlord company did in *Khurshid* when it initiated proceedings to enforce the termination notice before the Swedish Court of Appeal, a state may be held responsible for failing to protect human rights if the court's resolution of the dispute is not rights-compatible. This is a radical step, which has the potential to require fundamental changes to the legal relations between private individuals in countries that have ratified the ECHR, since it prevents private individuals from relying in court on established private law rights where that would cause harm to the interests protected by human rights. As Richard S Kay says about this line of reasoning, it allows '[e]very disappointed litigant [to] raise a European human rights claim'.[71]

Of course, review of national court orders in purely private disputes should in theory require attention to be paid to the human rights of the private parties on both sides of the dispute. This is not the case when legislation or executive acts are reviewed, since the state does not have rights, only interests. This is important because balancing of the competing rights of private parties could be expected to allow some leeway for private parties to act in ways that would be unacceptable for state actors, by virtue of rights such as the right to respect for private property, autonomous choice and intimate life – although, in fact, the decision in *Khurshid* has been accused of paying insufficient attention to the values speaking in favour of enforcing the contract.[72]

In summary, notwithstanding the fact that individuals can assert their human rights only against states, *Khurshid* demonstrates that this does not prevent the injection of human rights norms into most human interactions. The reality is that international human rights law is used for a variety of purposes along a spectrum. At the one end of the spectrum it is used as a shield to protect individuals from abuse of power by the state. Here we are dealing with negative or defensive rights against the state, in accordance with the original purpose of international human rights law. At this end of the spectrum it is accurate to say that the aim is to regulate the conduct of states. In the middle of the spectrum, international human rights law has come to be used to remedy legislative or executive failures to prevent private actors from infringing the rights of other private actors. Here we are concerned with the imposition of positive duties on the legislative and executive organs of government to protect against private misconduct. At the opposite end of the spectrum, human rights law has emerged as a way of preventing domestic courts from enforcing or upholding private legal acts that cause harm to the interests protected by human rights, notwithstanding the fact that the actors are exercising what Frank Michelman describes as 'their ordinary rights, privileges and powers as accorded by (we assume) a generally benign body of background law.'[73]

Although this may be a desirable development, such conduct can be described as 'governmental misconduct' only in a very technical sense of the term. It is already something of a stretch to describe the existence of gaps in the law or executive failures to prevent private individuals from violating rights as involving governmental violations of human rights. If the state can also be held responsible for judicial rulings in private matters, the nexus with governmental wrongdoing becomes even more difficult to discern. Although the case is nominally brought against the state, the same practical effect is achieved as would be achieved if international human rights law had direct horizontal effect and private parties could assert their human rights directly against other private parties.[74] The conceptual difference between (a) private parties having legal duties not to violate human rights and (b) courts having legal duties not to assist private parties who seek to rely on otherwise unobjectionable private laws where such reliance would be incompatible with human rights is not non-existent. It is, though, very fine, and it is hard to see what practical difference it makes. Substantively, international human rights law is being used in circumstances such as these to regulate private individuals, not states, and the ascription of responsibility to the state via its courts is merely a legal stratagem for getting around the obstacle that private parties cannot sue other private parties for breach of their human rights.

Related developments are evident at the domestic level, although some courts are not willing to go quite as far as the ECtHR in ascribing liability for human rights violations to courts. For instance, in a case dealing with the application of the Canadian *Charter of Rights and Freedoms* to common law litigation between private individuals, the Supreme Court of Canada rejected the idea that the mere fact that a court has made an order in a case between two private parties removes it from the private sphere, turning it into the exercise of governmental power reviewable for its compatibility with rights. McIntyre J stated:

> [w]hile in political science terms it is probably acceptable to treat the courts as one of the three fundamental branches of Government, that is, legislative, executive, and judicial, I cannot equate for the purposes of *Charter* application the order of a court with an element of governmental action . . . It is [the courts'] duty to apply the law, but in doing so they act as neutral arbiters, not as contending parties involved in a dispute. To regard a court order as an element of governmental intervention . . . would . . . widen the scope of the *Charter* application to virtually all private litigation. All cases must end, if carried to completion, with an enforcement order and if the *Charter* precludes the making of the order, where a Charter right would be infringed, it would seem that all private litigation would be subject to the *Charter*.[75]

However, while the Supreme Court of Canada rejects the idea that court orders must be compatible with the *Charter* rights, it does endorse a weaker form of indirect horizontality, in terms of which Canadian courts ought to develop the common law that governs relations between private persons in terms of the human rights values contained in the *Charter*. This development can also be observed in other jurisdictions, such as Germany, South Africa and the United Kingdom.

I conclude that Beitz's and Raz's picture of the purpose of international human rights law is over-simplified. It seems that Beitz and Raz too readily infer from the absence of direct horizontality in international human rights law, which was a practical choice, devoid of moral significance, to the strongly state-centric conclusion that international human rights law is essentially concerned with regulating the vertical relations between individuals and states. The truth is that it has also come to be used to regulate horizontal relations between private individuals, and to subject private actors, as well as governments, to human rights standards, even to the extent of making international human rights applicable to judicial decisions in *inter se* litigation. Since human rights are not directly justiciable against private individuals, this development required some legal acrobatics. The solution was found in the idea that governments are responsible for violating human rights when they fail to prevent violations of rights by private individuals, including by the conduct of their national courts in permitting private individuals to rely on otherwise unobjectionable private law rules when they come into conflict with human rights. The state can in this way be made the formal subject of legal complaint. While this strategy yields the desired result, it should not obscure the fact that the real dispute in these cases is between individuals, not between an individual and the state. Although the complaint is addressed to the state as a formal matter, the idea that the state has breached human rights is tenuous as a substantive proposition. Practically speaking, one might as well allow individuals to sue other individuals for breach of their human rights. The idea of human rights law as a special body of norms with a limited reach, the impact of which is confined to delinquent states, has all but disappeared.

Since Beitz and Raz believe that a normative theory of human rights should reflect an understanding of the purpose of the practice of human rights, the phenomenon of indirect horizontality undermines their argument that the concept of human rights is a moral concept that applies specifically to how states treat the individuals within their jurisdictions. Of course, there might be reasons derived from ordinary moral reasoning for thinking that violations of human rights constitute a distinctive form of moral wrongdoing that can be committed only by states. That is not, however, what Beitz and Raz argue.

7 The tensions in Beitz's and Raz's conceptions of human rights

Raz explains that 'in a way' his approach is not about human rights at all but about the practice of human rights.[76] This is presented as a virtue of his approach, by contrast with traditional conceptions of human rights, which he regards as deficient because their understanding of human rights 'is so remote from the practice of human rights as to be irrelevant to it'.[77] For instance, Raz says they do not show why the rights they identify as human rights (universal rights that people have by virtue of their humanity) should be recognized as setting limits to state sovereignty.[78] Traditional conceptions do not illuminate the practice of human rights.[79] Nor do they provide a basis for criticizing human rights practice, since they fail to show why the practice should be governed by their concerns. Raz writes: '[t]here is no point in criticizing human rights practice on the ground that it does not fit the traditional human rights ethical doctrine. Why should it?'[80]

In response, I have argued that dependence on international human rights practice is in one way problematic, because it commits Beitz and Raz to the implausible view that in circumstances in which only domestic bodies are warranted in taking action against states that have violated moral rights/urgent interests that they are under a duty/responsibility to protect, the rights/interests in question cannot count as human rights. I have argued that it is hard to see what is morally special or distinctive about these measures being warranted at the international level. I have also argued that in important respects Beitz's and Raz's theories are at some distance from the practice, making their theories susceptible to the same charges Raz levels against traditional conceptions. I have argued, in particular, that the use of human rights to limit state sovereignty or to recommend limits on state sovereignty does not loom large in the practice of international human rights, and, furthermore, that sometimes when states are subject to external interference, the intention is not to prevent or remedy misconduct on their part in any meaningful sense.

It seems that the first problem arises out of the fact that Beitz and Raz are seeking to accommodate desiderata that pull in opposite directions – not only to solve the problem of narrowness that confronts Rawls by including more rights in the category of 'human rights', but also to locate the solution in the international practice of human rights, so as to claim practical relevance for their theories in line with their preferred methodology. The problem, though, is that although the practice helps them to articulate a political account of human rights that is broader than Rawls's, it also forces them to distort the solution, by insisting that measures for protecting rights that are not intrinsically international must be warranted at the hands of outsiders before we can talk of human rights. When it comes to Raz's claim about human rights and state sovereignty, it seems that Raz is trying to bolt normative beliefs he finds independently attractive onto the practice of human rights, again to support the argument that, unlike traditional conceptions of human rights, his account can be used to assess the practice of human rights. This requires him to make some questionable assertions about the practice, so as to make good on the claim that his normative theory is a theory about the practice.

The normative belief to which Raz is attracted is Rawls's view that human rights serve the function of morally justifying limits on the internal autonomy of regimes or, as Raz puts it, limits on the sovereignty of states. However, Raz does not wish to defend this conception of human rights from the perspective of moral theory. Instead, in line with his rejection of abstract philosophical reasoning in theorizing about human rights (the vice of traditional conceptions of human rights), Raz's conception is supposed to emerge from observation of actual human rights practice. Thus responsiveness to practice is supposed to provide a methodologically satisfactory basis for retaining Rawls's attractive view that there is a connection between human rights and moral limits on sovereignty, in the same way that responsiveness to practice is supposed to provide a methodologically satisfactory basis for rejecting Rawls's unattractive view that the role of human rights is limited to justifying forcible intervention. The problem, though, is that this is difficult territory to inhabit.[81] The difficulty lies in attempting to combine the following claims: (a) human rights are a way of preventing state misconduct by permitting restrictions on their sovereignty when they treat their citizens in certain way; (b) human rights are rights whose violation justifies a range of measures, among which are consensual and non-coercive measures such as criticism; (c) the task of a normative theory of human rights is to secure relevance by answering the moral questions that arise out of observation of the practice of human rights.

Raz is committed to claim (b), since it solves the narrowness problem faced by Rawls's account. However, Raz is also morally attracted to claim (a), and claim (a) is difficult to combine with claim (b), in light of the fact that consensual and non-coercive measures are not plausibly seen as limits on sovereignty. Claim (a) is also difficult to square with claim (c), since the practice of human rights does not rely on or recommend sovereignty-restricting measures to any great extent in response to violations of what it regards as human rights. In an attempt to reconcile these various claims, Raz is obliged to take the implausible view that monitoring by international bodies, which is the primary non-coercive measure for encouraging human rights compliance in the practice, is an interference with state sovereignty. It is even more implausible to say this about some of the other non-coercive measures used in the practice of human rights to encourage compliance, such as capacity building and reform of global rules. Since it is not true to say that these facilitative measures would otherwise (ie, in the absence of a human rights violation) be prohibited by the value of state sovereignty, this may explain why they do not figure in Raz's account. As a result, Raz's account of the moral function served by human rights does not adequately reflect the role they play within the practice of human rights and is still too narrow relative to the practice, even if not as narrow as Rawls's. Hence claim (c) is not vindicated.

Rawls's account does not suffer from the same tensions, because his theorizing is not constrained by the practice of human rights. This provides him with the conceptual space to argue that the class of human rights should be confined to rights that justify forcible intervention, and since forcible intervention does limit the internal autonomy of states, Rawls is able to preserve the internal coherence of his account. Of course, internal coherence is not the same thing as plausibility, and Raz and Beitz are not alone in finding the narrowness of Rawls's account implausible. The question, however, is whether it is possible to sever the aspects of Rawls's theory that Raz and Beitz find implausible from the aspects they find plausible. They seek to justify their selective approach to the different elements of Rawls's theory by reference to the practice of human rights. I have suggested that this forces them to misdescribe some aspects of the practice, undermining their central claim that their accounts of human rights are practically relevant, and raising the same question Raz asks about traditional conceptions of human rights: why should the practice conform to their conceptions of human rights?

Notes

1 I am grateful to participants at a workshop at King's College London and at seminars at the University of Sydney and the University of Melbourne for their valuable suggestions. I would also like to thank Carolyn Adams, Brian Opeskin, Paul Taylor and Aleardo Zanghellini for their very helpful comments. Guy Lewis and Alex Whitelum provided research assistance.
2 Charles Beitz, *The Idea of Human Rights* (Oxford: Oxford University Press, 2009), p. 42.
3 Joseph Raz, 'Human Rights Without Foundations', in *The Philosophy of International Law*, edited by Samantha Besson and John Tasioulas (Oxford: Oxford University Press, 2010), p. 337.
4 Raz, 'Human Rights Without Foundations', p. 327.
5 Joseph Raz, 'On Waldron's Critique of Raz on Human Rights', University of Oxford Legal Research Paper Series, no 80/2013. SSRN: http://ssrn.com/abstract=2307471, p. 3.
6 Beitz, The Idea of Human Rights, p. 102.
7 Raz, 'Human Rights Without Foundations', p. 336.
8 Beitz, The Idea of Human Rights, p. 109.
9 Beitz, The Idea of Human Rights, p. 109.
10 Beitz, The Idea of Human Rights, p. 106.
11 Raz, 'Human Rights Without Foundations', p. 328.
12 Beitz, *The Idea of Human Rights*, pp. 33–40, 101, 116.
13 Raz, 'Human Rights Without Foundations', p. 328, fn. 21.
14 Raz, 'Human Rights Without Foundations', p. 328.
15 John Tasioulas, 'Are Human Rights Essentially Triggers for Intervention?', *Philosophy Compass* 4, no. 6 (2009): p. 944.
16 Raz, 'Human Rights Without Foundations', p. 328; Joseph Raz, 'Human Rights in the Emerging World Order', *Transnational Legal Theory* 1 (2010): p. 42.
17 Beitz, The Idea of Human Rights, p. 133.
18 Raz, 'Human Rights Without Foundations', p. 322.
19 Raz, 'On Waldron's Critique of Raz', p. 6.
20 Raz, 'Human Rights Without Foundations', p. 327.
21 Raz, 'Human Rights Without Foundations', p. 329.
22 Raz, 'Human Rights Without Foundations', p. 329.
23 Beitz, The Idea of Human Rights, pp. 137–141.
24 Raz, 'Human Rights Without Foundations', p. 332.

25 Raz, 'Human Rights Without Foundations', p. 334.
26 For a different argument in support of the claim that the state-centric view is not an accurate reflection of the function of human rights in the practice of human rights, see Cristina Lafont, 'Global Governance and Human Rights', in *Human Rights, Human Dignity, and Cosmopolitan Ideals*, edited by Matthias Lutz-Bachmann and Amos Nascimento (Surrey: Ashgate, 2014), pp. 55–58.
27 John Rawls, *The Law of Peoples* (Cambridge: Harvard University Press, 1999), pp. 37–38, 79–81.
28 Raz, 'Human Rights in the Emerging World Order', pp. 43–44.
29 Beitz, The Idea of Human Rights, p. 140.
30 Beitz, The Idea of Human Rights, p. 168.
31 See, eg, James Griffin, 'Human Rights and the Autonomy of International Law', in *The Philosophy of International Law*, edited by Samantha Besson and John Tasioulas (2010), pp. 342–343; Allen Buchanan, 'Taking the Human out of Human Rights', in *Rawls's Law of Peoples: A Realistic Utopia?*, edited by Rex Martin and David Reidy (Oxford: Blackwell Publishing, 2006), pp. 150–168.
32 See, eg, James Nickel, 'Are Human Rights Mainly Implemented by Intervention?', in *Rawls's Law of Peoples: A Realistic Utopia?*, edited by Rex Martin and David Reidy (Oxford: Blackwell Publishing, 2006), pp. 270–271.
33 Beitz, The Idea of Human Rights, pp. 32–34.
34 Raz, 'Human Rights in the Emerging World Order', pp. 43–44, 46.
35 Beitz, The Idea of Human Rights, p. 101.
36 Raz, 'Human Rights in the Emerging World Order', pp. 43–44.
37 For discussion of these issues, see Yuval Shany, 'Toward a General Margin of Appreciation Doctrine in International Law?', *The European Journal of International Law* 16, no. 5 (2005): p. 907.
38 Martin Scheinin, 'International Human Rights in National Law', in *An Introduction to the International Protection of Human Rights*, 2nd ed., edited by Raija Hanski and Markku Suksi (Turku: Institute for Human Rights, 2000), p. 422.
39 Raz, 'On Waldron's Critique of Raz', p. 5.
40 Stephen Gardbaum, 'Human Rights as International Constitutional Rights', *The European Journal of International Law* 19, no. 4 (2008): p. 749, 767; David Cole, 'Are Foreign Nationals Entitled to the Same Constitutional Rights as Citizens?', *Thomas Jefferson Law Review* 25, (2003): pp. 372–374.
41 Gardbaum, 'Human Rights as International Constitutional Rights', p. 751.
42 Louis Henkin, 'Human Rights and State "Sovereignty"', *Georgia Journal of International and Comparative Law* 25 (1996): pp. 40–41.
43 Johan van der Vyver, 'Sovereignty and Human Rights in Constitutional and International Law', *Emory International Law Review* 5 (1991): p. 324.
44 Gardbaum, 'Human Rights as International Constitutional Rights', pp. 752, 766–767.
45 Raz, 'Human Rights Without Foundations', p. 337.
46 Raz, 'Human Rights Without Foundations', p. 337.
47 For additional reasons to be sceptical about this claim, see John Tasioulas, 'Towards a Philosophy of Human Rights', *Current Legal Problems* 65, no. 1 (2012): p. 24.
48 Louis Henkin, 'That "S" Word: Sovereignty, and Globalization, and Human Rights, et cetera', *Fordham Law Review* 68, no. 1 (1999): p. 5.
49 Frédéric Mégret, 'Nature of Obligations', in *International Human Rights Law*, 2nd ed., edited by Daniel Moeckli, Sangeeta Shah and Sandeesh Sivakumaran (Oxford: Oxford University Press, 2014), pp. 114–115.
50 Jane Connors and Markus Schmidt, 'United Nations', in *International Human Rights Law*, 2nd ed., edited by Daniel Moeckli, Sangeeta Shah and Sandeesh Sivakumaran (Oxford: Oxford University Press, 2014), pp. 381–384.
51 Christine Wotipka and Kiyoteru Tsutsui, 'Global Human Rights and State Sovereignty: State Ratification of International Human Rights Treaties, 1965–2001', *Sociological Forum* 23, no. 4 (2008): p. 750.
52 Connors and Schmidt, 'United Nations', pp. 363–365.
53 Raz, 'Human Rights in the Emerging World Order', p. 46, fn 8.

54 Raz, 'Human Rights in the Emerging World Order', p. 42.
55 For a related criticism of Raz's concept of state sovereignty as 'idiosyncratically hyper-protective', see Tasioulas, 'Towards a Philosophy of Human Rights', p. 24.
56 Gerd Oberleitner, 'Does Enforcement Matter?', in *The Cambridge Companion to Human Rights Law*, edited by Conor Gearty and Costas Douzinas (Cambridge: Cambridge University Press, 2012), p. 262.
57 Raz, 'Human Rights Without Foundations', p. 332.
58 Adam McBeth, 'Every Organ of Society: The Responsibility of Non-State Actors for the Realization of Human Rights', *Hamline Journal of Public Law and Policy* 30, no. 1 (2008): pp. 42–43.
59 For discussion, see Murray Hunt, 'The "Horizontal Effect" of the Human Rights Act', *Public Law* (1998): p. 423; Stephen Gardbaum, 'The Structure and Scope of Constitutional Rights', in *Comparative Constitutional Law*, edited by Tom Ginsburg and Rosalind Dixon (Cheltenham: Edward Elgar Publishing, 2011), pp. 391–396.
60 Andrew Clapham, *Human Rights Obligations of Non-State Actors* (Oxford: Oxford University Press, 2006), p. 1.
61 For discussion, see Clapham, Human Rights Obligations of Non-State Actors, ch. 8.
62 *Kontrová v Slovakia*, Appl. no. 7510/04, Judgment of 31 May 2007.
63 *X and Y v Netherlands* (1986) 8 EHRR 235.
64 *X and Y v Netherlands* (1986) 8 EHRR 235, para. 23.
65 Stephen Gardbaum makes this point in the context of discussing the horizontal application of constitutional rights: Stephen Gardbaum, 'Where the (State) Action Is', *International Journal of Constitutional Law* 4, no. 4 (2006): p. 769.
66 Gardbaum, 'Where the (State) Action Is', p. 766.
67 Stefan Somers, 'Protecting Human Rights in Horizontal Relationships by Tort Law or Elaborating Tort Law from a Human Rights Perspective', *European Human Rights Law Review*, no. 2 (2015): p. 159.
68 Gardbaum, 'Where the (State) Action Is', pp. 764–765.
69 Khurshid Mustafa and Tarzibachi v Sweden (2011) 52 EHRR 24.
70 For an argument in favour of upholding this distinction in the context of US constitutional law, see Richard Kay, 'The State Action Doctrine, the Public-Private Distinction, and the Independence of Constitutional Law', *Constitutional Commentary 10* (1993): 329, p. 348: 'only a lawmaking act may violate the Constitution. A reprehensible exercise of power by an individual within a framework of unobjectionable law presents no constitutional question.'
71 Richard Kay, 'The European Convention on Human Rights and the Control of Private Law', *European Human Rights Law Review*, no. 5 (2005): p. 479.
72 Peter Webster, 'Contract Law and Human Rights', in *Private Law and Human Rights: Bringing Rights Home in Scotland and South Africa*, edited by Elspeth Reid and Daniel Visser (Oxford: Oxford University Press, 2013), pp. 327–328.
73 Frank Michelman, 'Rawls on Constitutionalism and Constitutional Law', in *The Cambridge Companion to Rawls*, edited by Samuel Freeman (Cambridge: Cambridge University Press, 2003), p. 415.
74 Somers, 'Protecting Human Rights in Horizontal Relationships by Tort Law', p. 161.
75 *RWDSU v Dolphin Delivery Ltd* [1986] 2 SCR 573, pp. 600–601.
76 Raz, 'On Waldron's Critique of Raz', p. 7.
77 Raz, 'Human Rights Without Foundations', p. 323.
78 Raz, 'Human Rights Without Foundations', p. 334.
79 Raz, 'Human Rights Without Foundations', p. 324.
80 Raz, 'Human Rights Without Foundations', p. 328.
81 See also Tasioulas, 'Towards a Philosophy of Human Rights', p. 24.

8 Human rights, doubts and democracy

James Allan

In this chapter I will be voicing some doubts. There will be doubts about some of the usually offered foundations or underpinnings for human rights claims. There will be other doubts tied to both the political and the moral conceptions of human rights. Then there will be doubts about the ease with which any type of human rights dominated worldview and programme for future action can co-exist with a worldview that puts democracy front and centre. Some of my doubts will be aimed at matters peripheral to the broader human rights worldview, some at core level strands. Some of the scepticism will be mild, some rather strong.

I will then finish with a consideration of Charles Beitz's approach in his *The Idea of Human Rights*[1] to weigh up whether Beitz successfully wards off or redirects these doubts of mine. In building up to that consideration I will offer no overarching theories, just some arguments to the effect that significant portions of what is claimed on behalf of the human rights worldview stand up rather poorly to scrutiny and that such a worldview has great difficulty co-existing with any vigorous understanding of democracy. Of course, even were all doubts correct, it may well also be true that this human rights worldview is still on balance a force for good, that its costs are outweighed by its benefits. Nevertheless, this chapter will proceed on the assumption that such sentiments are no basis for suppressing these doubts.

1 Doubts about foundations

When one claims that North Koreans have a right to free speech or that the homeless in New York City have a right to housing or that Shia Muslims or Christians or Bahai in Saudi Arabia have a right to freedom of conscience and religion what sort of claim is being made? What is the foundation or basis for these sort of human rights claims?

Most lawyers can tell you that rights are entitlements, or protections, or guarantees of a sort. Some will go on to note that analytically-speaking a right amounts to an 'others must' claim.[2] If I have a right to free speech then others must let me speak. Similarly, if you have a right to housing then someone or some agency must provide you with housing. Those rights, those 'others must' claims, are linked – they are correlated – to duties. A duty, then, is an 'I must' claim. My duty to care for my children is an 'I must' claim. So their right ('others must') is my duty ('I must').

One could go further with this analytical understanding of rights. One could continue by noting that rights and duties are themselves tied together by the concept of rules. Any right you care to mention I can transliterate into the form of a rule: 'She has the right to free speech' becomes 'There is a rule that allows her to speak her mind in the following circumstances'. Of course, the language of rules does not trigger the same frisson of self-entitled excitement as does the language of rights. But analytically-speaking, they are the same: a right is a rule.

Yet that sort of analytical understanding of rights only takes us so far. Yes, it provides insight into the sort of claim that is being advanced, and how it relates to other demands. But such Hohfeldian-type analyses of rights take us no closer to answering a more fundamental question about the source or origin of these rights. From where do these and other rights claims originate? What is the basis or source of these claims, these assertions of such things as a free speech right or a housing right?

Any answer will start by noting that once you see that a right can be transliterated into a rule, you can ask those questions I have just asked in blunter terms: where does the rule come from that lays down what you are claiming? You can then notice, as well, that rights – broadly speaking – are of two sorts. First off, there are rights (or rules) where we all can see the basis of the claim. These are legal rights (or rules). They might be spelt out in a statute, emerge from a line of cases, be fleshed out of some amorphous constitutional provision by top judges using a best-fit Dworkinian Justice Hercules interpretive approach,[3] or maybe even traced back to custom. Yet whether you like the substance of these legal rights, or not, their source will be overwhelmingly patent and clear. You can say why these legal rights, these legal rules, exist, and none but a few anarchists will disagree that they do in fact exist.[4]

However, in other circumstances it is plain that we are not talking about legal rights, but instead about non-legal or moral rights. This is the second sort of rights claim that can be advanced. Indeed the previous examples with which I began this section, with my mooted rights to free speech in North Korea, to housing in New York City, and to freedom of religion in Saudi Arabia, might all be most laudable ones to fulfil. They are not, though, claims about the actual legal systems now in existence in those jurisdictions. Rather, they are moral claims; claims whose source must be traced back to theories or assertions about the moral world.

Hence notice this big – nay, huge – difference between the legal realm (including rights claims within that realm) and the moral realm (including rights claims within that realm). Claims about whether someone in fact even possesses certain rights, certain 'others must' entitlements, in the moral realm are often highly contestable and debatable. Smart, well-informed, nice people do not agree about whether a particular claimed moral right actually exists or not. There is reasonable disagreement[5] whether the moral rights being claimed in fact actually do exist in some mind-independent sense, whether they can persuasively be argued to rest on foundations that show the claims are good ones. On the plane of 'do these claimed rights even exist at all', the doubts are many orders of magnitude greater in the moral realm than the legal realm. At this first step moral rights claims are vastly more open to doubt, and so to the same much greater extent more contestable, than legal rights claims.

Put differently, in the legal realm we overwhelmingly know if a claimed right or rule happens to exist in some particular jurisdiction. Disagreement there is focused on the desirability or otherwise of such a legal right, on whether to keep, amend or repeal it. In the moral realm, by contrast, disagreement occurs a step earlier. It occurs when one person makes a claim that some non-legal right X (a right to free speech in North Korea, perhaps, or one to freedom of religion in Saudi Arabia, maybe) in fact exists and another person disputes that claim. He says it exists; she says it does not.

That means that for non-legal rights claims the question of foundations – why it is you say some particular rights claim happens to exist – matters. There is no non-debatable, non-contentious answer as to the source or genealogy of these sort of rights.

Why does this distinction matter in a discussion on the topic of human rights? It matters because the modern day vocabulary of human rights is one that sits abreast the legal rights/non-legal rights divide. It finesses the distinction. It is a little bit of one and a little bit of the other. To varying extents, depending upon speaker and context, the language of human rights attempts to have it both ways at once – to offer something of the aspirational moral world of the 'ought' while at the same time giving you the concrete, enforceable, here-and-now legal world of the 'is'.

We can see this if we momentarily focus more narrowly on justiciable bills of rights, at least in the common law world. They sit partly in the legal realm, being entrenched in a constitution (and so giving top judges a power to strike down or invalidate statutes as one sees in the United States and Canada) or being enacted via a statute (and so giving top judges a souped-up interpretive power to re-write legislation via a reading down provision as one sees in the United Kingdom and to a lesser extent in New Zealand). They also sit partly in the aspirational, moral realm to the extent that they fail to lock in answers as to how far the enumerated rights protections extend. Put differently, the more a bill of rights is treated as a 'living tree'[6] or 'living constitution' instrument whose meaning can change and alter and shift over time at the point-of-application – in part due to the interpreting judges' shifting moral judgements – the more such an instrument sits astride the legal/non-legal divide. Of course, the moral can even become the legal when five of nine Supreme Court Justices extend what a right to a fair trial now means[7] or do the same with the right to vote.[8]

The point, though, is that the moral and the legal are intertwined with justiciable bills of rights.[9] And my broader claim in this chapter is that that same concatenation or commingling is at work with human rights more generally. The extent of this commingling will vary depending upon the grounds or foundations one offers for thinking some particular non-legal right actually exists. Let us turn next, therefore, to the various bases or foundations generally offered as underpinning human rights of the non-legal 'free speech in North Korea' variety. I will generalize here and note my doubts and scepticism as we go along.

1.1 Human rights as moral rights

If a human rights claim is being advanced, and it is clear that that claim is not being advanced on the 'as things actually are today in this jurisdiction' plane, then most often what you will be hearing is a moral claim. Its source or foundation will lie in morality. Accordingly, the plausibility of that rights claim will vary directly with the underlying plausibility of the moral theory on which it rests. Hence if you are sceptical of the persuasiveness of some moral theory – or indeed sceptical of the meta-ethical position it takes – then you will to the same extent be sceptical of the non-legal rights claim which it underpins and supports.

Let me briefly run through some of the more obvious moral foundations said to provide a basis for thinking various claimed moral rights do in fact exist; that they have a plausible source or basis outside of a particular evaluator's own subjective moral sense or judgement or druthers.[10]

A. The most venerable, and historically influential, are all those moral theories related to or that draw on theism and a benevolent, theistic God who creates a world in which some conduct is wrong and some right. In that sort of world there will be non-legal rules that we humans can discover in two ways. They might be revealed to us by divine revelation. Alternatively, they might have been infused into the structure of the universe in such a way that we humans can reason to them; we can discover them on our own without recourse to any divine revelation. Yet what we are discovering or finding is only there because God put it there.

It is uncontroversial to say that thinking along those lines lies at the heart of the natural law tradition of Augustine and Aquinas. We can debate its influence on the sort of Jeffersonian claims about 'we hold these truths to be self-evident' in the American Declaration of Independence[11] or on modern day natural law theory of the sort that John Finnis provides.[12] What cannot be denied is that the theistic worldview has driven much of the West's moral theorizing; that it has been extremely influential in historical terms. Likewise, it is clear that if its premises are correct – if a benevolent, theistic God created the world in such a way that humans can reason to right moral conduct, and hence to non-legal rules governing right action, and hence to non-legal rights – then the foundations of moral rights are secure. Individual humans may sometimes reason incorrectly and make incorrect claims, but the moral rights do exist. And they exist because they have a lineage going back to a benevolent, omnipotent God.

As it happens I am highly sceptical of this foundation for all the reasons that J.L. Mackie and indeed David Hume give.[13]

B. A related type of moral theory that provides the needed foundations for plausible, convincing moral rights claims are what I am categorizing as 'all natural law theories without God'. Clearly this is a big group, especially in our modern day more secular times. Just as clearly there will be reasonable disagreements about whether certain theories and thinkers fall into this category or the previous one. So we can debate not just about where to slot Finnis as noted previously, but also about where to put a 'we are required to treat all people (or all rational agents) as *ends* not *means*' Kantian deontological theory, and no doubt plenty of others.

That said, there are also plenty of modern day moral theories that are indisputably secular (placing no reliance whatsoever on a theistic God in the background) while at the same time offering the same sort of end results as category **A** previously explained. Let me nominate Ronald Dworkin as fitting clearly into this category. Dworkin builds a theory of law, and a theory of rights, out of a theory of how to interpret. We are to take all the jurisdiction's settled laws, its first 13 chapters in the chain novel, and we are to build the best fitting background political morality that explains and justifies those inherited materials. So, for Dworkin, there can be no clear line between law and morality. Moreover, a super human Justice Hercules will be able to create this best background fit in such a way that in any dispute that reaches a top court – most obviously one involving rights-related disputes – one answer will be weightier and have more gravitational pull than any other. That will be the one right answer, the answer that gives the most integrity to the settled laws.[14]

Now it may well be that that sort of 'building a theory of law out of a theory of how to interpret' requires one to be a moral realist to make it work. Dworkin himself denies this at first, distinguishing between external and internal scepticism,[15] but later says that he is a moral realist; that he rejects non-cognitivism.[16] Regardless of the exegetical disputes about Dworkin's theory, it is clear that Dworkin offers an account in which there are rights in a non-subjective (and indeed more than just inter-subjective) sense. He gives us a secular foundation for making such rights claims.

Again, it is a separate matter whether one finds Dworkin's theories persuasive. I do not.[17] In my view, the same goes for all theories of moral rights that rest on more than Humean, non-cognitivist, feeling or sentiment-driven grounds.

C. It is not clear where to put social contract or agreement theories that seek to provide a foundation for human rights. If the goal is to offer a theory of rights in pre-institutional terms, then these do so. We might put Locke here (though perhaps also in category **A**). And Rawls. It seems true to me that by asking a conditional hypothetical question ('What would some reasonable or "behind the veil of ignorance" person prefer or pick if that person had this information or that?'), you are not creating a mind-independent standard. You are creating something akin to (but clearly not exactly the same as) an Adam Smith 'impartial spectator' or 'well informed person at the time' standard.[18] This sort of approach gives you a pre-institutional basis for your claims; but at the same time it does not seem to me to really rise up to being a mind-independent standard or basis for your claims.

Still, you do end up with a foundation for your non-legal rights claims; or rather you get one if you decide such social contract, agreement theories are persuasive. Again, I am sceptical. Imputing opinions and values and beliefs to a hypothetical (never actually having existed) being seems to me to be prone to collapsing into a thinly disguised 'this is what I, the maker of the theory, would have valued or believed had they asked me' game. You get out of the imagined agreement or contract what you put in. In Rawlsian terms, if you come to the task as a risk-averse person then the reasonable-seeming outcome of the 'veil of ignorance' imaginings will be a risk-averse one. But there are many real-life people in the world who are not risk averse. So, I have plenty of doubts that this social contract or agreement avenue will provide a solid foundation for non-legal rights claims.

Of course many readers will disagree with my broad doubts about the plausibility and persuasiveness of category **A**, **B** and **C** type attempts to provide a solid foundation for human rights. They will think one or more of these moral foundations is persuasive. If they are correct and I am not, then they have their basis – a moral basis – for making 'free speech in North Korea' type non-legal rights claims. If not, some other foundation can be sought.

1.2 Human rights as tools to advance the general welfare

If you are a utilitarian, or more generally a consequentialist, then seeing human rights as tools to increase or advance the general welfare is a moral understanding of human rights. For non-consequentialists it is not. Put differently, if you give human rights a utilitarian foundation, some people (most obviously utilitarians, but other consequentialists as well) will consider that to be a moral foundation. Other people (non-utilitarians and non-consequentialists) predominantly will not. For my purposes this is just a classificatory dispute that I can side-step. I give this a separate sub-section solely to note the classificatory disagreement.

As I noted in a previous footnote (see fn 10), I think that the appeal of utilitarian-type theories depends in part upon one's answer to the meta-ethical question of the status of moral evaluations. If you are a moral realist or moral objectivist, for whom moral claims are supposed to have mind-independent status (so your Kantians and deontologists and theologically-driven theorists and more), then the appeal of an inter-subjective utilitarian standard of right and wrong is not obvious, and perhaps close to zero. Why go for the half-hearted option when you believe you have the real thing? By contrast, if you are a non-cognitivist or moral sceptic (so your Humeans and Blackburns and Mackies and more),[19] it seems to me that the appeal will be greater. If moral evaluations have no higher mind-independent status, if they are a function at core of the sentiments and feelings that humans happen to have, then utilitarianism (and consequentialism more generally) can offer you a way out of raw subjectivism, a way to avoid what Bentham scathingly deemed 'sympathy and antipathy' or 'I happen to like it' and 'I don't happen to like it' pontificating.[20] You can at least achieve an inter-subjective standard of right and wrong that escapes raw subjectivism, albeit falling short of any mind-independent status.

Whether you agree with me that non-cognitivists are more likely to find utilitarianism attractive, or not, let me briefly run through the basic way in which a utilitarian would understand non-legal rights claims.

The right thing to do for utilitarians is to aim for conduct and actions that will increase the general welfare (everyone in the specified group being counted equally to start, with Bentham advocating a 'greatest happiness of the greatest number' test).[21] Make human happiness or welfare the sole 'good-in-itself' and then aim for those likely future good consequences that will maximize that happiness (or that will keep to a minimum unhappiness or pain in situations when only bad things are on the menu).

But as modern day utilitarians realize, we can often achieve better overall outcomes by the indirect pursuit of the good rather than by attempting to maximize the good on a case-by-case basis.[22] Put more bluntly, part of the modern day sophistication of utilitarianism involves the realization that sometimes best consequences are achieved by laying down clear rules, and always following them even though we know going in that all rules will at times produce sub-optimal results, will be over-inclusive and under-inclusive. In other words, we can accept the fact that no rule will ever have a 100 percent hit rate, a perfect record of producing good consequences every single time that it is honestly applied. Yet, despite that, and the less than 100 percent hit rate, it will nevertheless be the case that in some situations opting for a rule will deliver better overall consequences (all things considered, on average, over time) than case-by-case decision-making aimed at good consequences in each individual case.

One example sometimes given of this is a 'who can vote?' rule. Let us say a rule lays down something along the lines that 'any citizen 18 years of age and older, not declared mentally unfit by a doctor' can vote. That sort of rule clearly is sub-optimal; it clearly has a less than 100 percent hit rate. There will be 17 year olds well-versed in civic education who look far more qualified to vote than scores of 19 or 50 or 60 year olds. Yet such 17 year olds will, sub-optimally, be barred. Obversely, there will be know-nothing, alcoholic 45 year olds who have not read a newspaper in 20 years; under the rule they can vote.

Yet the point is that such a rule delivers better consequences than any non-rule alternative. To see this, imagine that you tried to decide who can vote by striking committees of people who would interview potential voters and then make decisions on a case-by-case basis. Not only would the costs of such a scheme be huge, the overall hit rate would be lower than that achieved with the rule. No real life human being, or group of human beings, will ever have a 100 percent hit rate of opting for the better consequences choice any more than any rule would. Plus there are the various frailties that flow from being a limited biological creature; there is the possibility of succumbing to corruption (say, excluding from voting bunches of those obviously on the other side of politics to you); there is the chance of moral failures (say, opting to exclude blacks from voting); and more.

So Rule Utilitarianism says that sometimes (as with who can vote) you do better by having rules and just applying them. This is not true in all situations, of course. To see this just consider how we decide who can drive – here we go for case-by-case decision-making, despite knowing that that, too, is far from perfect (as you can see by noting all the teenage boys who manage to pass their driving tests).

But the point is that rules are sometimes the best way to achieve the greatest happiness, which for utilitarians is the moral outcome. And as rules are just the obverse of rights, we can see that a utilitarian need not be restricted to the legal world of 'is'; she can make a calculation that there *ought* to be a rule to further free speech or freedom of religion in North Korea or Saudi Arabia, despite such rules being lacking there at present. The utilitarian is not conflating the 'is' and the 'ought'.[23] She is saying, in effect, that good consequences would go up if there were such a rule, such an enforceable rule, and so there should be one. We ought to work towards enacting one, towards creating such a legal rule.

As a non-cognitivist myself, I see the appeal of utilitarian and consequentialist moral theories, in least-bad terms if nothing else. That said, utilitarianism has well-known weaknesses[24] such as being incredibly perfectionist (treat the poor in Africa as counting equally to your own children) and being open to sacrificing the individual in certain extreme situations. So I am mildly sceptical here about whether most people will find a consequentialist/utilitarian foundation for human rights all that attractive.

1.3 Human rights where no foundations given – just assume they exist

Another approach to understanding human rights can be put quite frankly and simply. On this approach you just ignore the issue of foundations as far as possible. You sweep the question under the carpet and pass along in silence. The thinking here goes something as follows: if a commitment to fundamental human rights is the foundation of political legitimacy, then we just have to assume such human rights (whenever we stray into the non-legal realm) actually exist. Or as Stephen Smith puts it, without in any way endorsing such an approach, and in regards to the related issue of equality:

> Just as in one kind of philosophy elusive but indispensable things like causation, time, space and continuity of personal identity are not so much observable facts *in the world* as commitments or categories we *bring to and impose on the world*, so equal moral worth is a starting point or necessary presupposition that we assume in order to deal with the normative and political world as it is. That presupposition need not be justified . . . on any other grounds.[25]

Fellow contributor to this book, Sonu Bedi, makes a basically related point by saying that one can

> view human rights in light of their function or role in international politics and law . . . [and so one can] contend that the justification for [human] rights need not be based on some moral or philosophical account of human nature but rather [on] an instrumental view of the role of rights in international discourse.[26]

But of course that is just a backhanded way of saying that core issues related to foundations can be ignored or assumed away. It is not unlike saying, 'these things are a force for good in the world, so don't ask too many questions about them'.

If you want the same basic attitude to foundations in terms that amount to caricature, then you can think of this school of thought as the one that just begins by looking at what Eleanor Roosevelt did with the Universal Declaration of Human Rights back in 1948 and moves on from there, as though that is all the foundation you will ever need. You ignore all deeper questions and doubts about foundations; you assume them away.

Of course you can give a consequentialist defence to this 'ignore or assume away foundations' approach. You will just need to make arguments for why best consequences flow from simply assuming certain human rights exist, and from ignoring any further questions about how to provide them with solid foundations. You will focus on their most desirable scope of application, or on how best to make them enforceable, and waste little time on more fundamental queries. To be blunt, my suspicion is that more than a few lawyers adopt precisely this attitude, or make this consequentialist calculation. In some situations it may well be the sensible route to take.

That said, offering no reasons for why you are so intensely committed to something, to the human rights worldview or to the existence of particular human rights, is far from satisfying for others, and possibly even for you too. Speaking for myself, I am more than a little sceptical of this attitude, and of the apotheosis of things that are put beyond questioning and seldom, if ever, justified. I think that sort of attitude and approach to foundations in fact has bad long-term consequences. I accept, though, that this 'just ignore foundational issues' strategem is not an uncommon approach or attitude.

2 Doubts about finessing foundations

An alternative to simply assuming away the question of what are the plausible foundations of human rights is to assert that people do not need to agree on foundations in order to discuss and debate, say, their proper reach. In other words, we might be able to finesse this question of foundations.

This is most plausible where all the disputants agree that some set of human rights have a non-conventional, perhaps even a mind-independent, existence; it is just that none of them can agree on what the foundation actually is. So as regards some particular human rights claim the Kantian says the foundation for the claim flows from the fact that we are all required to treat people as ends, not means. The Christian says it flows from God's edict to love everyone, even one's enemies. The liberal egalitarian traces it to the obligation to treat all people with equal respect, or perhaps to the human dignity of everyone. And so on and so on. The idea is that you do not need agreement on foundations in order to move the debate to the next level, and indeed to settle a good many questions at that next level.

Again, I confess to being somewhat sceptical about how far this attempt to finesse the issue of foundations can take us. Clearly there can be meaningful human rights discussions and moral discussions within groups of like-minded people – the utilitarians can talk to the utilitarians, the Kantians to the Kantians, the egalitarians to the egalitarians and so on. But when there are no shared premises the danger is of the sort of incommensurability described by Alisdair McIntyre.[27] This is the world in which rights-related arguments (on the justness of some war, say, or the acceptability of abortion, or on some equality-related issue) seem completely cogent and persuasive on their own premises and presuppositions, but in which polar opposite conclusions can be reached when founded on differing premises. It is more like ships passing in the night than a bracketed clashing of ideas and narrowing of options. As McIntyre puts it:

> Every one of the arguments is logically valid or can easily be expanded so as to be made so; the conclusions do indeed follow from the premises. But the rival premises are such that we possess no rational way of weighing the claims of one as against another. For each premise employs some quite different normative or evaluative concept from the others, so that the claims made upon us are quite of different kinds.[28]

In other words, this is the possibility that the attempt to finesse foundations leaves us with a world in which those who disagree with one another on rights-related issues (and who do not share foundational premises) will talk at each other, yes, but not so much with each other. They will lack any agreed arbiter or final appeal mechanism for resolving and ending disagreements. When you begin from different starting points, in fact from different core conceptions of what grounds and gives life to human rights, you simply will not get the sort of winnowing and narrowing and agreeing that is desired and hoped for by proponents of the 'let us just put to one side our disagreement about foundations and see if we cannot get agreement further up the food chain' gambit.

Personally, I lean towards the McIntyre view. I have a good deal of scepticism about any likely prospects for success when the strategy is to finesse the question of the foundations of human rights. Take away the shared premises and the Finnisian natural law adherent will differ from the liberal egalitarian on the correct reach and force of the right to freedom of religion; the Kantian will differ from the utilitarian on the effect of a right to equality; the list goes on and on, even as to whether certain rights do or do not exist. Hence, any move to descend from the Olympian heights of disagreement-finessing moral abstractions down to the quagmire of the day-to-day charting of the exact scope and specific requirements of human rights looks unlikely to bring much agreement, at least to me. Foundations matter; they matter when it comes to mapping how human rights ought to play out. So I have my doubts that this variant of the finessing option can take us very far.

There is a different variant, though, of the finessing gambit. Here what you finesse is not the widespread disagreement about the core foundations for non-legal human rights. Instead, on this second variant, what you finesse is the divide between legal and non-legal human rights. I mentioned above, briefly, how justiciable bills of rights can be understood in this way – how they sit in the legal world and yet, when top judges appeal to morality to decide cases in the Hartian penumbra of doubt, how they also can be seen as sitting partly in the aspirational, moral realm. The moral understanding of five of nine judges on a Supreme Court can become law; their moral judgements can move the coverage provided by some right from the purely moral to become part of the here and now legal.

That same second variant of the finessing gambit can arguably be seen in the international law realm as well. Indeed this might be a better way to understand the Bedi quotation above.[29] It depends upon the extent to which one thinks that international law rules are in a sense, or when first laid down, non-legal rules at the domestic level, and yet over time can become legal rules on that same level or plane.

So take an international, multilateral rights-related convention or treaty. Pick one of the many whose substantive provisions are articulated in vague, amorphous moral abstractions pitched up in the Olympian heights of disagreement finessing terminology. As far as the municipal law of most any Western liberal democracy is concerned these rights-related international law conventions, these amorphously articulated human rights, are not enforceable in a domestic legal system – not directly at first in any straightforward way. (And this is even clearer if you pick, instead, any non-democracy in the world you care to choose, an authoritarian one-party state, a theocracy, take your pick. The laid down international law right will have next to no effect or bearing on the domestic legal system in such non-democracies.) But in our Western liberal democracies we may see that over time judges appeal to these international law rights (and so rules), first perhaps when deciding administrative law matters; then as defeasible presumptions when interpreting statutes; maybe even ultimately when interpreting constitutions. Over time the non-legal becomes, to varying extents, the legal. That is the finesse.

Notice, in addition, that with this second variant of the finesse the source of your human rights is plain; the source is evidently some man-made, laid down rule/right. You need go no further back than that. Put differently, if you have some multilateral convention or bill of rights to point to then you can ignore the issue of foundations; you can justify all you need to justify based on 'an instrumental view of the role of rights in international discourse'[30] or some similar basis. Or such is the general approach at the heart of this second variant of the finessing gambit.

For those, like me, who generally have significant doubts about the success and persuasiveness of providing solid (moral?) foundations for non-legal human rights claims, this second finessing approach is not without attraction. That said, it carries with it disadvantages as well as advantages. The former are almost all related to the undemocratic nature of having unelected judges and an international elite of unelected committee members monitoring rights-related treaties and indeed a swathe of other unelected participants being the people who are giving specific content to these vague, amorphous human rights provisions as they move, here and there, from the non-legal realm to the legal one.

I now leave behind the issue of the foundations of human rights, and turn to the issue of how the human rights worldview does or does not mesh with a preference for democracy and democratic decision-making.

3 Doubts about the human rights worldview easily co-existing with democracy

In many ways this second main theme of my chapter is the more important one. Yet, as I have just published a book that deals with my concerns about the decline of democracy in five of the oldest democracies in the world,[31] and as some of my doubts here overlap with the themes in that book, I will be brief in this section. I limit myself to pointing out areas of concern – reasons for worrying that a human rights worldview does not co-exist easily with a commitment to democracy.

Start with any full-blooded understanding of human rights as moral rights. For those who see human rights in those terms, there is clearly room to doubt how great the pull of democracy will be for them. If some human right enunciates a mind-independent standard of what is correct and proper moral treatment, then it is not obvious why that claim or moral obligation should lose out just because a majority of one's fellow citizens see things differently. In addition, the pull of a supposedly 'reason-based', court-focused decision-making procedure[32] may well prove to be very great, its counter-majoritarian credentials notwithstanding. Indeed, democracy for such people is likely to be seen as just one good amongst many, and not one immune from the 'civilizing effects' either of a strong judiciary interpreting a potent bill of rights or of the demands of rights-related international law, or most probably of both.

Let me put it this way. If you see rights in non-consequentialist, 'strong rights' terms,[33] as setting out claims that have a basis or foundation over and above the way humans happen to feel about things, then being told that a majority of your fellow citizens feel otherwise is unlikely to be a knock-out argument for you.[34] It will have a prudential and procedural pull, yes. I have hefty doubts, though, that it will for many such proponents have a substantive pull.

Of course one *can* make a strong rights, or deontological, argument on behalf of democracy. Jeremy Waldron does something along those lines with his 'you are not treating others as autonomous agents worthy of respect unless they have an equal say in decision-making, even over rights-related issues' type argument. This is how Waldron grounds his 'right to participate', his 'right of rights'. Waldron does not rest it on consequential foundations.[35]

So my doubts here are *not* that giving human rights a moral foundation (of the **A**, **B** or **C** sort outlined above) must ineluctably undermine one's commitment to democracy; rather it is an empirical claim that for many it does.

At this point it is necessary to make clear what I mean by democracy, and in particular that I understand it in a thin, procedural sense.[36] In other words, when you think of democracy as a procedure for making decisions in a world where smart, nice, well-informed people will and do regularly disagree, democracy does not guarantee good outcomes. Yes, you might on average think those outcomes have a better likely batting average, or hit rate, than any other way of making society-wide decisions. But that assertion about what plays out best in the world of politics does not change the fact that democracy on this procedural, majoritarian, letting the numbers count understanding just describes a way of making decisions. It is not a guarantee of the goodness or rightness or superior moral credentials of those decisions in any or all instances.

Issues can and do arise, in other words, where the majority speaks and you think it has spoken foolishly or wrongly or in a panic.

A quite different approach is to think of democracy in much fatter, more morally pregnant terms. Indeed, many people[37] do just that; they use the term *democracy* to mean a great deal more than the process of majoritarian decision-making. For them, being a democracy and describing some country's system as 'democratic' carries with it an additional assertion that the decisions taken have reached a certain level of goodness or acceptability or rights-respectingness. In other words, for them, the noun *democracy* and the adjective *democratic* do not simply refer to *how* decisions are made, they also (to some extent or other) refer to the quality of those decisions.

People who use the word *democracy* in this fat, morally pregnant way want it to tell you two things, one about how a decision was made and another about the goodness or appropriateness of that decision. Democracy, on this view or understanding, means both a statement that decision-making is being done by some majoritarian process as well as a claim that the decisions pass some pre-established moral threshold.

This fat, substantive, morally-laden understanding of democracy is not, in my view, a desirable one. If decisions are made on a fair, open, majoritarian basis then it is better to be able to say 'country X is a democracy, but one that now ignores many individual rights and tramples on various economic freedoms' than to say it is not a democracy. We need to keep separate the issue of how a country makes its key decisions, on the one hand, and on the other whether some or all of us think those decisions are generally or overwhelmingly rights-respecting or freedom-protecting or morally palatable.

Put bluntly, there are good grounds for leaving yourself room to be able to say 'that country is a democracy, but it is doing very wrong-headed, even wicked, things'. And that is true despite you, and I, also thinking that most of the time, overwhelmingly perhaps, democracies do not do wicked things or even that no other decision-making procedure would, on the whole, make better decisions.

To be clear, then, when I assert that it is those who see human rights as resting on strong rights, full-bloodedly moral foundations who may well find the pull of democracy less than determinative, it is to this thin, procedural sense of democracy that I refer. Inflate your conception of democracy in a big way, make it sufficiently expansive and morally-charged, and chock full of the need for liberal and rights-respecting outcomes to count as democratic, and quite plainly the most robustly moral foundations for human rights can co-exist with the demands of democracy.

Hence my scepticism about the ease with which the grounded-in-morality human rights worldview and democracy are able to co-exist relates to my preferred thin understanding of democracy.

It gets worse. Even those who prefer to see human rights in consequentialist terms, or who seek to finesse the issue of foundations by making various human rights conventions and treaties their starting point, even for them the human rights worldview can be difficult to reconcile with a robust commitment to democracy. Take treaties. In the Westminster world these have highly diminished democratic credentials, being entered into under the prerogative power with no veto in the elected legislature – unlike in the United States where treaties are taken seriously, and hence where many fail to get through the US Senate. Or take customary international law. A less democratic way to make law is hard to imagine. Or take the International Court of Justice. Many of the judges on this court come from jurisdictions that by no stretch of the imagination could be described as democratic. And their manner of appointment looks pretty awful too. The same, or worse, goes for the membership of the committees that monitor human rights conventions.

Put bluntly, there is a huge democratic deficiency in the making of this type of law. As I make and defend that very point at length elsewhere,[38] I content myself here with this abbreviated listing of the areas or headings of democratic deficiency. If you accept these claims I make about the enervated nature of the democratic credentials of international rights-related law, notice that any attempt to finesse the foundations of human rights themselves (and that emphatically includes the second variant of the finesse outlined above) does not free you from this other deficiency, this undesirable emasculation of democracy. Yes, you avoid the highly contentious and debatable arguments encountered when seeking to provide a moral foundation for human rights, and you do so by simply making your starting point some laid down, constructed-by-humans, international treaty or convention or some customary international law ruling. You start with something that sits astride the legal/non-legal divide and you thereby side-step or finesse the question of foundations, at least in a way. But this finesse or side-step does not in any way at all reduce the democracy-enervated nature of your starting point.

Or for the purposes of this chapter let me put it in these terms: my suspicion is that the human rights worldview cannot easily co-exist with any full-blooded commitment to democracy. In fact I have a great many doubts indeed that they can easily co-exist. Of course, as I said at the start of this chapter, a good many people may well decide that cost (in terms of the emasculation of democratic input) is outweighed by the benefits such a worldview brings with it. But such costs there will be.

4 Doubts about the Beitz approach

Having set out my various doubts about the foundations and underpinnings of human rights as well as my doubts about how easily, if at all, the human rights project or practice meshes with a preference for democracy and democratic decision-making, I am now in a position to finish this chapter by considering whether these doubts of mine are alleviated in the picture of human rights that is set out by Charles Beitz in his *The Idea of Human Rights*.[39] Now, despite the fact that Beitz offers a sophisticated model of human rights that forswears the moral approach – of the need explicitly to ground one's understanding of human rights in one or more of the category **A**, **B** or **C** type ways set out above – in favour of an approach that focuses on the actual practice of human rights as one finds it today, it is nevertheless easier if I begin with the democracy question first and then turn to foundations afterwards. Why is it easier to take my two main themes in that order? Simply because Beitz's entire discussion of democracy is focused on something totally different to the concerns and doubts I raised above. My concern is that the human rights practice or structures we find in existence are seriously undermining the scope for democratic decision-making in the oldest and best-established democracies in the world. Beitz neither denies nor ever addresses that claim. His focus[40] is quite different. He wonders whether there is a defensible right to political participation, a right to democracy,[41] that can be teased out of the earlier case he makes for a political conception or approach to understanding human rights. Along the way Beitz considers whether democratic institutions deliver better rights-respecting consequences as well as issues connected to the transition to democracy and more. But he nowhere raises the prospect that his human rights model actually enervates or emasculates democracy in well-established existing democracies. With his sights trained on non-democracies and whether the existing human rights practice can be understood to encompass a right to democracy, my doubts as set out above never make it on to Beitz's radar.

Accordingly, as far as my second theme is concerned, my claim that the human rights worldview cannot easily co-exist with democracy is not addressed. Beitz in no way at all alleviates those doubts I raise. He is focused elsewhere.

Things are much more complicated with my first theme, the issue of foundations or underpinnings for human rights claims. Here, I concentrate on how Beitz's model for understanding human rights affects the doubts I have raised above. As I have just noted, Beitz forswears the moral approach.[42] And I say 'forswears' as opposed to 'rejects as implausible' because Beitz never explicitly commits himself to arguing that natural rights are philosophically false or wholly unconvincing. Instead, he simply says that this line of argument does not mesh with what we see in practice when we observe the human rights practice that actually exists and operates in international law. And that is not quite the same thing. You might aptly describe Beitz as a not-terribly-interested agnostic when it comes to natural rights.

Why should we insist that international human rights conform to a received philosophical conception rather than interpret them, as they present themselves, as a distinct normative system constructed to play a certain special role in global political life?[43]

Beitz rejects what he calls 'agreement theories'.[44] These are not the same as the conditional hypothetical social contract theories I described above. No, these are theories that look to see what does happen to exist in the world across cultures and then tries to speculate on what might be agreed to, based on a 'common core' or 'overlapping consensus' of what has been observed.[45] Beitz is more explicitly critical of this approach, and rejects it.[46]

What Beitz offers instead, as his positive case, is a model that first looks to what happens actually to exist as far as the existing practice of human rights is concerned and then extrapolates from that. It is very much a model that begins from an 'is'. And in some ways one is left wondering if there are elements of deriving an 'ought' from that 'is'[47] – such as when arguments are made about whether some right or set of rights might defensibly be extended or boundaries moved. And even if Hume's Law is not being breached when doing any of this, on what basis – on what implicit foundation or underpinning – is the extension being justified? More is going on in Beitz's account than a straight out empirical description of what happens at some particular point to exist, as he concedes. My own reading of Beitz is that there are traces of social contract thinking;[48] there are fairly big doses of consequentialist or utilitarian underpinnings – that we look at what happens to exist and then ask ourselves if that existing practice on balance delivers good consequences[49] – though I am equally sure that Beitz would not himself like to be thought of as offering a utilitarian defence; and throughout there is the sort of 'just assume they exist' or 'just begin with what Eleanor Roosevelt wrote down back in 1948 and move on from there' type thinking that I sketched above,[50] and that comes close at times to side-stepping the 'why are these things desirable' question. Certainly the core foundations of the Beitz model come from facts on the ground, from what was laid down after the Second World War, with the various later human rights conventions and protocols and even customary international law 'advances' or new interpretive outlooks adding to the mix.

Interestingly, Beitz himself insists on separating the normative question out from the others. He argues that the query 'What are human rights?' can solicit three types of answers; (a) one that gives an analysis of the concept of a human right; (b) one that gives an account of the content of human rights; and (c) one that gives an explanation of the reason-giving force of human rights.[51] Beitz's practical approach does not concern itself with the third of these, he says, though he does turn to address it in chapter 6.[52] Yet I am not so sure that the tripartite distinction is as neat as Beitz wishes it to be. For Beitz to be correct, *(a)* and *(b)* have to be answered in non-normative terms, perhaps wholly in such terms, on the 'is' level. I suspect that is not the case, not even for Beitz. Nor am I at all certain that Beitz's attempts to rebut the charge that his practical conception gives too much authority to the status quo are convincing. Most clearly he says 'In response, a practical conception need not take the details of present practice as beyond criticism.'[53] Yet any criticism has to be founded or premised on some moral worldview.

If I am wrong, notice that when Beitz comes to address the normative questions in chapter 6 – most generally the question of whether 'the [human rights] practice is of a kind we have reason to endorse and support'[54] – the most forceful sort of persuasive reply is a straight-out utilitarian one, that this practice delivers good consequences, on average, over time.[55] Now as I am a 'this is the least-bad theory on offer' consequentialist myself, I am not unhappy with that sort of reply. But I suspect more than a few readers would be.

I also wonder about the extent to which the legal/non-legal distinction (this time not via a bill of rights but rather via expanding international law norms) is being finessed.[56]

Perhaps most worryingly for Beitz himself, though not necessarily for me, nothing that I saw in the normative case that Beitz makes for human rights and the practice of human rights strikes me as inconsistent with a J.L. Mackie error theory.[57] In other words the 'should we support the existing human rights practice' can be answered quite well indeed (in consequentialist terms) even if it also be the case that no non-legal or no non-positive law (including international law) account of human rights can be given. And even if people think it can be given, but they are mistaken. To be blunt, even if human rights did not exist – in the sense that no plausible foundations or underpinnings could be given for them, or at least nothing other than some sort of utilitarian account – they would still fit in quite well with Beitz's practical model. We could be living in a Richard Rorty[58] and David Hume non-cognitivist, 'sentimentalist' world (as I believe we are) where all attempts to provide foundations outside of what-the-law-happens-to-be dissolve into consequentialist ones and Beitz's account could in a way work. We could even be living in a world where most people believed they weren't living in a Humean/Rortyian world, but in fact they were (so a Mackie world), and still Beitz's account could in a way work. I am not at all sure if Beitz himself would consider that a plus. On balance, I do.

None of this is to deny that Beitz offers a fascinating account of human rights. Nor is it to deny that his side-stepping of the need for a moral account to some extent tends to increase the plausibility of that account, because such a side-stepping does tend to increase the plausibility of Beitz's position.

Nevertheless, the Beitz account of the question of the foundations or underpinnings of human rights does not alleviate all, or even many, of the doubts I enumerate above. To the extent that Beitz's account is most plausibly seen as founded on an implicit sort of consequentialism, to that extent it tends to line up with my own views.

But the doubts set out above largely live on, even in the face of a Beitzian practical account.

In conclusion, let me reiterate that I have not offered here any overarching theories. I have simply attempted to enumerate some of my scepticism and doubts about aspects of, and possible foundations that might be used to underpin, the modern human rights edifice. And I have noted my scepticism, too, as regards how easily this edifice is able to co-exist with any vigorous commitment to democratic decision-making. And I have finished by holding up those doubts to the practical account offered by Charles Beitz to see how things stand in the light of that Beitzian account.

Notes

1 Charles Beitz, *The Idea of Human Rights* (Oxford: Oxford University Press, 2009).

2 See Wesley Newcomb Hohfeld, *Fundamental Legal Conceptions as Applied in Judicial Reasoning* (Yale: Yale University Press, 1919) for the best known analytical conception of rights. The next few paragraphs draw on Hohfeld and repeat an argument I made in James Allan, 'The Idea of Human Rights', *Bond Law Review* 25, no. 1 (2013), pp.1–12.

3 See Ronald Dworkin, *Taking Rights Seriously* (Cambridge: Harvard University Press, 1978), ch. 7.

4 Of course the exact reach or parameters or scope of coverage of this legal right or that will still be unclear at the margins and so highly debatable at these peripheries. Or to make the point in Hartian terms, these legal rights/legal rules will inevitably have a 'penumbra of doubt' or 'open texture' where there are good reasons for thinking the right/rule applies as well as good reasons for thinking it does not. See H.L.A. Hart, *The Concept of Law* (Oxford: Clarendon Press, 1961).

5 In the context of bills of rights, and more particularly the undesirable nature of such instruments, Jeremy Waldron often puts weight on this notion of reasonable disagreement when it comes to rights-related issues. See Jeremy Waldron, *Law and Disagreement* (Oxford: Oxford University Press, 1999); Jeremy Waldron, 'The Core of the Case Against Judicial Review', *The Yale Law Journal* 115 (2006): p. 1346. For my analysis of Waldron's writings on bills of rights see James Allan, 'Jeremy Waldron and the Philosopher's Stone', *San Diego Law Review* 45 (2008): p. 133.

6 This phrase comes from Lord Sankey in *Edwards v Canada (Attorney General)* [1930] AC 124, the 'Persons Case'.

7 See the UK case of *Regina v A* [2001] UKHL 25.

8 See the Canadian case of *Sauvé v. Canada (Chief Electoral Officer)* 3 SCR 519 (2002), or even the Australian case of *Roach v Electoral Commissioner* 233 CLR 162 (2007), which did this without a bill of rights (as I set out in James Allan, 'The Three "R"s of Recent Australian Judicial Activism: *Roach*, *Rowe* and (no) 'Riginalism', *Melbourne University Law Review* 36 (2012): p. 743.

9 I say this as a strong opponent of bills of rights. For a small sample see James Allan, 'Bills of Rights and Judicial Power – A Liberal's Quandary?' *Oxford Journal of Legal Studies* 16 (1996): p. 337; James Allan, 'Rights, Paternalism, Constitutions and Judges', in *Litigating Rights: Perspectives From Domestic and International Law*, edited by Grant Huscroft and Paul Rishworth (Oxford: Hart Publishing, 2002), p. 29; James Allan, 'A Modest Proposal', *Oxford Journal of Legal Studies* 23 (2003): p. 197; James Allan and Grant Huscroft, 'Rights Internationalism Coming Home to Roost?' *San Diego Law Review* 43 (2006): p. 1; James Allan, 'Portia, Bassanio or Dick the Butcher? Constraining Judges in the Twenty-First Century', *King's College Law Journal* 17 (2006): p. 1; James Allan, 'Jeremy Waldron and the Philosopher's Stone'; James Allan, 'Meagher's Mischaracterisations of Majoritarianism',

King's Law Journal 20 (2009): p. 115; James Allan and Michael Kirby, 'Public Conversation on Constitutionalism and the Judiciary between Professor James Allan and the Honourable Michael Kirby', 33 *Melbourne University Law Review* 33 (2009): p. 1032; James Allan, 'Statutory Bills of Rights: You Read Words In, You Read Words Out, You Take Parliament's Clear Intention and You Shake It All About', in *The Legal Protection of Human Rights: Sceptical Essays,* edited by Tom Campbell, K.D. Ewing and Adam Tomkins (Oxford: Oxford University Press, 2011): p. 108; James Allan, *The Vantage of Law: Its Role in Thinking about Law, Judging and Bills of Rights* (Farnham: Ashgate, 2011); James Allan, *Democracy in Decline: Steps in the Wrong Direction* (Montreal & Kingston: McGill-Queen's University Press, 2014).

10 Jeremy Bentham described this as a person's 'sympathy and antipathy' sentiments – 'I like it' or 'I don't like it'. See Jeremy Bentham, *An Introduction to the Principles of Morals and Legislation* (Oxford: Clarendon Press, 1907), ch. 16, p. 305. Certainly the attraction of utilitarianism, Bentham's preferred moral worldview, goes up considerably if all moral theories that make claims to having a mind-independent status are false or unpersuasive. Put differently, an inter-subjective standard of right and wrong (achieved by counting everyone equally to start and then going for what maximizes happiness or welfare or preferences) looks better than raw 'I happen to find that I like this' subjectivism. So if all moral theories that make less ephemeral, more mind-independent claims are for you ultimately unconvincing, then the sort of inter-subjective standard proposed by Bentham and by consequentialists more generally will be a least-bad option. At least I have argued as much. I have claimed that consequentialist moral theories are most attractive to those who find implausible and unpersuasive all the alternatives that offer standards of right and wrong that are not contingent on the way human sentiments happen to be. See my James Allan, *Sympathy and Antipathy: Essays Legal and Philosophical* (Farnham: Ashgate, 2002), especially the last chapter.

11 See United States Declaration of Independence (1776), preamble.

12 See John Finnis, *Natural Law and Natural Rights* (Oxford: Oxford University Press, 2011).

13 See J.L. Mackie, *The Miracle of Theism: Arguments for and Against the Existence of God* (Oxford: Oxford University Press, 1982) and see David Hume, *Dialogues Concerning Natural Religion* (published posthumously by his nephew after Hume's death in 1776; Kemp Smith edition, Bobbs-Merrill, 1947).

14 See, for instance, Dworkin, *Taking Rights Seriously,* and Ronald Dworkin, *Law's Empire* (Cambridge: Harvard University Press, 1988).

15 See Dworkin, *Law's Empire.*

16 See Ronald Dworkin, 'Objectivity and Truth: You'd Better Believe It', *Philosophy & Public Affairs* 25, no. 2 (1996): 87, and see James Allan, 'Truth's Empire – a Reply to Ronald Dworkin's "Objectivity and Truth: You'd Better Believe It"', *Australian Journal of Legal Philosophy* 26 (2001): p. 61. Notable non-cognitivists include Simon Blackburn (and his quasi-realism), Jeremy Waldron, J.L. Mackie and H.L.A. Hart.

17 See James Allan, *The Vantage of Law: Its Role in Thinking About Law, Judging and Bills of Rights* (Farnham: Ashgate, 2011). Those who share my scepticism of the persuasiveness of Dworkin's theories are many, including A.W.B. Simpson and Brian Leiter.

18 Oddly enough, much of modern American originalism constitutional interpretation theory has forsworn the search for actual intended meaning ('intentionalism') in favour of original public meaning, which involves constructing a hypothetical well-informed person at the time and asking what he or she would take the legal provisions to mean. This is the same game in a different guise. See, for example, Keith Whittington, 'On Pluralism Within Originalism', in *The Challenges of Originalism,* edited by Grant Huscroft and Bradley Miller (Cambridge University Press, 2011), pp. 70–86. Justice Scalia of the US Supreme Court also more or less falls into this category.

19 As it happens I find this camp the more plausible one myself. See James Allan, *A Sceptical Theory of Morality and Law* (New York: Peter Lang, 1998).

20 J.L. Mackie offers a sort of hybrid possibility; he offers an error theory. Mackie argues that most people believe they are making mind-independent moral claims when they make them; it is just that they are wrong. So for Mackie we in fact live in a non-cognitivist world but many people think, and feel as though, they are living in a moral realist one. See J.L. Mackie, *Ethics: Inventing Right and Wrong* (London: Penguin, 1977).

21 See Bentham, *An Introduction to the Principles of Morals* and Jeremy Bentham, *A Fragment on Government* (first published 1776, 2001), p. 93.

22 See, for example, how the non-utilitarian Larry Alexander makes the point in, Larry Alexander, 'Pursuing the Good – Indirectly', *Ethics* 95 (1985): p. 315.

23 Indeed Bentham was adamant that 'wants are not means – hunger is not bread': Jeremy Bentham, 'Anarchical Fallacies', in *The Works of Jeremy Bentham, Vol. 2,* edited by John Bowring (Edinburgh: William Tate, 1843), p. 501. Bentham was well aware of the dangers of the naturalistic fallacy, of breaching Hume's Law. Hume makes his famous 'you can't derive an "is" from and "ought"' point in David Hume, *A Treatise of Human Nature*, edited by L.A. Selby-Bigge (Oxford: Oxford University Press, 1978), p. 469.

24 Well known critics of utilitarianism include Dworkin, *Taking Rights Seriously,* pp. 232–238, 269, 275–276, chs. 9 and 12, *inter alia* and John Rawls, *A Theory of Justice* (Cambridge: Harvard University Press, 1971).

25 Steven Smith, 'Equality, Religion, and Nihilism', *San Diego Legal Studies Paper* 14–169 (2014): pp. 9–10.

26 Bedi chapter of this book, first page of that chapter.

27 See Alistair McIntyre, *After Virtue,* 2nd ed. (Notre Dame: University of Notre Dame Press, 1985).

28 McIntyre, *After Virtue*, p. 8.

29 See footnote 26 above and the main text to that footnote.

30 Bedi, this volume, fn.26 above.

31 See Allan, Democracy in Decline.

32 Steven Smith sets out this allure and then argues that judges, in fact, no more rely on reason than do legislators. See Steven Smith, 'Judicial Activism and "Reason"', in *Judicial Activism: An Interdisciplinary Approach to the American and European Experiences,* edited by Luis Pereira Cotinho, Massimo La Torre, and Steven Smith (New York: Springer, 2015), pp. 21–30.

33 For my distinction of 'strong rights theories' and 'weak rights theories' see James Allan, 'Bills of Rights and Judicial Power – a Liberal's Quandary', *Oxford Journal of Legal Studies* 16 (1996): p. 337.

34 Larry Alexander makes this point in his Larry Alexander, 'What Is the Problem of Judicial Review?' *Australian Journal of Legal Philosophy* 31 (2006): p. 1.

35 See Waldron, *Law and Disagreement* and see James Allan, 'The Travails of Justice Waldron', in *Expounding the Constitution: Essays in Constitutional Theory,* edited by Grant Huscroft (Cambridge: Cambridge University Press, 2008), pp. 161–183.

36 The next page repeats Allan, *Democracy in Decline.*

37 For example, the Nobel Prize winning economist Amartya Sen. See Amaryta Sen, 'Democracy as a Universal Value', *Journal of Democracy* 10 (1999): p. 8. See also Ronald Dworkin, *A Bill of Rights for Britain* (Chatto & Windus, 1990), p. 43: '[d]emocracy is not the same thing as majority rule, and that in a real democracy liberty and minorities have legal protection'.

38 See Allan, *Democracy in Decline*, pp. 83–107.

39 Beitz, The Idea of Human Rights.

40 See Beitz, The Idea of Human Rights, pp. 174–185.

41 Beitz's answer is a qualified 'no'. See Beitz, *The Idea of Human Rights,* pp. 179–181 and especially Beitz, *The Idea of Human Rights,* p. 182 and 185.

42 See, in particular, Beitz, *The Idea of Human Rights,* ch. 3, pp. 48–72; see also Beitz, *The Idea of Human Rights,* p. 103.

43 Beitz, The Idea of Human Rights, p. 68.

44 Beitz, *The Idea of Human Rights,* ch. 4, pp. 73–95.

45 Beitz, The Idea of Human Rights, p. 76.

46 For example, Beitz, *The Idea of Human Rights,* p. 88.

47 In other words, of breaching Hume's Law or the naturalistic fallacy. See Hume, *A Treatise of Human Nature.*

48 For instance, see Beitz's various reliances on Rawls, Beitz, *The Idea of Human Rights,* pp. 96, 100, 102. And likewise the many built-in qualifiers Beitz requires of what is 'reasonable' (see Beitz, *The Idea of Human Rights,* p. 106 *inter* alia) are just another way of asking conditional hypothetical normative questions – what counts as 'reasonable' not being a value-free

criterion. The same goes for determining what is 'objectionable'. The same goes for building a model that 'abstracts from [existing] particulars'. See Beitz, *The Idea of Human Rights,* p. 106.

49 See Beitz, *The Idea of Human Rights,* 126 and the first bits of ch. 6.
50 See Section 1c. above.
51 Beitz argues for this tripartite distinction at Beitz, *The Idea of Human Rights,* pp. 104–105.
52 Beitz, The Idea of Human Rights, pp. 126–159.
53 Beitz, The Idea of Human Rights, p. 105.
54 Beitz, The Idea of Human Rights, p. 126.
55 Perhaps that means it is more of a rule utilitarian reply.
56 I cover this earlier in this chapter.
57 I discuss Mackie's offer of hybrid possibility and error theory above. See also Mackie, *Ethics: Inventing Right and Wrong.*
58 See Beitz, The Idea of Human Rights, p. 103.

Part III

Accommodating economic rights

9 Two conceptions of social and economic rights

Basic needs versus equality

Octavio Luiz Motta Ferraz

Despite their widespread recognition both in international human rights law and domestic constitutional law, many supporters of so-called social and economic human rights (e.g. rights to health, education, housing, social security) complain that these rights have been consistently neglected by states and the international community, especially in comparison to the attention given to so-called civil and political rights such as freedom of expression, freedom from torture, the right to a fair trial, etc. '[T]he international community as a whole continue to tolerate all too often breaches of economic, social and cultural rights which, if they occurred in relation to civil and political rights, would provoke expressions of horror . . .', claimed the leading UN committee entrusted with monitoring these rights in an often quoted statement.[1]

This perceived neglect is often blamed on one, all or a combination of some of the following factors: the political power of those who benefit from the neglect of social rights; the current dominance of neoliberal ideology; a mistaken analytical dichotomy between positive and negative rights; and a false empirical claim that social rights are costly whereas civil and political rights are not.[2]

These explanations have always seemed to me somewhat unconvincing and incomplete. In this chapter I argue that an important, and perhaps main, difficulty faced by social and economic rights[3] is the *lack of a stable consensus* about the interrelated issues of their actual justification and content, i.e. *why these rights are genuine human rights* and *what concrete positive duties they entail?* In my view, disagreement about these fundamental questions is much larger, more genuine and deeper than it is acknowledged in the literature. Ambivalence about and opposition to these rights (depending on how they are formulated) is in my view much more widespread, and includes not only the self-interested and powerful, nor just the ideologically conservative or confused, but also progressive academics and activists, and a sizeable proportion of the poor.[4]

If this is correct, supporters of social rights should focus more on trying to advance a positive argument in favour of social rights, i.e. one that attempts to give plausible and persuasive answers to those questions of justification and content and muster consensus among the still large and diverse constituencies that disagree about them, rather than spend so much energy and effort deriding what they see as self-serving, malicious or misguided arguments of opponents of social rights.

I start by arguing why, in my view, the current prevalent strategy of many social rights supporters seems to miss this crucial explanatory cause for such perceived rights neglect: the lack of consensus on their justification and content, i.e. their *indeterminacy* (Section 1). I then discuss two potential candidates for conceptions of social rights that address those fundamental questions of justification and content and could potentially generate the badly needed consensus over these rights: the basic needs conception (Section 2) and what I call the equality conception (Section 3). I argue that the latter is superior to the former and should be embraced by social rights supporters as a potential good strategy to give these rights teeth.

1 The 'neglect' of social rights

Why does it seem, to many, that social rights are neglected in comparison to civil and political ones? If the issue were simply lack of implementation, or volume of violations, it would be hard to support this claim, especially in developing countries,[5] where civil and political rights are also violated on a daily basis and a large scale, and sometimes perhaps even more than social and economic rights. China and Cuba are examples that readily come to mind. But this seems to be also true of non-communist countries. To cite a brief example, almost 60 thousand people are murdered every year in Brazil, many thousands by the police, in situations that are much more plausibly described as summary executions than self-defence.[6] The right to life (a civil and political one) is therefore violated on a large scale in Brazil, perhaps more than the rights to health and education, for instance, where the Brazilian state invests reasonably large proportions of its GDP.[7]

But perhaps social rights supporters do not mean, by 'neglect', that these rights are more violated than their civil and political counterparts. What they mean, possibly, is that when these rights are violated, the reaction seems weaker than when civil and political rights are breached. No 'expressions of horror', to use the UN committee's statement quoted earlier, are forthcoming from the international community, when social rights are violated. This seems a bit more plausible,[8] but then the question is 'Why?', and the answers often given by social rights supporters seem unconvincing, or so I shall argue.

Self-interest of the powerful, be it through direct and blunt exercise of their power (e.g. corruption, tax evasion etc), be it via more subtle propagation of libertarian philosophy and neoliberal political ideology,[9] may of course have a role to play in the lack of strong condemnation by the so-called international community when states around the world invest less than they might in the provision of health, education and other socio-economic goods and services. To claim that this is the chief or one of the main explanations for the perceived neglect of social and economic rights seems, however, implausible.

The powerful are quite able, of course, to protect their wealth against taxation and redistribution through both direct political influence and evasion and corruption.[10] This has an obvious bearing on the ability of states to provide social and economic goods to the population. It does not explain, however, the paucity of condemnation of such practices in comparison to condemnations of torture, murder, political persecution etc. Nor does the propaganda that the wealthy are able to generate through control of media outlets and so-called 'independent' think-tanks.[11] Though these are somewhat influential, I doubt they would by themselves be capable of completely drowning out condemnations of social rights violations. We must therefore look beyond the opposition by the powerful to try and understand social rights neglect.[12]

I am also not convinced that alleged misconceptions (deliberate, induced or simply ignorant) about social rights as being exclusively 'positive' and costly plays that important a role. It is now well established that civil and political rights also entail positive duties that are resource-dependent, and often very costly, such as the maintenance of courts and police forces, the electoral system etc. But repeating this point *ad nauseam* will not resolve the important underlying problem that positive and costly duties raise for *all rights*.

The problem, and here is where in my view lies the main reason for the perceived neglect of social rights, is that positive and costly duties depend on and compete against each other for resources that are not only limited but often very unevenly distributed in modern societies. This raises intractable questions for the definition of the content of *all* rights, it is important to reemphasise, pertaining to the complex and controversial fields of distribute justice and social policy. How much economic inequality, if any, can a society justly allow to exist? Or, to put it another way, how much taxation, redistribution and spending ought a society to implement in order to provide public services such as security, education, health, etc? How much ought society to spend on these services? Should private education and health services be forbidden? Should education and health services be always free at the point of use? Should there be a minimum core of provision for everyone or a higher optimal equal level? Should any conditions be attached to access to social benefits and services?

I could go on and on listing the myriad intractable questions involving both normative and practical difficult issues (over which reasonable disagreement is fierce) that need to be answered so that we can have a more concrete idea about what positive duties rights actually entail. But my point should be sufficiently clear by now. Social rights supporters seem to have been focusing too much on at best secondary explanatory causes for the perceived neglect of social rights and too little on the main one: the high indeterminacy of their content, which stems from the intractable and controversial normative and practical questions that specifying positive and resource-dependent duties entail.[13]

It is mainly this indeterminacy that, in my view, fuels the ambivalence and opposition to these rights that still exist from many situated across the political ideological spectrum – sometimes at the opposite end to libertarianism and neoliberalism – including the poor,[14] and helps to explain their perceived neglect. It is not simply that the powerful, the gullible and the ignorant don't care or don't see that social rights are being violated across the world. It is rather, mostly, that even those who are deeply bothered about poverty and its consequences find it hard to conceptualize this in terms of concrete duties corresponding to these rights.

If social rights are to become effective tools in the promotion of health, education, housing and other socio-economic interests that so many are deprived of in our unequal world, this problem of indeterminacy has to be overcome. We need a plausible and persuasive conception of these rights, i.e. one that can muster a reasonable degree of consensus around both why these socio-economic interests ought to be regarded as rights (justification) and what concrete duties these rights give rise too (content).

This is no easy task, of course, but it is the only way of overcoming the perceived 'neglect' of social rights. How can we criticize societies and the international community for neglecting these rights in the absence of a reasonably wide consensus on the specification of their content? How can violations of these rights be identified and acted upon without such consensus?

In the next sections of this chapter I try to contribute to this effort by discussing two different possible approaches to the task. I call them, for reasons I hope will become clear later, the 'basic needs conception' and the 'equality conception' of social rights.[15] I argue in Section 2 that the former, although seemingly the most popular among social rights supporters in academia, legal practice and human rights activism, cannot fulfil the purposes mentioned above. I then defend the latter as a more promising way forward (Section 3).

2 The 'basic needs conception' of social rights

The idea of basic needs, despite raising significant debate in the philosophical literature, is very intuitive and well established in ordinary public discourse.[16] Food, water, basic housing, minimum standards of health and education are needs that we all have and are basic in the sense that their fulfilment is needed not only for survival but is also instrumentally essential to the enjoyment of all our other needs (we can call them non-basic needs) and preferences in life.[17] An intuitive and popular way of conceiving of social rights, therefore, is to think of them as rights that protect or guarantee the interests that we all have in satisfying these basic needs. I will call this the 'basic needs conception' of social rights.

There may of course be disagreement between proponents of the basic needs conception in terms of its more precise specification, particularly as to what needs are to be considered basic, what level of satisfaction of these needs should be protected and whether the duty to protect or guarantee these needs is subject to any conditions. Some may even dislike the terminology I am using here. But all the authors share the understanding that satisfaction of our needs in health, education, housing, food and social security is what social and economic rights are supposed to protect. Under the basic needs conception, an individual's inability to satisfy these basic needs as specified and at the level specified by the particular conception, amounts, *per se*, to an infringement of his or her social and economic rights, that is, a *prima facie* violation of that right.

I will distinguish between two main versions of the basic needs conception, the strong and weak versions. This distinction is based on the *strength of social rights* under these conceptions. By strength I mean the capacity of the right to generate duties that have a reasonably clear content and can be immediately claimed by right-holders (i.e. not easily limited or overridden by countervailing considerations). The distinction will hopefully become clearer later when I discuss each conception in more depth.

2.1 Strong basic needs conceptions

Good examples of strong basic needs conceptions can be found in the work of Tom Campbell, David Beetham and David Copp.

For Campbell, for instance, 'the core violation of human rights that is properly associated with extreme material poverty is the failure to respond effectively to poverty by those who are able to do so.'[18] For Beetham, 'in a world rich in resources and the accumulation of human knowledge, everyone ought to be guaranteed the basic means for sustaining life, and those denied these are victims of fundamental injustice.'[19] For Copp, 'the better off have a duty to pay their share until the point is reached that the worst off are enabled to meet their basic needs'.[20]

These are all good examples of what I am calling strong versions of the basic needs conception because the only countervailing consideration that may justify limiting the immediate duty to guarantee basic needs is what we may call *strict feasibility*, i.e. that one 'is able to do so' without himself falling below the level of basic needs satisfaction, or, to use the formulation of Peter Singer in a famous paper 'without thereby sacrificing anything of comparable moral importance'.[21] Moreover, given the high level of wealth and inequality in the world as a whole and within most countries, that condition is very easily reached by many. It is very likely, therefore, that this duty will not be defeated by the countervailing consideration of strict possibility in most scenarios. The duties generated by this basic needs conception of social rights are accordingly very strong.

Can the strong basic needs conception help us overcome the crucial problem of the indeterminacy of social rights discussed in the previous section? The test is whether this conception is capable of generating a reasonably clear and persuasive specification of the content of these rights.

I will leave aside, for the purposes of this chapter, the controversial issue of whether the positive duties corresponding to social rights should be confined to the national state or not. The only condition, i.e. countervailing consideration of this conception, *strict feasibility*, i.e. ability to aid at no comparable sacrifice, is of course easier to overcome within a cosmopolitan framework of social justice. It suffices to recall, here, that the wealth of the 1% richest people in the world amounts to US$110 trillion, that is, 65 times the total wealth of the bottom half of the world's population, where most of those deprived of basic needs are (or all of them depending on one's definition).[22] So, if ability to aid applied globally, there would be no question that a small sacrifice by rich individuals across the world or rich states would be sufficient to raise all the global needy above the basic needs threshold. But the geographical scope of global justice is a highly contested field among philosophers and the wider public, so, to avoid unnecessary complication, I will focus only on the narrower yet still relevant and complex national realm in order to evaluate competing conceptions of social rights.[23]

Another intricate issue I need to set aside for the purposes of this chapter is the one about the identity of the duty holder in the realm of social rights, i.e. the state and non-state actors such as individuals, corporations etc. For the sake of simplicity I will just assume that the primary duty holder is the national state, and that individuals and companies are responsible only indirectly through the duty to pay taxes and obey other related regulations.[24]

Even thus restricted, i.e. to the national realm and to states as the primary duty holders, the strong version of the basic needs conception would easily overcome the condition of strict feasibility in many countries in the world.[25] We can leave aside, therefore, the issue of feasibility and ask whether the strong conception is plausible at least in this large number of countries. A central plank of that conception, to recall, is that it is irrelevant what brought the predicament of the needy about. The mere fact that some are needy and resources are available to enable them to satisfy basic needs at no comparable sacrifice to others is a sufficient reason to ground immediate duties on others to aid the needy. The focus is exclusively on need and feasibility.

A great virtue of this conception is its clarity. The duties corresponding to social rights are reasonably clear and concrete, i.e. to provide those in need with the resources required to bring them above the threshold of needs deprivation. As Campbell makes clear, it is based on what he calls the 'uncomplicated moral duty of humanity', i.e. 'on the propriety of the elemental response of aiding another human being arising from seeing, imagining, or knowing of the suffering of that being irrespective of who is suffering or why that suffering came about.'[26]

This clarity, however, comes in my view at the cost of plausibility. As much as I accept the cogency of Campbell's and others' argument that one ought to aid those in desperate need whenever one is able to do so without sacrificing anything of comparable moral importance, many would deny that this moral duty corresponds to a *right* of those in need, i.e. an entitlement to demand such aid no matter what brought about the situation of inequality between the needy and the better-off. To put it another way, *need alone* is not a sufficient reason, in many people's view, to ground a right's claim. A right's claim, for many, requires the crucial element of a 'justified grievance', i.e. that one 'has been wronged' by another to use Buchanan's apt phrase.[27]

This distinction between duties of different moral status and consequences is familiar in the moral philosophy literature, sometimes portrayed with the dichotomy duties of beneficence-duties of justice.[28] As put by Beitz, a beneficence reason 'would count in favour of an action just in case the action would contribute to the satisfaction of another person's interests, independently of considerations about any historical or contemporary relationship one might have with that person.'[29] Allen Buchanan argues forcefully in his article 'Charity and Justice' that this distinction is 'both difficult to draw and of limited significance in ethical theory',[30] in particular against those who claim, like Robert Nozick, that duties of justice are always negative in nature, which would immediately rule out social and economic rights. But I believe that the distinction remains relevant enough to explain the strong intuitions of many non-libertarians that aiding those in need simply because they are suffering is a moral duty of different status from that of compensating those in need as a result, for example, of harm or exploitation. Many would regard the latter as duties of justice to which there are corresponding rights.[31]

Singer himself recognises the important obstacles for the acceptance of his argument, stating that it would require a change in 'the whole way we look at moral issues – our moral conceptual scheme – . . . the way of life that has come to be taken for granted in our society'.[32] And so does Campbell, who acknowledges that moral progress would be required by those who fail to grasp the moral force of the obligation to unconditionally aid the needy. As he puts it:

> Charity, seen in terms of humanitarian obligations, must cease to be regarded 'mere charity'. In relation to such phenomena as extreme poverty, failure to act when you are able to do so at little cost to yourself, must come to be seen as being just as morally culpable as actually bringing it about.[33]

I am not so sure that those changes in the prevailing moral intuitions of most people advocated by Singer and Campbell, even if realistic, are in fact desirable. To use a classic example from moral philosophical debates, the child-drowning-in-the-shallow-pond case, although I believe that there is a moral duty on any passer-by to save the child, I do not think that failing to comply with that duty should necessarily be regarded as 'just as morally culpable' as pushing the child in the pond with the clear intent of killing her. I believe there may be important reasons to distinguish not only between acts of charity and acts of justice, but also for grading moral culpability at different levels depending on the conduct of the individual. But I will not enter into this discussion here. For my purposes, all I want to argue is that given the significant disagreement that persists regarding the strength of the humanity-based moral duty to unconditionally aid the needy, and the seemingly reasonable view that such duty belongs to the realm of beneficence and charity and not justice and rights,[34] the strong basic needs conception of social rights is not, at least at present, a promising avenue to pursue in the quest to overcome the indeterminacy of these rights.[35]

Does the weak version of the basic needs conception fare any better?

2.2 Weak basic needs conceptions

Many social rights supporters, although they seem at first to adopt a strong version of the basic needs conception, in fact adopt what I will call a *weak* version. I call it weak, following the criteria explained above, because the duties generated by social rights under this conception are rather indeterminate and the right can be more easily overridden when compared with the strong version just discussed.

After stating (or implying) that social rights are rights to the satisfaction of basic needs, proponents of the weak version go on to specify several countervailing considerations (or conditions) that, when present, would justify the limitation of these rights. Cecile Fabre, for instance, states that 'a bill of social rights would lay on the state . . . an obligation to promote our interest in resources, that is, to give us the resources minimally necessary for us to lead what everybody would agree is a decent life', but then adds that this is 'subject to the equality and priority principles and to the availability of resources.'[36]

They can only, therefore, 'secure provision that might be regarded as adequate given the level of social and economic development that obtains, given other people's prospects for a decent life, and given certain expenditures that are simply unavoidable, like national defence and police forces (it is also necessary to defend the people you are going to house and feed), courts, working of the government, and so on.'[37]

A similar formulation is found in David Bilchitz. In the beginning of his book, he quotes some statistics on world poverty and claims that they 'are sufficient to indicate that these rights are more honoured in the breach than in the observance',[38] seemingly endorsing strong rights to the satisfaction of basic needs. Later in the book, however, it becomes evident that the duties generated by these rights are significantly qualified. This is how he puts it:

> [E]ach individual has certain fundamental interests that are the necessary prerequisites for leading lives of value. A concern by a society with the equal importance of lives will entail that each being ought to have their fundamental interests protected. Whenever the fundamental interests of a being are infringed, that being suffers severe harm and has a *prima facie* case that society ensures these fundamental interests are protected. [But] respecting and upholding conditional rights may take place in circumstances of scarcity, and involves action by agents who have their own interests. There are thus morally relevant features of the world in which rights are to be realized that would, in several circumstances, justify a failure to realize fully the conditional right.[39]

As the passages cited from these authors suggest, the main potential obstacle for what is often called (misleadingly in my view as I will argue later) the 'full realization' of social rights to basic needs protection is the fact of resource scarcity, i.e. the existence of many other competing claims on available resources that may limit or defeat the duty to provide basic needs to everyone. But this, one might say, is not much different from the feasibility condition of the strong version discussed above, and must anyway feature in any plausible conception given the well established principle of 'ought implies can'.

It is true, but a closer look at Fabre, Bilchitz and other proponents of what I am calling weak versions of the basic needs conception reveal that they go beyond this strict feasibility condition and add a further, and much more complex, countervailing consideration, which we may call *burdensomeness* following their own terminology. Fabre highlights the importance of 'other people's prospects for a decent life'. Bilchitz puts a lot of emphasis on the existence of 'agents who have their own interests'. Both are in line with more general philosophical accounts of the nature of human rights, such as John Tasioulas', who regards *possibility and burden* as necessary tests in the definition of the content of human rights corresponding duties, or, as he aptly puts it, the 'conditions that need to be satisfied for the threshold from interests to duties to be crossed.'[40]

Unlike in the strong version of the basic needs conception, therefore, it is not just ability to aid (I called it *strict feasibility*) that may limit the scope of the duties corresponding to social rights, but also the burden on others that these duties might entail.

This further condition may appeal to many as necessary to avoid the counterintuitive implications of the strong conception I highlighted above. Many believe that the mere existence of an interest in having one's basic needs satisfied does not automatically translate into human rights duties even when the strict feasibility condition is met (the strong version's implausible claim, or so I agued). As Jeremy Waldron has well put in an early piece:

> To acknowledge that P has a *right* to X is to acknowledge that someone, possibly the person doing the acknowledging, has a duty or responsibility to secure it for P. That's what stating '*P has a right*' means. Nothing analogous is true (or straightforwardly or uncontroversially true) of the language of needs.[41]

But is *burdensomeness* the missing element that, together with possibility (i.e. strict feasibility) can make the basic needs conception fulfil the difficult task of overcoming the problem of indeterminacy? To recall, we need a plausible and persuasive conception of these rights, i.e. one that can muster a reasonable degree of consensus around both why these socio-economic interests ought to be regarded as rights (justification) and what concrete duties these rights give rise too (content). I do not think so, for the reasons I turn now to discuss.

2.2.1 Burdensomeness

The weak versions tend to proceed in two stages in the determination of the duties entailed by social rights. Firstly, it defines the right, a right to the satisfaction of basic needs as we saw (first stage). Then it assesses whether the countervailing considerations (possibility and burdensomeness) obtain and therefore justify non-satisfaction of these needs (second stage).[42] Given the possibility, at least in principle, that the right will not 'survive' the second stage, i.e. that either possibility or burdensomeness, will limit or defeat the duty to guarantee basic needs, we ought to call the right and its corresponding duties in the first stage as prima facie, or 'conditional' to use Bilchitz expression. I think the idea of *prima facie* or conditional rights is conceptually awkward and will say more on this later.[43] But this is not the main problem with the weak basic needs conception. The main problem is, rather, with the countervailing consideration (or condition) of *burdensomeness*. It does not seem to provide a useful approach to determine with the necessary degree of clarity and plausibility the content of the duties that correspond to social rights.

The first problem is that the distinction between possibility and burdensomeness seems fuzzy. One could plausibly argue, for instance, that what is possible in terms of strict feasibility, that is, resource availability, cannot by definition be regarded as too burdensome. What else could have a stronger claim on existing resources than the fulfilment of the right to the satisfaction of basic needs, if there is indeed such a right? This is from where the strong conception draws most of its intuitive appeal. If there is indeed a human right to the satisfaction of basic needs, it seems fitting with the idea of rights as 'high priority norms', to use James Nickel's phrase, that the only countervailing consideration capable of overriding it is a real impossibility of satisfying those needs without sacrificing something of comparable moral importance, such as the basic needs of other individuals, or their other fundamental rights, such as life, physical integrity, etc. If burdensomeness is defined in this narrow way,[44] it collapses into possibility (i.e. strict feasibility as I called it above), and there is no real distinction between the weak and the strong conceptions, and the same criticism I raised against the latter would apply to the former.[45]

But some of the authors I cited above as proponents of the weak conceptions do seem to view burdensomeness as going beyond and above possibility. David Bilchitz is one of them. As well as possibility (he calls it simply 'scarcity'), he argues that there must be a 'space' in which individuals should be able to 'pursue their projects beyond the basic, whilst other individuals lack even the basic necessities'.[46] Encroaching on this space would in his view be too burdensome (a large 'sacrifice' in his terminology) and as such it would justify not fulfilling the prima facie right to basic needs.[47] I have already noted the counter intuitiveness of such an argument, and Bilchitz's choices of examples of potential excessive burdensomeness (ballet dancers who might need to give up one morning to help the needy; fashion lovers who might need to forgo a new trendy jumper) seems to help make that point.[48]

The other important problem I want to raise about the concept of burdensomeness is that, unless we define it narrowly as possibility (strict feasibility) it becomes rather unhelpful, due to its high indeterminacy, in our quest to specify with a reasonably degree of precision the content of social rights duties. As Bilchitz himself seems to admit, unless we take a more objective line on this question, we are left with highly subjective, and therefore variable, individuals' views of what constitutes excessive burden, or 'large sacrifice', to the point of having to accept the implausible claim that small limitations in the pursuits of the ballet dancer and the fashion lover would be unjustified even if for the sake of fulfilling the fundamental rights of the needy. In the end, thus, burdensomeness, even if plausible as an additional condition beyond possibility, seems to provide us with no useful tool.[49]

2.2.2 Indeterminacy and rights

I have claimed so far that neither version of the basic needs conception can help us determine the content of social rights in a sufficiently clear and plausible manner, i.e. in a manner that overcomes the problem of their normative indeterminacy which fuels, I argued, their perceived neglect in comparison to their civil and political counterparts. The strong version seems *too* strong, as it defends the existence of duties to guarantee everyone's basic needs simply because this is currently possible, in our world of reasonably abundant resources. As I argued, there is no widespread consensus around the existence of such a duty, and to the extent that there is, many would think of it as a duty of beneficence, or humanity, i.e. with no corresponding rights. The weak version does not fare much better. Rather than correcting the problem of the strong version, it adds to it. It starts with the same implausible claim that everyone has a right to the satisfaction of their basic needs simply because they are needy, but then weaken it with an implausible, and elusive condition: ***burdensomeness.*** Social rights are thus only ***prima facie*** rights to the satisfaction of basic needs, or definite rights to the satisfaction of basic needs whenever this is not ***too burdensome*** on society.

Even if the weak version were not implausible as I argued it is, it is certainly rather indeterminate. It is not surprising, therefore, that so many people still have doubts whether these are 'real', 'genuine' rights, or whether 'rights language' is applicable to them, as they seem to fall outside of what Tasioulas calls 'the core or focal concept' of human rights, or their 'basic normative idea'.[50]

Goodin and Beitz, for instance, state that '[t]he distinctive point of rights . . . is to enable us to make claims and demands against one another, and to identify particular agents of whom we would be justified in saying that they would be wrong not to act as the right requires.'[51] For Campbell, 'rights discourse is the language of priority. To have a right is to have something that overrides other considerations in both moral and legal discourse.'[52]

Ronald Dworkin expresses a similar idea with the term right in the 'strong sense'. As he put it:

> In most cases, when we say that someone has a 'right' to do something, we imply that it would be wrong to interfere with his doing it, or at least that some special grounds are needed to justify any interference.[53]

If this core, focal concept of human rights is correct, then conceptions such as the weak basic needs one just discussed is at the very least conceptually awkward.[54] This problem has of course not escaped those who adopt the weak basic needs conception. Bilchitz, for instance, puts forward the following argument in defence of his conception: '[It] helps to express the idea that there is a moral loss, something deeply disturbing that occurs when not all can be provided with life-saving health care, food, water, and shelter.'[55] Jeff King, despite not using the language of *burdensomeness*, admits that a social right corresponding to which there is only a vague duty towards its realisation 'looks at first sight more like a promise to try than a real guarantee'.[56] But he goes on to argue that 'it would be false to say that [such] a duty . . . is incompatible with it being a real or even justiciable standard. It does not make rights-language inapplicable'.[57]

At any event, whether rights language is applicable or not to such indeterminate claims as those resulting from the weak basic needs conception is not crucial to my point. At the very least, such claims would be of limited use to individuals as they would not be able to derive any immediate and concrete benefit from having these *prima facie* rights. If all one can claim under social rights is that the state makes an effort to progressively guarantee them in an unspecified future and within an unspecified amount of resources, so long as this is not too burdensome on society, these are very vague and weak moral claims, call them rights or not. As James Griffin has appropriately stated about the right to health, but which would apply in my view to social rights in general: 'A right to health must specify, at least roughly, the level of health we have a right to; otherwise the right is too indeterminate to be useful as a social claim'.[58]

It should be no wonder that these rights appear to be so neglected, as this highly indeterminate conception seems to be the most prevalent among international lawyers, officials and activists.[59] Is there a way of conceiving social rights in a manner that overcomes the flaws of both versions of the basic needs conception, i.e. one that generates normatively plausible and reasonably clear duties corresponding to social rights? This is what I will try to defend in the next section.

3 The 'equality conception'

My proposed conception is based on the idea of equality of concern and respect, or equal importance (I will call it the 'equality conception' for short). It shares with the basic needs conceptions the intuition that social and economic rights are ultimately about the protection of individuals against deprivation of basic needs such as health, education, housing, food and water. Yet not simply because basic needs' deprivation is a morally regrettable state of affairs that, in our world of reasonably abundant resources, could be remedied with relative ease, i.e. without comparable sacrifice on the part of the better off (the strong basic needs conception), or without excessive burden on society, whatever that means (the weak basic needs conception). The former, as I claimed earlier, can generate only a weaker duty of beneficence, or humanity, at least according to the prevailing consensus in most Western societies, whereas the latter is not only implausible but also indeterminate in that burdensomeness is at the same time too weak to defeat basic needs satisfaction and too vague to allow a reasonably clear definition of the content of social rights.

In my view, to implicate unequivocally the human rights discourse and its corollary of strong (i.e. clear and immediately claimable) duties, the situation of basic needs deprivation must also feature a grave injustice. It is therefore necessary to go beyond deprivation *per se* and inquire into its causes. Deprivations that come about as a result of grave injustice can be unequivocally identified as violations of social and economic rights. Our question, thus, is not simply whether someone is incapable of satisfying basic needs and it is feasible to help them, but whether his or her deprivation is attributable to a grave injustice. This connection with grave injustice would put social rights on much firmer ground in my view.

The challenge is of course to define what grave injustice is. If this is too indeterminate, then we will not achieve a reasonably clear determination of the content of social rights, our other important aim. I suggest that grave injustice should be interpreted through the idea of equality in the sense proposed by Ronald Dworkin, that is, not of sameness (equal treatment), but of equal concern and respect, or equal moral importance (treating people *as equals*).[60] When basic needs deprivation results from treatment that fails to respect individuals' fundamental status as equals, it is gravely unjust and, as a consequence, a violation of their human social rights.

Equality in this sense allows us to distinguish between inequalities in basic needs satisfaction that are not unjust, and therefore do not represent a violation of human social rights from those that do. It is not difficult to come up with extreme examples of both. If a person deliberately chooses, for example, to lead a life of total leisure and no work (the proverbial 'surfer' in political philosophy debates, or the 'grasshopper' in the famous Aesop fable) despite having the opportunity to gain a living sufficient to satisfy his basic needs, it would be odd for him or her to claim that they have a right that society provides for his basic needs as a matter of justice, i.e. equal concern and respect.[61] There may still be other good moral reasons for anyone to do so (beneficence, humanity etc, especially under conditions of abundance), but these, I emphasise, are not reasons that most people believe can ground human rights. On the other hand, when someone is not able to satisfy her basic needs due to racial or gender discrimination, for instance, a blatant and grave injustice occurs, i.e. a failure to be treated as an equal by society.

This egalitarian conception of social and economic rights is perhaps better expressed in the familiar language of equality of opportunity. These rights may therefore be formulated as rights to an *equal opportunity* to have one's basic needs satisfied, rather than as rights to the satisfaction of basic needs. James Nickel seems to be expressing a similar view when he states:

> A viable system of social rights will require most people to provide for themselves and their families through work as long as they have access to appropriate opportunities, education and infrastructure. Government-implemented social rights provide guarantees of availability (or 'secure access'), but it should not be necessary for government to supply the necessary goods in more than a small fraction of cases.[62]

To illustrate my proposed conception through a concrete example, let me invoke the famous South African case of *Grootboom*, where a group of homeless individuals on the verge of being evicted from private land where they had erected provisional shacks complained to the Constitutional Court that this represented a violation of their right to housing. If one adopts the basic needs conception, there is no doubt that this right is *prima facie* violated if the eviction is carried out, since the basic need to housing of the group will go unmet when they become homeless. Under the strong version, the violation is also definitive, as South Africa is arguably wealthy enough, as a country, to enable everyone to enjoy a minimum standard of housing at no comparable sacrifice to other needs of the population; under the weak version, it is only a *prima facie* violation, since we would still need to know whether South Africa has also a definitive duty to immediately provide Ms Grootboon and her group with housing, something I argued no proponent of the weak version has so far successfully proven, as it involves defining the elusive concept of *burdensomeness.* Under the equality conception here proposed, there is no automatic recognition that the right to housing has been violated, *prima facie* or definitively, as there is no right to the satisfaction of the basic need to housing in the first place, but rather a right to the equal opportunity to satisfy that need. We must therefore also inquire into the causes that led to the situation of basic needs deprivation of the claimants to see if these causes implicate inequality of opportunity for the satisfaction of basic needs in housing, which would qualify as a grave injustice.

The following simplified fictional scenarios will help me to clarify the differences between my conception and the basic needs ones and show, I hope, its higher plausibility:

1. The homeless belong to an ethnic group that has been systematically discriminated within their reasonably wealthy country, suffering enormous disadvantages in terms of opportunities for education and work, and being also restricted in their freedom of movement within their country (any resemblance to real events is no pure coincidence!).
2. The homeless belong to no particular group, have had ample opportunity to access education and work in their reasonably rich country, yet have decided freely not to make use of those opportunities and thus ended up with no means to satisfy their own basic needs (any resemblance to fanciful and unrealistic examples used in political philosophy debates is no pure coincidence!).
3. The homeless is only one group among several other homeless groups in their extremely poor country, where resources are very evenly distributed yet simply insufficient to enable everyone to enjoy a minimally decent standard of housing.
4. The homeless were victims of a purely natural catastrophe, say a hurricane, that wiped out their houses.
5. The homeless suffer from an extremely rare and debilitating disease that make them unable to work and for which there is no available treatment (or only at an extremely high cost).

The basic needs conceptions would see all these scenarios as implicating violations of human rights, although only *prima facie* violations in some of them, depending on whether the strong or weak version is adopted. The strong version would see definitive violations in all scenarios but for perhaps scenario 3, where it is simply unfeasible to provide housing to everyone. The weak version would regard all scenarios as *prima facie* violations of social rights, apart yet again from scenario 3 that would fail the condition of possibility, it is hard to say how the others would be considered as they would need to pass the elusive test of 'burdensomeness' as well. The equality conception would regard only scenario 1 as a clear violation of social and economic rights. All other scenarios would be instances in which, although beneficence or humanity might entail a variable moral duty to help the needy depending on the more specific characteristics of the particular scenario, there is no grave injustice and therefore no issue of human rights implicated. This is because in all these scenarios apart from scenario 1 the cause of deprivation cannot be attributed to an inequality of opportunity to satisfy basic needs, which would unequivocally implicate grave injustice and therefore human rights discourse. In scenario 2 equal opportunities were available but deliberately not taken. In scenario 3 opportunities are lacking yet equally lacking to everyone due to the extreme poverty of the country.[63] In scenario 4 the cause of basic needs deprivation is a natural event, not inequality of opportunity. The same goes for scenario 5.

It is important to emphasise again that my claim is not that there is no moral duty to help the individuals in these scenarios, but only that such duties cannot be unequivocally grounded on justice reasons and therefore do not command the necessary consensus to ground social and economic rights.[64] I am also aware of the limitations of these fictional scenarios. In the real world the actual causes of basic needs deprivation are of course significantly more complex and obscure, and will be often simply impossible to ascertain with any degree of accuracy. Some might therefore claim that my proposed conception of social rights is just as indeterminate as the weak basic needs conception I have criticized above.[65] If this is the case, then my proposed conception cannot indeed be the cure for the intractable indeterminacy of social rights, even if, in my view, it is more normatively plausible than either version of the basic needs one. We would then need simply to accept that the language of human rights has at present little more than rhetorical effect in the debate about our moral obligations to address poverty.

I want to suggest, however, a way in which this indeterminateness might be at least mitigated and social rights might be more precisely defined under the equality conception. Our main obstacle, as already noted, is in the intractable complexity and obscurity that plagues our knowledge of the causes of basic needs' deprivation.[66] Richard Arneson has put this in a stark manner in an insightful paper when discussing the related ideas of personal responsibility and deservingness:

> The idea that we might adjust our distributive-justice system based on our estimation of persons' overall deservingness or responsibility seems entirely chimerical. Individuals do not display responsibility scores on their foreheads, and the attempt by institutions or individuals to guess at the scores of the people they are dealing with would surely dissolve in practice into giving vent to one's prejudices and piques. The criminal justice system has a difficult time making reliable determinations of an individual's guilt or innocence with respect to the charge that she committed a particular criminal act; the thought that we could construct a distributive-justice system that assesses people's lifetime responsibility is surely a nonstarter.[67]

I agree with Arneson, but the measures we are able to implement in the real world of policy don't need to fit perfectly the best principles of the realm of theory. We could bypass the extraordinary difficulties in establishing the exact causes of basic needs deprivation by adopting a presumption. We could set minimum levels of basic needs satisfaction below which we would presume that individuals would not fall *but for* injustice, i.e. had they been guaranteed equal opportunity to satisfy basic needs. This minimum level would be the content of social rights that everyone would be entitled to claim, entailing corresponding duties on others to guarantee that minimum immediately. Setting this minimum will of course present some challenges, but these should not be insurmountable, an issue I shall return to later.

For now I just want to emphasize the legitimacy of this strategy. We make people pay compensation on a 'balance of probabilities' that they have caused others harm by negligent conduct. We lock people up in jail even if we cannot be 100% sure that they are responsible for the crime they have been accused of, presuming their guilt if it can be established 'beyond reasonable doubt'. We use these and other presumptions in our legal systems because, without them, it would be simply impossible to attribute civil and criminal responsibility.

I believe the presumption of social responsibility that I am proposing for the implementation of the equality conception of social rights can be justified on similar grounds. Deprivation of basic needs is a dreadful and morally regrettable thing, as the basic needs conceptions rightly stress, and especially in a context of relative abundance of resources like that of our present world and most countries within it. Given an equal opportunity to satisfy their basic needs, e.g. through equal opportunity for education and employment, it is reasonable to assume that most people would be able to satisfy their basic needs. In an ideal world, we would not only be able to guarantee equal opportunity to everyone but also know who nonetheless ended up deprived despite having had equal opportunity. In our imperfect world, equality of opportunity clearly does not obtain anywhere, and we cannot be sure, as already discussed, whether someone's deprivation is solely, partly, and to what extent, a result of inequality of opportunities (i.e. circumstances beyond individuals' control). But we have plenty of (and growing) empirical evidence that most cases of basic needs deprivation can be plausibly and largely attributed to inequality of opportunity.

Ethnicity, place of birth, mother's and father's education and occupation have been found in recent empirical studies to explain a significant part of variations in household income and consumption levels in several countries both in the developing and the developed world.[68] The World Bank has produced an index, the Human Opportunity Index (HOI) focusing on children up to the age of 16 and their access to a set of basic services and goods. It shows, again, that circumstances over which individuals have no control whatsoever determine significantly their unequal access to these basic services.[69] In such a context, I suggest that we are more than justified to adopt the presumption of injustice as a way to tackle the indeterminacy in the causes of deprivation. To repeat, when individuals fall below a certain minimum level of basic needs satisfaction we should presume that they have suffered grave injustice (i.e. inequality of opportunity). Social and economic rights corresponding duties are best conceived, thus, as duties to guarantee that no one falls below that minimum threshold.

The remaining challenge is to define with some degree of precision what these minimum thresholds of health, education, housing, food and water are. But this is something that we should be increasingly able to do with the aid of the growing empirical data available and some innovative and exciting methodology being currently developed by experts. To give one recent example, Fukkuda-Parr, Lawson-Remer and Randolph have developed a methodology that allows us to set what countries at different levels of economic development, as measured by GDP *per capita*, should be able to afford (economic feasibility) basic needs satisfaction of the population. They call it the 'Achievement Possibilities Frontier' (APF) and calculate it for a set of 16 basic needs indicators related to health, education, food, housing and work. They calculate the APF through a sophisticated and long-standing economics framework (the 'Production Possibility Frontier') that shows the maximum output of a good possible result for any given resource input. By plotting the value of a given socio-economic indicator against GDP *per capita* for all countries and for a period of a decade, they are able to define with a great degree of precision at what level of resources (GDP *per capita*) a country should be able to achieve full satisfaction of a given socio-economic indicator. To give a couple of examples, to provide access to improved sanitation to 100% of the population, a GDP *per capita* of just $3,970 is sufficient; to also eliminate stunting in children the GDP *per capita* required is $7,806.[70]

This and other empirical efforts, which will for certain continue to be developed and improved, can be used in the specification of the minimum thresholds needed for the implementation of the equality conception. Lack of access to improved sanitation, for instance, should be regarded as a violation of social rights almost anywhere in the world. We can use the same approach with the other social and economic rights. To know whether these rights are being respected we need to know first what the APF is for the relevant country. Countries that have achieved the APF yet the population still lacks the corresponding basic needs ought to be regarded as presumptive violators of the corresponding social rights, unless they can prove robustly that opportunities are equally distributed for everyone to satisfy those needs.

4 Conclusion

I have claimed in this chapter that both versions of the most prevalent conceptions of social rights are inadequate. I called them basic needs because commentators see these rights as rights to the guarantee of basic needs satisfaction so long as this is possible (strong version); or possible and not too burdensome on society (weak version). The strong version, although not implausible from the perspective of pure feasibility (the world, and most countries in it, is indeed rich enough to guarantee in principle everyone's basic needs satisfaction at a reasonably high level), is nonetheless implausible from a normative perspective. There is no stable consensus at present on the existence of a strong, justice-based moral duty to guarantee everyone's satisfaction of basic needs simply because it is possible to do so. There is perhaps more consensus on the existence of a beneficence or humanity-based duty based purely on ability to aid, but beneficence or humanity are not reasons that command a wide enough consensus at present as grounds for duties that correspond to rights. The weak version, in turn, is inadequate for the following reasons. It starts from the same implausible claim that everyone has rights to basic needs satisfaction. It then conditions that right not only to possibility, but also to *burdensomeness.* Burdensomeness seems an implausible condition to place on fundamental rights. The very idea of human rights implies special priority over other interests and goals, so it seems implausible to allow for more than possibility (i.e. strict feasibility) as a countervailing consideration that may limit or defeat these rights. Even if this is incorrect, excessive burden is a highly indeterminate idea. This indeterminacy represents a great obstacle to the use of social rights as a meaningful social tool.

Both basic needs conception seem to fail, thus, in the crucial task of providing a plausible and reasonably clear definition of the concrete duties that these rights give rise to. It is not surprising, then, that these rights seem to be neglected, and that so many are sceptical of their status as genuine rights. Bernard Williams' statement when commenting on the right to work is a good illustration of the problem:

> I think that it may be unfortunate that declarations of human rights have, though for understandable reasons, included supposed rights of this kind. Since in many cases governments cannot actually deliver what their peoples are said to have a right to, this encourages the idea that human rights represent merely aspirations, that they signal goods and opportunities which, as a matter of urgency, should be provided if it is possible. But that is not the shape of a right. If people have a right to something, then someone does wrong who denies it to them.[71]

I have suggested that a different conception may be able to overcome this difficult problem of indeterminacy. Rather than rights to the guarantee of basic needs satisfaction, we ought to conceive of social rights as rights to an *equal opportunity* to satisfy basic needs, derived from a more fundamental right to equal concern and respect. As well as more plausible and therefore capable of mustering the badly needed consensus (denial of equal opportunity to satisfy basic needs is an almost universally recognized grave injustice) this conception is able to generate reasonably clear duties corresponding to these rights. All we need to do is adopt a strong presumption that, given a certain level of resources, anyone lacking in basic needs satisfaction has been denied an equal opportunity to satisfy these needs. Under this conception, the question to be asked in the definition of social rights' entitlements would be the following: what minimum level of health, education, housing etc can we safely presume that, given a certain level of aggregate resources in the relevant society, everyone would be able to achieve had they had equal opportunities to do so? This minimum level, which can vary from country to country according to their economic development or be applied universally (a difficult question I did not attempt to answer in this chapter), is what everyone should be guaranteed as their social rights.

Notes

1 UN Committee on Economic, Social and Cultural Rights, Statement to the World Conference, UN Doc. E/1993/22/ (2010), p. 83, para 5. Many academics and activists have made similar claims. David Bilchitz, for instance, states that social rights are 'more honoured in the breach than in the observance', see David Bilchitz, *Poverty and Fundamental Rights: The Justification and Enforcement of Socio-Economic Rights* (Oxford: Oxford University Press, 2008), p. 1. Margot Salomon urges in a similar vein that 'equal attention and urgent consideration . . . be given to the civil, political, economic, social and cultural rights', see Margot Salomon, *Global Responsibility for Human Rights: World Poverty and the Development of International Law* (Oxford: Oxford University Press, 2007), p 122.

2 Salomon, *Global Responsibility,* p. 122, fn.1. The latter two may be held in ignorance or deliberately propagated by the powerful. See, for instance, Paul Hunt: 'Bluntly, many of those in positions of power and privilege do not wish this to happen. They do not want a redistribution of power within and between societies. Many of them wish to preserve the status quo. Thus, they and their ideological allies keep raising objections. As one objection is dispatched, they raise another. The Hydra's heads multiply.' See Paul Hunt, '*Power, Suffering, and the Struggle for Dignity: Human Rights Frameworks for Health and Why They Matter,* book review', *Human Rights Quarterly* 38, no. 4 (2016): pp. 1138, 1142. See also Paul O'Connel, 'The Death of Socio-Economic Rights', *Modern Law Review* 74, no. 4 (2011): pp. 532–554. See Kate Young, *Constituting Social Rights* (Oxford: Oxford University Press, 2012), p. 5: 'The separation of rights into categories endures due to the bifurcation of human rights into two foundational international human rights covenants, a bifurcation itself premised on analytical distinctions that have been long criticized.'

3 Jeff King has helpfully distinguished five different senses of social rights, two moral: social human rights (universal), and social citizenship rights; and three legal: international social rights (designed to mirror social human rights), legislative social rights and constitutional social rights. My focus here is on a conception of social human rights that could then help us interpret international social rights. But the discussion is also relevant, in my view, for all other senses. See Jeff King, *Judging Social Rights* (Cambridge: Cambridge University Press, 2012), pp. 18–19.

4 They may of course be misguided or influenced by propaganda from the powerful, but this is another issue that we can only fruitfully approach once we have answers to those fundamental questions of justification and content.

5 A brief perusal of reports by human rights NGOs chiefly concerned with civil and political rights, such as Amnesty International and Human Rights Watch, would suffice to see this.

6 'Violent deaths in Brazil surge to peak of 58,000 amid Olympic safety fears', The Guardian, 9 October 2015, www.theguardian.com/world/2015/oct/09/violent-deaths-in-brazil-surge-to-peak-of-58000-amid-olympic-safety-fears; Robert Muggah, 'How did Rio's police become known as the most violent in the world?', The Guardian, 3 August 2016, www.theguardian.com/global-development-professionals-network/2016/aug/03/rio-police-violent-killing-olympics-torture.

7 According to the latest available data Brazil spends 5.9% of its GDP on Education and about 4% on health. See The World Bank, 15 March 2017, http://data.worldbank.org.

8 Although it is an empirical question to which it would be hard to find an accurate answer.

9 I am not equating libertarianism with neoliberalism. Although there are interconnections between them, and both are hostile to the idea of social rights, they are different in that the former is a philosophical, and therefore openly normative theory of justice, whereas the latter is an economic theory that attempts (unsuccessfully in my view) to remain neutral to normative concerns. Whereas the former opposition to social rights is due to the alleged injustice of limiting property rights for redistributive purposes, the latter's opposition to social rights is allegedly based on the bad consequences for the economy and well-being of everyone when governments tax and spend too much in social policies. For an interesting explanation and challenge of the latter from a surprising source see Jonathan Ostry, Prakash Loungani and Davide Furceri, 'Neoliberalism: Oversold?' *Finance and Development* 53, no. 2 (2016): pp. 38–41.

10 See Gabriel Zucman, *The Hidden Wealth of Nations: The Scourge of Tax Havens* (Chicago: University of Chicago Press, 2015).

11 See George Monbiot, 'Think of a Tank', 12 September 2011, www.monbiot.com/2011/09/12/think-of-a-tank/.

12 Pierre Dardot and Christian Laval's *The New Way of the World: On Neoliberal Society* (London: VersoBooks, 2014), seem to me spot on in their diagnosis of neoliberalism as not simply an economic free market theory imposed in a forceful and conspiratorial way by those who benefit from it, but rather as a mentality (or rationality as they put it) based on the paramount idea of competition that is currently accepted by many and permeates all spheres of human life.

13 This is not, of course, a problem that affects only positive duties. The content of negative duties that correspond to some very well established rights will also often raise debate. What is the threshold of severity that separates torture from inhuman, cruel and degrading treatment? Does freedom of expression include the right to offend members of ethnic or religious groups? Should prisoners have the right to vote?

14 Due for instance to the individualistic and conservative nature of the idea of rights, to inequalities in access to Justice, to the over legalization of social issues etc. See, for instance, Mark Tushnet, 'The Critique of Rights', SMU Law Review 47 (1994): p. 23; Richard M. Titmuss, 'Welfare "Rights", Law and Discretion', *Political Quarterly* 42, no. 2 (1971): p. 113; Robert E. Gooding, *Reasons for Welfare: The Political Theory of the Welfare State* (Princeton: Princeton University Press, 1988). For a good discussion, see King, Judging Social Rights, ch. 3, section III.C.

15 A similar, perhaps identical distinction is made by others using the terms humanity and justice, or beneficence and justice. See, for instance, Thomas Campbell, 'Poverty as a Violation of Human Rights', in *Freedom From Poverty as a Human Right: Who Owes what to the Very Poor?* edited by Thomas Pogge (Oxford: Oxford University Press, 2007).

16 For a seminal philosophical discussion see David Braybrooke, *Meeting Needs* (Princeton: Princeton University Press, 1987).

17 The expression 'basic needs' seems to have become prominent in the literature on development in the late seventies, when the 'basic needs approach' to development was promoted as an alternative to the exclusively economic, growth-centred approach. See Dharam P. Ghai, et al., *The Basic Needs Approach to Development: Some Issues Regarding Concepts and Methodology* (Geneva: ILO, 1977).

18 Campbell, 'Poverty as a Violation of Human Rights', p. 62.

19 David Beetham, 'What Future for Economic and Social Rights', *Political Studies* 43 (1995): p. 44.

20 David Copp, 'The Right to an Adequate Standard of Living: Justice, Autonomy and the Basic Needs', *Social Philosophy and Policy* 9, no. 1 (1992): 231; David Copp, 'The Right to an Adequate Standard of Living: Justice, Autonomy and the Basic Needs', in *Welfare Rights*

and Duties of Charity, vol. 5, edited by Carl Wellman (London: Routledge, 2002), p. 206. See also Henry Shue, *Basic Rights: Subsistence, Affluence and US Foreign Policy* (Princeton: Princeton University Press, 1980), although Shue's argument for basic rights is instrumental.

21 Although Peter Singer does not use the language of human rights, see Peter Singer, 'Famine, Affluence, and Morality', *Philosophy and Public Affairs* 1, no. 1 (Spring 1972): p. 229, See also, for the same rationale, Peter Unger, *Living High and Letting Die: Our Illusion of Innocence* (New York: Oxford University Press, 1996).

22 Oxfam, 'Working for the Few: Political Capture and Economic Inequality', 2014, www.ox- fam.org/sites/www.oxfam.org/files/bp-working-for-few-political-capture-economic-inequality-200114- summ-en.pdf.

23 As will hopefully be clear, the arguments I will develop are equally relevant for social rights within a cosmopolitan global justice framework.

24 For interesting discussions of so-called non-state actors' potential duties, see Aoife Nolan, 'Holding Non-State Actors to Account for Constitutional Economic and Social Rights Violations: Experiences and Lessons from South Africa and Ireland', *International Journal of Constitutional Law* 12, no. 1 (2014): p. 61; Colm O'Cinneide, *Taking Equal Opportunities Seriously: The Extension of Positive Duties to Promote Equality* (London: Equality and Diversity Forum/Equal Opportunities Commission, 2003), p. 120. See also Laura Valentini's analysis of Transnational Corporations as potentially fulfilling human rights needs in this volume.

25 I have no space to develop this any further here, but there is enough and robust empirical evidence of this in the development literature. World GDP per capita in 2013 was $10,613. 126 countries in the world have GDP per capita higher than $8,000 and 161 have GDP per capita higher than $4,000. See Central Intelligence Agency (CIA), 'The World Factbook', 2012, www.cia.gov/library/publications/the-world-factbook/. For some interesting recent data, see Sakiko Fukkuda-Parr, Terra Lawson-Remer and Susan Randolph, *Fulfilling Social and Economic Rights* (Oxford: Oxford University Press, 2015). See text below with some of their findings.

26 Campbell, 'Poverty as a Violation of Human Rights', p. 65.

27 I use here the terminology of Allen Buchanan, 'Charity and Justice', *Ethics* 97 (1987): p. 572.

28 Another popular distinction is that between perfect and imperfect obligations, attributed to Kant. But see George Rainbolt, 'Perfect and Imperfect Obligations', *Philosophical Studies: An International Journal for Philosophy in the Analytic Tradition* 98, no. 3 (2000): p. 233, registering at least eight different ways in which the distinction is formulated by different authors.

29 Charles Beitz, *The Idea of Human Rights* (Oxford: Oxford University Press, 2009), p. 167.

30 Buchanan, 'Charity and Justice', p. 574.

31 Beitz seems to be of the same view: 'it is controversial whether reasons of beneficence are strong enough, in themselves, to require anyone to undertake substantial sacrifices for the benefit of persons unknown to them, particularly when the sacrifices take the form of continuing commitments rather than one-off transfers.' See Beitz, *The Idea of Human Rights,* p. 167. Although he seems at first to endorse Buchanan's position he then goes on to distinguish between ordinary reasons of beneficence and strong reasons of beneficence, the latter obtaining when three conditions are present (urgency, feasibility and reasonably moderate costs), all of which apply to global poverty, and to claim that the latter gives rise to requirements of action. Yet, as he makes it clear, he does not mean that these reasons are 'conclusory or non-defeasible', although he does not specify what 'weighty conflicting reasons' would be capable of outweighing 'strong beneficence'. See Beitz, *The Idea of Human Rights,* p. 168. See also Richard Miller, 'Beneficence, Duty and Distance', *Philosophy and Public Affairs* 32 (2004): p. 357; Garett Cullity, *The Moral Demands of Affluence* (Oxford: Clarendon Press, 2004).

32 Singer, 'Famine, Affluence, and Morality', p. 230.

33 Campbell, 'Poverty as a Violation of Human Rights', p. 69.

34 The criminal law systems of different countries provide a good indication of this disagreement. Many countries do, other do not, criminalise omissions to help others in danger. Those that do, like France, apply a much lower sanction than that of murder. Article 223–226 of the French Penal Code is a good illustration: 'Art. 223–226 Quiconque pouvant empêcher par

son action immédiate, sans risque pour lui ou pour les tiers, soit un crime, soit un délit contre l'intégrité corporelle de la personne s'abstient volontairement de le faire est puni de cinq ans d'emprisonnement et de 75 000 euros d'amende. Sera puni des mêmes peines quiconque s'abstient volontairement de porter à une personne en péril l'assistance que, sans risque pour lui ou pour les tiers, il pouvait lui prêter soit par son action personnelle, soit en provoquant un secours.'

35 Campbell has explained how need and justice are separate and only contingently linked as, for instance, when need comes about as a result of harm and exploitation. If there is a universal obligation to relieve need 'whatever its origin', it must be based, he claims, correctly in my view, on humanity, not justice. An obligation to relieve poverty has therefore 'twin sources', justice and humanity, but only the latter can justify an unconditional (universal in Campbell's language) obligation. Where I disagree with Campbell is in his suggestion that we 'may even perhaps be led to give priority to humanity over justice in those cases where they conflict'. See Thomas Campbell, 'Humanity Before Justice', *British Journal of Political Science* 4 (1974): p. 16. I am also not sure whether we really need to import inhumanity into the justification of anti-poverty rights, as claimed by Campbell in a more recent article as I believe that most cases of poverty can be safely attributed to injustice, as I will argue below. See Campbell, 'Poverty as a Violation of Human Rights'.

36 Cecile Fabre, *Social Rights under the Constitution* (Oxford: Oxford University Press, 2000), p. 157.

37 David Bilchitz, *Poverty and Fundamental Human Rights* (Oxford: Oxford University Press, 2007), pp. 31–32.

38 Bilchitz, Poverty and Fundamental Human Rights, p. 2.

39 Bilchitz, *Poverty and Fundamental Human Rights*, pp. 80–81. Another well-developed and sophisticated account of the weak basic needs conception is defended by Virgilio Afonso da Silva, *Direitos Fundamentais: Conteudo essencial, restrições e eficácia. Malheiros* (Saraiva: São Paulo, 2009). Unfortunately, there is no English version available.

40 In another paper, Tasioulas mentions that duties corresponding to human rights must 'represent practicable claims on others given the constraints created by general and relatively entrenched facts of human nature and social life in the modern world' See John Tasioulas, 'The Modern Reality of Human Rights', in *Freedom From Poverty as a Human Right: Who Owes What to the Very Poor?* edited by Thomas Pogge (Oxford: Oxford University Press, 2007), p. 78.

41 Jeremy Waldron, 'Rights and Needs: The Myth of Disjunction', in *Legal Rights: Historical and Practical Perspectives*, edited by Austin Sarat and Thomas R. Kearns (Ann Arbour: University of Michigan Press, 1996), p. 94.

42 One usual objection to basic needs approaches, which would apply also to the strong version, is the difficulty of defining basic needs in health, education, housing etc that. As I have already mentioned above, I think it is possible to define with a reasonable degree of precision what basic needs are.

43 A similar point was made by James Nickel: 'The danger is that prima facie rights will provide no guidance in the cases where guidance is needed most.' See James Nickel, *Making Sense of Human Rights: Philosophical Reflections on the Universal Declaration of Human Rights* (Berkley: University of California Press, 1987), p. 44.

44 This is how James Nickel seems to define burdensomeness. The justification of specific rights 'requires showing that the burdens imposed by a proposed right are justifiable. . . . that the normative burdens they impose on people not be ones that are destructive to life or health, that deprive people of fundamental freedoms, or that treat people in ways that are severely cruel and unfair.' See Nickel, *Making Sense of Human Rights*, p. 78.

45 This seems to be the case of Cecile Fabre judging from the following passage of her book, where she explains her priority principle to adjudicate between individuals interests: 'According to the priority principle, if you have more functionings than I do, your interest in being brought to the minimum threshold is not important enough to be protected by a right to be less interfered with than me; by contrast my interest in having as many functionings as you do, or at least in having more than I currently have, is important enough to be protected by such a right.' Fabre, *Social Rights Under the Constitution*, p. 31.

46 Bilchitz, Poverty and Fundamental Human Rights, p. 77.

47 Bilchitz, Poverty and Fundamental Human Rights, p. 77.

48 'It is possible, for instance, that a person who ties his projects very closely to buying clothes and being fashionable may well regard it as a substantial sacrifice to have to forgo buying expensive clothes.' The only example of potential acceptable burden he gives is that of a commercial lawyer. For a longer discussion of Bilchitz argument see my review of his book, 'Poverty and Human Rights', *Oxford Journal of Legal Studies* 28, no. 3 (2008): pp. 585–603.

49 Bilchitz himself admits it as the issue which is 'most difficult to answer'; see Biltchitz, *Poverty and Fundamental Human Rights*, p. 79.

50 For instance, 'the basic normative idea that enables us to make the best sense of what we pre-reflectively identify as the discourse and practice human rights – or the human rights culture . . . they are normative, or reason- giving, standards of a certain kind.' See John Tasioulas, 'On the Nature of Human Rights', in *The Philosophy of Human Rights: Contemporary Controversies,* edited by Gerhard Ernst and Jan-Christoph-Jan Heilinger (Berlin: de Gruyter, 2012), p. 17. Although, interestingly, Tasioulas himself is not concerned with indeterminacy: 'it is almost always the case that, for any given right, its effective realization will depend on a more precise specification of its associated duties – the content of the duties and their bearers – than pure moral reasoning itself will yield. The more precise specification will be provided by some mode of social fiat, such as social convention or positive law. But it will be a demand of pure moral reasoning itself that convention or law take up the slack in these cases, and the convention and law must operate within rough but objective parameters identified by that reasoning. . . . To create a properly workable standard in each case, we must supplement the deliverances of pure moral reasoning with publicly accessible standards detailing what counts as torture or who is entitled to what level of health care from whom.' See John Tasioulas, 'Towards a Philosophy of Human Rights', *Current Legal Problems* 65, no. 1 (2012): pp. 17–18.

51 Charles Beitz and Robert Goodin, 'Basic Rights and Beyond', in *Global Basic Rights*, edited by Charles Beitz and Robert Goodin (Oxford: Oxford University Press, 2009), p. 14.

52 Tom Campbell, *Rights: A Critical Introduction* (New York: Routledge, 2006), p. 3. See also James Griffin, *On Human Rights* (Oxford: Oxford University Press, 2008), pp. 35–37.

53 Ronald Dworkin, *Taking Rights Seriously* (London: Harvard University Press, 1977), p. 188.

54 Some would describe it as a 'manifesto right' (O'Neil), or, even fiercer, as a 'hopelessly utopian gesture' in the words of Tasioulas, see Tasioulas, 'The Modern Reality of Human Rights', p. 79. The purported right to happiness, for instance, seems to provide a clear example of such a 'right' as it fails most of these core conditions simultaneously.

55 Biltchitz, Poverty and Fundamental Human Rights, p. 217.

56 King, Judging Social Rights, p. 36.

57 He then uses a technical distinction, common in other areas of law, between obligations of result and obligations of conduct to try to defend this point. While obligations of conduct require from duty holders 'steps in a certain fashion, without achieving any particular result', obligations of result requires duty holders 'to achieve a result with discretion as to the means'. In his view, the indeterminacy of social rights corresponding duties simply indicate they are obligations of conduct. I find the argument unpersuasive. Obligations of conduct in other areas of law have a much greater degree of concreteness than the progressive obligation to fulfil social rights. Take King's example of the obligation to 'behave reasonably', a classic case of an obligation of conduct recurrent in tort law. The duty not to cause harm through unreasonable behaviour, even in complex cases such as medical negligence, can usually be specified to reasonable detail with the help of medical experts. Even in extremely complex surgical procedures where surgeons cannot guarantee success, for instance, there are nonetheless consensual state of the art techniques and procedures she must follow in order to fulfil her obligation of conduct and not incur in negligence. The same is not true of the obligation to 'take expeditious steps to the maximum of available resources' to fulfil social rights. See King, *Judging Social Rights*, p. 36.

58 Griffin, *On Human Rights*, p. 100. Nickel seems to be making a similar point when he talks of 'rights that are undersupported by their associated duties and hence misleadingly formulated. If we proclaim a specific right to food or education, but support it only with duties to try to ensure the availability of food or education, the right is undersupported. A more accurate description of the right would be to say that people have a right that their

governments try to provide food or education.' See Nickel, *Making Sense of Human Rights*, p. 151. I have no space to discuss here attempts made within the weak basic needs conception to make it stronger through the idea of a minimum core. My own view is that it does not succeed due to its implausibility (the distinction between core and non-core rights is artificial) and lack of clarity, as no specific proposal is put forward on how to define the so-called minimum core. For a good survey of the literature, see Young, *Constituting Social Rights.*

59 This is partly due, in my view, to the unhelpful language used in the formulation of these rights in the International Covenant, where their corresponding duties are qualified with the ambiguous expressions 'maximum available resources' and 'progressive realization'.

60 Ronald Dworkin, *Taking Rights Seriously* (Cambridge: Harvard University Press, 1977), p. 370.

61 For a good entry point to this debate and an interesting argument see Philippe Van Parijs 'Why Surfers Should Be Fed: The Liberal Case for an Unconditional Basic Income', *Philosophy & Public Affairs* 20, no. 2 (Spring 1991), pp. 101–131.

62 Nickel, *Making Sense of Human Rights*, p. 148. For a similar argument focused on the right to health see Norman Daniels, *Just Health: Meeting Health Needs Fairly* (Cambridge: Cambridge University Press, 2008), especially chapter 12.

63 Unless, of course, one adopts a global approach to social justice, whose discussion I have deliberately not engaged with in this chapter.

64 This point is in my view overlooked by Elisabeth Anderson when she claims that liberal egalitarians would allow the needy to perish whenever their deprivation cannot be attributed to circumstances beyond their control. See Elisabeth Anderson, 'What Is the Point of Equality?', *Ethics* 102, no. 2 (1999): 287.

65 These complexities is part of what attracts some, like Campbell, to what he calls the 'uncomplicated moral duty of humanity' as the best basis for social rights: 'Here we come up against the initial difficulty . . . not because widespread and severe poverty is less significantly morally than deprivation of the right to vote or systematic torture, but because the causes and cure of poverty are much more elusive, much more controversial, and challenging than most other human rights déficits.' See Campbell, 'Poverty as a Violation of Human Rights', p. 58. See also the interesting article by Allen Buchanan, 'A Right to a Decent Minimum of Health', *Philosophy and Public Affairs* 13, no. 1 (1984): 55. Buchanan suggests enforced beneficence and a plurality of other reasons as the most plausible justification for a right to a decent minimum of health.

66 Another important problem is that even our choices are partly pre-determined by our circumstances. 'If one's preferences are themselves influenced by disadvantage during the period of their formation, any sophisticated theory of psychology should not hold the individual responsible for their consequences. Of course, what these authors fear is that there is a danger of sacrificing liberalism: one could argue that a slippery slope leads from including the effect of circumstances on effort as a circumstance to denying people freedom of choice. To say we must be aware of the slippery slope is not the same as saying that we should assign the person complete responsibility for his preferences once he reaches the age of consent. Slippery slopes should be treated with care, not abolished.' See Anders Bjorklund, Markus Jantti and John E. Roemer, *Equality of Opportunity and the Distribution of Long-Run Income in Sweden* (Bonn, Institute for the Study of Labor, 2011), p. 26.

67 Richard Arneson, 'Egalitarian Justice Versus the Right to Privacy', *Social Philosophy and Policy* 17, no. 2 (2000): p. 97. One further problem highlighted by Arneson is related to privacy: the problem is that versions of egalitarianism that seek to accommodate concerns of personal responsibility and deservingness appear to require for their implementation vast amounts of what would otherwise be private and merely personal information about people's lives. See Arneson, 'Egalitarian Justice Versus the Right to Privacy', p. 107.

68 Francois Bourguignon, Francisco H. G. Ferreira and Marta Mendez, 'Inequality of Opportunity in Brazil', *Review of Income and Wealth* 53, no. 4 (2007): p. 615; Francisco Ferreira and Jeremie Gignoux, 'The Measurement of Inequality of Opportunity: Theory and Application to Latin America', *Review of Income and Wealth* 57, no. 4 (2011): p. 652; Arnaud LeFranc, Nicolas Pistolesi and Alain Trannoy, 'Equality of Opportunity and Luck: Definitions and Testable Conditions, With an Application to Income in France', *Journal of Public Economics*

93 (2009): p. 1189; Joseph Stiglitz, *The Price of Inequality: How Today's Divided Society Endangers Our Future* (New York: W.W. Norton & Company, 2013).

69 Jose R. Molinas, et al., Do Our Children Have a Chance? The 2010 Human Opportunity Report for Latin America and the Caribbean (Washington: The World Bank, 2010).

70 Sakiko Fukkuda-Parr, Terra Lawson-Remer and Susan Randolph, *Fulfilling Social and Economic Rights* (Oxford: Oxford University Press, 2015).

71 Bernard Williams, *In the Beginning Was the Deed: Realism and Moralism in Political Argument* (Princeton: Princeton University Press, 2005), p. 73.

10 The politics of human rights and finance

David Kinley

On 23 December 2001, Argentina's President Adolfo Rodriguez Saá announced that his government would not be repaying a forthcoming instalment due on a large segment of the country's external debts, thereby precipitating the biggest sovereign debt default in history. All told, Argentina's sovereign debt – comprising bonds issued by the state and sold on the global capital markets – stood at $82 billion. It was the President's first day in office.

Though not entirely unexpected – Argentina had endured nearly a decade of economic recession that had recently reached crisis levels with widespread rioting resulting in 26 deaths and the ousting of two of Mr Saá's presidential predecessors in just two weeks – the default nevertheless triggered a cascade of dire consequences. The most immediate and direct result was Argentina being effectively locked out of the international capital markets. International banks and other financiers simply refused to lend to the country and those that were already holding defaulted bonds sued the state for their full repayment. With borrowing no longer an option, the only avenue open to the government to keep paying its bills, the salaries of its employees, and the costs of running its public services and welfare programmes, was to print money.

This is precisely what it proceeded to do, after first jettisoning the peso's peg to the United States dollar, which action led directly to accelerating inflation and an exacerbation of the economic and social woes that precipitated the default in the first place. Unemployment soared to 21.5%, salaries and wages were slashed, welfare programmes were cut or abandoned and people's bank accounts were frozen. Stable foods became so expensive that hunger and malnutrition posed a serious and growing problem (and this in a country that had long been considered the breadbasket of South America), while the economy shrank, by 4.4% in 2001, and by 10.9% in 2002.[1] Social and political unrest also continued, with regular mass protests aimed at the government's handling of the crisis. President Saá himself lasted only four days in the position, and his successor (Eduardo Duhalde) held the Presidency for just 16 months.

Living standards and human rights protections of Argentinians suffered accordingly. With nearly 60% of the population living in poverty, and 25% living in extreme poverty, people were neither able adequately to maintain human rights standards themselves, nor to rely on the state to step in to help them do so.[2] With the economy in meltdown, society in turmoil and the government paralyzed by political conflict and incompetence, the safety-net of public services failed at the very time it was most needed. The health system in particular was squeezed from both sides, with an enormous spike in people needing medical assistance at the same time as the health budget was being severely cut. Even basic medicines and medical procedures were either unavailable or interminably delayed, and the health of the old, the young and the poor were seriously jeopardized.[3]

The civil unrest also raised the undesirable spectre of the army in government. Having endured 30 years of military dictatorship that had ended in 1983, Argentinians were especially resentful of the government's 'criminalization of social protest' at this time. The use of the military for civilian control marked increases in instances of killings, torture and excessive use of force by the security forces,[4] as well as a supine judiciary that failed to exercise any effective oversight of these encroachments on basic civil and political rights, all added to a sense of a society in crisis.[5]

One of the government's greatest challenges during this period was to negotiate the terms upon which it could restructure the defaulted bonds. The reconstruction of such enormous debts was never going to be easy, and as a matter of fact the resolution has been long and torturous. It took nearly 10 years (in two stages: 2005 and 2010) before Argentina was able to settle on new repayment terms regarding the majority of its creditors, who together held 92% of the debt. These creditors accepted repayment at the level of roughly 30 cents in the dollar, and while a 'haircut' of 70% was evidently a substantial loss, it was, as they collectively accepted, better than nothing and likely to be as good as they would get.[6] However, even then, it was not until 2016 that this particular episode in Argentina's sovereign debt history was finally brought to a close.

On the face of it, these initial settlements offered the Argentinian government a 'get out of jail' card. However, no agreement had been reached with the so-called 'holdout' creditors, who commanded the outstanding 8% of the defaulted debt. Many of these, in the meantime, had sold their debt, at hugely discounted prices,[7] to hedge funds (disparagingly labelled 'vulture funds') specializing in recovering distressed debt. The vulture funds had duly pursued repayment of the defaulted bonds in full, including accumulated interest, which was estimated to amount to some $15 billion by early 2013.[8] In effect, the country was held to ransom. One of the reasons why the dispute with the holdouts dragged on for so long was because of the inclusion of 'Rights Upon Future Offers' (RUFO) clauses in both sets of restructured bonds in the 2005 and 2010 settlements which prohibited the government volunteering better deals to the holdouts. The existence of the RUFO (or *pari passu)* clauses, together with the absence of a collective action clause in the sovereign bonds as originally issued (which would have compelled all bondholders to agree to any restructured deals once a certain threshold level of agreement among bondholders had been reached – typically 75% or 80%),[9] had two perverse and, for Argentina, especially damaging consequences.

First, some of the holdouts successfully sued Argentina in the US courts. These same creditors had previously sought court orders, with limited success, in other national jurisdictions to impound Argentinian state assets such as aircrafts of the national airline, overseas deposits of the Central Bank, the Presidential plane, and even an Argentinian Navy training ship.[10] In the US however, one holdout hedge fund NML Capital, had prevailed in all 11 actions it had brought against Argentina in the New York District Court for recovery of its debt.[11] Then, in June 2014, NML obtained a US Supreme Court judgment confirming its unfettered rights of discovery in respect of Argentinian assets held anywhere in the world that might be acquired by NML in executing the outstanding judgments in its favour.[12] In effect, this gave NML the green light to pursue Argentina for the total of $2.5 billion (comprising principal and accumulated interest) it claimed it was owed by country. As NML had paid just under $50 million for $220 million of Argentina's defaulted bonds in 2002,[13] the Supreme Court order represented what was potentially a staggering 5,000% return on investment.[14]

More damaging for Argentina, however, was the fact that this judgment was then used as the basis for a further US District Court ruling that barred the Argentine government from paying interest to the holders of the restructured bonds until it had first paid its debt to NML and other holdout creditors. Argentina was now in an impossible situation, caught between its contractual obligations to its bondholders (by way of the RUFO clauses prohibiting paying the holdouts any more than the holders of the restructured bonds) and the court ordered demands of NML (which included an injunction against any financial institution facilitating Argentina's payment of interest on the restructured bonds).[15] In the end, and despite intense negotiations with its creditors facilitated by a court-appointed mediator, Argentina complied with neither side's demands, and so by failing to pay the interest due on its bonds, the government was once again in default.

The second detrimental consequence arose from the fact that the RUFO clauses were subject to a sunset provision, expiring at the end of 2014. In other words, come 1 January 2015, a critical impediment to Argentina agreeing to settle with the holdouts on terms better than offered to the restructured bondholders would have been removed. That is, if Argentina wanted to settle.[16]

The answer to that question came 10 months later in November 2015 when Argentina elected right-wing Mauricio Macri to the Presidency on a mandate to fix the economy. Shortly after taking office the Macri government opened negotiations with the holdouts and by late February 2016 it had reached agreements with nearly all of them. But at a considerable cost. Overall, Argentina agreed to pay $7.1 billion, on terms that amount to a write down of just 25% for these bondholders, compared to the 70% loss accepted by the 2005 and 2010 restructured bondholders.[17]

With the door now open to raising capital on the international financial markets for the first time in 15 years, Argentina looks like turning a new page in its troubled economic history over the past 60 years. Time will tell, but in any event the country's recovery is likely to be long and challenging.[18]

There are many lessons to be learned from this complicated saga, but in respect of how to approach the human rights dimensions of such events there seems to be one enduring message. It is that the human rights standards enjoyed by the least able in society are very often the first and the most to suffer when a state faces sovereign debts of such dimensions as to cripple its financial capabilities. For it is those dependent on state welfare, those reliant on public services (in health, education, housing, power, water and food), that typically shoulder the cuts to services as a government strives to repay its mounting external debts. The economic imperative – at least up to the point of a debt restructuring or default – simply trumps the moral, and even legal, imperatives that states are obliged to honour their commitments under international human rights treaties. I say 'even legal', because under the UN International Covenant on **Economic, Social and Cultural Rights** (ICESCR), for example, a state is obliged to utilize 'the maximum of its available resources' to ensure the full realization of the rights in the Covenant. 'The implication' being, as Cephas Lumina, the former UN Independent Expert on Foreign Debt and Human Rights in his report of his mission to Argentina in 2013, that the state must ensure the adequate protection of these rights 'before using public resources to achieve other state objectives unrelated to human rights, such as debt service'.[19] In practice, however, that is often not the order of priority employed by heavily indebted states.

1 Lessons of politics and economics

Political lessons can also be drawn for human rights' intersection with the world of high finance. That is, lessons in the broad sense of the many machinations of the political economy, including the political drivers and outputs of finance in so far as they impact on the standards of living of ordinary people and the human rights-respecting capacities of nations. Finance is vital to human rights. It is essential in enabling individuals themselves to achieve and satisfy standards of rights enjoyment that they expect and warrant, and it is indispensible to governments to provide basic rights protection for those unable to provide for themselves. Behind the question of what moneys are spent on protecting human rights, there lie foundational questions of whether and how finance is raised, earned or otherwise obtained. Human rights standards are therefore affected both by the accumulation and dispersal of finance.

As they stand, such broad statements are unlikely to attract any serious quarrel. Over the past 15 years or so there has been a steady rise in academic and policy-making interest in, and basic understanding of, the enabling role of finance, as well as the human rights consequences of its absence, squander or theft. A number of UN human rights treaty bodies, especially the Committee on Economic, Social and Cultural Rights, have made explicit reference to the budgetary choices made by states in light of their obligations under the ICESCR.[20] UN Special Rapporteurs have incorporated economic and financial analyses in their reports under their respective mandates, including those working on the right to water (on questions of privatization);[21] the right to housing (mortgage finance);[22] on the right to food (commodities trading);[23] the right to health (access to and pricing of essential medicines);[24] foreign debt (sovereign debts default and restructuring);[25] and on extreme poverty and human rights (tax policy).[26] A small number of human rights academics have outlined the complexity of the finance/human rights relationship,[27] or warned of the dangerous gap in understanding between the two fields,[28] and made some initial suggestions as to reform.[29] Policy reviewers, such as the now well-established 'rightingfinance' commentary,[30] and a recent report from the Institute for Human Rights and Business,[31] have sought to enliven debate on the present and possible future nature of the relationship in actual practice.

Welcome and important though these incursions into finance are, the community of human rights scholars, activists and policy makers have barely scratched the surface of what finance does, and is capable of doing, in ways that profoundly impact levels of respect, protection and promotion of human rights.

There is, for example, a natural tendency to focus on public sector finances – that is, the capacity of, and means by which, governments raise and spend public funds. But this tells only half the story. For it is upon private/personal financial means that the vast majority of people rely to fulfil their human rights needs as best they can. The state's role in the financial provision of human rights protection is facilitative, rather than direct; supplementary, rather than wholesale. International human rights law requires states to provide adequate levels of security, order and fairness, as well as access to basic health care and educational facilities, which obligations, in practice, states honour to widely differing degrees. In fact, most people rely on their own efforts and means to provide life's basic necessities, to foster families and friends, and to building and governing communities. The garnering of sufficient financial resources (large or small) by individuals and their families to attend to these human rights needs depends mainly on people living off the fruits of their labours, or by selling their produce, possessions or skills. The state's broader role in this is to help establish and maintain economic conditions that provide people with the employment, trading or transactional opportunities to obtain an income and build wealth, no matter how modest. The availability and access to finance, in other words, directly enables both governments and individuals to protect, respect and promote human rights needs and obligations.

Finance – or more accurately, the financial system – also dictates human rights' fortunes in ways that are indirect, but no less significant. Local economies are today materially shaped by the exigencies of global finance, such that the capacity of states, communities, families and individuals to deliver on human rights expectations may be positively or negatively affected by the circumstances far beyond their control, knowledge or even awareness. The need for human rights discourse to engage more thoroughly with the political intrigues of finance, both locally and globally, is imperative.

2 The thrall of finance

As an essential feature of economic relations, finance has long impacted on how individuals and communities obtain the desired social derivatives of the good (or at least better) life. In one form or another, finance governs almost every aspect of our lives. Every day and everywhere, people are using the financial system to borrow to build homes and businesses, to insure their health and death, to invest in their futures through education and pension funds, to feed and clothe themselves and their children, to receive payment for their labours or the goods they sell, and to help others in need.

Increased wealth brings benefits, especially to those most in need. The marginal utility of increased wealth for the world's poorest can be very significant. According to World Bank data, global levels of absolute poverty have dropped from 42.15% of the world's population in 1981 to 10.68% in 2013.[32] For those lifted out of abject poverty, this can mean the difference between bare survival and a life with prospects and plans, no matter how modest. Access to formal financial services of any kind can also impact significantly on people's lives. Nearly everyone in rich states has had direct exposure, or access, to formal financial services – even if for some (and especially the less well off), the experience have been chastening or harmful. For most people in poor states, access to regulated, or even semi-regulated, financial services may be entirely novel, and despite being expensive by Western standards (interest rates on micro-finance loans, for example, are notoriously much higher than rich country loan rates),[33] nevertheless opens doors of opportunity not previously available. It is precisely this potential to transform lives that has helped fuel the exponential growth of mobile money services in some of the world's poorest states across sub-Saharan Africa.[34] Finance, it is clear, can be benign, safe and convenient; a force for good that protects and promotes human rights.

But finance can also cause great harm to people's human rights standards. For the poor, and for poor states, its absence or inadequacy is compelling. Monetary poverty for those who remain abjectly poor (the above-mentioned 10.7% of the global population – some 767 million people) is a key factor in their lack of basic rights to adequate food, health care, education and housing.[35] Disparities in wealth are huge between the haves and the have nots, as are their relative capacities to secure human rights that follow therefrom. Today, 'the richest 10% of adults own 87% of all wealth, and the top 1% account for almost half of all assets in the world.'[36] And the gap is widening. By virtue of the simple but exponential power of compound interest, those with interest-attracting capital are, according to Thomas Piketty, getting richer much quicker than those with little or no capital.[37] No less significantly, the human rights standards of many in developing states are further undermined by the huge flows of illicit finance (including monies from corruption, tax evasion and theft) out of the world's poorest states, currently running at over $1 trillion per annum,[38] an amount equivalent to more than eight times global aid provided to those same developing countries.[39]

Globalization has been the vector through which the fortunes of finance have been funnelled, both to the good and bad effects for human rights. As nearly all states have become richer, so have their citizens, albeit in often highly unequal proportions with the already haves getting far more than the have nots (or have little). Yet it is possible now, as modern globalization approaches its middle age, to see distinct differences between how citizens in developed states respond to wealth disparities, as compared to those in developing or emerging economies. In rich world democracies, sustained and gross iniquities of wealth distribution have fed the widespread anger and discontent that lies behind such system-bucking electoral outcomes as the United Kingdom's Brexit and Donald Trump's ascendency to the US presidency. It is not surprising, therefore, to find that in the West today there is significantly less enthusiasm for globalization and the head-long pursuit of international free trade.[40] This is contrast to many states in the developing world where support for globalization, warts and all, is generally much higher, and even increasing in those countries whose GDP has grown fastest in recent years, such as India, Indonesia, the Philippines and, most of all, Vietnam.[41] It seems that the people of these states believe they stand to gain from even modest increases in wealth, and that the prospect or potential of further and greater social gains from increases in disposable income emboldens their viewpoint.

Irrespective of where any of us sit on this spectrum of responses to globalization, the fundamentals of finance upon which our greater global economic integration has been built have shifted. From the crude manipulation of currency exchange rates that enrich autocrats in Asia and Africa to the sophisticated rigging of lending rates between banks that benefit bankers in Europe and North America, a combination of light-touch regulation, untrammelled access to debt, and the fetishization of greed has transformed finance from a boringly predictable servant of the economy to its capricious master.[42]

Social concerns, including human rights impacts, are externalities from a financial system's perspective – irrelevant to its functioning and someone else's responsibility (namely, the state). Finance's job is being done when the monetary pie is grown as large as possible, no matter the consequences of the process, nor the distribution of the gains, provided some 'trickles down' through the rest of society. The state's regulatory role ought to be minimalist, or at least no more than is necessary to ensure that the pie-enlarging system functions as efficiently as it can.[43]

However the consequences cannot be overlooked; least of all by states encumbered by significant obligations under international human rights law or under their own constitutions and other domestic laws.[44] Financial capacity is, as noted earlier, recognized in these instruments as an essential pre-requisite to the adequate protection and promotion of human rights. The efficient and effective functioning of finance is of critical importance and not therefore something that those concerned with human rights can afford to ignore. But efficacy cannot be a *raison d'etre*. And certainly not when efficacy is sought in order to claim even greater rewards for the few, while the gains for many are minimal or non-existent. Above all, it cannot be a valid excuse not to manage finance in ways that advance human rights goals rather than allow the system to disregard or flout them.

Yet this precisely what has been happening. Whether by design or inadvertency, human rights goals have been marginalized and standards maligned through the globe-spanning regulatory edifice that finance, with the active support of states, has built for itself. The sovereign debt crisis that was allowed to accrue over decades in so many of the world's poorest states, and its lingering aftermath, is a poignant symptom of this malaise, and the Argentinian experience just one of its latest presentations.

Many of these states are, or have been, considerably worse off than Argentina. Léonce Ndikumana and James Boyce have documented the long, lamentable history of poor African states taking on more debt than they can ever hope to repay. A toxic combination of corrupt and larcenous leaders, weak and unstable economies and imprudent (at best) or callous and greedy lenders has, in nearly all of these cases, brought the borrowing state to the edge of ruin. The leaders and lenders have done exceedingly well out of the transaction and have left the poor state's citizens (and often the generations that follow them) to pay the bill. 'This is disastrous for African development', as Ndikumana and Boyce put it, precisely because 'private incentives are not aligned with the public good.'[45]

3 Reclaiming finance

The important point here is to recognize that none of this was inevitable; the consequence of the irresistible force of finance, as it were. The system that has created these problems, or at least the conditions in which they have been able flourish, has been a political exercise; one born of the self-perpetuating, persuasive power of finance over our economies and systems of government. Financiers have infiltrated the government agencies meant to regulate them through the so-called 'revolving door', and have held legislatures hostage by convincing them that what is good for the finance sector is good for the economy and society.[46] Bankers have tagged themselves the smartest guys in the room and demanded to be paid accordingly – we 'tell the corporate lawyers what to do and make much more money', as one Wall Street interviewee told anthropologist Karen Hoh.[47] And tax regimes systematically favour the rich over the poor, capital over income, and big corporations over small – as Warren Buffett famously illustrated when he compared his effective tax rate (17.7%) with that of everyone else working in his office (which averaged 32.9%),[48] and as reflected in the elaborate, highly profitable, and legal, tax avoidance schemes employed by many of the world's largest corporations.[49]

As a consequence of the successful exercise of political power over the past 30 years, limits on bank borrowing have been relaxed and debt levels (of governments, companies, banks and individuals) have all soared; regulatory controls of capital markets loosened, and extreme risk-taking institutionalized.[50] Most incredibly, financiers have effectively recast the social contract between governments and their citizens, whereby states not only encourage the banking sector to ratchet up debt and risk, they effectively guarantee the system against collapse by underwriting big banks with public money. The state-funded bank bailouts following the 2007/08 global financial crisis – which for the US alone necessitated a total Federal Reserve commitment in excess of USD$29 trillion[51] – were, collectively, the most expensive example of financial moral hazard the world has ever seen.

The management of sovereign debt has been swept up in this powerful tide of financial pre-eminence with, as we have seen, predictably malign effects for poorer states. However, the history of sovereign debt over the last 20 years or so has also provided some grounds for cautious hope that politics and finance can be used in ways that have more benign impacts.

The very acknowledgement that some sovereign debts are odious is itself an important step forward. An odious debt may provide sufficient reason to question the erstwhile sanctity of the debt contract, on the grounds that its illegitimate provenance (having been used in ways that 'were not beneficial or were harmful to the interests of the population')[52] renders it unenforceable against subsequent governments and citizens of the relevant state. Given those who have inherited such a debt, the reasoning goes, were neither consenting parties to the original contract nor its beneficiaries, so they ought not to be left to shoulder servicing the debt.

The moral arguments against the injustice of such inherited debts, quite apart from their ruinous economic impacts on many developing states, gave rise to a turn-of-the-century wave of political pressure to forgive part or all of such debts. Public lenders (developed states and multilateral development banks) backed the establishment of the Highly Indebted Poor Countries (HIPC) initiative in 1996 (to be supplemented by the Multilateral Debt Relief Initiative (MDRI) in 2005), which has provided a process and conditions by which these lenders have forgiven debt.[53] Some have argued that this display of moral conscience has coincided with a growing 'respect for actual self-determination, human rights, and internal governance' in international relations, which has had the direct – if somewhat unexpected – effect of 'undermin[ing] the most stringently statist approaches to sovereign debt, in which assessments of the nature and efficacy of internal rule are considered irrelevant.'[54] The UN General Assembly has also formulated a set of *Basic Principles on Sovereign Debt Restructuring Processes* that underline 'the obligation of sovereign debtors and their creditors to act in good faith and with a co-operative spirit to reach a consensual rearrangement of the debt of sovereign States'.[55] And, more particularly, the UN Human Rights Council endorsed a set of *Guiding Principles on Foreign Debt and Human Rights* in 2012 that seek to 'strike an appropriate balance between the obligations of States arising from their external debt arrangements and under international human rights law.'[56]

Progress in this respect has been made mostly in the public sector sphere with state-based lenders. Debt relief extended to poor states by private creditors has been meagre, even when these states default and the loan is restructured. Economist John Wright has noted that after defaults and restructuring, the debt-to-GDP ratios of low income countries in respect of private creditors rose by an average of 50%, and for sub-Saharan states it more than doubled.[57] In other words, where some, or even many, public sector creditors are prepared to forgive debts when poor states reach crisis points, private creditors are not.

The rapacity of the private sector in this area is most strikingly illustrated by the single-minded behaviour of vulture funds (such as those involved in Argentina's case as discussed above), when they purchase distressed or defaulted debt (including poor states' sovereign debts) cheaply and then purse the debtor, often by way of litigation, for full repayment. While nearly all public lenders have agreed not to sell their debts to such funds,[58] no such commitment has been forthcoming from private sector banks. The deleterious economic, social and human rights impacts of such exploitative pursuit of debts,[59] as well as the paradoxical effects they have on countries that are at the same time receiving debt relief under the HIPC initiative, has prompted both political and regulatory responses. Belgium and the UK, for example, have both enacted legislation that effectively prohibits vulture funds from litigating within their respective national jurisdictions,[60] though in the US courts, as discussed above in respect of NML Capital's pursuit of Argentinian assets, the practice is still alive and well.

4 Beyond the thrall

Finance's thrall is broad and powerful. But where the political will exists, neither finance in general, nor specifically the management of sovereign debt, are beyond regulatory control and reform. Beyond the necessary political motivation, much depends on the levels of institutional competence and accountability if financial relations are to be regulated in ways that protect and promote human rights. For even in apparently relatively discrete matters such as the taking on and servicing of sovereign debt, the ramifications can be far-reaching and profound. In the Argentinian story, for example, there are few commendable players. Banks, governments, courts, creditors and debt collectors, have all evidenced various combinations of blindness and bastardry.[61] Argentina's prior history of defaults, and a recent history of poor governance and naïve economic management, would tend to point blame for the national catastrophe squarely at the government. But responsibilities can also be traced back to the financial institutions that extended credit, who were neither blameless, nor innocent victims in the transactions. The 'animal spirits'[62] that drive the highs and lows of finance (of which the 2007/08 global financial crisis is just the latest in a long line of such boom/busts) vividly illustrate how bankers are quite capable of entering into financial arrangements with debtors whom they know, or have not taken care to determine otherwise, are unlikely to be able properly to service the debt, let alone repay it. Just as impecunious aspirant home owners who are poor money managers can be enticed to take on debts far beyond their means (in so-called sub-prime mortgages), so international finance is littered with examples of similarly poorly run countries borrowing way beyond their capacity. Understanding the mercenary culture of finance as much as the technicalities of how it functions are key to achieving a fairer political reconciliation of finance and human rights.

The power and prevalence of finance is a fact of life in modern society. It is therefore neither pragmatic nor politic to ignore or shun its machinations, no matter how repellent and detrimental its impacts can sometimes be. This is especially important for those who wish to harness the best features of finance, while at the same time seeking to redirect or reform other features, to yield greater societal benefits, including wider and deeper human rights protections. The task of better understanding finance, let alone changing it, is challenging, but it cannot and must not be avoided. Engagement between finance and human rights requires both sides to reach across the divide to be sure.

In this context, my concern in this chapter with how it might be achieved from the human rights side in the particular circumstance of the management of sovereign debt, is but one part of a large puzzle. But it does provide some pointers in the right direction. In addition to the above-mentioned UN's 2012 *Guiding Principles on Foreign Debt and Human Rights basic*, academic and practitioner Danny Bradlow, for example, has formulated a tightly reasoned argument for applying the much broader UN *Guiding Principles on Business and Human Rights 2011* (UNGPs),[63] to sovereign debt restructurings which, as he notes, 'carr[y] high risk[s] of having adverse human rights impacts on at least some of the stakeholders'.[64] The particular value of Bradlow's contention lies in its focus on the human rights responsibilities of commercial, or private, lenders which, as we have seen, are often flying beneath the radar of socially-aware sovereign debt management. The UNGPs, he concludes, offer a set of human rights expectations that can be fairly made of financial businesses within the 'complex economic, financial and political contexts' in which sovereign debt restructurings are negotiated.[65]

Another innovative perspective on the problem has come from Juan Pablo Bohoslavsky's work as the UN Independent Expert on the Effects of Foreign Debt and Human Rights. He argues that the foundational international law principle of *pacta sunt servanda*,[66] can be used as a vehicle to reconcile a state's sovereign debt obligations with its human rights obligations. The two sets of obligations are, on their face, equally imposing on states. However, there are crucial differences. A state's debt is typically established by way of a contract between the state and the public or private sector creditor. International human rights obligations, on the other hand, are established through international legal instruments entered into directly with other states, and indirectly with the state's own people. Though debt obligations are normally binding, they are not absolute. As such, Bohoslavsky reasons, they are subject to limitations where meeting the debt obligations would seriously diminish the state's capacity to protect basic human rights, such as where a heavily indebted poor state is forced to direct public funds to debt repayments that might otherwise be used for welfare payments or other social services.[67]

These examples of bridging initiatives are relatively minor, and somewhat legally-oriented, but they are significant and have distinct political undertones. Soft and hard international law arguments can provide a leading edge in building consensus (among governments and even bankers, as well as civil society) that wider considerations must be taken on by financiers when they lend to poor states and how they pursue their repayment. The expectation being not only that the lenders acknowledge these broader social dimensions to their otherwise commercial transactions, but also that they shoulder greater responsibilities for the consequences of their actions.

5 Conclusion

In one of his perceptive forays into the philosophy and practice of human rights, Amartya Sen has suggested that perhaps one of the reasons why human rights activists are so often 'quite impatient' with expressions of intellectual scepticism of such rights is because 'many of those who invoke human rights are concerned with changing the world rather than interpreting it'.[68] If there is overriding motivation behind a political approach to human rights then it must be to try to merge these two perspectives. In the context of the subject matter of this chapter, I have striven to do so by interpreting, albeit through the particular case of poor countries' sovereign debt, how the world of finance works from the perspective of human rights; what problems it causes, as well as pointing towards the benefits it can bring. Above all, it is important to recognize that finance and human rights are necessarily and intimately related aspects of human society. Neither exists, nor can flourish, in the absence of the other, no matter how often their separation is casually assumed or fervently asserted. Their interdependency is unavoidable, even if the consequences of their intersection can crush as well as liberate the lives of countries, communities and individuals. This is the nature of the realm of politics in which finance and human rights co-exist. For although human rights comprise important moral and legal claims in the ways societies operate today, they are also and always creatures of politics – moulded, facilitated, challenged and compromised by political forces.

Notes

1 World Bank, 'Poverty and Equity Databank – Argentina', 2016, http://povertydata.worldbank.org/poverty/country/ARG.

2 See Carlos G. Fernández Valdovinos, 'Growth, Poverty and Social Equity in Argentina', *World Bank, En Breve,* no. 82 (November 2005): pp. 1–4.

3 The former UN Independent Expert on Foreign Debt and Human Rights, Cephas Lumina, for example, reported that during the crisis infant mortality rates in the poorer northern parts of the country had risen to 25 per 1,000 live births (it was 17 for the country as a whole in 2003, compared to 8 per 1,000 live births in Chile in that year), see Cephas Lumina, *Report on Mission to Argentina 18–29 November 2013,* UN Doc A/HRC/25/50/Add3 (2 April 2014), para.14 and World Bank data on infant mortality rates by country, available at World Bank, 'Mortality Rate, Infant (per 1,000 Live Births)', 2016, http://data.worldbank.org/indicator/SP.DYN.IMRT.IN.

4 Human Rights Watch, in its 2002 country report on Argentina, noted that 'police killed some 266 people in the last six months of 2000 and the first six months of 2001' in protests held across the country; see Human Rights Watch, 'Argentina', 2016, www.hrw.org/legacy/wr2k2/americas1.html.

5 See Inter-American Commission on Human Rights, 'Visit to Argentinian Republic', Press Release, 6 August 2002.

6 See Matt Levine, 'Argentina's Bond Fight Come Down to Its Worst Bonds', *Bloomberg View*, 8 February 2016.

7 See below, at notes 13 and 14 and accompanying text.

8 J.F. Hornbeck, 'Argentina's Defaulted Sovereign Debt: Dealing With the Holdouts', Congressional Research Service, 6 February 2013, p. 8.

9 Which constitutes, for Argentina, a potentially extremely costly oversight in legal drafting, if – as some duly did (see below) – the holdouts obtain court orders in their favour regarding repayment, or are able to negotiate financial settlements with Argentina on terms far more generous terms than those extended to the other bondholders. See Jon Hartley, 'Argentina's Default: Lessons Learned, What Happens Next?', *Forbes*, 4 August 2014.

10 See Shane Romig, 'Argentina Grounds President's Plane', *Wall Street Journal*, 7 January 2013.

11 In yet another legal drafting twist to this saga, Argentina was deemed to be unable to defend its assets by claiming sovereign immunity on account of the broad waiver of sovereign immunity claims that Argentina had agreed to in the terms of the original bonds contracts – as noted by the US Supreme Court in the judgment cited in the following note.

12 *Republic of Argentina v. NML Capital, Ltd.*, 134 S. Ct. 2250 (decided 16 June 2014)

13 See Independent Expert Lumina, *Report on Mission to Argentina*, note 2, at para. 32.

14 Though the size of the debt owed to NML had previously been estimated at $1.33 billion in an earlier District Court case. See *NML Capital, Ltd. v. Republic of Argentina*, Nos. 08-cv-6978(TPG), 09-cv-1707(TPG), 09-cv-1708(TPG), 2012 WL 5895784 (S.D.N.Y. Nov. 21, 2012)), but even this figure promised a return of around 2,700%.

15 NML Capital, Ltd. v. Republic of Argentina. On which issue, see further, Anna Gelpern and Mark Weidemaier, 'Injunctions in Sovereign Debt Litigation', Yale Journal on Regulation 31 (2014): p. 189.

16 The Argentine Congress had also previously passed legislation (the so-called Lock Law) that had in effect enshrined the RUFO, *pari passu* clauses in domestic law.

17 Katia Porzecanski, Charlie Devereux and Bob van Voris, 'Paul Singer Cuts Deal With Argentina After Ugly, 15-Year Dispute', *Bloomberg News*, 1 March 2016. Argentina's Lock Law referred to in the previous note was also, necessarily, repealed and the US District Court lifted its injunction against the Argentina paying interest on its other sovereign bondholders, both executed shortly after the deal was concluded with the holdout creditors; see Mark Douglas, 'Sovereign Debt Update – March/April 2016', *Lexology*, 1 April 2016. This settlement also presaged the settlement of another, parallel claim against Argentina brought by some 50,000 Italian creditors before the International Centre for Settlement of Investment Disputes (ICSID) under a bilateral investment treaty between Italy and Argentina; see Caroline Simson, 'Argentina Settles Historic ICSID Row With Italian Bondholders', *Law360*, 2 February 2016.

18 See Moody's Investor Service, 'Argentina Still Faces Long-Term Challenges After Successful Return to Bond Market', 4 May 2016.

19 Report to the UN General Assembly, UN Doc. A/HRC/25/50/Add.3 (2 April 2014), para.37.

20 See, for example, the Committee's remarks regarding the allocation of public funds to protect the right to housing in the Concluding Observations to a number of states' periodic reports (summarized in Ben Saul, David Kinley and Jacqueline Mowbray, *The International Covenant on Economic, Social and Cultural Rights: Commentary, Cases and Materials* (Oxford: Oxford University Press, 2014), pp. 946–951, and in respect budgets to promote of the right to health, see the Committee's General Comments No.3 (1991) and no. 14 (2000).

21 See Report of the Special Rapporteur on the Human Right to Safe Drinking Water and Sanitation (Catarina de Albuquerque), A/HRC/24/44 (11 July 2013).

22 See UN Special Rapporteur on the Right to Housing, Raquel Rolnik, *Annual Report: Right to Housing and the Financial Crisis* (4 February 2009), A/HRC/10/7, para. 43

23 See Special Rapporteur on the Rights to Food, Olivier de Schutter, *Food Commodities Speculation and Food Price Crises*, Briefing Note No.2 (September 2010).

24 See Report of the Special Rapporteur on the Right of Everyone to the Enjoyment of the Highest Attainable Standard of Physical and Mental Health on the Impact of TRIPS on the Right to Health, A/HRC/11/12 (31 March 2009).

25 Relevant reports of the two holders of this mandate are discussed below.

26 Report of the Special Rapporteur on Extreme Poverty and Human Rights, Magdalena Sepúlveda Carmona, on Taxation and Human Rights, UN Doc. A/HRC/26/28 (22 May 2014).

27 Mary Dowell-Jones, 'Financial Institutions and Human Rights', *Human Rights Law Review* 13, no. 3 (2013): p. 423.

28 Aoife Nolan, 'Not Fit for Purpose: Human Rights in Times of Financial and Economic Crisis', *European Rights Law Review* 4 (2015): p. 358, and Mary Dowell-Jones and David Kinley, 'Minding the Gap: Global Finance and Human Rights', *Ethics and International Affairs* 25, no. 2 (2011): pp. 183–210.

29 David Kinley, Necessary Evil: A Human Rights Journey Into the Dark Heart of Finance (New York: Oxford University Press, 2017), ch. 7.

30 See *rightingfinance*, at www.rightingfinance.org/.

31 Institute for Human Rights and Business (IHRB), *Human Rights and Sustainable Finance: Exploring the Relationship*, Inquiry Working Paper 16/01 (February 2016), prepared for the UN Environmental Program Inquiry on the Design of a Sustainable Financial System.

32 Using the poverty line of $1.90 per day (at 2011 purchasing power parity); see World Bank, 'Poverty', 2016, http://data.worldbank.org/topic/poverty.

33 For data and an explanation of this phenomenon, see Pablo Cotler and Deyanira Almazan, 'The Lending Interest Rates in the Microfinance Sector: Searching for Its Determinants', *The Business and Economics Research Journal* 6, no. 1 (2013): p. 69.

34 On the exponential growth of mobile money accounts in developing countries, especially in Sub-Saharan Africa, see World Bank, 'Global Payment Systems Survey 2015' (October 2016 Update), pp. 7–8.

35 Classified as less than $1.90 per day; see World Bank, 'Poverty: Overview', 2016, www.worldbank.org/en/topic/poverty/overview.

36 Credit Suisse, Global Wealth Report 2015, p. 13.

37 Thomas Piketty, *Capital in the Twenty-First Century* (Cambridge: The Belknap Press of Harvard University Press, 2014), see Table 7.2, p. 248.

38 See Dev Kar and Joseph Spanjers, *Illicit Financial Flows From Developing Countries: 2004–2013* (Washington, D.C.: Global Financial Integrity, 2015), in which the authors estimate the annual total for 2013 (the latest available) to be $1.090 trillion; see Table X1, p. vii. The report notes that the annual average increase in illicit financial flows over the past decade has been 6.5% – nearly twice that of global GDP.

39 Total global aid or 'Official Development Assistance' (ODA) in 2014 was $135 billion; see OECD, 'Development Aid Stable in 2014, But Inflows to Poorest Countries Still Falling', 8 April 2015.

40 See, 'League of Nationalists', *The Economist*, 19 November 2016, especially the graph entitled: 'Enough to go around? Attitudes towards globalisation against change in GDP per person'.

41 See, 'League of Nationalists', *The Economist*. In respect of the more sedate (but still high) levels of support for globalization China, another fast growing economy, see Ben Baden, 'WTO Accession, Globalization and a Changing China', *China Business Review*, 1 October 2011.

42 For an overview of this shift, see David Kinley, *Necessary Evil*, ch. 3.

43 See John Quiggin, *Zombie Economics: How Dead Ideas Still Walk Among Us* (Princeton, NJ: Princeton University Press, 2010), for an excoriating as well as entertaining review of such perspectives.

44 As for example, is the case with Argentina – on which point see Sabine Michalowski, *Unconstitutional Regimes and the Validity of Sovereign Debt: A Legal Perspective* (Hampshire: Ashgate, 2007), ch. 7.

45 Léonce Ndikumana and James Boyce, Africa's Odious Debts: How Foreign Loans and Capital Flight Bled a Continent (London: Zed Books, 2011), p. 13.

46 Simon Johnson, 'The Quiet Coup', *The Atlantic*, May 2009.

47 Karen Ho, *Liquidated: An Ethnography of Wall Street* (Durham: Duke University Press, 2009), p. 39.

48 Interview with Tom Brokaw, NBC, 29 October 2007, www.youtube.com/watch?v=Cu5B-2LoC4s

49 See Oxfam, 'Broken at the Top: How America's Dysfunction Tax System Costs Billion in Corporate Tax Dodging', 2016.

50 Adair Turner, Between Debt and the Devil: Money, Credit and Fixing Global Finance (Princeton: Princeton University Press, 2015).
51 See James Felkerson, *$29,000,000,000,000: A Detailed Look at the Fed's Bailout by Funding Facility and Recipient*, The Levy Economics Institute of Bard College, Working Paper No.698 (December 2011).
52 Robert Howse, *The Concept of Odious Debt in Public International Law*, UNCTAD Discussion Paper no.185, (July 2007), p. 2.
53 For details of the processes and the debts that have been forgiven, in part or whole, see IMF, 'Fact Sheet: Debt Relief Under the Heavily Indebted Poor Countries (HIPC) Initiative', 20 September 2016.
54 Odette Lienau, Rethinking Sovereign Debt: Politics, Reputation, and Legitimacy in Modern Finance (Cambridge, MA: Harvard University Press, 2014), pp. 194, 196.
55 See *Resolution Adopted by the General Assembly on 10 September 2015*, UN.Doc. A/RES/69/319 (29 September 2015). Alongside the insistence on the good faith behaviour of both creditors and debtors, the principles also cover respect for the rule of law, and the need to take into account of the social, economic and human rights costs of any restructured agreements entered into.
56 See *Report of the Independent Expert on Foreign Debt and Human Rights*, UN Doc. A/HRC/20/23 (10 April 2011), at para.16; the text of the *Guiding Principles* themselves are appended to this report.
57 Mark Wright, 'Restructuring Sovereign Debts With Private Sector Creditors: Theory and Practice', in *Sovereign Debt and the Financial Crisis: Will This Time Be Different?* edited by Carlos Primo Braga and Galli Vincelette (Washington, DC: World Bank, 2010), pp. 295–296.
58 See Paris Club, 'Press Release on the Threats Posed by Some Litigating Creditors in Heavily Indebted Poor Countries', 22 May 2007.
59 On which see Report of the Human Rights Council Advisory Committee on the Activities of Vulture Funds and the Impact on Human Rights, UN Doc. A/HRC/33/54 (20 July 2016), and UNCTAD, Vulture Funds in Action: Social and Economic Impacts (Background Note, 26 October 2016).
60 Belgium has two relevant laws – one enacted in 2008, that prohibits litigation involving funds originally disbursed as aid, see 'Loi visant à empêcher la saisie ou la cession des fonds publics destinés à la coopération internationale, notamment par la technique des fonds vautours', 6 April 2008, and another, in 2015, that limits the amounts recoverable by a litigant to that which the debtor state paid (via earlier debt restructuring arrangements) to repurchase the loan, thereby effectively removing the incentive to sue, see 'Loi relative à la lutte contre les activités des fonds vautours', 12 July 2015. This second Belgian law was in fact modelled on the approach taken in UK's *Debt Relief (Developing Countries) Act 2010.*
61 For an account of the players in this den of iniquity, see Paul Blustein, *And the Money Kept Rolling In (and Out): The World Bank, Wall Street, the IMF and the Bankrupting of Argentina* (New York: Public Affairs, 2005).
62 As John Maynard Keynes famously labelled the multifarious human emotions that determine economic behaviour in the final chapter of John Maynard Keynes, *General Theory of Employment, Interest and Money* (London: Palgrave Macmillan, 1936), p. 161.
63 UN Human Rights Council, Guiding Principles on Business and Human Rights: Implementing the United Nations 'Protect, Respect and Remedy' Framework, UN doc. A/HRC/RES/17/4 (6 July 2011).
64 Daniel Bradlow, 'Can Parallel Lines Ever Meet? The Strange Case of International Standards on Sovereign Debt and Business and Human Rights', *Yale Journal of International Law Online* 41, no. 2 (2016): pp. 201, 202.
65 Bradlow, 'Can Parallel Lines Ever Meet?', p. 237.
66 Report of the UN Independent Expert on the Effects of Foreign Debt and Other Related International Financial Obligations of States on the Full Enjoyment of All Human Rights, Particularly Economic, Social and Cultural Rights (4 August 2015), UN Doc. A/70/275, paras. 33–60.
67 Report of the UN Independent Expert, para.50.
68 Amartya Sen, *The Idea of Justice* (Cambridge: Harvard University Press, 2009), p. 356.

11 Human rights, the political view, and transnational corporations

An exploration

*Laura Valentini**

1 Introduction

Recent debates on the philosophy of human rights have been polarized between so-called 'orthodox' and 'political' views. The former understand human rights as fundamental entitlements all human beings hold against every capable agent (individual or corporate), just by virtue of their humanity. The latter see human rights as entitlements human beings hold against *particular* types of agents only: political ones.[1] In this chapter, I focus on the latter, political view.

Several proponents of this view converge in regarding *states* as the sole agents bearing primary human-rights duties vis-à-vis their citizens, and the international community as bearing secondary ones vis-à-vis all human beings.[2] This focus on states seems problematic. In our increasingly globalized world, states often lack the capacity to secure human rights for their citizens. Since 'ought implies can', states that lack the relevant capacity cannot plausibly be burdened with primary responsibility to *secure* human rights now, but only with the long-term responsibility to develop the capacity to fulfil them. Yet the conclusion, seemingly implied by the political view, that when states are weak, no agent carries primary responsibility for securing some people's (citizens') human rights seems implausible. This is all the more so given the existence of non-state actors that *could* do a great deal to secure the human rights of those individuals. Among such agents, much attention has been recently given to transnational corporations (henceforth TNCs). These are the non-state actors I discuss here.

I assume that an ability to account for TNCs' human-rights duties is a *prima facie* desideratum of a plausible theory of human rights. I then ask whether the political view can meet this desideratum, and answer in the affirmative. In developing this answer, I proceed as follows. In Section 2, I offer a sympathetic reconstruction of the political view, and of the reasons it offers for regarding states as the primary bearers of human-rights responsibilities. Two rationales are particularly relevant: what I call 'capacity' and the 'authority-plus-sovereignty package'. In Sections 3 and 4, I characterize TNCs as distinctive types of agents, and argue that, while – in given circumstances – they may have the capacity to secure human rights, they seem to lack the 'authority-plus-sovereignty' package. In Section 5, building on the existing literature on the responsibilities of corporations, I show how the apparent authority-plus-sovereignty gap exhibited by TNCs may be filled. I note, with others, that by *de facto* enjoying some of the privileges associated with sovereign authority, agents (like TNCs) also acquire some of the *duties/responsibilities* associated with it.[3] This gives us a rationale for treating agents that are normally regarded as belonging to the 'private' realm (e.g., TNCs) as 'political', and thus fit for carrying primary human-rights responsibilities vis-à-vis their immediate subjects. In Section 6, I address two objections, and thereby further clarify the implications of the proposed argument. Section 7 concludes.

Let me make three points of clarification. First, this chapter is not meant to offer a defence of the political view of human rights. Its only aim is to address one possible objection against it, namely, that it cannot account for the (intuitively plausible) role of TNCs as bearers of primary responsibilities for human rights. In doing so, the chapter offers (what I hope is) an appealing construal of the political view, but the arguments it provides fall short of a full defence of it.[4] Second, the chapter is developed from a broadly normative individualist perspective on political morality, one that takes individual human beings as ultimate objects of moral concern, entitled to the basic conditions for leading their lives in pursuit of their ends and goals. Third, and finally, there has already been considerable debate about the role of TNCs in relation to human rights; and the conclusion that these corporate entities should bear human-rights duties by virtue of their *de facto* 'political role' is not a new one.[5] The chapter builds on these contributions to show how the human-rights duties of TNCs may be justified from a perspective on human rights, i.e., the political one, which may appear to have little room for them.[6]

2 Human rights, the political view, and the state

In this section, I offer a sympathetic construal of the political view – though one that is not representative of every 'member' of the 'political family' – and specifically of its justification for identifying states as the primary bearers of the duties correlative to human rights.

2.1 Human rights and the political view

From a structural point of view, human rights are what Wesley Hohfeld called 'claim rights', involving duties owed to others.[7] More specifically, claim rights have three components:

(1) a right-holder;
(2) a particular object;
(3) a duty bearer.

Different approaches to human rights may be distinguished based on how they understand each component, including the political view.[8]

Regarding the first component – i.e., *right-holders* – virtually every approach to human rights accepts that all human beings are in principle fit for holding such rights. The political view is no exception.[9]

Regarding the second component, once again most approaches converge in characterizing the *object* of human rights in terms of secure access to fundamental – social and material – goods needed to lead a decent life.[10] Different views, however, fill the list of fundamental goods differently, and some of them do so in ways that have been described as distinctively 'political'.[11] In some cases, the identification of the relevant goods occurs by articulating the 'public reason' of international society, and this is what allegedly makes it 'political'.[12] In other cases, the goods to be placed on the list are chosen by taking into consideration political feasibility constraints.[13] For present purposes, I bracket off the object dimension of political views on human rights, and limit myself to discussing rights that any plausible view (political or otherwise) would have to include in its list: e.g., life, bodily integrity, freedom from torture, shelter, sanitation, and so forth.[14]

Finally, let me turn to the *bearers* of the duties correlative to human rights. Proponents of the political view argue that the relevant bearers are only political agents: states and the international community. Specifically, states are *primary* bearers of human-rights duties vis-à-vis their citizens, and the international community is a *secondary duty bearer* vis-à-vis everyone in the world.[15]

Primary duty bearers are under *stringent obligations* to *secure* the objects of human rights for a relevant set of individuals. More specifically, securing these objects involves three kinds of duties: to *respect, protect, and fulfil* human rights.[16] Duties to respect human rights require their bearers not to undermine others' access to the objects of human rights. Duties to protect human rights involve taking measures (e.g., enforcement) aimed at preventing others from undermining right-holders' enjoyment of the objects of human rights. Duties to fulfil human rights require their bearers to positively provide right-holders with access to the objects of their human rights. Take, for instance, the right to freedom of religion. Respect for this right requires duty bearers not to prevent right-holders from practising their religion. Protection of this right involves preventing *others* from interfering with right-holders' freedom of religion. Finally, fulfilling the right to freedom of religion requires providing individuals with the means to practise their religion and creating a broader environment conducive to respect for freedom of religion. Whenever capable primary duty bearers fail to secure the objects of human rights, be it through lack of respect, protection or fulfilment, they perpetrate human-rights *violations*.

Secondary bearers, by contrast, have 'remedial' responsibilities to cater for human rights, which are triggered whenever primary bearers disregard their obligations, or are unable to discharge them.[17] These remedial responsibilities are often less demanding than primary ones. And failure to discharge them gives rise to human-rights unfulfilments, rather than violations proper.[18]

To better understand the relationship between primary and secondary responsibilities for rights more generally (as opposed to human rights specifically), consider the difference between parental and third-party duties of care towards children. Parents are bound by stringent duties to do what they can to give their children access to the goods they need to become well-functioning adults. When parents fail to honour these duties, third parties in a position to help acquire secondary, remedial duties to address the situation. These remedial duties are arguably less demanding than parents' primary duties of care. Third parties should help neglected children, if they can do so at reasonable cost to themselves, but are typically permitted to offer a more minimal level of assistance than parents. From a structural point of view, third parties' duty to help needy children is akin to one of beneficence – it lacks clear recipients and is constrained by weighty considerations of costs.[19] Irresponsiveness to this duty arguably does not result in *violations* of the rights of particular children, but in a wrongful failure to contribute to the fulfilment of children's rights generally.

With these conceptual preliminaries at hand, in what follows, I focus on how the political view characterizes primary and secondary human-rights *duty bearers* in particular. Why, one might ask, should we limit the range of duty bearers to states and the international community, as the political view does?

2.2 Desiderata for the identification of duty bearers

A number of proponents of the political view have defended a state-centred conception of human rights, by (a) insisting that the concept of human rights should be responsive to human-rights practice and (b) noting that human-rights practice has been largely (though not exclusively) state-centred.[20] As critics of the political view have pointed out, however, consistency with practice is not a convincing rationale for state-centrism. The plausibility of the political view thus depends on there being other, non-status-quo dependent reasons for regarding states as holders of primary human-rights responsibilities. In particular, proponents of the political view must explain why *it makes moral sense* to regard states as the relevant primary duty bearers, and the international community as holding remedial responsibilities.

I suggest that, to 'make moral sense', an account of responsibility for human rights should:

(1) satisfy the ought-implies-can proviso;
(2) explain

  (a) the distinctive wrongness of human-rights violations, and
  (b) the appropriate reactions to human-rights violations.

In other words, the account should satisfy general constraints on the imposition of duties, and stand in reflective equilibrium with our considered judgements about human rights.[21]

With respect to (1), just like any duties, human-rights duties can only bind agents who have the capacity to respect, protect and fulfil them – nothing more needs to be said in relation to this criterion. With respect to (2)(a), violations of human rights involve a *distinctive* affront to *dignity*.[22] Any normative outlook on human rights – and specifically of who should bear human-rights duties – must be able to account for this morally salient and widely accepted fact.[23]

With respect to (2)(b), human-rights violations, unlike other types of rights-violations, trigger international concern as an appropriate response.[24] While an isolated murder, within an otherwise well-ordered state, would seldom be described as a human-rights violation, and would not appropriately generate concern on the part of the international community, human-rights violations do. Yet, the right to life, violated in the murder case, is also a human right. The explanation for this difference, then, cannot rest on considerations about right-holders or content. Rather, it must refer to who the relevant duty bearers are.

On what strikes me as the most promising version of the political view, regarding states as primary bearers of human-rights duties, and the international community as a secondary bearer, allows us to make best sense of human rights' moral distinctiveness, consistently with the 'ought implies can' constraint.

2.3 Political agents as human-rights duty bearers

A focus on states *qua* primary duty bearers allows the political view to meet the above-mentioned desiderata to the extent that states exhibit two features: (i) capacity and (ii) what I call the 'authority-plus-sovereignty package'.[25] As I suggest later, on the version of the political view I sketch, each feature is individually necessary, and the two are jointly sufficient, for an agent to carry primary responsibility for human rights.

2.3.1 Capacity

At least under normal circumstances, states are particularly well placed to secure the objects of human rights for their citizens. And since, as we have seen, ought implies can, state capacity gives us a *prima facie* reason for attributing primary human-rights responsibility to states. The reason is only *prima facie*, however. Not all agents capable of performing a morally valuable action have a duty to perform it.[26] For example, a wealthy industrialist may have the resources to secure the human rights of a multiplicity of individuals, and yet we would be reluctant to conclude that this is a sufficient reason for holding him responsible for their human-rights protection and fulfilment. For instance, Bill Gates might have sufficient economic power to provide secure access to food, shelter, and sanitation to the inhabitants of a small village in the developing world, and yet we would not typically consider him a human-rights violator for not doing so. By contrast, if the government of the state in which the village is located altogether neglected its inhabitants, and failed to provide them with access to fundamental material and social goods (while having the capacity to do so), we would probably condemn it as a human-rights violator. Why? Because of its authoritativeness and sovereignty, says the political view – at least on the present construal of it.[27]

2.3.2 Authority-plus-sovereignty

States are comprehensive ruling institutions characterized by special privileges. These privileges have both an inward and an outward dimension. First, states have *de facto authority* vis-à-vis their citizens, namely a socially accepted right to rule them, coupled with their obligation to obey. Second, states are *sovereign* vis-à-vis outside agents, and thus entitled to external non-interference.

This bundle of *de facto* privileges is key to statehood. However, the existence of these privileges – and, consequently, of the social artefact of statehood – is only legitimate if states rule their subjects consistently with their most important (i.e., human) rights.[28] When an entity is recognized as a state, it is invested with privileges that can only be justified, from a normative individualist point of view, by assuming it has special responsibilities to 'look after' its members. States may only legitimately govern their citizens if they provide them with decent enough background conditions against which they may pursue their ends and goals. This, in turn, requires at least respect for human rights.

States' possession of the authority-plus-sovereignty package allows a political approach to human rights to make sense of both the distinctive wrongness of human-rights violations and the appropriate normative reaction to them (in line with the second desideratum outlined in Section 2.2 above). First, human-rights violations are particularly harmful to dignity because the state, the *authoritative agent* presumed to be acting on behalf of its citizens and to look after their interests, blatantly fails to do so.[29] 'Official disrespect', namely the kind of disrespect displayed by authorities – as Pogge puts it – conveys the message that the entire community (domestic and, indirectly, international – insofar as the latter recognizes the authority of states) fails to acknowledge the fundamental entitlements of the victim.[30] A private person's murder of a fellow citizen, and a state official's execution of a political protester are both wrong, and both rights violations. However, on the political view, only the latter counts as a human-rights violation. Why? Because only the latter embodies a distinctive form of wrongdoing, a special violation of dignity, since precisely those agents who are presumed to act on behalf of their subjects and protect their interests perpetrate it.[31]

By way of (distant) analogy, consider again child/parent relations. The reason why a parent's failure to provide for her child strikes us as distinctively morally wrong – more so than a stranger's identical neglect – is that the parent has special moral obligations towards the child, and is granted a certain sphere of authority/sovereignty over the child in order to discharge those obligations. In a similar fashion, the existence of a comprehensive authoritative relationship between the state and its citizens explains why state-sponsored violence or neglect towards them amounts to a distinctive form of wrongdoing: a human-rights violation.

Second, human-rights violations trigger international concern because they are linked to state *sovereignty*. When a state fails to secure the objects of its citizens' human rights, it is no longer performing its morally mandatory functions, and those individuals who live under its power require outside protection. The in-principle right to non-interference states enjoy is thus forfeited.[32] A murder – perpetrated by private persons – does not appropriately generate the same type of international concern. Rather, it triggers domestic concern, on the part of the domestic legal system. Once again, by way of distant analogy, when parents fail appropriately to take care of, or directly harm, their children, their actions and omissions are cause for 'external' concern. Neglectful or abusive parents lose their immunity from external interference in raising their children.

So far, I have argued that – on a plausible version of the political view – (i) capacity and (ii) the authority-plus-sovereignty package are each individually necessary and jointly sufficient conditions for bearing primary human-rights duties. This gives us a relatively straightforward explanation for the emphasis the political view places on states, and allows this view to make sense of many wrongs we would intuitively call human-rights violations. There is, however, a set of circumstances in which people lack access to the objects of their human rights, and yet the political view seems unable to identify any primary responsibility-bearers who may be accused of violating those rights. This occurs when states *lack the capacity* to secure the objects of their citizens' human rights.

To be sure, proponents of the political view would insist that, in such cases, the international community has remedial responsibilities to deal with such human-rights deficits.[33] But, as I have mentioned, these are more elusive, secondary responsibilities to assist the needy, somewhat akin to duties of beneficence. Failure to discharge them would not result in human-rights violations proper, but in human-rights deficits or unfulfilment.

The implication that, when states lack capacity, no human-rights violator *proper* may be found, appears problematic. This is all the more so, given the existence of other agents who (a) are knowingly involved in people's lack of access to the objects of some of their human rights and (b) have the capacity to provide this access to them. Specifically, as recent discussions within and outside the scholarly community show, particular types of corporate agents deserve scrutiny when citizens of weak states lack secure access to the objects of human rights: transnational corporations (TNCs).

3 TNCs, states, and human rights: the capacity gap

What are transnational corporations (TNCs)? They are large-scale commercial enterprises operating in a plurality of different countries. Familiar examples of such corporations include oil giants such as Shell, textile giants such as Nike and H&M, food and drinks giants such as Nestlé and Coca-Cola, retailers such as Wal-Mart, as well as many others.[34]

The power and influence that these actors exert on states and the global economy cannot be overstated.[35] In 2009, 44 TNCs figured among the world's top 100 largest economic entities. Just to give a flavour of the scale of this phenomenon, in 2009 Wal-Mart's and Shell's revenues were each greater than the GDPs of countries like Thailand, Portugal, Malaysia, the Philippines, Hungary, and Peru – to mention only a few.[36]

In addition to their economic power, TNCs are particularly well placed to (a) shape state regulation to their advantage through aggressive lobbying and (b) evade it when it obstructs their business interests, by operating in multiple countries, and relocating wherever they are likeliest to make the most profit. It is thus unsurprising that TNCs would often choose developing countries as the locus of their manufacturing activities. These countries most desperately need the investment and job opportunities created by TNCs, and are typically less willing to or capable of enforcing demanding labour standards. Low production costs mean lower prices, and lower prices mean greater competitiveness: exactly what TNCs look for.[37]

TNCs' mobility and economic power are also partly responsible for global dynamics with perverse effects, such as tax competition, whereby countries are incentivized to lower taxes on foreign capital in order to attract and retain investment. Once again, although most countries are affected by this phenomenon, its most serious effects are felt by developing ones.[38]

TNCs' largely unchecked power and their ability to affect individuals' access to fundamental goods have generated much debate. Cases of TNCs' complicity in government-sponsored rights abuses, as well as instances of TNC-sponsored abuses, have received significant media attention.[39] Consider, for instance, the following ones:

Unocal in Myanmar (Burma): In 1996, Unocal was sued in the U.S. for complicity in human-rights abuses perpetrated by the Myanmar military – including rape, torture, and murder – to force local villagers to build the 'Yadana' pipeline, running from Myanmar to Thailand. The case was settled in 2005. Unocal committed to compensating villagers and to contributing funds to ameliorate their living conditions.[40]

Coca Cola in Colombia: Coca Cola was accused of being indirectly responsible for the employment of paramilitary squads that have intimidated workers, and threatened – as well as killed – union leaders on Colombian premises.[41]

(This case, which generated much public discussion, was eventually dismissed.[42])

The first of the above cases involves TNC-complicity with government-sponsored human-rights abuses. The second involves accusations of TNC-abuse against a socio-political background, such as the Colombian one, characterized by 'weak statehood'.[43] When statehood is weak, the government has little ability to exercise control – either territorially or with respect to a given issue-area – and TNCs have greater scope to engage in what would otherwise be illegal activities with impunity. These include violations of bodily integrity, damages to the environment with serious repercussions on local populations' access to clean water and nutrition, and violations of fundamental labour rights – including exploitative working conditions and child labour.

Cases such as these have caused much concern in the international community, and sparked UN activities aimed at bringing TNCs to account for their actions, in the name of human rights. In 2003, this culminated in a set of UN *Draft Norms on the Responsibilities of Transnational Corporations and Other Business Enterprises with Regard to Human Rights*, stating that:

> Within their respective *spheres of activity and influence*, transnational corporations and other business enterprises have the obligation to promote, secure the fulfilment of, respect, ensure respect of and protect human rights recognized in international as well as national law.[44]

These draft norms were met with criticism – on the part of business representatives as well as states – and never gained legally binding status. They were followed, in 2011, by the

United Nations *Guiding Principles on Business and Human Rights*, developed under John Ruggie's lead.[45] These principles set forth somewhat more modest guidelines according to which:

> Business enterprises should respect human rights. This means that they should avoid infringing on the human rights of others and should address adverse human rights impacts with which they are involved.[46]

Although the emphasis on respect for human rights only – as opposed to respect, protection, and fulfilment – may appear as a step back from 2003, the existence of the UN *Draft Norms* first, and of the *Guiding Principles* later, is testimony to the prominence gained by the issue of TNCs and human rights in international discourse. Even more importantly, it is a manifestation of the widespread conviction that TNCs should be regarded as bearers of human-rights responsibilities.[47] Is the political view capable of accommodating this conviction?

4 TNCs, human rights, and the political view: the authority-plus-sovereignty gap

Note that, if the political view were unable to account for the human-rights responsibilities of TNCs in cases of *complicity* with government abuses, this would not be particularly troublesome.[48] In such circumstances, the political view can still point to a human-rights violator: the government. TNCs' acquiescence in, or indeed encouragement of, such violations is deeply morally problematic, of course, but may not itself count as a human-rights violation. While we can certainly consider TNCs complicit, the human-rights violators remain states.[49]

The situation becomes more complex, and more troubling for proponents of the political view, where TNCs operate in areas of weak governance, not reached by state regulation.[50] Here, as we have seen, TNCs can act in ways that deprive individuals of secure access to at least some of the objects of their human rights – e.g., through inhumane labour standards, violent security practices, and environmental degradation – but without governments having the capacity to place constraints on them and bring them to account for their actions. Could TNCs, from the perspective of the political view, be considered primary bearers of some human-rights responsibilities in such cases?

To answer this question, we need to remind ourselves of which features, on the political view, make certain agents appropriate primary bearers of human-rights responsibilities – i.e., *capacity* and the *authority-plus-sovereignty* package – and ascertain whether TNCs exhibit them.

4.1 Capacity

As the foregoing discussion shows, the satisfaction of the capacity criterion on the part of TNCs is rather unproblematic. In a multiplicity of different circumstances – including in areas of weak or, even more so, failed statehood[51] – companies have the ability both to undermine and to secure access to the objects of some key human rights for those falling 'within their spheres of influence' – an expression I will make more precise later in the text.[52] In other words, TNCs are often able to fill at least part of the capacity gap left by weak states. Things appear less straightforward, though, once we turn to the second feature human-rights duty bearers must exhibit: the authority-plus-sovereignty package.

4.2 Authority-plus-sovereignty

In the case of TNCs, the 'package' may seem to be missing. In our moral universe, TNCs are not sovereign authorities. Instead, they are voluntary ventures, speaking on behalf of private interests, and devoted to the pursuit of profit. Moreover, instead of being themselves sovereign, they are fit for being regulated by sovereign entities, who are in turn the primary bearers of human-rights responsibilities.

TNCs are transnational 'private associations' in relation to the state system. As John Rawls explains, private associations pursue particularistic ends, in line with their members' wills.[53] The pursuit of their ends ought to be constrained by the state, to secure the demands of justice, a subset of which is what we call human rights. But it would be contrary to the commitment to respect for persons underpinning (justice and) human rights to require private voluntary associations to become themselves primary vehicles of justice; to consider the realization of justice as one of their *goals*. There exists a 'division of moral labour' between public institutions and private associations, one that is integral to the aim of justice: giving each the space to pursue his or her own conception of the good.[54]

As recently argued by Chiara Cordelli, applying standards of public justice to private institutions would conflict with their specific purpose.[55] For example, it would be contrary to the point and purpose of a women's only association to practise non-discrimination – which is what justice otherwise requires – and allow men to join.[56] To the extent that justice and human-rights protection are meant to enable individuals freely to pursue their goals, it is self-defeating to force them to *pursue* human-rights protection in their private capacities.

If securing human rights were the job of TNCs, so the argument goes, these would no longer be TNCs, they would altogether change their nature. They would cease to be the expression of particularistic interests and ends, and become vehicles of justice.[57] And if free enterprise is an institution we should value both intrinsically – as an expression of individual freedom – and instrumentally – as a means of creating wealth – then TNCs should not be burdened with responsibilities to protect and fulfil human rights.

In light of the above, the problem for the political view is that, in some circumstances, *states have a capacity gap* – hence they cannot act as the primary bearers of human-rights responsibilities – while *TNCs* appear to exhibit *an authority-plus-sovereignty gap* – hence, even if TNCs are capable of both preventing and securing access to the objects of some human rights, moral reasons are lacking for regarding them as primary bearers of human-rights obligations.

This conclusion may be disappointing, but it also shows why the popular slogan 'with power comes responsibility' is insufficient to establish the role of TNCs as primary responsibility-bearers for human-rights protection. As argued earlier, power (capacity) is necessary but not sufficient for primary responsibility: authority-plus-sovereignty must also be present, at least from the perspective of the political approach to human rights. Unless TNCs' (apparent) authority-plus-sovereignty gap can be closed, the political view will be unable to identify them as primary bearers of human-rights duties.

5 Bridging the authority-plus-sovereignty gap

As several contributors to the literature on business and human rights – such as Steven Ratner, Florian Wettstein, and David Karp – have pointed out, although our standard conceptualization of TNCs classifies them as 'private associations', their *de facto* political role in contexts of weak statehood warrants a change in perspective.[58] In certain contexts, some

TNCs have both some *de facto* authority and some *de facto* sovereignty (a) vis-à-vis a given set of people and (b) relative to important issue areas. In turn, as explained in previous sections, the existence of these *de facto* privileges can only be justified if they are consistent with securing the fundamental rights of those within TNCs' spheres of influence. Let me elaborate on these points.

First, like states, powerful corporations in areas of weak governance are ruling institutions vis-à-vis *at least* their employees, who may be regarded as full members: they set some of the most consequential ground-rules affecting their existence, and enforce them.[59] They define a good number of aspects of their workers' lives, and their totalizing dimension contributes to their being perceived as the 'only authority around'. In the words of Florian Wettstein, 'an increasing number of people spend well over 75 percent of their active time . . . under the *direct rule* and supervision of the corporation'.[60] If a local employee of a TNC is supposed to work 16 hours every day for the corporation, then a very large portion of their time will indeed be spent under the corporation's rule. And to the extent that supervisors consider employees under an obligation to obey the company's rules, and have the means to enforce those rules, the corporation in question may be said to have *de facto* authority at least over its local employees with respect to important areas of their lives.

If *de facto* authority is associated with human-rights responsibilities in the case of states, then it is not clear why it should not also be so associated in the case of TNCs.[61] Again, by parity of reasoning, when these responsibilities are not discharged, a distinctive affront to human dignity occurs. The only or main 'authority around', the main official structure governing people's lives in a certain area, conveys a systematic lack of recognition of its subjects' humanity.

A critic might object that this fails to acknowledge a very significant difference between states and TNCs: while membership in the former is, typically, non-voluntary, membership in the latter is acquired through an act of will, such as signing a contract. This, it might be thought, has important implications for the moral standards we apply to states and TNCs. States' non-voluntariness places them under stringent obligations to behave in ways that all members could accept, such as by respecting human rights. Since membership in TNCs is voluntary, however, we can presume that members have *accepted* their terms of operation, which in turn exempts them from being subject to stringent human-rights requirements.

There are two possible lines of response to this objection. The first questions the link between non-voluntariness of membership and human-rights obligations. The suggestion that, for an agent A to have human-rights obligations towards another agent B, B must be subject to A's rule *non-voluntarily* has counter-intuitive implications also in the case of states. Although it is true that most citizens have not consented to becoming members, there are instances in which membership is consensual. Consider immigrants who, without being under duress, freely decide to move to a different country and acquire citizenship there. Imagine, say, an Italian citizen, Mario, moving to Canada for his love of Canadian nature and becoming a Canadian citizen. It would seem odd to suggest that, since his membership of Canada is voluntary, the Canadian state has no human-rights duties vis-à-vis him. If this is correct, then it is mistaken to argue that non-voluntariness of subjection is necessary for one to hold human rights against an authority.

But even setting this argument aside, and holding on to the thought that non-voluntariness matters to human-rights duties, we could still defend the conclusion that TNCs wield human-rights responsibilities vis-à-vis *the most vulnerable of their members.* This is because, while it is plausible to say that shareholders, CEOs, and high-ranking employees voluntarily join TNCs, in areas where states are weak and poor, factory workers must often join

TNCs' production lines non-voluntarily, i.e., due to the 'lack of acceptable alternatives'.[62] It is better to be employed in sweatshop conditions than to starve.[63] To the extent that local employees of TNCs may not be seen as voluntarily consenting to work for them – i.e., their consent is given under duress, because all alternatives are unacceptable – then just like states in relation to most of their citizens, TNCs qualify as comprehensive non-voluntary authorities towards them. And *if* carrying human-rights obligations is conditional on non-voluntariness of subjection, then, in relation to at least some of those falling under the authority of TNCs, this condition is met.

In addition to *de facto* authority, in areas of weak statehood, TNCs have *de facto* sovereignty, i.e., *de facto* immunity from external interference on the part of the state within which they operate.[64] Here too, as with states, this *de facto* immunity may only be legitimate to the extent that it is consistent with responsibility for an adequate set of human rights. From a political perspective on human rights, then, there seems to be no normatively consistent rationale for treating states as in-principle bearers of duties correlative to human rights, but not TNCs, when the letter exhibit the authority-plus-sovereignty package. TNCs' avoidable failures to secure access to some fundamental goods for their members are also violations of human rights, which rightly trigger international concern.

In sum, whenever TNCs are functionally sufficiently state-like, their *de facto* authority and sovereignty, just like those of states, can only be legitimate if they are accompanied by primary human-rights responsibilities. And TNCs' violations of human rights both carry a special harm to dignity and appropriately generate international concern.[65]

6 Objections: how much responsibility?

I have suggested that, from the perspective of the political approach to human rights, TNCs may be appropriately regarded as primary bearers of human-rights duties. But regarding TNCs as primary bearers of human-rights duties does not yet tell us how extensive their responsibilities for human rights are. This question might raise two opposite worries: that the view I have sketched requires either too much or too little of TNCs. In what follows, I consider each worry in turn. In doing so, I further elaborate on the nature of TNCs' human-rights responsibilities.

6.1 Over-demandingness

It might be argued that placing primary human-rights responsibilities on TNCs requires too much of them. After all, TNCs are commercial enterprises, and trying to secure human rights (at least) for their local employees in areas of weak statehood may make them commercially unviable.

When it comes to the issue of how demanding TNCs' human-rights duties are, two broad views are available. On what one might call the 'maximalist view', TNCs should have the same duties as capable states; the protection of human rights should be their main goal. TNCs operating in areas of weak governance would have to act so as to provide access to basic goods such as shelter, food, sanitation, medical assistance, and education to those falling within their 'jurisdiction'. In other words, from a maximalist perspective, TNCs would have to take up the job of the state in the relevant areas. What is more, if the 'correct' list of human rights also included entitlements to political participation – something on which I have remained agnostic here – TNCs would have to become internally participatory, giving all those falling under their authority something like a right to vote on their internal organization, regulations, and policies.[66]

The maximalist view is probably the one a critical reader is concerned about, and rightly so. This view is unappealing for two reasons: one concerns its consequences, the other its in-principle moral appropriateness (independently of consequences). First, placing such extensive responsibilities on TNCs could, in the long run, be potentially counter-productive, at least on the plausible assumption that it is desirable for the state itself to bear human-rights obligations. States, after all, do not have private interests, at least vis-à-vis their citizens. Instead, 'their job' is to provide a background framework within which citizens' private interests can be pursued. Unlike states, powerful corporations do have private interests, and are thus, by their very nature, less well suited to taking up human-rights responsibilities than states are.[67] Forcing TNCs to acquire the entire set of demanding state-like responsibilities would thus make it harder for states themselves to develop the necessary capabilities to eventually regain full primary responsibility for human rights. If a situation in which primary responsibility for human rights is in the hands of states is preferable to one in which such responsibility is shared between states and corporations, we should be sceptical of the maximalist view.

Second, although some TNCs may have the 'crude capacity' to secure *all* of the objects of human rights for those within their jurisdiction (i.e., *at least* local employees), their having the capacity is insufficient to establish their being under a duty to do so. Capacity is only necessary for duty. As we have seen, in addition to capacity, considerations about an agent's morally salient features also matter.[68] In this respect, I have pointed out that, in some circumstances, TNCs are relevantly state-like in that they exercise inescapable authority, and act as sovereigns with respect to (a) a certain set of individuals and, crucially, (b) a certain set of important dimensions of their lives. These considerations must be taken into account when thinking about the human-rights duties borne by TNCs. This leads me to consider the second account of the demandingness of the human-rights duties of TNCs.

On what I call the 'proportional view', these duties need to be circumscribed to the *areas of authority* distinctive of TNCs' operations. These plausibly include labour standards, environmental protection, and the provision of security – though an accurate account of the relevant issue areas can only be given on a case-by-case basis. Relative to these areas of authority, TNCs are primary bearers of human-rights responsibilities vis-à-vis their local employees. This means that they have duties to respect, protect and fulfil their human rights in these areas. Respect for human rights requires that TNCs abide by the kinds of constraints that the legal system of a human-rights respecting state would place on them. Such constraints would plausibly feature prohibitions on child labour, on tolerating inhumane working conditions, on polluting and degrading the environment, on adopting brutal security practices and so forth. In addition, TNCs also have responsibilities to do more – i.e., to protect and fulfil human rights – by trying to foster an environment where decent labour standards are respected, where employees' physical safety is protected, where their access to health is promoted.

That said, even if rather demanding, the duties just discussed would not require TNCs to become, all of a sudden, the main education, housing, and welfare providers within a particular area. Such heavy, comprehensive requirements are not appropriately tailored to the significant, but still limited, authority TNCs exercise. Given TNCs' circumscribed authority, and their nature as commercial enterprises, placing the full set of demanding human-rights duties on them would go beyond what they could be *reasonably expected to do*.

As suggested by Steven Ratner, TNCs are relevantly state-like in some respects, but not in all respects, and their human-rights duties should reflect this fact.[69] Most importantly, their duties to *protect and fulfil human rights* would not have to be so demanding as to undermine their commercial viability. After all, most duties are conditional on their cost not being excessive for their bearers; and what counts as excessive costs typically depends on the bearer in question. Most would agree, though, that placing duties on agents so demanding as to potentially extinguish the agents themselves would fail to meet the 'reasonable costs' caveat, under any specification of it. If this is right, then it is arguably plausible to consider TNCs' duties to protect and fulfil human rights conditional on their continued commercial viability: a TNC that is not commercially viable would simply cease to exist.[70] What is more, demanding so much of TNCs as to making them commercially unviable could have adverse effects on local populations who rely on the employment opportunities offered by TNCs for their subsistence.

In sum, on the 'proportional' view, content-wise, TNCs would have more positive responsibilities vis-à-vis their employees – i.e., their 'subjects' – than they would under a human-rights protecting state; yet their human-rights responsibilities would not be as demanding as those of a well-functioning state, given that: (a) the issue areas on which they would apply would be fewer and (b), unlike the duties to 'protect and fulfil' falling onto states, TNCs' would be constrained by considerations of commercial viability.

The status of TNCs' duties, and the appropriate reaction to their violation, differs depending on whether a human-rights protecting state exists or not. In the former case, failure to discharge these responsibilities would qualify as a violation of law, and would appropriately trigger intervention on the part of the state. If a capable state, however, failed to pass or enforce laws prohibiting the relevant repugnant behaviours, *that state itself* would be a primary bearer of human-rights responsibilities for the said violations. In the latter case – i.e., in areas of weak governance – TNCs that failed to constrain their behaviour in accordance with human-rights requirements, within their spheres of authority, would be correctly classified as human-rights violators, and directly accountable to the international community.

Finally, to further dispel the over-demandingness worry, let me note, following David Karp, that it is entirely up to TNCs to decide whether to operate in areas of weak governance, where they would acquire *de facto* authority and sovereignty, and hence the relevant human-rights duties.[71] Nobody forces TNCs to act as agents with some primary responsibilities for human rights. The only burden placed on them is a prohibition on taking advantage of the lack of state regulation in weak governance zones, and perpetrate human-rights abuses and neglect as a result.

6.2 Under-demandingness

Others might worry that, even if the political view is capable of including TNCs within the group of primary bearers of the duties correlative to human rights, this is not enough. TNCs' duties are limited to their capacities and areas of authority, which in turn suggests that they won't be able to secure all human rights for everyone living in areas of weak statehood. For example, what about those who are not employees and so are not directly under the authority of TNCs, and yet, living in the vicinity of their industrial plants, are deeply affected by their operations? And what about many others who lack secure access to the objects of their human rights? Although the political view can *partly* respond to the worry concerning human beings whose human rights have no primary duty bearers, it is still likely to leave some people without primary human-rights protection.

A few points can be made in response. First, recall that my conclusion is stated in modest terms – I have argued that *at least* local employees have human rights against their TNC-employer. This does not exclude the possibility of extending the scope of human-rights holders further, if the relevant authority relationships between the individuals in question and TNCs obtain. Second, while the argument offered here has focused on TNCs, it is in principle extendable to other agents as well, as long as they exhibit capacity and the authority-plus-sovereignty package. Even if TNCs are not sufficient to secure all the human rights of everyone living in areas of weak statehood, other agents might be in a material and moral position to fill the gaps.

Third, TNCs, just like every other agent part of the international community, have general duties to do what they reasonably can to bring about effective authoritative institutions capable of securing human rights.[72] International reforms strengthening state sovereignty, the establishment of more equitable trade and financial institutions, and of an effective system of human-rights monitoring, are everyone's duty. Yet, these are duties to bring about human-rights respecting capacity, and as such, they cannot be *correlative to human rights* strictly understood.[73]

The problem, then, is not that the political view is insufficiently demanding. Rather, the problem is that, as things are, we lack institutions with the capacity to guarantee the fulfilment of human rights worldwide.

7 Conclusion

In this chapter, I have offered a sympathetic reconstruction of the political view on human rights, and considered whether it has conceptual room for conceiving of TNCs as primary bearers of human-rights duties. To the extent that the political view is associated with a purely state-based account of primary human-rights responsibilities, it is considered unable to account for the human-rights duties of non-state actors. A deeper inquiry into the moral underpinnings of the political view has revealed that what makes states appropriate primary bearers of human-rights responsibilities is their possession of the authority-plus-sovereignty package (coupled with their capacity to secure human rights). Drawing on the literature on the moral responsibilities of corporations, I have suggested that TNCs in areas of weak governance meet both the 'capacity' and 'authority-plus-sovereignty' conditions. I have thus concluded that the political view has the conceptual resources to account for the primary human-rights obligations of TNCs. While my discussion has cast some favourable light on the political view, it has not provided a full defence of it. Such a defence would require a systematic comparison with competing views, for which I do not have the space here. Still, I hope that the chapter has shown that the political view has more conceptual and normative resources than ordinarily thought.

Notes

1 There are several senses in which human rights may count as political. Here, I focus on the most prominent one. See Laura Valentini, 'In What Sense Are Human Rights Political? A Preliminary Exploration', *Political Studies* 60, no. 1 (2012): pp. 180–194.

2 See, for example, Charles Beitz, *The Idea of Human Rights* (Oxford: Oxford University Press, 2011); Joseph Raz, 'Human Rights without Foundations', in *The Philosophy of International Law*, edited by John Tasioulas and Samantha Besson (Oxford: Oxford University Press, 2010), pp. 321–338; John Rawls, *The Law of Peoples: With "The Idea of Public Reason Revisited."* (Cambridge, MA: Harvard University Press, 1999); Andrea Sangiovanni, 'Justice

and the Priority of Politics to Morality', *Journal of Political Philosophy* 16, no. 2 (2008): pp. 137–164; Ronald Dworkin, *Justice for Hedgehogs* (Cambridge: Harvard University Press, 2011), pp. 332–344.

3 Here, I use the terms 'duties' and 'responsibilities' interchangeably.

4 For a defence of a middle-way between political and non-political views, consistent with the perspective defended here, see Laura Valentini, 'Human Rights, Freedom, and Political Authority', *Political Theory* 40, no. 5 (2012): pp. 573–601. For an alternative middle-way, see Pablo Gilabert, 'Humanist and Political Perspectives on Human Rights', *Political Theory* 39, no. 4 (2011): pp. 439–467.

5 See, e.g., Steven Ratner, 'Corporations and Human Rights: A Theory of Legal Responsibility', *Yale Law Journal* 111, no. 3 (2001): pp. 443–545; John Ruggie, 'Business and Human Rights: The Evolving International Agenda', *American Journal of International Law* 101, no. 4 (2007): pp. 819–840; Florian Wettstein, *Multinational Corporations and Global Justice: Human Rights Obligations of a Quasi-Governmental Institution* (Stanford: Stanford Business Books, 2009); David Karp, *Responsibility for Human Rights: Transnational Corporations in Imperfect States* (Cambridge: Cambridge University Press, 2014).

6 See, e.g., Cristina Lafont, 'Accountability and Global Governance: Challenging the State-Centric Conception of Human Rights', *Ethics and Global Politics* 3, no. 3 (2010): pp. 193–215.

7 Wesley Newcomb Hohfeld, 'Fundamental Legal Conceptions as Applied in Judicial Reasoning', *The Yale Law Journal* 26, no. 8 (1917): pp. 710–770.

8 Although different approaches to human rights typically offer a unified rationale for the way they interpret each dimension, the three dimensions are logically separable, and I shall treat them as such in what follows.

9 'In principle' here is meant to allow for two possible restrictions: (1) on some views, children do not (yet) have human rights and (2) any given agent really does have a human right to X only if suitable duty bearers can be identified.

10 See, e.g., Thomas Pogge, *World Poverty and Human Rights: Cosmopolitan Responsibilities and Reforms* (Cambridge: Polity, 2008). This also includes theorists like Griffin, if we understand a decent life as one in which human beings' normative agency is protected. See James Griffin, *On Human Rights* (Oxford: Oxford University Press, 2008).

11 For discussion, see John Tasioulas, 'Are Human Rights Essentially Triggers for Intervention?', *Philosophy Compass* 4, no. 6 (2009): pp. 938–950; Valentini, 'In What Sense Are Human Rights Political?'

12 Rawls, The Law of Peoples.

13 Raz, 'Human Rights Without Foundations'; Sangiovanni, 'Justice and the Priority of Politics to Morality'; Valentini, 'In What Sense Are Human Rights Political?'

14 The reader may simply include whatever rights he/she regards as *sine qua non* of any plausible list of human rights.

15 Beitz, The Idea of Human Rights; Rawls, The Law of Peoples.

16 See Asbjørn Eide, 'The New International Economic Order and the Promotion of Human Rights. Report on the Right to Adequate Food as a Human Right', 1987, UN Doc E/CN.4/Sub.2/1987/23. Cf. the original tripartite categorization of duties in Henry Shue, *Basic Rights: Subsistence, Affluence, and U.S. Foreign Policy,* 2nd ed. (Princeton: Princeton University Press, 1996). For discussion, see Lafont, 'Accountability and Global Governance'.

17 For the related (but not identical) distinction between primary and secondary agents of justice, see Onora O'Neill, 'Agents of Justice', *Metaphilosophy* 32, nos. 1–2 (2001): pp. 180–195. For the notion of remedial responsibility, see David Miller, 'Distributing Responsibilities', *Journal of Political Philosophy* 9, no. 4 (2001): pp. 453–471.

18 I borrow the notion of an unfulfilment or under-fulfilment from Pogge, *World Poverty and Human Rights.*

19 Allen Buchanan, 'Justice and Charity', *Ethics* 97, no. 3 (1987): pp. 558–575.

20 Rawls, *The Law of Peoples*; Beitz, *The Idea of Human Rights*; Sangiovanni, 'Justice and the Priority of Politics to Morality'.

21 For the notion of 'reflective equilibrium', see John Rawls, *A Theory of Justice* (Oxford: Oxford University Press, 1999).

22 This is not to say that human-rights violations uniquely undermine human dignity, but that they do so in a distinctive way.
23 See the discussion of 'official disrespect' in Pogge, *World Poverty and Human Rights*, ch. 2.
24 On the 'international concern' dimension of human rights, see Beitz, *The Idea of Human Rights.*
25 Cf. Valentini, 'Human Rights, Freedom, and Political Authority'.
26 Karp, Responsibility for Human Rights, ch. 5.
27 Cf. Julio César Montero, 'Human Rights, International Human Rights, and Sovereign Political Authority: A Draft Model for Understanding Contemporary Human Rights', *Ethics & Global Politics* 7, no. 4 (2014): pp. 143–162.
28 Note that I am treating this as a necessary condition for legitimate authority/sovereignty, not as a sufficient one. There may be other, further conditions, on which I remain agnostic here.
29 For a more extensive treatment of this point, see Laura Valentini, 'Dignity and Human Rights: A Reconceptualization,' manuscript, 2016.
30 Pogge, World Poverty and Human Rights.
31 Cf. Christian Barry and Nicholas Southwood, 'What Is Special About Human Rights?', *Ethics & International Affairs* 25, no. 3 (2011): pp. 369–383.
32 For a particular emphasis on this aspect of human rights, see Raz, 'Human Rights without Foundations'. Note that human-rights violations are a necessary, but not a sufficient, condition for the justifiability of outside interference in a state's affairs.
33 I use this term because, since there are no agents with the capacity to bear primary human-rights responsibilities, the language of violations appears out of place.
34 Surya Deva, 'Human Rights Violations by Multinational Corporations and International Law: Where from Here', *Connecticut Journal of International Law* 19, no. 1 (2003): pp. 1–57.
35 Jordan Paust, 'Human Rights Responsibilities of Private Corporations', *Vanderbilt Journal of Transnational Law* 35, no. 3 (2002): pp. 801–825, 802.
36 The comparison has been drawn by Tracey Keys and Thomas Malnight, looking at data from the 2009 ranking of Fortune Global, 500 and the IMF's data on countries' GDP. For the full list see www.globaltrends.com/knowledge-center/features/shapers-and-influencers/66-corporate-clout-the-influence-of-the-worlds-largest-100-economic-entities. For scepticism about GDP-turnover comparisons, see Tim Worstall, 'GDP for a Country Is Not the Same Thing as Turnover for a Business', *Forbes*, www.forbes.com/sites/timworstall/2011/06/28/gdp-for-a-country-is-not-the-same-thing-as-turnover-for-a-business/.
37 Ratner, 'Corporations and Human Rights', pp. 461–465.
38 Thomas Rixen, 'Tax Competition and Inequality: The Case for Global Tax Governance', *Global Governance: A Review of Multilateralism and International Organizations* 17, no. 4 (2011): pp. 447–467.
39 For this distinction, see Ratner, "Corporations and Human Rights', p. 449.
40 Rachel Chambers, 'The Unocal Settlement: Implications for the Developing Law on Corporate Complicity in Human Rights Abuses', *Human Rights Brief* 13, no. 1 (2005): pp. 14–16. See also, Business and Human Rights Resource Center, 'Unocal Lawsuit (re Myanmar)', 2014, https://business-humanrights.org/en/unocal-lawsuit-re-myanmar.
41 Sibylla Brodzinsky, 'Coca-Cola Boycott Launched After Killings at Colombian Plants', *The Guardian*, July 24, 2003, www.theguardian.com/media/2003/jul/24/marketingandpr.colombia.
42 François-Xavier Bagnoud, 'Coca-Cola Lawsuit (re Colombia)', *Business & Human Rights Resource Centre*, 2014, https://business-humanrights.org/en/coca-cola-lawsuit-re-colombia. Similar lawsuits have also been brought against the banana giant Chiquita. See David Voreacos, 'Chiquita Executives Must Face Claims Over Colombian Torture', *Business & Human Rights Resource Centre (Reported From Bloomberg)*, 2016, https://business-humanrights.org/en/chiquita-executives-must-face-claims-over-colombian-torture.
43 Thomas Risse, 'Governance Under Limited Sovereignty', in *Back to Basics: State Power in a Contemporary World*, edited by Martha Finnemore and Judith Goldstein (New York: Oxford University Press, 2013), pp. 78–104.
44 United Nations, 'Draft Norms on the Responsibilities of Transnational Corporations and Other Business Enterprises with Regard to Human Rights', 2003, 4, www.unhchr.ch/

huridocda/huridoca.nsf/(Symbol)/E.CN.4.Sub.2.2003.12.Rev.2.En?Opendocument, emphasis added.

45 From 2005 to 2011, John Ruggie served as the UN Secretary General Special Representative for Business and Human Rights.

46 John Ruggie, 'Guiding Principles on Business and Human Rights. Implementing the United Nations "Protect, Respect and Remedy" Framework', 2011, www.ohchr.org/Documents/Publications/GuidingPrinciplesBusinessHR_EN.pdf.

47 For forceful defences of this conclusion, see Ratner, 'Corporations and Human Rights', Wettstein, *Multinational Corporations and Global Justice*, and Karp, *Responsibility for Human Rights*.

48 For a comprehensive discussion of corporate complicity in human-rights abuses, see Wettstein, *Multinational Corporations and Global Justice*, pp. 295–305.

49 Similar considerations apply if governments outsource responsibility to TNCs.

50 For extensive discussion, see Karp, *Responsibility for Human Rights*.

51 For the latter, see David Karp, 'Transnational Corporations in "bad States": Human Rights Duties, Legitimate Authority and the Rule of Law in International Political Theory', *International Theory* 1, no. 1 (2009): pp. 87–118.

52 Ratner, 'Corporations and Human Rights'.

53 John Rawls, *Political Liberalism: Expanded Edition* (New York: Columbia University Press, 2013), Lecture VII.

54 For discussion see Samuel Scheffler and Véronique Munoz-Dardé, 'The Division of Moral Labour', *Proceedings of the Aristotelian Society, Supplementary Volume* 79, no. 1 (2005): pp. 229–284.

55 Chiara Cordelli, 'The Institutional Division of Labor and the Egalitarian Obligations of Nonprofits', *Journal of Political Philosophy* 20, no. 2 (2012): pp. 131–155.

56 For a related discussion of the Rawlsian idea that different regulative principles apply to different contexts/practices, see Meckled-Garcia, 'On the Very Idea of Cosmopolitan Justice: Constructivism and International Agency', *Journal of Political Philosophy* 16, no. 3 (2008): pp. 245–271.

57 Cf. the remarks about agents' public vs private nature in Karp, *Responsibility for Human Rights*, ch. 6.

58 Ratner, 'Corporations and Human Rights'; Wettstein, *Multinational Corporations and Global Justice*; Karp, *Responsibility for Human Rights*. Ratner, Wettstein and Karp emphasize aspects of TNCs that render them relevant political actors. Their starting point, though, is not the political conception of human rights, or at least not the version of the political conception I have sketched here. Wettstein, for instance, argues that human rights 'make their normative claim for unconditional respect not merely vis-à-vis governments but against everyone' (see Wettstein, *Multinational Corporations and Global Justice*, p. 285). He then argues that the *de facto* political power possessed by corporations – i.e., their ability to affect the basic functioning of society in a variety of ways, without being effectively challenged, hence acquiring a position of authority – justifies placing primary responsibility for human rights on them. See his 'Beyond Voluntariness, Beyond CSR: Making a Case for Human Rights and Justice', *Business and Society Review* 114, no. 1 (2009): pp. 125–152, esp. pp. 141–142. Karp too thinks that 'all moral agents have responsibilities both to *respect* human rights and also to *refrain from harming* human rights' (see his *Responsibility for Human Rights*, p. 5, added emphases). But when it comes to responsibilities to *protect and provide for* human rights, he defends what he calls the 'publicness' approach. This approach grounds the human-rights responsibilities of transnational corporations in their taking up a public, authoritative role through providing public goods for certain groups of people. See Karp, *Responsibility for Human Rights*, p. 148. For related discussion, see also O'Neill, 'Agents of Justice'.

59 This also explains why, just like governments, TNCs are deemed appropriate subjects of public accountability demands. See Mathias Koenig-Archibugi, 'Transnational Corporations and Public Accountability', *Government and Opposition: An International Journal of Comparative Politics* 39, no. 2 (2004): pp. 234–259. In the main text I say 'at least' because it is an open question, and one I will not explicitly address here, whether local populations affected by TNCs but not 'directly under their rule' may still count, in some weaker sense, as falling under their authority. To the extent that TNCs *require and enforce* non-obstruction with

their operations on the local populations, they may be said to exercise some degree of authority over them as well – with the associated normative consequences. Cf. the discussion of the position of outsiders vis-à-vis the state in Arash Abizadeh, 'Democratic Theory and Border Coercion No Right to Unilaterally Control Your Own Borders', *Political Theory* 36, no. 1 (2008): pp. 37–65.

60 Wettstein, Multinational Corporations and Global Justice, p. 214, added emphasis.
61 See Karp, Responsibility for Human Rights, p. 150.
62 Serena Olsaretti, *Liberty, Desert and the Market: A Philosophical Study* (Cambridge: Cambridge University Press, 2004), ch. 6.
63 Ratner, 'Corporations and Human Rights', p. 509.
64 See Wettstein, Multinational Corporations and Global Justice, ch. 7, for discussion.
65 Cf. Ratner, 'Corporations and Human Rights'.
66 Thanks to Anca Gheaus for raising this point.
67 Thanks to Caleb Yong for pointing this out to me.
68 Karp, Responsibility for Human Rights.
69 Ratner, 'Corporations and Human Rights', pp. 493, 511ff.
70 Thanks to Suzy Killmister and Helen Irving for helpful discussion of this point.
71 Karp, Responsibility for Human Rights, p. 149.
72 On the idea of a natural duty to support and create just institutions, see Rawls *A Theory of Justice*, 293–300. For its application to the international context, cf. Shue, 'Mediating Duties', *Ethics* 98, no. 4 (1988): pp. 687–704.
73 See Valentini, 'Human Rights, Freedom, and Political Authority'.

Part IV

Beyond the nation state?

12 The absence of horizontal effect in human rights law

Domestic violence and the intimate sphere

Sonu Bedi

Domestic violence is a global problem. Recent studies show that violence that takes place in the home or family is still a pressing concern.[1] Feminists have argued that sustaining the private or intimate sphere makes it difficult to address domestic violence.[2] Human rights law and, in particular, the Convention on the Elimination of All Forms of Discrimination Against Women (1981) (CEDAW) represent extant efforts to bring the language of human rights to bear on the problem of domestic violence. This invites us to consider these efforts in light of the distinction between the political and moral or orthodox conception of human rights. Although this distinction is a familiar one in recent work in the philosophy of human rights, its relationship to domestic violence and the intimate sphere has gone largely unnoticed.

Those who defend the orthodox conception view human rights, at least in certain respects, as rights that humans hold independent of social, legal, or political factors,[3] whereas the political conception of human rights views human rights as constitutive of their function or role in international politics and law.[4] I show that human rights law addresses the problem of domestic violence by contemplating only states, not individuals, as the relevant duty bearers of rights. Whereas the political conception informs this feature of human rights law, its orthodox counterpart challenges it. If human rights are 'right[s] we have simply in virtue of being human',[5] as the orthodox conception contends, this means that both individuals and states must count as duty bearers. I argue that, as a result, the orthodox conception goes further than its political counterpart in undermining the private or intimate sphere and the way it shields domestic violence.

I draw from the distinction between the horizontal and vertical effect of rights in making this argument. By 'rights', I mean those claims of justice that are conceptually independent from and more fundamental than democratic outcomes. Throughout the chapter, unless specified otherwise, by 'rights' I mean either constitutional or human rights. A vertical effect constrains state or governmental power: a right is violated only when a political body acts or fails to act in a certain way. The relationship is vertical, because there is a higher body (the state) and the individuals that compromise it. A horizontal effect constrains non-state or private actors: an individual may violate the rights of other individuals.

Although the horizontal/vertical effect distinction is a familiar one in comparative constitutional law,[6] it is largely absent in the philosophical work on human rights. I argue that the political conception affirms only a vertical effect of human rights, in line with extant human rights law. It fails to affirm the idea that individuals in the home or family are recipients of human rights duties. The orthodox conception, in contrast, goes further, explicitly contemplating individuals as recipients of such duties. This poses a challenge to the private or intimate sphere and, in turn, an under-theorized response to domestic violence. It also more directly explains why a state's failure to address such violence is a human rights violation.

This chapter proceeds in three parts, suggesting ever more progressive ways to combat domestic violence in line with the approaches to human rights elucidated above. First, I suggest that the problem of the intimate sphere and its relationship to domestic violence arises with the absence of horizontal effect. I look to *Castlerock v. Gonzales* (U.S. 2005) (held that a state is not constitutionally obligated to prevent domestic violence) to illuminate this problem under the United States Constitution. Second, I outline how *Lenahan (Gonzales) v. United States* (2011), an Inter-American Commission human rights case, and treatises such as CEDAW, hold states responsible for domestic violence. Although human rights law, in line with the political conception, goes further than American constitutional law, it does not contemplate the perpetrators of domestic violence as violating the rights of their victims. Third, drawing from John Locke and Martha Nussbaum, I argue that the orthodox conception goes beyond the vertical effect of rights, placing duties directly on individuals. This poses a fundamental challenge to the private or intimate sphere, representing a powerful response to domestic violence.

1 The intimate sphere and the absence of horizontal effect under the U.S. Constitution

Liberalism's commitment to the intimate sphere entails that there are certain activities or relationship that are outside the scope of justice. One way to understand this sphere in light of written constitutions is due to the absence of horizontal effect in the home or family. If private individuals cannot violate the constitutional rights of their family members to be free from physical violence, this leaves individuals outside the scope of a constitution. This informs the feminist critique of liberalism and its inability to address domestic violence.[7] In so far as there is an absence of horizontal effect, there is no direct challenge to the intimate sphere under a constitution.

This absence is evident in the United State Supreme Court's jurisprudence on domestic violence, jurisprudence that makes clear that violence between private individuals in the family or home does not count as a rights' violation under the U.S. Constitution. As a general matter, the Constitution only has vertical effect. The Bill of Rights along with various other constitutional rights applies just to actions by government. These amendments and the constitutional rights they contain apply to Congress and, by implication, the states. The Fourteenth Amendment reads in part that 'nor shall any State deprive any person of life, liberty, or property without due process of law; nor deny to any person within its jurisdiction equal protection of the laws.'[8] In the *Civil Rights Cases* (1883) the Court makes clear that the Fourteenth Amendment reaches only actions by the state, not actions by private or non-state actors. While these constitutional rights have vertical effect – constraining the state or government – they do not have direct horizontal application.[9]

In fact, in two important cases, the Court has rejected a principle of horizontality in the case of domestic violence, making clear that victims do not suffer rights' violation under the Constitution. This is why domestic violence is a legislative not court driven process in the United States.[10] In *DeShaney v. Winnebago* (1989) the Court held that a Wisconsin county Department of Social Services (DSS) did not violate the Constitution by failing to protect a child who was beaten and placed in a coma by his father. Over a four-year period, Joshua DeShaney's father beat him on numerous occasions. During that period, the DSS made numerous visits to the father's house, documenting the abuse. But DSS did not remove the child from the home. Ultimately, the father inflicted such severe injuries on Joshua DeShaney that he placed the boy in a coma. Randy DeShaney, the boy's father, was tried and convicted for child abuse. He committed a crime under Wisconsin law.

The question faced by the Court was whether the DSS violated the due process clause by depriving the child of his rights to life or liberty. The Court held there was no presumptive constitutional violation, because there was no state action:

> [N]othing in the language of the Due Process Clause itself requires the State to protect the life, liberty, and property of its citizens against invasion by private actors. The Clause is phrased as a limitation on the State's power to act, not as a guarantee of certain minimal levels of safety and security.[11]

Although the Court does not deploy the language of horizontal effect, it makes clear that the Constitution's purpose 'was to protect the people from the State, not to ensure that the State protected them from each other. The Framers were content to leave the extent of governmental obligation in the latter area to the democratic political processes.'[12] The Framers contemplated that issues such as domestic violence would be undertaken by states and their respective police powers. This is another way of saying that private or non-state individuals cannot violate constitutional rights. Randy DeShaney's violent act did not trigger a constitutional breach.

More recently, in *Castlerock v. Gonzales* (2005), the Court held that a Colorado police department did not violate the Constitution by failing to enforce a restraining order, a failure that led to the murder of three girls by their father. Whereas *DeShaney* held that there was no general constitutional duty to prevent violence by private individuals in the home, *Castlerock* went further holding that there is no specific duty to enforce a police restraining order. Jessica Gonzales secured a restraining order against Simon Gonzales, her estranged husband and father of their three children. Gonzales notified the police that her husband had unexpectedly taken the children. The police failed to investigate and later that night he killed the children, only to be killed by the police in a shoot out later. Citing *DeShaney*, the Court held that this did not violate the Constitution and in particular the due process clause:

> In light of today's decision and that in *DeShaney*, the benefit that a third party may receive from having someone else arrested for a crime generally does not trigger protections under the Due Process Clause, neither in its procedural nor in its 'substantive' manifestations.[13]

There is no constitutional benefit, precisely because of the absence of horizontal effect. Gonzales' husband did not violate the rights of his daughters. He committed murder but he did not violate their constitutional rights. Hence, the state had no constitutional duty to protect the children from their father.

Even the dissenting opinion in *Castlerock*, like its counterpart in *DeShaney*, does not affirm a principle of horizontality. 'It is perfectly clear . . . [that the] Federal Constitution itself . . . [does not grant] respondent or her children any individual entitlement to police protection.'[14] Rather, according to the dissent, Colorado had created an obligation to protect the children, cognizable under the Constitution, precisely because it issued a restraining order under the state's own laws and policies. In other words, once the state had created a system of procuring restraining orders, the Constitution may apply. Here too the dissent concedes that individuals cannot violate the rights of others.

Ultimately, this leaves violence that occurs in the family to the 'democratic political process.' Through this process, the relevant demos can decide to establish a department of social services, a police force, or a system of obtaining restraining orders. The Constitution, though, does not require it, precisely because it leaves the intimate sphere – and violence in the family or home – outside of its grasp. Leaving the issue of domestic violence to legislative majorities means that these majorities may decide *not* to take such violence seriously. And with no recourse to the language of rights, there is very little victims of domestic violence can do. Consider that Congress enacted the Violence Against Women's Act (VAWA) in 1994 in order to address the problem of domestic violence. Congress made extensive findings, over a four-year period, conducted a range of interviews to conclude, in part, that states were not doing enough to combat such violence. As one report states:

> [b]ias and discrimination in the [state] criminal justice system often deprive[ ] victims of crimes of violence motivated by gender of equal protection of the laws and the redress to which they are entitled.[15]

To be clear, in these state criminal justice systems, domestic violence was already a crime. But this proved insufficient. Congress found that states often neglected to prosecute perpetrators of domestic violence or ensure the protection of victims. The VAWA sought to address such violence by providing federal funds for social programmes, training, and prevention. The VAWA also provided victims with the ability to sue their perpetrators in federal court. Yet, in *United States v. Morrison* (2000) the Court struck down this part of the act reasoning that Congress exceeded its powers in crafting such a legal remedy.

Even in the case of the VAWA, Congress had to enact legislation to address the problem – not something that was required by the Court. After all, if perpetrators of such violence do not violate the rights of their victims under the Constitution, it is difficult for these victims, as evidenced in *DeShaney* and *Castlerock*, to seek redress from a constitutional court. Add insult to injury, the Court invalidated Congressional efforts to curb domestic violence.[16]

2 Human rights law and the political conception

Jessica Gonzales appealed the decision in *Castlerock* to the Inter-American Commission on Human Rights (hereafter 'the Commission'), a commission that the United States has not ratified. In *Lenahan v., the United States* (2011) (Jessica Gonzales had changed her name to Lenahan) held that the United States violated the human rights of Lenahan's children. I argue that this decision goes further than American constitutional law by holding states responsible for failing to protect victims of domestic violence under human rights law. However, it also does not adopt the horizontal effect of human rights. This is because human rights law is generally vertical in nature. In line with the political conception, the relevant duty bearers are still the relevant member states.

Consider that the Universal Declaration of Human Rights adopted by the United Nations General Assembly in 1948 lists a schedule of basic rights including the 'right to life, liberty, and security of person'[17] and the right not to 'be subjected to torture or to cruel, inhuman or degrading treatment or punishment.'[18] The Declaration makes clear that '[a]ll human beings are born free and equal in dignity and rights.'[19] But the Declaration itself is addressed only to member states:

> Whereas Member States have pledged themselves to achieve, in co-operation with the United Nations, the promotion of universal respect for and observance of human rights and fundamental freedoms.[20]

The Declaration does not place duties on individuals not to violate the rights of others. Although Article I of the Declaration says that individuals 'should act towards one another in a spirit of brotherhood,'[21] this very general statement does not explicitly contemplate horizontal effect. Rather, the Declaration is a vertical only regime, where duties are placed on member states.

This is borne out by human rights treaties such as the Convention Against Torture and Other Cruel, Inhuman or Degrading Treatment or Punishment (1987) that defines torture as 'inflicted by or at the instigation of or with the consent or acquiescence of a public official or other person acting in an official capacity.'[22] The Convention applies the duty not to torture only to those individuals who are acting in an 'official capacity.'[23] Only state actors may violate a right not to be tortured. The very definition of torture excludes 'pain or suffering' inflicted by a private, non-state affiliated individual in order to illicit some kind of information. If I inflict pain on my neighbour in order that he reveal his bank account password and information, I have not committed torture. I have not violated his human rights. Or consider the more recent International Convention for the Protection of All Persons from Enforced Disappearance (2010) that defines 'enforced disappearance' as 'the arrest, detention, abduction or any other form of deprivation of liberty by agents of the State or by persons or groups of persons acting with the authorization, support or acquiescence of the State.'[24] So if I were to kidnap my neighbour, I would not have committed an enforced disappearance. The Convention only places duties on state actors or those who are affiliated with the state. In both these cases human rights law is vertical in nature. It does not impose duties on individuals.[25]

This does not mean that human rights law is blind to actions by private individuals. Human rights treatises sometimes require that states pass domestic legislation effectively ensuring that individuals do not violate the rights of others. For instance, the International Convention on the Elimination of All Forms of Racial Discrimination (1969) (ICERD) defines racial discrimination and then goes on to say that:

> Each State Party shall prohibit and bring to an end, by all appropriate means, including legislation as required by circumstances, racial discrimination by any persons, group or organization.[26]

Similarly, and important to the argument of this chapter, the CEDAW also adopts a broad definition of discrimination, in this case discrimination against women. It is worth noting that the United States has not ratified CEDAW.[27] Like ICERD it requires that:

> States Parties condemn discrimination against women in all its forms, agree to pursue by all appropriate means and without delay a policy of eliminating discrimination against women and, to this end, undertake . . . To take all appropriate measures to eliminate discrimination against women by any person, organization or enterprise.[28]

Both ICERD and CEDAW require states to pass legislation, taking 'all appropriate' means or measure to end racial and gender discrimination by private individuals.

But even in these cases, human rights law does not adopt horizontal effect. These conventions do not place duties directly on individuals. Rather, they constrain individuals only indirectly, still imposing on states the duty to pass legislation that would prohibit or end discrimination.

This informs the political conception of human rights. According to the political conception, these rights are not independent of legal, government or social recognition. Rather, 'human rights are understood primarily as international norms that aim to protect fundamental human interests and/or secure for individuals, the opportunity to participate as members in political society.'[29] It makes sense then that such rights will generally impose duties only on states, because states are powerful entities that generally have the monopoly of force over their citizens. John Rawls in fact, considers states and not individuals as the central entities that have standing in his account of human rights.[30]

This is why Thomas Pogge rightly remarks that an 'ordinary assault in a pub' does not constitute a 'human-rights violation,' pointing to an issue of who may violate human rights.[31] Likewise, Laura Valentini says that the relevant duty bearers in human rights are not 'other individuals but political institutions.'[32] And she sees this as informing the political conception of human rights.[33] Although he does not invoke the vertical/horizontal distinction, Christian Tomuschat makes clear that 'human rights violations can, in principle, be committed only by states and/or the persons acting on behalf of the state.'[34]

The political conception has the potential to go further than the U.S. Constitution by imposing human rights based duties on states to prevent domestic violence. The Commission, in line with CEDAW, does just that, holding 'a State's failure to act with due diligence to protect women from violence constitutes a form of discrimination, and denies women their right to equality before the law.'[35] The Commission reasons that:

> As with all fundamental rights and freedoms, the Commission has observed that States are not only obligated to provide for equal protection of the law. They must also adopt the legislative, policy and other measures necessary to guarantee the effective enjoyment of the rights protected under Article II of the American Declaration.[36]

But in concluding that the United States violated the human rights of Lenahan, the Commission did not adopt the horizontal effect of rights. Nowhere did the decision say that Lenahan's ex-husband violated the rights of her children, placing duties directly on individuals. Rather, the Commission places the relevant duty on the states for 'International instruments in general require State parties not only to respect the rights enumerated therein, but also to ensure that individuals within their jurisdictions also exercise those rights.'[37] The United States violated human rights law, according to the Commission, precisely because it did not protect Lenahan and her children. The decision holds that 'human rights obligations' are 'not only negative in nature' but also 'require[] positive action from States.'[38]

The Commission couples this argument by explicitly recognizing that 'Gender-based violence is one of the most extreme and pervasive forms of discrimination, severely impairing and nullifying the enforcement of women's rights.'[39] It then goes on to hold that 'Various international human rights bodies have moreover considered State failures in the realm of domestic violence not only discriminatory, but also violations to the right to life of women.'[40] In this way, CEDAW and the Commission explicate this positive right in the context of a commitment to gender equality. Often scholarly work views domestic violence as an issue of gender discrimination.[41] Under this view, the state's failure to address domestic violence is evidence of structural or institutional sexism.

The political conception may very well have the resources to respond to the problem of domestic violence by arguing that the public/private divide itself is up for democratic renegotiation.[42] Charles Beitz argues that human rights are 'dynamic.'[43] Directly speaking to the public/private distinction, Seyla Benhabib contends:

> All struggles against oppression in the modern world begin by redefining what had previously been considered 'private', non-public and non-political issues as matters of public concern, as issues of justice, as sites of power which need discursive legitimation.[44]

This discursive, democratic process is one that is not given prior to politics or deliberation. This may permit the political conception to reclassify an issue or problem, such as violence that takes place in the family or home, as a human rights concern.

> The underlying problem with addressing domestic violence is the absence of horizontal effect. Rather than responding to this problem directly, the political approach (understood in a reflexive or dynamic way) seems to focus on its symptoms. This approach challenges the rigidity of the public/private divide in order to permit human rights discourse to acknowledge and address such violence.

Although this approach is significant, it still seeks to address domestic violence within a vertical only regime. Even though it permits victims to appeal to the language of human rights, for example, in the form of a right to ensure gender equality, the rights' violator is still the state. Treaties like CEDAW, in line with *DeShaney* and *Castlerock*, do not contemplate *perpetrators* as violating the rights of their victims. The state is the only culprit in discriminating against women by failing to protect them. Human rights law may go further than the U. S. Constitution but it does not go far enough in contemplating the horizontal effect of human rights. That is, there is no direct horizontal effect of a right to be free from physical violence in the home or family under human rights law. Rather, the language of rights arises from positing an affirmative or positive right for the state to engage in 'due diligence' or 'to take appropriate measures' to 'combat domestic violence.' This permits the political conception to address domestic violence in light of human rights discourse while still placing obligations only on the state.

In approaching the problem of domestic violence in a vertical fashion, human rights law, and the political conception that informs it, does not challenge the intimate or private sphere. By contemplating only states as possible rights' violators, the political conception does not seek to collapse the idea that there is an intimate area off limits to the reach of justice. After all, this is why human rights law places the duty on the state and not on the Simon Gonzales i.e. the perpetrator of domestic violence.

3 The orthodox conception and horizontal effect

I argue that the orthodox conception poses a more progressive response to domestic violence by actually challenging the existence of the intimate sphere. I draw from John Locke and Martha Nussbaum to explicate the horizontal effect of human rights. Although these are two very different accounts of rights both reflect the core implication of the orthodox conception, one where duties apply directly to individuals.

Locke's account of pre-political rights and the ends of government in his *Second Treatise of Government* inform the moral conception of human rights and, in turn, the principle of horizontal effect. According to Locke:

> The *state of nature* has a law of nature to govern it, which obliges every one: and reason, which is that law, teaches all mankind, who will but consult it, that being all *equal and independent*, no one ought to harm another in his life, health, liberty, or possessions.[45]

Individuals in the state of nature can violate the rights of others. If you physically harm me unjustifiably, you have violated my right to life or liberty. Rights are pre-political, precisely because they can be 'possessed independent of (logically prior to) civil society.'[46] This explains why the rise of government is necessary. In the state of nature, our enjoyment of rights is 'uncertain' and 'constantly exposed to the Invasion of others.'[47] The social compact arises as a more satisfactory method of securing the rights to life, liberty, and property. For Locke, individuals do not give up their rights in civil society. We only relinquish our power to punish violations of such rights.[48]

Although this is a familiar and admittedly brief account of Locke's argument, its relationship to the principle of horizontal effect has gone largely unnoticed. It is precisely because these rights are pre-political, that they must apply between and among individuals. Certainly, government may violate our rights by kidnapping us or arbitrarily killing or putting us in jail. But these rights also constrain individuals. As Locke makes clear: 'The Obligations of the Law of Nature, cease not in Society . . . Thus, the Law of Nature stands as an Eternal Rule to all Men, *Legislators* a well as others.'[49] This means that for Locke horizontal and vertical effect are both central to his conception of rights. Of course, legislators may not violate the obligations of the law of nature, obligations to protect the rights to life, liberty, and property. But importantly, individuals must also abide by these rights. Just as in the state of nature, I violate your rights by unjustifiably killing or physically harming you, so too do I violate your rights with the rise of government by doing so. This is why James Griffin claims that human rights are 'right[s] we have simply in virtue of being human.'[50] Being a human being is sufficient in order to possess human rights.

Under Locke's account, then, domestic violence ought to be a human rights' violation. Interestingly, Locke never uses the words 'private (or intimate) sphere' in the *Second Treatise.* Rather, he deploys a distinction between paternal and political power. Locke makes clear that 'these two powers, political and paternal, are so perfectly distinct and separate; are built upon so different foundations, and given to so different ends.'[51] For Locke, paternal power unlike political power is not exercised over equals. Both children and wives are under the authority of their father or husband; authority that itself precedes the rise of government. This is why Carole Pateman's classic feminist critique of social contract theory highlights Locke's sexism. For Locke, 'women's subjection to men was natural, and so outside of and irrelevant to the continuing controversies and struggles over political power in the state and economy.'[52] It may be hard to square Locke's argument with a robust commitment to gender equality. I do not seek to engage this debate here.

Relevant to the argument of this chapter is that Locke makes clear that violence committed within the family is wrong. That is, the paternal power does not permit a father or husband to kill or physically abuse those under his care: it 'gives the husband no more power over her life than she has over his.'[53] Similarly, Locke says that parents do not have complete power over their children. This power is 'for the help, instruction, and preservation of their offspring', but there is 'no reason why it should be thought to extend to life and death, at any time, over their children, more than over any body else.'[54]

This means that paternal power does not extend to issues of life and death, to acts of violence. By speaking in the language of power, Locke specifically contemplates that this power is limited. Simply equating paternal power to the existence of the intimate sphere (again, Locke does not actually deploy those words) obscures this point. The notion of a sphere connotes a wholly separate realm of activity that is not subject to rights' limitations. It suggests a vertical only regime where rights do not constrain private or non-state actors. But power, whether exercised by husbands or the state, is subject to such limitations. Power is often limited. The language of 'powers' versus one of 'spheres' implies as much.

This means a husband that commits violence against his wife or his children, as Randy DeShaney and Simon Gonzales did, violates their rights – rights that these individuals have always possessed. This is a central implication of the pre-political feature of a right to life; a feature that means private individuals can be possible right violators within the home or family. Horizontal effect stands alongside the political/paternal distinction. Although these are separate kinds of powers, exercises of either can trigger a rights' violation. Just as the state may violate your right to be free from unjustified physical violence – political power may be limited (vertical effect), individuals in the home or family may violate it – paternal power may be limited (horizontal effect).

Ironically, Lockean liberalism is often seen as creating rather than addressing the problem of domestic violence and the intimate sphere,[55] and as informing rather than undermining the theory of rights espoused in the Constitution.[56] But in so far as Locke's account justifies a principle of horizontality where violent acts committed in the home or family are rights' violations, this may invite a reappraisal of the value of his account and its relationship to the Constitution.

We can also arrive at the importance of horizontality without the need to affirm pre-political rights and the often-contested assumptions that underlie them. Martha Nussbaum's account of justice proffers the idea of a 'basic social minimum' that 'focuses on human capabilities, that is, what people are actually able to do and to be – in a way informed by an intuitive idea of a life that is worthy of the dignity of the human being.'[57] Nussbaum does not seek to justify her approach on metaphysical grounds. Her approach, unlike Locke's, is self-consciously political, not pre-political. In fact, she envisions, in line with John Rawls's notion of political liberalism, an overlapping consensus where those from different kinds of conceptions of the good can accept her account.[58]

Central to her approach is a commitment to human dignity; a commitment, according to Nussbaum, that has 'broad cross-cultural resonance and intuitive power.'[59] This kind of dignity means that a human beings

> 'have worth as an end, a kind of awe-inspiring something that makes it horrible to see this person beaten down by the currents of chance – and wonderful, at the same time, to witness the way in which chance has not completely eclipsed the humanity of the person.'[60]

She contends that individuals from various cultural and religious backgrounds can affirm such dignity, and in turn, a core set of capabilities. She identities ten such capabilities including: 'life, bodily health, bodily integrity, sense, imagination, and thought, emotions, practical reason, affiliation, other species, play and control over one's environment.'[61]

These capabilities are, for Nussbaum, better and more powerful ways to understand the idea of rights. To secure a right to something is nothing other than to ensure that an individual is capable of doing something, of exercising her aforementioned core capabilities. In fact, the language of capabilities rather than rights directly challenges the public/private distinction:

> The discourse of human rights originated in Western societies that relied strongly on the private/public distinction; the sphere of rights was typically imagined as the public sphere, and the family was typically imagined as a private sphere to which the discourse of rights had no applicability. Indeed, this way of thinking of rights has been one of the major impediments to winning recognition for women's rights as human rights. The concept of capabilities has no such baggage to jettison, and the idea of being able to do or be something is obviously applicable inside the family, as well as outside of it.[62]

This idea of being able to exercise one's core capabilities both inside and outside the family is crucial to the argument of this essay. Many of the core capabilities are relevant to the problem of domestic violence. In particular, Nussbaum further specifies 'bodily integrity' as:

> Being able to move freely from place to place; having one's bodily boundaries treated as sovereign, i.e. being able to be secure against assault, including sexual assault, child sexual abuse, and domestic violence; having opportunities for sexual satisfaction and for choice in matters of reproduction.[63]

Nussbaum makes clear that with regards to domestic violence, the 'capability of bodily integrity is so directly involved here that there would seem little point in further detail.'[64] It's obvious that threat of such violence serves to compromise an individual's exercise of this capability in the family or outside of it.

If women's capabilities are thwarted by such violence, and this much is clear, it does not matter that such violence is committee by private actors. If 'bodily integrity' is a core capability that democracies must ensure, it does not matter whether state or non-state actors compromise it. The right to be free from physical violence, in turn, must also apply to individuals in the family or home.

In fact, Nussbaum explicitly criticizes the idea that a state's failure to act constitutes no violation under a constitution. According to her, the 'capabilities approach insists that all fundamental entitlements require and deserve state action for their protection, and that all must be supported, or else basic justice, minimal justice, has not been done. The benchmark is not absence of intervention, it is actual capability: people must be put in a position in which they can really do or be the thing in question.'[65] This suggests that Nussbaum would be critical of *DeShaney* and *Castlerock*, precisely because 'social and political institutions should be chosen, at least in part, with a view to promoting at least a threshold level of these human capabilities.[66] Obviously, 'social and political institutions' diminished these victims' human dignity by failing to promote their core capabilities.

But Nussbaum's account and, as a result, the orthodox conception go further by contemplating that private individual may be right violators in line with a principle of horizontality. She explains that even after the Bill of Rights of the Constitution was incorporated against the states (its original purpose was only to constrain the federal government), these rights did not reach 'discrimination by private actors.'[67] This is why, as Nussbaum says, '[s]exual harassment, for example, is illegal only because of legislative action, and not as a constitutional matter.'[68]

The orthodox conception, as evidenced by Locke and Nussbaum, poses a fundamental challenge to the intimate sphere, precisely because individuals can violate the human rights (capabilities) of others. Like the political conception, this means that states may violate the human rights of the victims of domestic violence by not protecting them through laws and polices. But the orthodox or moral conception goes further by contemplating perpetrators as right violators. Because the orthodox conception views human rights as 'right[s] we have simply in virtue of being human' this necessarily entails that domestic violence constitutes a direct human rights violations.[69]

In this way, the orthodox conception more straightforwardly explains why a state's neglect in prosecuting and preventing domestic abuse is indeed a human rights violation. Consider a state where gender based violence is severe problem. The political and legal system does not adequately respond to such violence, failing to treat it as seriously as it does other acts of violence. How does the political conception explain that this state is a human rights abuser, if the acts of violence are not violations of human rights? Put differently, what explains the fact that the state has a duty to prevent domestic violence under human rights law, if the individuals themselves who perpetrate such violence do not have such a duty? Any such explanation will have to offer some tortured justification connecting the acts of domestic violence to the conclusion that the state but not the individual perpetrator is a human rights violator.

The orthodox conception, in contrast, simply contends that the perpetrators of domestic violence are committing human rights violations. The fact that the state does not do enough to reduce such violations explains why the state violates human rights. Under the orthodox conception, the perpetrators of this violence are indeed human rights violators. By failing to prevent and curtail these human rights violations, the state fails to protect the human rights of the victims of this kind of violence. The connection between the acts of domestic violence and the responsibility of the state is straightforward. The state violates human rights, because it does not do enough to curb individual human rights' violations within its jurisdiction.

Certainly, the fact that the orthodox conception provides distinctive grounds for directly criminalizing domestic violence does not itself provide a remedy where the state is not responsive to such grounds. But this misses the importance of the normative force of a human rights claim. For once we, including individuals, activists, non-governmental organizations, and human rights' committees, publish state reports and draw on human rights norms to 'call out' perpetrators of domestic violence as direct human right violators, we have the resources to attempt to change existing sexist norms and practices by challenging the intimate sphere.

Once we appreciate the force of the orthodox conception as I have outlined it here, we realize that it does not matter that domestic violence takes place within the family or home. This does not extinguish or mitigate its seriousness. The orthodox conception, in effect, recognizes the power and domination that often exist within families and relationships. Bringing the language of human rights to bear on the perpetrators of domestic violence – treating such private actors as similarly culpable under human rights law as their state counterparts – represents a more forceful objection to domestic violence. The intimate sphere holds less salience under the orthodox conception, precisely because perpetrators have a duty under it not to violate the human rights of their spouses or children.

Somewhat ironically, the political conception, in line with extant human rights law, responds to domestic violence in an orthodox way. Although this conception contends that a state violates the human rights of victims of domestic violence by not adequately protecting them, it does not go as far as its moral or orthodox counterpart. The orthodox conception affirms both verticality (states violate human rights by failing to prevent domestic violence) and horizontality (perpetrators in a family or home violate the rights of their victims). In so far as human rights law is beholden to the political conception, we do not have the philosophical resources to challenge in a fundamental way the existence of the intimate sphere. In contrast, the orthodox or moral conception may provide a more thoroughgoing critique of this sphere.

Notes

1 See generally Domestic Violence Against Women and Girls, UNICEF Innocenti Research Centre, Florence, Italy (2000), www.unicef-irc.org/publications/pdf/digest6e.pdf.

2 See for example, Anita L. Allen, *Uneasy Access: Privacy For Women in a Free Society* (Totowka: Rowman & Littlefield, 1988), pp. 79–80; Kristin A. Kelly, *Domestic Violence and the Politics of Privacy* (Ithaca: Cornell University Press, 2003); Linda C. McClain, 'Inviolability and Privacy: The Castle, the Sanctuary, and the Body', *Yale Journal of Law and Humanities* 7, no. 1

(1995): p. 195; Catharine A. MacKinnon, *Feminism Unmodified: Discourses on Life and Law* (Cambridge: Harvard University Press, 1987); Susan Moller Okin, *Justice, Gender, and the Family* (New York: Basic Books, 1989); Carole Pateman, *The Disorder of Women: Democracy, Feminism and Political Theory* (Cambridge: Polity Press, 1989), pp. 118–140.

3 See for example Alan Gewirth, *Human Rights* (Chicago: University of Chicago Press, 1982); James Griffin, *On Human Rights* (Oxford: Oxford University Press, 2008); John Tasioulas, 'Are Human Rights Essentially Triggers for Intervention?' *Philosophy Compass* 4, no. 6(2009): p. 938.

4 See for example, Charles Beitz, *The Idea of Human Rights* (Oxford: Oxford University Press, 2009); Joshua Cohen, 'Minimalism About Human Rights: The Best We Can Hope For?' *Journal of Political Philosophy* 12, no. 2 (2004): p. 190; Kenneth Baynes, 'Toward a Political Conception of Human Rights', *Philosophy and Social Criticism* 35, no. 4 (2009): p. 371; John Rawls, *The Law of Peoples* (Cambridge: Harvard University Press, 1999); Pablo Gilabert, 'Humanist and Political Perspective Human Rights', *Political Theory* 39, no. 4 (2011): p. 439; Joseph Raz, 'Human Rights Without Foundations', in *The Philosophy of International Law*, edited by Samantha Besson and John Tasioulas (Oxford: Oxford University Press, 2010); Laura Valentini, 'In What Sense Are Human Rights Political? A Preliminary Exploration', *Political Studies* 60, no. 1(2012): p. 180.

5 Griffin, On Human Rights, p. 13.

6 See Stephen Gardbaum, 'The "Horizontal Effect" of Constitutional Rights', *Michigan Law Review* 102, no. 1 (2003): p. 387; Dawn Oliver and Jörg Fedtke, eds., *Human Rights and the Private Sphere: A Comparative Study* (New York: Routledge-Cavendish, 2009); Mark Tushnet, 'The Issue of State Action/Horizontal Effect in Comparative Constitutional Law', *International Journal of Constitutional Law* 1 no. 1 (2003): p. 79; Mark Tushnet, *Weak Courts, Strong Rights: Judicial Review and Social Welfare Rights in Comparative Constitutional Law* (Princeton: Princeton University Press, 2009).

7 See for example Allen, *Uneasy Access*; Kelly, *Domestic Violence*; McClain, 'Inviolability and Privacy; MacKinnon, *Feminism Unmodified*; Okin, *Justice, Gender, and the Family*; Pateman, *The Disorder of Women*, pp. 118–140; Robin West, 'Toward an Abolitionist Interpretation of the Fourteenth Amendment', *West Virginia Law Review* 94, no. 1 (1991): p. 111.

8 United States Constitution, Amendment XIV.

9 Now scholarly work has been critical of the state action requirement, positing alternative readings of the Constitution that avoid this requirement. See Erwin Chemerinsky, 'Rethinking State Action,' *Northwestern University Law Review* 80, no. 3 (1985): p. 503; Mark D. Rosen, 'Was Shelley v. Kraemer Incorrectly Decided? Some New Answers', *California Law Review* 95, no. 2 (2007): p. 451; West, 'Toward an Abolitionist Interpretation'. My purpose here is not to adjudicate this line of reasoning, only demonstrate that as a generally accepted principle the Constitution does not have direct horizontal effect. See generally Mark Tushnet, 'Shelley v. Kraemer and Theories of Equality', *New York Law School Law Review* 33, no. 1 (1988): p. 383. See also David P. Currie, 'Positive and Negative Constitutional Rights', *The University of Chicago Law Review* 53 (1986): p. 864.

10 Linda Gordon's classic account of the history of family violence in Boston demonstrates that social movements that included women, progressives, and reformers drew attention to the problem of such violence; see Linda Gordon, *Heroes of Their Own Lives: The Politics and History of Family Violence: Boston, 1880–1960* (Illinois: University of Illinois Press, 2002 [1988]), Gordon argues that only in the 1870s was family violence beginning to be seen as a social and hence political issue – subject to regulation by the state and not merely a personal matter.

11 *DeShaney v. Winnebago*, 489 U.S. 189 (1989) at 195.

12 *DeShaney* at 196.

13 *Castlerock v. Gonzales*, 545 U.S. 748 (2005) at 768.

14 *Castlerock* at 773, dissenting.

15 H. R. Conf. Rep. No. 103–711 (1994): 385.

16 See for example Julie Goldscheid, 'United States v. Morrison and the Civil Rights Remedy of the Violence Against Women Act: A Civil Rights Law Struck Down in the Name of Federalism', *Cornell Law Review* 96 (2000): p. 109; Catharine A. MacKinnon, 'Disputing Male Sovereignty: On United States v. Morrison', *Harvard Law Review* 114 (2000): p. 135; Louis J. Virelli III and David S. Leibowitz, 'Federalism Whether They Want It or Not: The New

Commerce Clause Doctrine and the Future of Federal Civil Rights Legislation After United States v. Morrison', *University of Pennsylvania Journal of Constitutional Law* 3 (2001): p. 926.

17 The Universal Declaration of Human Rights (UDHR), www.un.org/en/documents/udhr/index.shtml, Article 3.

18 UDHR, Article 5.

19 UDHR, Article 1.

20 UDHR, Preamble.

21 UDHR, Article I.

22 The Convention Against Torture and Other Cruel, Inhuman or Degrading Treatment or Punishment (CATOCIDTP), http://treaties.un.org/doc/Publication/UNTS/Volume%201465/volume-1465-I-24841-English.pdf, Article I.

23 CATOCIDTP, Article I.

24 International Convention for the Protection of All Persons From Enforced Disappearance. www.ohchr.org/en/hrbodies/ced/pages/conventionced.aspx, Article 2.

25 In so far as there exist horizontal duties in international law, they arise under international criminal law. See John H. Knox, 'Horizontal Human Rights Law', *The American Journal of International Law* 102 (2008): pp. 1, 28.

26 International Convention on the Elimination of All Forms of Racial Discrimination. http://treaties.un.org/doc/publication/UNTS/Volume%20660/v660.pdf, Article 2.

27 See generally Lisa Baldez, *Defying Convention: US Resistance to the UN Treaty on Women's Rights* (Cambridge: Cambridge University Press, 2014).

28 The Convention on the Elimination of All Forms of Discrimination Against Women (CEDAW). www.un.org/womenwatch/daw/cedaw/text/econvention.htm, Article 2.

29 Baynes, 'Toward a Political Conception of Human Rights', p. 375.

30 Rawls, The Law of Peoples.

31 Thomas Pogge, 'The International Significance of Human Rights', *The Journal of Ethics* 4 (2000): pp. 45, 47.

32 Valentini, 'In What Sense are Human Rights Political?', p. 182.

33 Valentini, 'In What Sense are Human Rights Political?', p. 182.

34 Christian Tomuschat, *Human Rights: Between Idealism and Realism* (Oxford: Oxford University Press, 2003), p. 309.

35 *Jessica Lenahan (Gonzales) and Others v. United States* (Inter American Commission on Hunan Rights (2011): Article 111.

36 *Lenahan*, sec. 108.

37 *Lenahan*, sec. 117.

38 *Lenahan*, sec. 117. See for example, CEDAW; Inter-American Convention on the Prevention, Punishment and Eradication of Violence Against Women (1995); International Covenant on Civil and Political Rights, (1976); International Covenant on Economic, Social and Cultural Rights (1976).

39 *Lenahan*, sec. 110.

40 *Lenahan*, sec. 112.

41 See for example, Elizabeth M. Schneider, *Battered Women and Feminist Lawmaking* (New Haven: Yale Press, 2000); Susan Schechter, *Women and Male Violence: The Visions and Struggles of the Battered Women's Movement* (Cambridge: South End Press, 1982); Catharine A. MacKinnon, 'Reflections on Sex Equality Under the Law', *Yale Law Journal* 100 (1991): p. 1281; Sally Goldfarb, 'Applying the Discrimination Model to Violence Against Women: Some Reflections on Theory and Practice', *American Journal Gender, Social Policy and Law* 11 (2003): p. 251; Goldscheid, 'United States v. Morrison'.

42 See for example Beitz, *The Idea of Human Rights;* Seyla Benhabib, *Situating the Self* (New York: Routledge, 1992); Seyla Benhabib, *The Rights of Others: Aliens, Residents, and Citizens* (Cambridge: Cambridge University Press, 2004); Seyla Benhabib, *Dignity in Adversity: Human Rights in Turbulent Times* (Cambridge: Polity Press 2011); Jean Cohen, *Regulating Intimacy: A New Legal Paradigm* (Princeton: Princeton University Press, 2002); Jürgen Habermas, 'Remarks on Legitimation through Human Rights', in *The Postnational Constellation: Political Essays*, edited and translated by Max Pensky (Cambridge: Polity Press, 2001), p. 116; Karen Zivi, *Making Rights Claims: A Practice of Democratic Citizenship* (New York: Oxford University Press, 2011).

43 Beitz, The Idea of Human Rights, p. 44.
44 Benhabib, *Situating the Self*, p. 100.
45 John Locke, Second Treatise of Government, ed. Peter Laslett (Cambridge: Cambridge University Press, 1988 [1690]), section 6.
46 A. John Simmons, *The Lockean Theory of Rights* (Princeton: Princeton University Press, 1992), p. 90.
47 Locke, Second Treatise of Government, section 123.
48 Locke, Second Treatise of Government, sections 127–131.
49 Locke, Second Treatise of Government, section 135.
50 Griffin, On Human Rights, p. 13.
51 Locke, Second Treatise of Government, section 71.
52 Carole Pateman, *The Sexual Contract* (Stanford: Stanford University Press, 1988), pp. 85, 91. See also Kelly, *Domestic Violence.*
53 Locke, Second Treatise of Government, section 81.
54 Locke, Second Treatise of Government, section 170.
55 Kristin Kelly, for instance, concedes that in 'fairness to Locke, it should be acknowledged that he does place unprecedented limitations on power granted to husbands.' See Kelly *Domestic Violence,* p. 25–26. These limitations over 'life and death' are 'very important to any discussion of battering.' See Kelly, *Domestic Violence,* p. 26.
56 Locke is often seen as 'America's Philosopher.' See Michael Zuckert, 'Natural Rights and Imperial Constitutionalism: The American Revolution and the Development of the American Amalgam', in *Natural Rights Liberalism from Locke to Nozick*, edited by Ellen Frankel Paul, Fred D. Miller, Jr., and Jeffrey Paul (New York: Cambridge University Press, 2005), p. 27; but see Garry Wills, *Inventing America: Jefferson's Declaration of Independence* (New York: Double Day, 1978), pp. 169–174. His conception of pre-political rights is taken as central to the underlying political theory of the United States Constitution. See generally Randy E. Barnett, *Restoring the Lost Constitution: The Presumption of Liberty* (Princeton: Princeton University Press, 2005); Michael Zuckert, *The Natural Rights Republic: Studies in the Foundation of the American Political Tradition* (South Bend: Notre Dame Press, 1996). In particular, some see the Declaration of Independence's commitment to pre-political rights as embodied in the Bill of Rights. See for example, Dan Himmelfarb, 'The Constitutional Relevance of the Second Sentence of the Declaration of Independence', *Yale Law Journal* 100 (1990): p. 169; Michael W. McConnell, 'Natural Rights and the Ninth Amendment: How Does Lockean Legal Theory Assist in Interpretation', *New York University Journal of Law and Liberty* 5 (2010): p. 1. See also Robert P. George, 'Natural Law, the Constitution, and the Theory and Practice of Judicial Review', *Fordham Law Review* 69 (2001): 2269; Hon. Diarmuid F. O'Scannlain, 'The Natural Law in the American Tradition', *Fordham Law Review* 79 (2011): p. 1513.
57 Martha C. Nussbaum, *Women and Human Development: The Capabilities Approach* (Cambridge: Cambridge University Press, 2001), p. 5; see also Martha C. Nussbaum, 'Capabilities as Fundamental Entitlements: Sen and Social Justice', *Feminist economics* 9, no. 3 (2003a.): p. 33.
58 See Nussbaum, *Women and Human Development*, p. 69. See generally Eric Nelson, 'From Primary Goods to Capabilities Distributive Justice and the Problem of Neutrality', *Political Theory* 36, no. 1 (2008): p. 93.
59 Nussbaum, Women and Human Development, p. 72.
60 Nussbaum, Women and Human Development, p. 97.
61 Nussbaum, Women and Human Development, pp. 79–80.
62 Martha C. Nussbaum, 'Women's Bodies: Violence, Security, Capabilities', *Journal of Human Development* 6, no. 2 (2005): pp. 167–183, 176.
63 Nussbaum, Women and Human Development, p. 78.
64 Nussbaum, 'Women's Bodies', p. 172.
65 Nussbaum, 'Women's Bodies', p. 176.
66 Nussbaum, Women and Human Development, p. 75.
67 Nussbaum, 'Women's Bodies', p. 176.
68 Nussbaum, 'Women's Bodies', p. 176.
69 Griffin, On Human Rights, p. 13.

13 The 'human' right to self-defence

Natural, institutional or political right?

Seumas Miller

1 Introduction: moral and institutional rights

My focus in this chapter is on the moral right to self-defence and, in particular, on the question as to whether this moral right is a natural, institutional or political right.[1] I argue that there is a natural (moral) right to self-defence, a legal (institutional and moral) right to self-defence and a political (institutional and moral) right to collective self-defence, but that these moral rights do not mirror one another since the natural right to self-defence does not depend on a necessity condition, and the necessity condition upon which the legal right to self-defence rests differs importantly from the necessity condition upon which the right to collective self-defence rests. As a preliminary to this exploration of these various (as it turns out) rights to self-defence I need to provide a characterization of the distinction between natural and institutional rights. I understand political rights to be a species of institutional rights; specifically, rights pertaining to political institutions.

Some moral rights, such as the right to life, right not to be tortured, right to (clean) air and water, and the right to freedom of movement, are evidently logically prior to social institutions. These moral rights depend on properties that we have *qua* human beings: the capacity to suffer physical pain, to freely move around and so on. Let us, therefore, refer to these moral rights as natural rights. By contrast, some moral rights, such as the right to vote, the right to a fair trial, and the rights to buy/sell land/labour, are logically dependent on social institutions. These moral rights presuppose institutions: democratic governments, courts of law, institutions of property, markets and so on.[2]

Natural rights bring with them concomitant moral obligations. For example, the right not to be killed has a concomitant obligation not to kill. Moreover, natural rights are such that discharging their concomitant obligations is always possible, at least in principle if not in practice. Thus murderers could refrain from killing innocents and torturers could refrain from engaging in torture. The obligations in relation to some positive natural rights, such as the right to (clean) air and water, and to basic foodstuffs and shelter might seem more problematic, given various economic and (especially) political obstacles.[3] However, I suggest that discharging these obligations is, at least in principle, possible, given the abundance of the earth's resources, the possibility of redesigning relevant institutions and so on. Further natural rights generate enforcement obligations, such as the obligation on the part of third parties to prevent attackers from killing innocent persons. Again, I suggest that enforcement of natural rights is always in principle possible, even if not in practice on some occasions, e.g. by the removal of natural rights-violating government at some point (even if not immediately).

Natural moral rights are often institutionalized, e.g. legalized. However, the fact that a natural moral right is institutionalized does not make it an institutional right in my above sense, i.e. a moral right which presupposes an institution. Of course, it is trivially true that all institutional rights are institutional rights. However, natural moral rights that are institutionalized do not *qua moral rights* presuppose institutions and are not, therefore, institutional moral rights in the required sense.

With respect to moral rights that are also institutional rights (in the sense of presupposing institutions) there is an important distinction germane to our purposes here between *general* institutional moral rights and *special* institutional moral rights. General institutional moral rights – and, for that matter, general institutional duties – attach to all members of a nation-state (or like polity).[4] General institutional moral rights depend in part on properties that we possess as human beings and in part on membership of a community with social institutions of the relevant kind. General institutional moral rights/duties attach to all or most members of a nation-state because they are logically dependent on institutions in which all or most members participate, e.g. right to vote, right to equality under the law, the obligation to obey the law. I note that some general institutional moral rights and duties transcend the nation-state by virtue of trans-national social institutions, e.g. the right to buy and sell in international markets. I also note that many general institutional moral rights are among *so-called* human rights, e.g. the right to vote.

Special institutional moral rights and duties are constitutive of institutional roles. As such, they are not rights or duties that are possessed by all members of a polity; rather they attach to (and are in part constitutive of) particular institutional roles, notably (given our concerns here) police officers and military personnel. For instance, police officers have an institutional duty – which is typically also a moral duty – to arrest lawbreakers. Again, military combatants have an institutional moral right, and indeed duty, to use lethal force against combatants of an enemy nation-state in a theatre of war – or, at least, they have such a right and duty if the war that they are fighting is a just war.

I have argued elsewhere[5] that special (institutional) moral rights and duties derive in part from the collective good that is the *telos* and, as such, constitutive of the institution in question. According to this normative teleological theory, social institutions have as their *raison d'etre* the provision of some collective good(s), such as national security (military), law and order (police), knowledge acquisition and dissemination (universities), food (agribusinesses), and so on. Being derived from the collective good produced or maintained by an institution, these rights and duties are not natural rights and duties, albeit they are moral rights and duties (as well as being institutional rights and duties). Moreover, special (institutional) moral rights do not feature in the lists of human rights proffered by the UN and other like institutions; special rights are not human rights in one widely accepted sense of that term.

According to my normative teleological account of social institutions the precise content, strength and context of application (e.g. jurisdiction) of the institutional rights and duties of institutional role occupants is determined in large part by reference to the purposes of those institutions and, in particular, by the relevant collective goods of those institutions, e.g. security, knowledge. Of course, some institutional rights are not also moral rights, e.g. the right to move one's pawn one space forward in chess, the right of full professors to free parking at a university. Moreover, in the case of some institutional rights that are also moral rights the collective goods from which they are derived themselves consist in part in aggregated natural rights. I shall shortly argue that the collective good of security is a case in point. Here I stress that security is a somewhat loose term and even in the more restricted senses in which I use it (of which more later) it does not reduce to an aggregate of (realized) natural rights, such as an aggregate of rights to life. Let me now turn to an analysis of the right to self-defence.

2 The natural right to self-defence

As already mentioned, the moral right to life and the related right not to be killed are possessed by virtue of properties we possess as human beings; these are natural rights. As such, the right to life and the right not to be killed are logically prior to social institutions and contrast with institutional moral rights, such as the right to vote, the right to a fair trial, and so on. Neither the right to life, nor the right not to be killed, are absolute moral rights. There are circumstances under which they can be forfeited or, at least, overridden. Perhaps the most salient circumstance is that of self-defence; it is generally agreed that killing in self-defence is sometimes morally justifiable.[6]

The standard conditions for Defender's morally permissible killing in self-defence of Attacker who poses a lethal threat to Defender are as follows:

(1) The lethal threat posed by Attacker is imminent.
(2) Attacker has no good (let alone decisive) moral justification for deliberately trying to kill Defender.
(3) Attacker will kill Defender unless Defender intervenes.
(4) It is necessary for Defender to intervene by killing Attacker, if Defender is to prevent Attacker from killing Defender.
(5) Defender's killing of Attacker is not disproportionate since it is a case of one life (that of Attacker who is at fault) for one life (that of Defender who is not at fault).

Relatedly the standard conditions for permissible killing of Attacker by Third Party in defence of Victim whose life is at risk from Attacker are as follows:

(1) The lethal threat is imminent.
(2) Attacker has no good (let alone decisive) moral justification for deliberately trying to kill Victim.
(3) Attacker will kill Victim unless Third Party intervenes.
(4) It is necessary for Third Party to intervene by killing Attacker, if Third Party is to prevent Attacker from killing Victim.
(5) Third Party's killing of Attacker is not disproportionate since it is a case of one life (that of Attacker who is at fault) for one life (that of Victim who is not at fault).

As is evident from the above two outlined sets of conditions, the standard conditions under which killing in self-defence is morally justified mirror the standard conditions under which killing in defence of others is morally justified. Nevertheless, there are some important moral differences between justified killing in self-defence and justified killing in defence of others, which the standard accounts fails to mention, let alone accommodate. Firstly, Defender has a moral right to kill Attacker in self-defence but *no* moral obligation to do so, even if it is necessary to preserve his or her own life. By contrast, Third Party has a moral obligation to protect Victim and, therefore, a moral obligation to kill Attacker, assuming it is necessary to do so to save Victim (and assuming, also, little or no cost to Third Party in doing so). For Defender has a moral right that Third Party protect him or her from the lethal threat of Attacker.

Secondly, the moral weight of the necessity condition, and the way it operates, in self-defence is different from its moral weight and the way it operates in the case of other defence and, therefore, the fact that the two sets of standard conditions mirror one another in these respects is misleading. According to the necessity condition it is morally permissible for Defender to kill Attacker only if it is necessary; likewise it is morally permissible for Third Party to kill Attacker only if it is necessary. Indeed, it is morally permissible for Defender or Third Party to kill Attacker only if the lethal threat is imminent and, arguably, this is so because it is necessary to kill Attacker if the lethal threat he or she poses is imminent. Nevertheless, the necessity condition does not underpin the moral *right* of Defender to kill in self-defence (and Defender has no moral obligation to do so), whereas it does underpin the moral obligation of the Third Party to kill in defence of another. Clearly, Third Party has no moral obligation to kill Attacker if it is not necessary to do so; indeed, it would be morally impermissible for Third Party to kill Attacker unless it was necessary. However, Attacker has no right not to be killed by Defender if Attacker mounts a deliberate and unjustified lethal attack on Defender and Attacker will kill Defender unless Defender intervenes. In short, I suggest that Attacker loses his or her right not to be killed by Defender, even if it is not necessary for Defender to kill Attacker to preserve Defender's life. Since this claim is not self-evident I will offer an extended argument for it in the next section. However, I note that this claim is accepted by a number of historically important philosophers, including John Locke.[7] I also note that notwithstanding this claim concerning Attacker's right not to be killed (or, at least, lack thereof), Defender may well have a moral obligation not to kill Attacker unless it is necessary to do so. Needless to say, any such obligation on the part of Defender to refrain from killing Attacker does not derive from Attacker's right not to be killed by Defender.[8]

3 Necessity condition

There are two general intuitions motivating my claim that Attacker's right not to be killed by Defender is not underpinned (even in part) by the necessity condition. Firstly, whether or not a person has such a fundamental right as the right not to be killed depends on properties of that person. It does not depend on whether someone else, such as the defender, has or does not have a capacity to defend himself. Secondly, if a person deliberately kills other people without any moral justification whatsoever, then that person has called into question their very entitlement to live; a person's right to live is not something that exists independently of the respect that that person has for the right to life of others. Let us now consider more closely the standard assumption that the necessity condition provides an underpinning, or at least one of the key elements of the underpinning, of the right not to be killed.

Suppose that there is a not insignificant possibility that Defender will be killed if he chooses the option of disarming, rather than killing, Attacker. Given the necessity condition, Defender would nevertheless be under a strong moral obligation to try to disarm Attacker. For given the necessity condition, Attacker has a right not to be killed if Defender can disarm Attacker. But surely, in this kind of case, Defender is not obliged to put his life at risk to preserve the life of someone who is deliberately and unjustifiably trying to kill him. So the necessity condition needs to be weakened to accommodate this kind of counter-example. It should read: Defender cannot disarm Attacker without putting Defender's life at risk.

But it might be the case that Defender's life is not at risk, but that he will lose an arm and a leg in the process of trying to disarm Attacker. Presumably, the condition needs to be further weakened to: Defender cannot disarm Attacker without either putting Defender's own life at risk or incurring serious harm to Defender.

But now what if Attacker has tried to kill Defender in the past and will try to kill Defender in the future (and neither the police nor anyone else is able to provide adequate protection for Defender)? Presumably, Defender is entitled to kill to prevent an otherwise unavoidable and certain future deadly threat of this sort. We now have a double-barrelled condition of the form: (a) Defender cannot disarm Attacker without putting Defender's own life at risk or incurring serious harm to Defender, or (b) Defender's disarming of Attacker will not remove an unavoidable and certain (probable?) future threat posed by Attacker to the life of Defender.

Unfortunately, even this heavily qualified and complicated condition is inadequate. Assume that Defender happens to be an agent-centered pacifist. Assume further that Defender will have to either severely wound or kill Attacker if he is to preserve his own life. Pacifist Defender has a threefold choice: (a) allow himself to be killed, (b) kill Attacker, or (c) severely wound Attacker by severing Attacker's weapon-using right arm. Defender chooses to allow himself to be killed, and is killed. In this scenario, the option of disarming rather than killing the attacker is available to Defender. Therefore, given the necessity condition, Attacker retains her right not to be killed. But in this pacifist scenario, this seems incorrect; surely Attacker does not have a right not to be killed. To see this, imagine that there is a non-pacifist Third Party with a gun who is unable to disarm Attacker, but who could kill Attacker and, thereby, preserve Defender's life. It is clearly morally permissible for Third Party to kill Attacker, and indeed our agent-centered pacifist Defender may thank Third Party for doing so. However, given the necessity condition, Attacker has a right not to be killed since Defender could have disarmed Attacker. Therefore, it would be morally wrong for Third Party to kill Attacker. The example shows that yet another modification of the necessity condition for losing one's right not to be killed is called for.

We have now arrived at the following proposition: a necessary condition for Attacker losing his right not to be killed is: (a) Defender cannot disarm Attacker without either putting his own life at risk or incurring serious harm to himself, and/or (b) Defender's disarming of Attacker will not remove an unavoidable and certain future threat posed by Attacker to the life of Defender, and/or (c) Defender chooses not to disarm Attacker, even though Defender knows that if he so chooses Attacker will kill him.

Even this host of qualifications is incomplete. For example, what of future threats to the lives of Defender's family? Surely Attacker does not have a right not to be killed by Defender if Defender knows that if he spares Attacker then Attacker will, at some future date, kill the members of Defender's family?

It is implausible that such a contingent, complex and changing set of facts about other agents (in this case, Defender) could ground a basic, negative, individual human right, such as the right not to be killed (in this case Attacker). Perhaps positive rights, institutional rights, and derived rights may go in and out of existence, depending on various contingent, complex and changing circumstances that are external to the bearers of those rights. And any right, including the right not to be killed, might be overridden, or its violator excused, on the basis of various, contingent, and external circumstances. But what is in question is whether the *existence* of a basic, negative, individual natural right could depend on such contingent, complex and changing circumstances that are external to the rights bearer. Surely such a natural right is only dependent on natural properties possessed by the rights-bearer *qua* human being. At any rate, I have argued that the required recourse to a wide variety of contingent, external circumstances for the existence of this natural right renders the claim that the necessity condition underpins the right not to be killed implausible. Accordingly, Defender retains his right not to be killed whereas Attacker does not, even in cases in which it is not necessary for Defender to use lethal force. In such cases, Defender is exercising his natural right to self-defence. Therefore, the natural right to self-defence is not underpinned by the necessity condition.

Nevertheless, as I suggested above, the necessity condition remains in force. For there are typically other moral considerations of a broadly social kind in play. If Defenders kill Attackers even when it is unnecessary to do so, then the deleterious consequences in terms of unnecessary loss of human life – including in all probability innocent human life, given the likelihood of mistakes and malevolent motives – and social conflict more generally will likely be very great. Accordingly, the legal right to self-defence morally ought to include the necessity condition in light of the broader social purposes (collective ends that are collective goods on my normative teleological account) served by the law, to wit to minimize loss of human life and social conflict. So the legal right of self-defence does not, and ought not, precisely track the natural right of self-defence. Moreover, as mentioned above, in well-ordered jurisdictions the imminence condition is derivable from the necessity condition. Hence, the legal right of killing in self-defence typically includes, and morally ought to include, an imminence condition.

Thus far I have argued, firstly, that there is a natural right to self-defence which is not underpinned by the necessity condition and, secondly, that the necessity condition, nevertheless, is and morally ought to be a key element of the underpinning of the legal i.e. general *institutional* right to self-defence. What of the special rights and duties of police officers and military combatants to use lethal force? How do they relate to the right, or as it turns out rights, of self-defence? I argue later that necessity understood in terms of institutional purposes (collective goods) is again highly germane and that there is a third notion of self-defence in play, namely, collective self-defence. I begin with the rights and duties of police officers.

4 Police officers' use of lethal force: self-defence and enforcing the law

The paradigm case of the use of lethal force by a police officer in well-ordered, contemporary, liberal democratic states in peacetime is a one-off encounter between the officer and an armed offender in a context in which the offender is threatening someone's life (either that of the officer or some third party) or has committed, or is about to commit, some other serious crime. The primary aim of the police officer is, or ought to be, to arrest but not kill the offender. Nevertheless, it is morally (and, typically, legally) permissible for the officer to use lethal force under the following conditions:

(1) the threat is imminent;
(2) it is necessary for the officer to use lethal force to protect the life of the police officer (or third party) or, at least, to prevent the commission of some other serious crime;
(3) the use of lethal force by the officer is not disproportionate to the threat posed by the offender, e.g. the offender culpably poses a threat to life;
(4) the officer's use of lethal force does not put the lives of innocent third parties at risk.

Importantly, it is morally impermissible for the police officer to use lethal force merely to prevent an offender escaping – even an offender guilty of a serious felony – if the officer's use of lethal force risks grievously harming an innocent bystander. Forced to choose between allowing an offender to escape and putting innocent bystanders at risk of serious harm, police officers must choose the former. Indeed, even if the lives (or other vital interests) of innocent bystanders are not at risk it may well be morally impermissible for an officer to use lethal force against an escaping offender. This would be so if, for example, the offender does not pose an immediate serious risk to anyone and could be arrested at a later time. These restrictions on police use of lethal force are due to two normative institutional features of policing.[9] First, the primary institutional purpose of police is to effect arrests rather than kill, or otherwise harm, offenders; indeed, police have a duty to use minimum coercive force in effecting arrests and, as far as possible, to protect offenders from harm. Second, a primary institutional role of police officers is to protect ordinary citizens from serious harm – and this typically trumps their other primary role of arresting offenders.

In addition to police use of lethal force in personal self-defence or to defend the lives of fellow officers or citizens there is an important third moral justification for police use of lethal force, namely, to realize the institutional purpose of enforcing the law. In short, police have an institutional right and, indeed, an institutional duty to use lethal force if it is necessary in order to uphold the law. Here we have the necessity condition again, but in this case the necessity in question derives from an institutional purpose, namely, to uphold the law.

Consider the case of armed suspects. A police officer has institutionally based moral duty to use lethal force against an armed person if:

(1) The person is rightly and reasonably suspected of serious crimes, (e.g. serious fraud).
(2) The person is using a firearm to avoid arrest.
(3) The only way to prevent the suspected offender from escaping is to use lethal force.

Notice that the officers would not be using lethal force in personal self-defence or defence of the life of another in this kind of scenario. If the officer merely wanted to avoid the loss of life then he should get back into his patrol car and drive back to the police station.[10] In response to this it might be insisted that, nevertheless, in refraining from driving back to the police station and persevering with his duty to arrest the armed offender the officer may end up shooting the offender dead in self-defence and that, therefore, the officer's use of lethal force is ultimately justified on grounds of self-defence. By contrast I have suggested that in these situations the police are using lethal force to enforce the law.

In these situations at the point at which the police decide to enforce the law in the knowledge that the offender will use lethal force to resist arrest, the police are not engaged in an act of self-defence. After all, to reiterate, at this point the police have another option, if they are primarily interested in preserving their own lives and/or that of the offender: get back into their patrol cars and return to the police station. Accordingly, at this point the standard self-defence justification and, therefore, the legal self-defence justification is not available to the police officer. It is not available since it is not necessary for the police officer to use lethal force to protect his life (or that of his fellow officers or other third party): the option of flight is available to the officer(s). However, it is necessary for the police officer to use lethal force if the officer is to enforce the law. Therefore, in these scenarios the moral (and institutional) justification for the police officer using lethal force is that it is necessary to do so if the law is to be enforced.[11]

The upshot of the discussion in this section is that police officers have – in addition to the natural (moral) right to self-defence and the legal (moral) right to self-defence possessed by all human beings and citizens, respectively – a special institutional (moral) duty to use lethal force to enforce the law and this institutional duty should not be confused with, and does not reduce to, their prior natural and legal rights to self-defence (or other defence). Moreover, this moral and institutional duty is underpinned by a necessity condition; however, it is not merely the necessity to prevent loss of life or limb (either one's own or that of others). Rather it is the necessity to uphold the law and, thereby, realize the collective good constitutive of the institution of the law.

5 The military use of lethal force and collective self-defence

Let us now consider the self-defence justification in the context of the military use of lethal force.[12] Wars and other armed conflicts involve armed forces. Moreover, the armed forces in question are collective entities. However, this does not entail that collective entities per se perform intentional actions; by the lights of individualism in its various forms, only the individual human occupants of the task-defined roles constitutive of such entities do that.[13] However, these individual role occupants perform joint actions as well as individual ones. A joint action consists of individual actions directed to a shared, interdependent end or goal (collective end, in my parlance) and typically this end could not be achieved by a single individual acting on his or her own.[14] Many complex joint actions involve large numbers of agents and take place over extended periods of time; military operations are a case in point.[15]

According to the *jus in bello* of traditional Just War Theory, conventional military conflict and, let us assume, armed conflicts in our somewhat wider sense, should be conducted in self-defence and according to the principles of military necessity, discrimination and proportionality.[16] The notion of self-defence in question is that of collective self-defence; nation-states fight just wars to defend the collective construed not merely as a set of individual human beings occupying a geographical areas, but also as a set of institutions in large part constituted by those individuals. So the 'self' in collective self-defence ought not to be confused with the 'self' in personal self-defence or, indeed, with the 'selves' afforded protection by police officers. Moreover, unlike in the instances of personal self-defence or in law enforcement, in military conflicts these principles predominately apply at the collective level rather than merely at the individual level. Let me explain.

At the collective level there is an ongoing war being fought by organizations; war is not simply fought at the level of any given single combatant's lethal actions considered as discrete, self-contained actions. This is, of course, not to deny that there is also an individual level and that it is in part constitutive of the collective level.

Let me now turn to the (normatively understood) institutional role of regular soldiers (understood broadly so as to include sailors, airmen etc. and their superior officers) in liberal democratic nation-states.[17] The institutional role of regular soldier can be defined in terms of (a) the collective end of protecting the moral rights of the members of the nation-state (including their rights *qua* institutional role occupants) from violation by persons from external communities/nations, i.e. the collective good of external security defended in wars of collective self-defence;[18] (b) by means of the use of lethal force, or the threat thereof; and (c) a jointly held obligation on the part of all adult members to protect fellow members from external threats, i.e. to provide the collective good of external security. This latter jointly held moral obligation could be discharged by, say, an all citizen-militia. However, in contemporary liberal democracies it is typically discharged by establishing standing professional armed forces (often supplemented in wartime by an armed force of citizen conscripts).

This jointly held obligation to (in effect) act in collective self-defence does not include infringing the rights of the members of other nation-states by, for example, engaging in wars of conquest on behalf of one's own national leadership. The so-called *jus ad bellum* is an attempt to spell out the relevant moral principles governing the decision to wage war, including by liberal democratic states. Moreover, there is a moral obligation on the part of military forces and individual combatants to comply with moral principles constraining the use of lethal force in wartime – an influential formulation of these being the various formulations of *jus in bello* (moral and legal) principles – such as not to intentionally kill innocent civilians (principle of discrimination), only to use an extent of lethal force that is militarily necessity (principle of military necessity) and, when lethal force is militarily necessary, to avoid a disproportionate extent of civilian deaths (principle of proportionality).

In the context of armed conflict between armed forces, each combatant in one's own armed force is an organizational element of a *standing joint* lethal threat to the enemy and, likewise, each enemy combatant is an organizational element of a standing joint lethal threat to one's own armed force. Consistent with my individualist analysis of joint action, joint lethal threats (standing or otherwise) are constituted by the potentially lethal actions of individual combatants and their leaders acting in concert, i.e. *jointly*. Accordingly, any given single combatant involved in an ongoing armed conflict is confronting (jointly with his fellow combatants and leaders) a standing joint lethal threat in relation to which (a) any single enemy combatant constitutes a threat element; and (b) any single, discrete lethal encounter with enemy combatants is simply a phase-element in the ongoing conflict.

Crucially, unlike in the paradigm cases of the application of the principles of necessity and proportionality governing the use of lethal force by police officers, the principles of military necessity and proportionality apply not only in relation to immediate goals, but also to medium and long term (military) collective ends, e.g. winning a battle, winning the war. Moreover, they apply differently. As we saw above, it is morally permissible for a police officer to use lethal force against an offender only if it *strictly necessary* in the circumstances; that is, there is no other option available. Thus police cannot justify an otherwise unjustifiable use of lethal force against an escaping (say) armed robber merely by recourse to some medium or long term law enforcement goal to 'win the war' against armed robbers. This is not the case in war. For it is morally permissible for a combatant to kill an enemy combatant, even if it is *not strictly* necessary to do so either to save his own life (or the life of a fellow combatant or civilian) or, indeed, to further the immediate, medium or long term (military) collective ends of the armed force to which he belongs. Rather, his killing an enemy combatant is necessary only in the sense that it is part of the rationally defensible means to achieve these collective ends, albeit in the context, of course, of appropriate moral weighing of these collective ends. (Of course, there are also side-constraints on the use of lethal force against enemy combatants, such as the impermissibility of killing those who have surrendered.)

Accordingly, generally speaking, the principle of necessity is different in military conflicts than in law enforcement contexts; and, of course, different than the one in play in personal self or other defence. To simplify, the principle of necessity in military conflicts is ultimately derivable from collective self-defence understood as the defence of the moral rights of members of a polity. Hence, the right to collective self-defence in the contexts in questions is essentially a political – and, therefore, institutional – right. Moreover, it is a jointly held right of the individual human members of a polity that is typically exercised (via a division of institutional labour) by the members of the armed forces of that polity. This is, of course, not to deny that there are situations in law enforcement (or, for that matter, in self-defence scenarios outside institutional settings), which are more or less the same morally speaking as those in military conflict and in which the morally required lethal response (or lack thereof) is identical, e.g. situations of personal self-defence or of defence of the life of a fellow officer/combatant. Regarding the differences consider, for example, that the use of lethal force by a military combatant is not necessarily in defence of an *imminent* threat to that combatant, his fellow combatants in that encounter or, for that matter, any other individual person present at that time and place. Thus, it is morally permissible in military conflict, but not in law enforcement or in personal self-defence scenarios involving ordinary citizens, to use the tactic of ambush whereby enemy soldiers are attacked and killed without warning and notwithstanding the fact that they do not constitute an imminent threat to anyone at that time and place. At the risk of overstating the point, in a theatre of war there is a presumption in favour of using lethal force against enemy combatants, if it serves a military purpose, whereas, as we saw above, in law enforcement there is a presumption in favour of arresting offenders (and, one might add, there is a presumption in favour of flight in the case of citizens under attack in well-ordered jurisdictions).

6 Conclusion

In this chapter I have argued that the so-called human right to self-defence is something of a misnomer. Properly understood, the right to self-defence comprises three distinct moral rights. There is a natural right to self-defence, a legal (institutional) right to self-defence, and a political (institutional) right to collective self-defence. Moreover, these three moral rights do not mirror one another. The 'self' defended by members of armed forces in wars of self-defence is a collective entity, namely, a polity comprised of rights-bearing individual human beings and the institutions constituted by them. Hence, the right to (collective) self-defence is a political (moral) right and a jointly held one. As such, this collective right to self-defence is obviously importantly different both from the natural right to self-defence of all human beings and from the legal (and moral) right to self-defence of ordinary citizens in well-ordered jurisdictions. Moreover, the natural right to self-defence is importantly different from the legal right to self-defence in that, unlike the corresponding legal right, the natural right to self-defence is not underpinned by the principle of necessity. Finally, the principle of military necessity is very different from the principles of necessity underpinning (respectively) the legal right to self-defence of ordinary citizens and the (institutional moral) duty of police officers to use lethal force to uphold the law. In each of these three kinds of case there is a necessity condition governing the use of lethal force as a means to *some* morally worthy end. However, the morally worthy ends in question differ: citizens use lethal force having as an end to save their own lives, police use lethal force having as an end to uphold the law, and military combatants use lethal force having as an end to win wars.

Notes

1 Henry Shue, *Basic Rights* (Princeton: Princeton University Press, 1996); James Nickel, *Making Sense of Human Rights* (Oxford: Blackwell, 2007); James Griffin, *On Human Rights* (Oxford: Oxford University Press, 2008).
2 I note that the set of rights referred to as 'human rights' in, for example, United Nations documents include both natural and institutional rights in my senses of those terms.
3 Thomas Pogge, *World Poverty and Human Rights* (Cambridge: Polity Press, 2008).
4 Or at least to all members who are adults, or perhaps rational adults or some such category.
5 Seumas Miller, *The Moral Foundations of Social Institutions* (Cambridge: Cambridge University Press, 2010).
6 Philip Montague, 'Self-Defence and Forcing the Choice Between Lives', *Philosophical Studies* 40 (1981): p. 207; Judith Jarvis Thomson, 'Self-Defence', *Philosophy and Public Affairs* 20, no. 4 (1991): p. 283.

7 John Locke, *Two Treatises of Government*, 2nd Treatise, ch. 3 (any edition). The argument in this section is taken from Seumas Miller, 'Killing in Self-Defence', *Public Affairs Quarterly* 7, no. 4 (1993): p. 325.

8 In Miller, 'Killing in Self-Defence', pp. 325–340, I elaborate an account along these lines, namely, the fault-based internalist (suspendable) rights-based account (FIST). On this account your natural right not to be killed by me is suspended if:

(i) You deliberately try to kill me and you will kill me if I do not intervene.
(ii) You are morally responsible for your action.
(iii) You do not have a good and decisive moral reason for trying to kill me.Note that while your right not to be killed by me is suspended if you culpably attack me, your right not to be killed by Third Party is not suspended if you culpably attack me, but is rather overridden in the case where it is necessary for Third Party to use lethal force. See also Seumas Miller, *Shooting to Kill: The Ethics of Police and Military Use of Lethal Force* (New York: Oxford University Press, 2016), ch. 2.

9 Seumas Miller and John Blackler, *Ethical Issues in Policing* (London: Routledge, 2005), ch. 1 and Miller, *Shooting to Kill*, ch. 4.

10 For further argument in relation to this point see Miller and Blackler, *Ethical Issues in Policing*, ch. 5, and Miller, *Shooting to Kill*, ch. 4.

11 For more detail on this point see Miller, *Shooting to Kill*, ch. 2.

12 Michael Walzer, Just and Unjust Wars: A Moral Argument With Historical Illustrations (New York: Basic Books, 1977).

13 Seumas Miller, 'Joint Action: The Individual Strikes Back', in *Intentional Acts and Institutional Facts: Essays on John Searle's Social Ontology*, edited by Savas L. Tsohatzidis (Dordrecht: Springer Press, 2007), pp. 73–92.

14 Seumas Miller, 'Joint Action', *Philosophical Papers* 11, no. 3 (1992): p. 275.

15 Miller, Moral Foundations of Social Institutions, ch. 1.

16 Walzer, Just and Unjust Wars.

17 Miller, *Shooting to Kill*, ch. 6.

18 See David Rodin, *War and Self-Defence* (Oxford: Clarendon Press, 2002) for a narrower (in my view too narrow) conception.

14 Beitz's two-level model of human rights and statelessness

Kylie Bourne

In 2015 Frontex, the European Border and Coast Guard Agency, reported that nearly two million people had crossed through main migration routes into the European Union. The majority of arrivals were from war-torn countries such as Syria, Afghanistan and Iraq. Significant numbers also arrived from Eritrea, Nigeria and Somalia while countries in other parts of the world, notably in Asia, were also receiving migrants hoping for asylum or resettlement.[1] In 2014 around 60 million people were displaced or stateless and seeking refuge or asylum somewhere in the world. This was the highest figure since the Second World War. 2015 and 2016 have seen similar numbers of people moving between and through borders.[2] These numbers are unprecedented, and the countries in which these people have arrived continue to struggle not only with the immediate needs of those arriving but also to clearly determine the extent of their obligations to the arrivals, and the role they have in fulfilling human rights claims made against them.

In this chapter I consider the human rights claims of stateless and displaced persons and how these may be fulfilled on Charles Beitz's two-level model of human rights. The millions of people fleeing across borders do so primarily because their basic interests cannot be effectively fulfilled by the government of the country from which they flee.[3] On Beitz's account, those fleeing turn towards the international community not merely for help but in its capacity as a guarantor of their human rights. But does this 'turning towards' the international community lead to the effective fulfilment of human rights claims? And if it does not, what does this tell us about the human rights of stateless persons? I argue that while Beitz's account attempts to provide for those without an effective state to fulfil rights claims, observed practice shows us that the description of the international community as a 'guarantor' of human rights is overstated.[4] I specially argue that this overstatement comes about because Beitz's account does not satisfactorily account for the implementation deficit in modern human rights practice. Further, I argue that by failing to take sufficient cues from current practice, Beitz's account, which eschews foundations, does not explain the quasi-foundational role of nationality in fulfilling human rights claims. In so doing, I underscore the difficulty that political approaches have in accounting for ideals outside the practice that appear to influence the content and scope of human rights claims in the first instance.

The chapter proceeds as follows: First, I provide a brief discussion of statelessness and provide a short overview of statelessness in contemporary global politics. Second, I outline Beitz's two-level model of human rights, drawing particular attention to the role of the international community as a guarantor of human rights for those whose claims cannot be effectively fulfilled by states. Third, I discuss Beitz's concept of 'observed practice' and suggest a more realist approach to this that foregrounds the implementation deficit and the quasi-foundational role that citizenship plays in current human rights practice. However, I do not suggest that this approach necessarily commits us to grounding the content of human rights in realism itself. Fourth, I discuss two criticisms of the political approach to human rights and the way that these manifest in discussions of statelessness. These criticisms are the political approaches necessary to the promotion of the status quo and, following Barry and Southwood, the conflation of the implementation mechanisms of human rights with a machinery that determines their content. Lastly, I suggest two ways that Beitz's account can be strengthened to afford stateless persons better protection of their human rights claims. I conclude that Beitz's model is a progression on orthodox conceptions of human rights because it allows human rights discourse to be practically informed without losing its dynamic and aspirational nature. Specifically, I argue that because Beitz's model considers human rights practice to be emerging we are able to recast aspects of his account as we become informed about the reality that the model represents and require a greater number of 'competent participants' in the fulfilling of the human rights claims of stateless persons.

1 Statelessness in the contemporary world

Statelessness can be caused in a variety of ways. Acts of government can suddenly revoke the citizenship of sections of a population, thus rendering them internally displaced in a country in which they may have lived for years. Since 2014, discussions of statelessness have tended to be contextualized by crises in migrations. Generally, human rights literature has distinguished between 'types' of migration of stateless persons and thus between *de jure* and *de facto* statelessness. In this chapter I use the term 'stateless persons' to encompass both of these groups. Article 1 of the *1954 Convention Relating to the Status of Stateless Persons*, defines a *de jure* stateless person as 'a person who is not considered as a national by any State under the operation of its law'. A *de jure* stateless person does not enjoy the nationality of any state and is 'the literally stateless.'[5] By contrast, the Convention defines *de facto* stateless people as those who have a nationality but whose status where they reside is not legal. Often *de facto* stateless persons are illegal, irregular or undocumented migrants with an inability to prove their legal identity, lacking the documentation necessary to prove their claim.[6] This distinction between *de jure* and *de facto* statelessness has been contested in recent years, especially as people migrate across borders in such great numbers from failed states, persecution and conflict. The United Nations High Commissioner for Refugees (UNHCR) protection to refugees covers not only these definitions of statelessness but also persons who come under an extended definition that is predicated on both the *1984 Cartagena Declaration of Refugees* and the *2004 EU Qualification Directive*. These include persons who have a 'valid reason for being unwilling to avail oneself of protection'[7] of a state and who in the country of their nationality 'face a real risk of serious harm not resulting from generalized violence or events seriously disturbing the public order.'[8]

The distinction between *de jure* and *de facto* statelessness can at times appear pejorative, with the implication that the *de facto* stateless are differently stateless in that their situation can involve a choice that is denied to *de jure* stateless. For example, mass media outlets have commonly cast economic migrants as *de facto* stateless, with the implication that they are entitled to lesser protections than the *de jure* stateless.[9] To the existing categories of statelessness, including those internally displaced and associated with migration, Jacqueline Bhabha adds another: 'effective statelessness', which she defines as the 'inability to prove formal nationality and legal immigration status despite having both.'[10] Effective statelessness effects, for example, children who are living within their own countries but who have not had their births registered. Statelessness is a complex concept and the circumstances of one stateless person may not resemble those of another, as these distinctions show. Article 1(1) of the Convention applies both in contexts of migration and non-migration, and there is a possibility that persons in migration contexts can be wrongly excluded from discussions of statelessness if the distinction between *de jure* and *de facto* statelessness is applied mistakenly. Further, as restricting statelessness to two categories fails to consider the effectively stateless, I will use the term 'stateless persons' to refer to those in *de jure*, *de facto* and effective contexts. It will refer to those who have no protection from their country of nationality, or who have a valid reason for being unwilling to avail oneself of this protection. I concede that there are important differences between these groups of people, and that each category may require dissimilar solutions. However, such a discussion lies outside the parameters of this chapter.

Statelessness gathered prominence as a human rights issue in the modern world between the First and Second World Wars, particularly as waves of people left Germany as the National Socialist Party came to government. Due to the large numbers of people left stateless after the Second World War, the United Nations proceeded to draft conventions aimed at protecting the rights and interests of those without an effective nationality. In 1948, three years after the United Nations was formed, the Universal Declaration of Human Rights (UDHR) was adopted by the United Nations General Assembly. Although it bares no force in law, the UDHR is an ideal standard held in common by member nations. Article 15 of the UDHR states that '[e]veryone has the right to a nationality' and that '[n]o one shall be arbitrarily deprived of his nationality nor denied the right to change his nationality [sic].'[11] Currently, the UNHCR has two conventions relating to statelessness. In addition to the 1954 *Convention Relating to the Status of Stateless Persons*, the *Convention of the Reduction of Statelessness* was adopted in 1961. The *Convention Relating to the Status of Refugees*, signed in 1951, and the subsequent 1967 *Protocol Relating to the Status of Refugees* are also directly relevant to stateless persons, particularly to irregular migrants. As of February 2017, there were 89 state parties to the 1954 Convention and 68 to the 1961 Convention.[12] In November 2014, the UNHCR launched 'I Belong', a ten-year campaign dedicated to the eradication of statelessness.[13]

People become stateless for a variety of reasons and the legacy of statelessness can pass down through generations. With single acts of legislation, for example, ethnic and minority groups can have their citizenship taken away and become stateless in the country in which they have resided all of their lives.[14] The Rohingya people of Myanmar, for instance, face institutional discrimination and are classified as foreigners by the country's Buddhist government.[15] The Rohingya live in the Rakhine province of Myanmar, where they account for nearly 90% of the population, but in 1982, the Burmese government enacted a law that denied the Rohingya citizenship in what many regard as their traditional homeland. Denied citizenship, the Rohingya people are therefore denied equal access to legal and political entitlements such as education, health and the legal system and they are subject to ethnic-based violence.[16] Combined, these conditions have prompted tens of thousands to flee to other countries, primarily by boat. The situation remains critical: some countries in the region, impoverished themselves, have agreed to offer temporary shelter to the refugees, but a permanent solution and regional response is yet to be determined.[17]

If, as in the case of the Rohingya, the citizenship of such people is not restored, their statelessness is inherited by proceeding generations. Others become stateless when fleeing from poverty, violence or persecution only to find themselves in circumstances just as dire. Such people have come to live in increasing numbers in emergency camps on the borders of states, with limited access to education, food and shelter. These camps may initially be intended as temporary and immediate solutions to house large numbers of arrivals, but they can themselves become more permanent and contested areas.[18]

In terms of the human rights literature, statelessness can be regarded as something of an exception. Hannah Arendt noted that the UN Declaration of Human Rights itself implied that 'everyone had political membership in a territorially defined nation state' such that the condition of stateless persons did not challenge the way that the emerging international system of human rights was being organized. Rather than the norm stateless was the exception, and this meant that statelessness 'left the system itself untouched.'[19] The effects of this approach have been long lasting and underscore the complexity of statelessness around the globe. There is an under-representation of the stateless in historical literature, perhaps itself an emblem of how entire groups of people can come to be omitted from not just the history of citizenship and nationalism but from moral theory too.[20] Consistent and reliable data is difficult to collect and explains why stateless population data is only publicly available for 75 states and further why qualitative analysis of this data is publicly available for only 45 states.[21] A central difficulty in understanding statelessness is that it is often 'hidden.' Stateless people have little if any documentation, are often not registered with state or international agencies and, with fear of expulsion from a territory, have learned to be 'invisible' even where they experience 'multifarious forms of discrimination and abuse.'[22]

Stateless people are found in all regions of the globe, although there are particular regions where stateless is pronounced. The UNHCR estimated that in 2014 more than 12 million people in the world are stateless and that a third of these are children.[23] Over 620,000 people have been rendered stateless as a result of state succession since 1974, and at least 20% of all states have populations that, although entitled to nationality under law, cannot acquire documentary proof of nationality.[24] In 2015 there were 40.8 million internally displaced persons, that is, displaced in their own country, accounting for 62% of the 65.3 million forcibly displaced persons worldwide.[25] Also in 2015, it was estimated that close to 60% of the world's internally displaced persons come from five countries: Syria, Columbia, historic Palestine, Sudan and Iraq.[26] This is the highest number of refugees and displaced persons since the Second World War.[27] Around two thirds of these refugees have been displaced for at least three years (which is called protracted displacement), while half of all people currently displaced because of conflict and war have been displaced for over ten years.[28]

Europe is currently experiencing the highest number of stateless arrivals since the Second World War when records began. In 2014, Germany received 800,000 claims for asylum, four times the number of the previous year.[29] The rate of first-time applicants dramatically increased,[30] with the most claims coming from people arriving from Syria, Afghanistan, Albania and Iraq.[31] In the first eight months of 2015, 20% more migrants arrived in Europe than had in the entire year of 2014. European countries have attempted a joint border protection operation and have agreed on several approaches to the situation that has come to be known as the 'European Migrant Crisis'. However many countries are yet to make good on the commitments that they had promised in 2015, so a permanent solution to the crisis continues to be negotiated.[32]

2 Beitz's two-level model of human rights

Like John Rawls and like Joseph Raz, Beitz presents a political conception of human rights. He claims that the practical conception of human rights relies on 'a construction of some kind' that 'abstracts from the particulars to describe in general terms the roles played by human rights in the public normative discourse of global politics.'[33] On this political conception, if we are to understand the function of human rights, we are compelled to look to current human rights practice. While Rawls and Raz emphasize the international role that human rights play in that they justify the external intervention in sovereign states, Beitz, crucially, includes in his conception a broader range of interventions including 'soft measures' found in international practice:

> Rawls' s understanding of the functions of human rights is narrower than what is found in present international practice. The differences are not only of exegetical interest . . . To the extent that judgements about the doctrine's contents depend on considerations about the concept's functions, it seems likely that a more expansive function would generate a broader view of the doctrine's normative range. One's grasp of the discursive role of human rights is of normative as well as descriptive interest.[34]

For Beitz, a model of human rights based on this political conception lets us comprehend the normative range of current practice. Fundamentally, human rights are not a moral category of their own and neither are they legal rights. Human rights are 'special' because of the role they play as norms of global political life. As such, human rights must satisfy three criteria. First, they must represent an interest sufficiently important enough to warrant political protection, in that they aim to protect individual interests against predictable threat to which they are vulnerable. Second, the human right must apply in the first instance to the political institutions of states. Third, the interest would be a suitable object of international concern. A state's failure to fulfil its first level responsibilities may be a reason for second level agents external to it to take action.[35] The content of human rights claims is also ascertained by these three questions (and I shall return to a discussion of this later).

Human rights thus serve a functional role and are thought of as action guiding in that they are 'supposed to provide reasons for actions for agents external to the societies in which they might be violated.'[36] These rights serve another purpose then, because they elucidate aspects of the structure and governance of states about which other states ought to be concerned. States that participate in human rights practice at a global level are expected to play a role as duty bearers in that practice, and to 'make explicit the kinds of linguistic commitments one would undertake if one were to participate in good faith in the discursive practice.'[37]

In his foregrounding of the role of practice in his model of human rights, Beitz stresses that this practice is emerging. Although it consists in considerable architecture such as treaties, agreements and international institutions, the practice is also defined by the political nature of the relationships between parties and by the kinds of discussions and interactions that they have. Participants of the practice engage in critical, reflective disagreement about the structure and value of the practice itself and this is a feature of the model. Through this disagreement Beitz claims that the model 'clarifies the subject matter of this type of disagreement.'[38] It grows in maturity as these disagreements are considered and worked through. He contrasts human rights practice with other 'mature practices' because, unlike these, human rights systems are not recognized for their 'institutional capacities for the authoritative resolution of disputes about the application of norms.'[39] Human rights practice is far from being an established, authoritative, or even exemplified by polished set of mechanisms that work evenly in the adjudication and enforcement of a set of wholly agreed-upon rights. Rather, the practice is uneven; it is sometimes cumbersome, and notable for weaknesses and sometimes glaring inconsistencies in its real-world implementation. Even so, Beitz characterizes these factors as indicators of an emerging global enterprise that shows promise: human rights can function as 'standards of aspiration', as 'shared moral language' and as 'ideals that guide efforts at political change by individuals and nongovernmental organisations.'[40] The practice may be emerging, and its elements immature by some standards, yet Beitz sees no reason to abandon the enterprise as failed. The emergence provides opportunities to understand the complexity of the scope of human rights and to consider 'which substantive values should count as parts of the public doctrine.'[41]

3 Observed practice and quasi-foundations

Given the complexity of statelessness in the modern world, it is unsurprising that questions about human rights claims arise, especially when statelessness is set against Beitz's deceptively neat two-level model. Two of many possible questions are my focus here: first, whether and to what extent questions of efficacy and implementation are considered part of the practice; and second, whether the role of nationality performs a quasi-foundational role in the modern practice of human rights, such that it practically grounds questions about the content and scope of human rights claims. The first of these questions concerns the extent to which we consider questions of implementation and efficiency as part of the modern practice of human rights.

Beitz argues that in defining what is a human right, it is 'self evident that we should take instruction from the public practice in conceptualising . . . [the right] . . . central terms.'[42] However, it is not clear whether and to what extent he considers matters of efficacy and implementation instructive insofar as the content or scope of human rights. What, for example, are we to make of implementation gaps in the practice? Are they to be tolerated as part of an emergent practice or are they somehow limiting of human rights claims themselves? In discussing the human rights of women for instance, Beitz advocates for a functional view where ideal concepts give way to pragmatism. This is so that the pertinent normative questions concern (a) the importance of the threatened interests, (b) the severity of the threats and (c) 'the feasibility and costs of protecting against them by means of human rights.'[43] The functional view is promoted as a way of 'sidestepping' conceptual objections about the existence of the human rights of women *per se*. The threats to the human rights of women are here considered to be not 'typically faced by men' and 'a special subject of concern.' The importance of the interests that are threatened determine their protection even though there is a conceptual question as to whether 'human rights should be "universal" in the sense of being claimable by everyone.' However, by sidestepping one conceptual issue and by making reference to costs and to feasibility, Beitz's account becomes vulnerable to criticisms in which human rights are contingent on the particular set of circumstances that include efficacy of implementation systems and even a general political appetite for the claims at all.

This is an issue that is encountered at several points through Beitz's account, and yet is never explicitly addressed by it. When discussing the various implementation mechanisms that in part constitute the practice, Beitz concedes that these 'are likely to be relatively ineffective', yet his criticism is largely aimed at systems by which states monitor and report on their human rights activities for which he notes there is 'very little systematic evidence about the efficacy of these processes.'[44] Beitz refers to the sceptical view of Emeilie Hafner-Burton and Kiyoteru Tsuitsui in which it is argued that 'governments often ratify human rights treaties as a matter of window dressing, radically decoupling policy from practice and at times exacerbating negative human rights practice', but implies that there is little other substantive work in this area.[45] This seems to be an opportunity missed. If human rights take cues for at least some of their content from observed practice, then it is beholden on us to understand this practice more fully, or at least to understand its broad and systemic weaknesses. Even if Beitz is correct in his claim that there is 'very little systematic' evidence about the efficacy of human rights mechanisms, there is nevertheless a body of scholarly work that analyses factors which influence implementation deficits in more general matters of international law. It is, for example, acknowledged that countries with a high degree of political stability and trust in political systems are more likely to comply with international or supra-national directives,[46] and that even where countries do comply with directives or to treaties to which they are signatories, this compliance is rarely achieved within agreed timeframes.[47] There is similar analysis regarding effective means of countering the implementation deficit in international environmental laws with compliance and enforcement mechanisms,[48] and in public international law more generally.[49]

My point is not that Beitz's account must be predominately empirically informed, or that it should necessarily address practical matters of implementation and the mechanisms through which human rights are institutionalized. Rather, it is to underscore the complexity of taking conceptual cues from observed practice, where this practice is difficult, cumbersome and subject to feasibility considerations. This appears to be critical in the issue of statelessness where, without an effective nationality, people turn to the international community as a guarantor of their human rights. The machinery of the practice is known to be slow and often inefficient, particularly when the international community must coordinate their efforts to fulfil the role of guarantor of human rights. Without building this into a practical account of human rights, it is too easy to conflate issues regarding human rights instrumentation with the existence conditions of human rights themselves. Christian Barry and Nicholas Southwood criticize Beitz's account in this way, arguing that:

> Beitz is surely correct that it is vitally important to pay attention to various kinds of contingent facts about the world global order – the existence of territorially defined states, the absence of world government, and so on – when considering how to *institutionalize* human rights. Moreover, it seems important to pay attention to facts about the way human rights are *currently* institutionalized.[50]

Barry and Southwood argue that taking conceptual cues from the practice can lead to the obscuring of the 'central distinction between human rights and the form in which they should be institutionalized.'[51] This leaves Beitz's account susceptible to an unfortunate conclusion: that where an implementation deficit fails to effectively fulfil the human rights claims of a stateless person, that person has no claim to those human rights. This would mean for example that where it is too difficult for a person to make an effective human rights claim, they do not have that human right. This would mean that where the efforts between countries cannot be effectively coordinated to house or settle an influx of stateless people from a warzone, the human rights of these people does not exist. In terms of statelessness, this would mean that when, in 2014 international efforts to grant a nationality or to safely return the 13.9 million newly stateless persons to their homelands resulted in only a fraction of these (126,800) being resettled, that it is only these 126,800 who – effectively – have a human right to a nationality.[52] It would mean that Europe's failure to resettle 90% of the stateless people arriving by boat in 2015 means that only 10% have this human right to be granted resettlement. Such conclusions are implausible: not only do they violate ideals of equality and fairness (to which Beitz's own account aspires),[53] but they make agreed principles within the practice vulnerable to what may be temporary issues of feasibility or of domestic political expediency.

Political expediency presents a particular challenge for practice-based accounts of human rights, especially in a political climate where tolerance for the rights of migrants is diminishing. This is especially the case where a person turns to the international community in their capacity as guarantor and when there is a smaller appetite for a country to participate in global efforts to fulfil the human rights claims of stateless people. For example, when in 2015 the Australian Prime Minister Tony Abbott refused direct appeals to offer asylum to a group of Rohingya, whose boat had strayed into Australian waters and which had been prevented at least five times from landing by both Thai and Malaysian authorities, he denied that Australia had an obligation to offer assistance to the asylum seekers.[54,55,56] Eschewing any responsibility for fulfilling human rights claims in the capacity of a guarantor, the Prime Minister proclaimed that the sole responsibility for resolving the situation lay with the government that had recently denied citizenship to an entire ethnic group of Rohingya residents: 'In the end the culprit is Burma, it is Burma where there is an issue.'[57] Australia was heavily criticized for this stance, which was compounded by other recent violations of international refugee law, specifically regarding non-refoulement and around the housing of asylum seekers in conditions that the United Nations had likened to torture.[58,59,60] Nevertheless, the Australian government dismissed the criticism, claiming that the country 'was sick of being lectured to' by the United Nations.[61] It is a mistake to assume that these feasibility considerations equate to existence conditions for human rights. It is a mistake to consider that where human rights claims of stateless people remain unfulfilled people like the Rohingya do not have these rights in the first instance.

Beitz's account of human rights attempts to ground the modern practice in 'a pragmatism that is germane to the thought processes of actual human rights policymakers.'[62] This is no easy feat, and the criticisms levelled at the account in this discussion are made in light of this achievement. Issues of pragmatism underscore the complexity of the human rights enterprise and they highlight dynamic tensions with it. If, as Onora O'Neill argues, rights can only co-exist with obligations, and these obligations are 'the creatures of convention, then so too are rights.'[63] If political accounts of human rights eschew theoretical foundations for these rights, then our cues for the fulfilment of them must be taken from the practice itself. Any account of human rights that is predicated on the practice must be able to explain deficits and inconsistencies in the implementation of these rights.

The way that the international community does coordinate its efforts to address statelessness brings to light the importance that nationality plays in the fulfilment of human rights claims in the modern practice. Contemporary efforts to combat statelessness turn on the assignment of an effective nationality, not only in crisis situations such as that currently being experienced in Europe, but also in formally coordinated efforts by bodies like the United Nations. For example, the UNHCR's iBelong campaign specifically encourages combating statelessness by offering stateless persons citizenship of a country that Beitz would label a 'competent participant' in the present international practice of human rights. For instance, one aim of the campaign is to have no child born stateless by 2024, and to do so the agency is working to improve access to documentation for children born in border camps as well as those internally displaced within state borders. Other milestones include granting or confirming nationality of non-refugee stateless persons in major non-refugee statelessness situations, introducing nationality laws that allow women to confer their nationality to their children on an equal basis as men, removal of all nationality laws which permit denial, loss or deprivation of nationality on discriminatory grounds.[64] Efforts by the international community to guarantee human rights appear to be closely tied to the institution of states. Through brokering citizenship arrangements for stateless people, the international community moves a stateless person from occupying a space in international law somewhere between the principles of state sovereignty and humanitarian intervention,[65] and towards a place where, through their belonging, they can effectively make human rights claims.

This approach means that Beitz's claim that the international community acts as a guarantor for human rights is not strictly correct. Where the international community does act for the human rights of the stateless, the action is not necessarily to guarantee their human rights *per se*, but rather to bring about effective access to a body (a state) that can act as a primary duty bearer of human rights. The international community in the practice then does not strictly act as a guarantor of human rights but effects to bring about a 'place in the world' for stateless people. There are strong Arendtian echoes here. If practice shows that human rights are predicated on a right to have rights via access to a state that can act as a primary duty bearer, then the stateless are particularly unlikely to have their claims fulfilled. Although Beitz's account eschews naturalistic and agreement conceptualization of the basis of human rights, the practice suggests that these rights are grounded in a particularly pragmatic way and that nationality acts as a *quasi-foundation* for human rights. Where an implementation deficit fails to connect a stateless person with an effective nationality, there is no foundation upon which their human rights claims can be fulfilled. While the international community may provide basis humanitarian assistance in crisis situations, such as camps on borders, human rights claims can only be guaranteed through an effective nationality. To the extent that the practice fails to provide the stateless with an effective nationality, their human rights claims cannot be guaranteed.

4 Statelessness as a predictable threat

One potential way to strengthen the human rights claims of stateless persons in Beitz's account is to recast the issue of statelessness as a predictable threat to urgent interests in the modern world. Statelessness is a pronounced problem and instances of wide-scale statelessness are predictable, as people cross borders to flee persecution, poverty and war. The current human rights architecture was not designed for the kind of scale of migration we see currently. Recasting this issue would allow the international community to identify possible situations of state succession before they occurred and to identify trends, promote co-operation pre-emptively and mobilize agencies like those of the United Nations.

However, even if statelessness can be recast as a predictable threat to urgent interests, Beitz's account would still need to address problems regarding implementation of preventative and reparative mechanisms. Familiar coordination problems are likely to exist between members of the international community who join in preventative efforts, and contributions of individual states are likely to be just as subject to fluctuations in political will. This is not to say that political will and co-operation between states cannot be stimulated, but rather that the practice shows us that implementation efforts are likely to be imperfect. Even signatories to refugee and statelessness conventions do not always fully participate in efforts to combat statelessness or even to uphold long-standing principles such as non-refoulement. Adding responsibilities around the prevention of statelessness to members of the international community may compound these coordination problems, even where political will can be galvanized. For instance, in September 2015 media images of the body of three-year-old Alan Kurdi, whose body had washed up on a Turkish beach, altered the tenure of the debate about Syrian migrants arriving in Europe by boat. Shocked by the images, European leaders formed more compassionate migration policies.[66] Two days after Alan's death, Germany admitted thousands of refugees who had been stranded in neighbouring Hungary.

Public responses sparked by the pictures of Alan's body were immediate and sympathetic. However, on the first anniversary of the drownings, European countries have resettled less than 10% of the number of migrants that was promised and another 4,000 people have died at sea in the ten months from January 2016 to November 2016 in an attempt to turn to the international community for asylum or resettlement.[67]

In short, Beitz's two-level model of human rights cannot effectively fulfil the human rights claims of stateless people. Without a stronger consideration of the implementation deficit and of the quasi-foundational role of nationality in observed practice, the model is vulnerable to conflating questions of instrumentation with existence conditions of rights themselves. However, the model does allow for the future emergence of mechanisms that could fulfil the human rights claims of the stateless, because the practice is discursive and in the process of maturing. Such mechanisms would need seriously to consider recasting statelessness as a predictable threat to urgent interests and to build stronger expectations about the participation of states in the practice as guarantors of human rights via membership of the international community.

Notes

1 European Commission: Humanitarian Aid and Civil Protection, 'Refugee Crisis in Europe', 2016, http://ec.europa.eu/echo/refugee-crisis_en.
2 United Nations High Commissioner for Refugees (UNHCR), 'Global Trends: Forced Displacement in 2015', 2016, www.unhcr.org/en-au/statistics/unhcrstats/576408cd7/unhcr-global-trends-2015.html.
3 Hugh Massey, 'UNCHR and De Facto Statelessness', *Legal and Protection Policy Research Series* (Geneva: United Nations High Commissioner for Refugees, 2010).
4 Charles Beitz, *The Idea of Human Rights* (Oxford: Oxford University Press, 2009), p. 108.
5 Jacqueline Bhabha, 'From Citizen to Migrant: The Scope of Child Statelessness in the Twenty-First Century', in *Children Without a State,* edited by Jacqueline Bhabha (Boston: The MIT Press, 2011), p. 1.
6 Bhabha, 'From Citizen to Migrant', pp. 1–2.
7 Massey, 'UNCHR and De Facto Statelessness', p. 62.
8 Massey, 'UNCHR and De Facto Statelessness', p. 66.
9 Mary Berry, 'Press Coverage of the Refugee and Migrant Crisis in the EU: A Content Analysis of Five European Countries', 2016, www.media-diversity.org/en/additional files/UNHCR_Cardiff_University_Report_on_EU_Press_Migrants_Coverage_201415.pdf.
10 Bhabha, 'From Citizen to Migrant', pp. 1–4.
11 United Nations, *Universal Declaration of Human Rights* [1948], accessed 12 December 2015, www.un.org/Overview/rights.html#a15.
12 Nations High Commissioner for Human Rights, (2017), accessed 16 February 2017, https://treaties.un.org/pages/ViewDetailsII.aspx?src=TREATY&mtdsg_no=V-3&chapter=5&Temp=mtdsg2&clang=_en and https://treaties.un.org/pages/ViewDetails.aspx?src=TREATY&mtdsg_no=V-4&chapter=5&clang=_en
13 UNHCR, 'Ending Statelessness Within 10 Years: A Special Report', 2014, accessed 21 March 2015, www.unhcr.org/546217229.html; UNHCR, 'A Campaign to End Statelessness: Concept Note', 2014, accessed 18 May 2015, www.unhcr.org/53174df39.html.
14 Ayten Gündoğu, *Rightlessness in an Age of Rights: Hannah Arendt and the Contemporary Struggles of Migrants* (New York: Oxford University Press, 2015). Gündoğu provides an such example in 2007 the Italian government put into effect an emergency decree that allowed nationals of other EU states to be summarily expelled if they were judged to be a threat to 'public safety.' As a result Roma minorities were effectively made stateless and deprived the possibility of appearing before the courts to appeal their expulsion orders.
15 Clara Tran, 'Who Are the Rohingya Fleeing Myanmar by Boat?', *ABC News Online*, 2015, accessed 25 May 2015, www.abc.net.au/news/2015-05-21/explainer-who-are-the-rohingya-fleeing-myanmar/6487130.

16 Tran, 'Who Are the Rohingya Fleeing Myanmar by Boat?'.
17 The Age, 'Nope Is Not Good Enough, Mr Abbott', 2015, accessed 26 May 2015, www.theage.com.au/comment/the-age-editorial/nope-is-not-good-enough-mr-abbott-20150522-gh7hne.html.
18 One such example of this is the 'jungle' that was established by stateless people in Paris in 2016. See www.aljazeera.com/news/2016/10/tent-cities-rise-paris-jungle-evacuation-161030074232527.html.
19 Beitz, The Idea of Human Rights, p. 11.
20 Institute on Statelessness and Inclusion, 'The World's Stateless', 2014, www.institutesi.org/worldsstateless.pdf.
21 United Nations High Commissioner of Refugees, *Global Action Plan to End Statelessness 2014–2024* (Geneva: United Nations High Commissioner for Refugees, 2014), p. 24.
22 Beitz, The Idea of Human Rights, p. 10.
23 United Nations High Commissioner for Refugees, 'Who Is Stateless and Where?', accessed 21 March 2015, www.unhcr.org/pages/49c3646c15e.html.
24 UNHCR, Global Action Plan to End Statelessness 2014–2024, pp. 15, 21, respectively.
25 UNHCR, 'Global Trends: Forced Displacement in 2015'.
26 John Cosgrave, Nicholas Crawford and Irina Mosel, '10 Things to Know About Refugees and Displacement', *Overseas Development Institute*, accessed 7 October 2015, www.odi.org/publications/9916-refugee-crisis-displacement-migration-idp-protracted.
27 BBC World News, 'Number Displaced Worldwide Hits Record High – UN', accessed 7 October 2015, www.bbc.com/news/world-33178035.
28 Cosgrave, Crawford, and Mosel, '10 Things to Know About Refugees and Displacement'.
29 The Economist, 'Europe's Migrant Acceptance Rates', accessed 6 October 2015, www.economist.com/blogs/graphicdetail/2015/09/daily-chart.
30 Eurostat: Statistics Explained, 'Asylum Quarterly Report', accessed 6 October 2015, http://ec.europa.eu/eurostat/statistics-explained/index.php/Asylum_quarterly_report.
31 Eurostat: Statistics Explained, 'Asylum quarterly report'.
32 European Parliamentary Assembly, 'PACE Urges Reform of 'dysfunctional' Dublin Asylum System, Creation of 'European refugee', accessed 6 October 2015, http://assembly.coe.int/nw/xml/News/News-View-EN.asp?newsid=5798&lang=2; Omar Dabbagh, 'Australia's refugee intake cuts questioned as European crisis deepens', *SBS News*, 4 September 2015, accessed 6 October 2016, www.sbs.com.au/news/article/2015/09/04/australias-refugee-intake-cuts-questioned-europe-crisis-deepens.
33 Beitz, The Idea of Human Rights, p. 106.
34 Beitz, The Idea of Human Rights, pp. 101–102.
35 Beitz, *The Idea of Human Rights*, pp. 109, 137.
36 Beitz, The Idea of Human Rights, p. 133.
37 Beitz, The Idea of Human Rights, p. 106.
38 Beitz, The Idea of Human Rights, p. 108.
39 Beitz, The Idea of Human Rights, p. 43.
40 Beitz, The Idea of Human Rights, pp. 43–44.
41 Beitz, The Idea of Human Rights, p. 45.
42 Beitz, The Idea of Human Rights, p. 11.
43 Beitz, *The Idea of Human Rights*, p. 189. The notion of 'strict feasibility' and costs is a topic touched on in Octavio Ferraz's chapter in this volume.
44 Beitz, The Idea of Human Rights, p. 34.
45 Emeilie Hafner-Burton and Kiyoteru Tsutsui, 'Human Rights in a Globalizing World: The Paradox of Empty Promises', *American Jurenal of Political Science* 110 (2005): p. 1373.
46 Risto Lampinen and Petri Uusikylä, 'Implementation Deficit: Why Member States Do Not Comply With EU Directives', *Scandinavian Political Studies* 21, no. 3 (1998): p. 231.
47 Phedon Nicolaides and Helen Oberg, 'The Compliance Problem in the European Union', *EIPAScope* 1 (2006): p. 13.
48 David Freestone and Ellen Hay, The Precautionary Principle and International Law: The Challenge of Implementation (London: Kluwer Law International, 1996).
49 Jan-Erik Lane, 'On the Growth in Normativity in International Relations,' *Journal of Politics and Law* 6, no. 1 (2013): p. 15.

50 Original Italics. Christian Barry and Nicholas Southwood, 'What Is Special About Human Rights?', *Ethics and International Affairs* 25, no. 3 (2011): p. 369.
51 Barry and Southwood, 'What Is Special About Human Rights?'.
52 UNHCR, 'Worldwide Displacement Hits All-Time High as War and Persecution Increase', 18 June 2015, www.unhcr.org/en-au/news/latest/2015/6/558193896/worldwide-displacement-hits-all-time-high-war-persecution-increase.html.
53 See, for instance, the discussion of the 'nondiscrimination' basis to justify the special promotion of the human rights of women, Beitz, *The Idea of Human Rights*, pp. 189–193.
54 UNHCR, 'High Commissioner Zeid: Pushbacks Endanger Thousands in Bay of Bengal', accessed 19 May 2015, www.ohchr.org/EN/NewsEvents/Pages/DisplayNews.aspx?NewsID=15960&LangID=E.
55 Aljjzerra, 'Migrants Rescued Off Indonesian Coast', accessed 23 May 2015, www.aljazeera.com/news/2015/05/scores-refugees-rescued-indonesian-coast-150520021111009.html.
56 George Roberts and James Bennett, 'Tony Abbott Rules Out Resettling Rohingyas in Australia, Indonesia Says It Is Obliged to', *ABC News Online*, accessed 26 May 2015, www.abc.net.au/news/2015-05-21/rohingyas-migrants-indonesia-says-australia-obliged-resettle/6486590.
57 George Roberts and James Bennett, 'Tony Abbott Rules Out Resettling Rohingyas in Australia, Indonesia Says It Is Obliged to', *ABC News Online*, accessed 26 May 2015, www.abc.net.au/news/2015-05-21/rohingyas-migrants-indonesia-says-australia-obliged-resettle/6486590.
58 Non-refoulement is considered an essential component of refugee status and of asylum and is a protection against returning a person to a country where a person has reason to fear persecution. See: www.unhcr.org/en-au/excom/scip/3ae68ccd10/note-non-refoulement-submitted-high-commissioner.html
59 The Guardian, 'UN Accuses Australia of Systematically Violating Torture Convention', 10 March 2015, www.theguardian.com/australia-news/2015/mar/09/un-reports-australias-immigration-detention-breaches-torture-convention.
60 Mary Crock and Hannah Martin, 'Finding Refuge in Australia: How Law and Policies Affect the Entitlements of Children Entering as Refugees and Humanitarian Migrants', in *Creating New Futures: Settling Children and Youth from Refugee Backgrounds*, edited by Mary Crock (Sydney: Federation Press, 2015), pp. 49–52.
61 Lisa Cox, 'Tony Abbott: Australians "sick of being lectured to" by United Nations', *The Sydney Morning Herald*, 2015, www.smh.com.au/federal-politics/political-news/tony-abbott-australians-sick-of-being-lectured-to-by-united-nations-after-report-finds-antitorture-breach-20150309–20150313z3j0.html.
62 Adam Etinson, 'To Be or Not to Be: Charles Beitz on the Philosophy of Human Rights', *Res Publica* 16 (2010): p. 441.
63 Onora O'Neill, 'The Dark Side of Human Rights', *International Affairs* 81, no. 2 (2005): p. 427.
64 The United Nations High Commissioner for Human Rights, '#IBelong', accessed 15 May 2015, www.unhcr.org/en-au/ibelong-campaign-to-end-statelessness.html.
65 Rebecca M.M. Wallace and Frazer A.W. Janeczko, 'The Concept of Asylum in International Law', in *An introduction to International Refugee Law*, edited by Rafiqual Islam and Hossain Bhuiyan (Lieden: Brill, 2013), pp. 133–134.
66 For example, Germany instituted an 'open door' policy and welcomed a million refugees. See: www.abc.net.au/news/2016-09-03/germanys-open-door-refugee-problems-12-months-on/7811116.
67 Patrick Kingsley, 'The Death of Alan Kurdi: One Year On, Compassion Towards Refugees Fades', *The Guardian*, 2016, www.theguardian.com/world/2016/sep/01/alan-kurdi-death-one-year-on-compassion-towards-refugees-fades.

Conclusion

An overview of political approaches to human rights

Rhiannon Neilsen and Tom Campbell

Human rights discourse is in danger of being overwhelmed by its own success not so much in terms of its material outcomes as in the ubiquity of its usage. Human rights have become not only the principal medium in which moral concerns are brought to bear on politics and economics, and indeed on almost every sphere of public human activity, but also the principal ingredient of the burgeoning field of human rights law. Its rhetoric is pervasive while being ill defined and variably applied in almost all dialogues which seek to prescribe moral weight and urgency or demand legal resolutions of certain wrongs.

These exponential developments have taken place despite the foundational weaknesses of the very idea of human rights. At a highly abstract level we can readily conceive of human rights as the rights which all human beings possess in virtue of the fact that they are human beings and endorse their moral significance over that of other rights as the source of stringent obligations to all humans. Yet, once we seek to turn this abstract formulation into more concrete terms, the intelligibility and significance of human rights discourse proves disquietingly elusive.[1] Cementing these notional constituent principles of human rights meets with legal, political and judicial complexities that are not assuredly or neatly rectified.

This process of concretization which renders abstract human rights discourse more specific, both with respect to the content and scope of such rights and in terms of location and force of their correlative obligations, can be short-circuited by going directly to human rights law of one sort or another.[2] However, this tactic simply bypasses the foundational questions as to the moral and epistemological basis of human rights which is a contingent and variable instantiation of the human rights it is designed to protect and promote. It loses in its sights the very moral pertinence and gravity that positions human rights with certain special statuses above other rights. There is a disjuncture between the orthodox formulations of human rights as philosophical articulations of moral rights and the laws that are supposedly borne from these abstractions. We still need to be enlightened as to the underlying moral reality that is said to undergird human rights and explain the special status of human rights law.

Here, we are brought to the realm of the moral considerations which bear upon the political and economic choices that, in a democracy, call for collective consideration, public discussion and collective decision-making. In part this involves the critical identification of the prime human values to which all can be said to universally hold to be true and sacrosanct, such as happiness, creativity, fulfilment of potential, autonomy, love and life itself. In part it involves moral scrutiny of the demands that we make on each other, involving restraint, assistance and co-operation, as we individually or collectively pursue that which we value. In part it requires the careful consideration of the standing agreements and arrangements that serve the morally acceptable collaborative endeavours that constitute human relationships, as well as the more complex institutional structures that are indispensable to sustainable human existence.

Within this complex framework of considerations it may be possible to filter the combination of factors which resonate within the discourse of human rights. Such rights, it may be said, are those things which have the greatest intrinsic value for us; that is, the things what we treasure above all else for their own sake, the things which may be said to constitute our basic interests. But this does not take us far enough. Rights cannot be reduced simply to the interests which attach to individuals. Rights are within the domain of social relationships. Rights are inseparable from duties we have with respect to the interests of others, and establishing what those interests are does not in itself tell us what these duties are but must be reasonable and achievable. Right declarations are in themselves proclamations of demands made to the self and others to have those rights met, and are by nature then innate and extrinsic.

Moreover, many human rights are clearly instrumental rather than or as well as being intrinsic, in that the interests they protect and promote are not, or are not solely, the interests of the right-holder. This applies to human rights as well as to rights in general. Thus the right to freedom of speech protects the interests of the persons whose right it is and serves the wider interests of those others who benefit from the flourishing of human debate. One person's rights to the freedom of speech in essence is a request for all other right-holders to respect that right by not impinging on the expression of that right as long as it does not serve to encroach on the rights of those others. Such rights are entrenched in and serve to bolster the social relationships between right-holders.

This is clearly muddied terrain, from which we cannot be extracted by a few simple self-evident moral beliefs or moral 'intuitions' which lay down what we must never or always do to and with each other. Much moral sifting of values, much reflection on who owes what to whom, and some awareness of how social and legal rules operate in diverse institutional frameworks, are part and parcel of the moral considerations that are required if we are to move defensibly from broad affirmations of general human rights to the sort of specific determinations that can serve to secure the sort of tangible benefits that are promised by human rights rhetoric. It's not that we are to settle on finite and final articulations of moral virtues encompassed in human rights and how this is to be operationalized in social and legal circles. To do so endangers the continual refinement of these duties as human beings advance in all fields, therein bringing new considerations to the fore (for example, certain rights associated with online presences that have yet to be fully explored). Rather, the present situation in human rights dialogues asks for clarity regarding the moral standards and values that are linked to human rights.

Sorting out these moral values and cognate moral duties associated with human rights is but one challenge faced by any attempt to explicate the idea of human rights. Another is the question or how we are to account for and defend not just the priority of human rights over other moral considerations but the practical superiority normally ascribed to human rights over existing social arrangements and current laws in force in actual legal systems. This would seem to require some very firm ontological basis, either in some empirical conception of nature, particularly human nature, or in an objective moral reality whose existence is not dependent on any human recognition, knowledge or application. Such a venture is likely to be laced with complexities, and may see compromises on the part of each approach that serves to dilute the coherence of the ontological basis altogether. Accounting for the priority of human rights – morally, legally, political and judicially – has long been a worthwhile pursuit of human rights, but its importance is more pronounced now than ever.

On the whole, it must be said, that, outside the scope of religious revelation, no such basis is available for making significant progress towards a clear and solid foundation for a universal body of human rights commanding general agreement even within particular cultural traditions. Both moral and philosophical disagreement would appear to vitiate the sort of consensus that could legitimate the position given to human rights in justifying and limiting the coercive conduct of individuals, states and corporations.

All this may be to give too much weight, however, to the concerns of that small minority consisting of politically aware intellectuals who demand proofs and certainties that are not to be found in the sphere of political morality and are unreasonably blind to the clear moral imperatives to prevent the sort of abuses to which bodies such as Amnesty International and Human Rights Watch draw our attention so convincingly on a daily basis. After all, very similar difficulties have been raised continuously since the time of the Universal Declaration of Human Rights (UDHR) in 1948, and indeed long before that, without halting the rise and rise of what may reasonably be called the triumph of the human rights movement in the 'age of human rights'.

There are plenty of signs, however, that the crisis in human rights is no mere philosophical impasse. The global human rights crisis is manifest in the constant controversies that arise over such attempts to pit human rights against the entrenched practices of states and corporations, in the conflict between 'east' and 'west', between Christian, Muslim and secularist, and between socialist and libertarian, and in the diversity of findings in different and indeed in the same human rights courts and other forums. The very success of human rights discourse in colonizing the fields of political debate, legal deliberation and international diplomacy is constantly bringing to light the paucity of their theoretical basis and the indecisiveness of their substance when it comes to the selection of practical implementations. However, the disappointments and setbacks are now endemic in the spheres of human rights and their philosophical accounts. Human rights theoretical virtues and consequence are seemingly selectively chosen, awarded and challenged legal, political or judicial arenas. There is clearly no simple way out of this crisis. At a time when state after state is embracing constitutional systems that draw on outdated conceptions such as natural rights, and international relations are being further and further articulated in terms of human rights, we have more need than ever to address the underlying intellectual problems and moral choices that lie behind current discontents in the multiplying fields of human rights. It is time that human rights dialogues became more than an abstract band-aid for moral injustices and a perceived skeleton key for practically realizing such rights.

The principal strategy offered in this book is a pragmatic one in that it directly addressed the variety of uses to which the language of human rights is put, the variety of issues which it is called upon to solve, and the variety of forums in which it is thought to be decisive. Taken together, this volume finds that what we cannot have is an overarching theory of human rights that suits all purposes and addresses all problems.[3] This involves us approaching human rights as a type or cluster of mechanisms which can be used in different contexts for a variety of different ends. It goes with this approach that the content, and indeed the form, of human rights will morph with the purposes and problems to which their mechanisms are addressed.

At a glance, this may appear to confront unapologetically the underlying assumption that has guided philosophical conceptualizations and applications of human rights since its liberal institutional inception: that human rights are universal and inalienable to all peoples in all contexts. Upon closer analysis, what we are proposing is something more conceptually coherent and empirically viable. The one-size-fits-all theory of human rights not only appears to have fallen short of reifying such moral imperatives in a practical sense, but it consistently highlights the incongruences between the abstract and the legal. By attempting to be true to an autonomous universalizing theory human rights finds itself struggling to articulate its moral poignancy and lacks decisiveness in legal applications. The reductionism of contemporary moral and legal human rights decision-making ultimately oversimplifies and distorts the incommensurable values that all contribute to the substance and form of human rights in context. Understanding human rights as collections of tools to be used in various scenarios to yield various results, rather than a ubiquitous, diluted, far-reaching theory, actually further ensures the universality of its usefulness and applicability. Looking at how human rights can be decisive in its different conceptions means its moral force will not continue to be lost in the gap between abstract explanations and political and legal institutions relating to human rights law.

We may call this approach a political philosophy of human rights partly because it focuses on the political uses of human rights and partly because it comes up with the thesis that the complex process of articulating human rights is ultimately a political matter which ought to take place primarily within political forums, rather than either as abstract moral reflection or on the basis of overriding legal findings.

We are thus freed from the unsupportable burden of producing a comprehensive moral philosophy or an autonomous legal theory of human rights. This does not mean, however that by proposing a political philosophy of human rights we are released from the task of filtering and formulating what may be called the principal human rights values or addressing the range and weight of correlative human rights duties in legal form. Nor can we bypass the challenges of institutionalization. To the contrary, a political philosophy of human rights draws on all these ingredients to provide practical clarification and guidance as to the choices available to us in a variety of very different contexts in which the discourses of human rights are deployed.

Clarifying these matters unveiled interesting aspects of prioritizing a political philosophy of human rights in different ways by each of the contributors. With the intent of traversing the divide between pre-political foundational justifications of human rights and emerging practices and institutions linked to human rights, the contributions, though varied, shed light on disparate aspects of the human rights debate in order to clarify its meaning and moral weight and (perhaps) holding certain political functions to account. These contributions, taken together in the press toward a scaffolding of a political philosophy of human rights, yield complex yet important issues for human rights debate today. This chapter elucidates these issues. It touches on the existence conditions and underlying strengths of human rights. It considers correlative duties and political functions. It demands a democratic core and attention afforded to economic rights. It begins with the crisis alluded to above.

1 The global human rights crisis

As voiced throughout this chapter, a dangerous split has developed between those who seek a foundational justification for human rights and those who simply wish to get on with promoting human rights. This split is manifest in those who want to promote what they call a political, or practical, analysis of human rights that is firmly anchored in human rights practice without going in for what might be called the philosophical or theoretical analysis of the nature of human rights and the moral sources their normative justification. The political approach points to the enormous gains in moral consciousness and the tangible gains in moral practice arising from the human rights movement as it has developed since the end of the Second World War. This movement, they argue, never did involve philosophical or theological or cultural agreement about the justification of human rights. Rather, the human rights movement aimed simply to obtain agreement amongst nations on some concrete human rights standards by reference to which nations could hold each other to account and move towards enforcement on a global scale, involving intervention into national states that violate such standards. They maintained that this could be achieved without agreement on the content, scope and enforcement of human rights as a whole and certainly without reaching a consensus on the moral or religious foundations of the human rights we choose to establish and enforce.

On the other side of the debate are those who are deploy concerns as to what might be called the moral and intellectual legitimation of the human rights movement, which, in their views, requires some demonstration of the intelligibility, authenticity and moral justification of human rights talk and the nature and content of the rights we seek to promote.

The emergence of this split has something to do with the overall failure of the philosophical approach to vindicate human rights and provide persuasive foundational principles to help us with the selection of what is to count as a human right. This is in contrast to the immense and largely unanticipated development of human rights in domestic and international politics. Such a phenomenon is particularly evident in the exponential world-wide growth of provisions for the constitutional protection of human rights and the increasing significance of international human rights law in the sphere of international relations. This has happened despite the ostensibly powerful critiques of human rights from many of those who seek to provide a reasonably rigorous analysis of the very idea of human rights in conjunction with a coherent and persuasive attempt to realize its potential.

It is these competing claims and the disjointed way in which the two approaches try to coalesce (amidst meticulous but important scepticism) that undergirds the crisis facing human rights. Ultimately, the orthodox conceptualizations of human rights that emphasize the *de novo*, evincible moral legitimation of human rights falls flat in practical realization; political approaches, with their concerns of tangibility, often forfeit the moral force that precisely prescribes the importance of the special status of human rights in the first instance. A political philosophy of human rights that does not lose sight of these ethical grounds in these legal, political and constitutional practices is the proposed departure point for future contributions to human rights studies. Tom Campbell in this volume, for instance, advances that the political approach can be altered to incorporate human rights morality and advocates a greater interactive relationship between the ethical justifications for human rights and its practice to achieve this aim. Providing a healthy note of caution to this, Caroline West encourages us to critically ask if it would be desirable to see a wide acceptance of the practical conception of human rights practice. Given its purely descriptive qualities, the practice-dependent theory of human rights may in fact place too much trust – and well-intentioned assumptions – on the people and institutions discharged with the responsibility to guarantee and protect human rights. In this sense (and nodding warily at the latest developments in international politics that has seen a rise in ethnocentric, religiously intolerant politicians and an increasing exasperation with liberal institutions), West argues that prioritizing a practical conception risks subverting the very ends that justify human rights practice.

Yet there is also problematic selectivity and inconsistency within these distinct approaches. For example, Denise Meyerson points out that Charles Beitz and Joseph Raz arbitrarily restrict the normative theorizing necessary for the advancement and relativity of human rights. Appearing to force a square into a circle, both narrow and distort their theories to such an extent that they become normatively implausible and misaligned with practice.

A reliance on international human rights practice for defining what meets the category of human rights problematically commits Beitz and Raz to the view that in the instance domestic bodies act against states because they have violated moral rights, such moral rights cannot count as human rights. Meyerson concludes that Beitz and Raz attempt to mesh 'independently attractive' normative beliefs with a 'recalcitrant practice'. Similarly, according to John Tasioulas, there is a gathering compromise position, which commits the modified orthodox approach with a political approach, which acknowledges its moral presuppositions, leaving the extremities engaged in quasi-scholastic hair-splitting. Contrary to the view that discourse of human rights is rampantly ambiguous as between moral aspiration and empirical prediction regarding political ascendancy, Tasioulas argues that the orthodox view is in fact 'parasitic' to such an account rather than rival to it.

Evidently, there is a crisis that faces human rights. The need to resolve these tensions is urgent and genuine. In an effort to further understand the fractures and agreements within these debates, the volume highlighted the centrality of the existence conditions and underlying strengths of human rights.

2 The existence conditions and the underlying strengths of human rights

Married to the global human rights crisis is the alleged existential inadequacy of orthodox definitions of human rights as those rights that all persons have in virtue of their humanity. Debates about existence conditions necessarily shape conceptual and practical paths toward a coherent political philosophy of human rights. One such is between those who see human rights as powerful normative forces and those who think that human rights are not real unless they are marked by observable social and political recognition through the institutionalization of rules involving a degree of understanding and enforcement. Duncan Ivison's sustained insistence in this volume that such practical recognition is an indispensable part of the existence conditions for human rights, and that such existence conditions are related to practical effectiveness by pointing to the overall situatedness of human rights, is a profound example of the latter. It illustrates claims that human rights serve the interests of a specific societal group with distinct historical, social, legal, political, traditional and cultural structures. By viewing human rights in this way, the diverse language of rights can be translated and re-negotiated across groups – and that this should be encouraged rather than syphoning all groups into the singular language of liberal democratic human rights.

These two houses – those orthodox that believe that individuals have human rights in virtue of being human and those that maintain that institutions are critical to human rights existence – may be able to come together. Moving away from dividing extant claims of universal truths and toward a multifaceted and fluid conception that accepts the normative existence of such rights, while simultaneously accepting the necessity for political institutions to realize these claims, the former is utopian rhetoric without the latter, and the latter lacks moral force or necessity without the former. Suzy Killmister ultimately elects a hybrid account of human rights based on dignity that sees human rights as constituted through social norms, thereby dismissing the traditionalist claim that human rights are necessarily pre-institutional while congenitally recognizing the role pre-institutional rights have within such social norms. She also allows space for 'moral foundations' to speak to human rights as a political construct, making the important distinction between *being dignified* – acting in a dignified way – and *having dignity* – which is not inherent to persons, but rather gained in the instance the agent is subject to normative standards. Striking a balance between orthodox and political conceptions, Killmister agrees with the anti-foundationalist/ anti-orthodox conception of human rights without rejecting the normative necessity of human rights. Conversations like these concern the existence conditions of human rights. It leads to questions like: if a right is not recognized, even theoretically, does it exist? Do rights necessarily require a degree of recognition (by someone or something, and indeed, who?) of their existence to be brought into existence? In both the orthodox and political conceptions of human rights, such rights are acknowledged to exist – what is debated is *how*.

Settling upon positive presentations of human rights values, including the distinctive content of equal worth, dignity, respect for persons, capabilities, and human rights duties, including their grounding in justice, humanity and prudence, as well as determining what exactly awards human rights its distinctive 'moral' or 'urgent' quality are further speculations borne out of these debates. What should the underlying core content of human rights encompass? What is the criteria that entitles one to a human right, and are these prerequisites for defining a human right?[4] Why *these* grounding principles? What sets these aside from other rights claims in a way that is 'special' and what awards them this status? Who has a voice in deciding this? Who is silenced? In this volume, by concentrating on questions relating to review of human rights' ontology, epistemology and purpose, Jovana Davidovic maintains that it is possible to have an account of human rights that is grounded in practice, rather than seeking the normativity that accompanies natural rights dialogues. She asks what exactly counts as a conceptual account of human rights and what the purpose of such an account would be. Killmister follows a more foundational path which argues for grounding the normativity of human rights on human dignity, whilst adopting a *political* analysis of the role of dignity in human rights discourse and practice. Establishing the existence conditions for human rights alongside the underlying normative strengths and criteria for human rights are imperative to responding to the short-falls of extant human rights discourses.

Grappling with the necessary existence conditions and innate moral strengths of human rights continue to occupy this space. Entering into the political function via various analytical contributions, the volume raises interesting points concerning correlative human rights duties from the macro (international) to micro (individual). It forcefully appraises the long-held belief that has shrouded human rights responsibilities which claims states, and often only states, are accountable for individuals' human rights protection and actualization. This examination is a testimony to our own responsibility as students, scholars, lawyers and practitioners of human rights, to remain critical of the expectations we can reasonably make of others and ourselves.

3 Correlative duties and the political functions of human rights

A coherent political philosophy of human rights is by its very nature concerned with the political functions of human rights. Congenital to this is putting human rights to work in different spheres as judicial review, corporate social responsibility, humanitarian intervention, legislative scrutiny, international trade, global poverty and statelessness. Such emphasis on the political functions of human rights and identifying correlative duties are spurred by the necessity to determine who – or what – can or should be regarded as duty bearers for realizing and protecting human rights in such instances. Rights are demands with reciprocal expectations; to expect a right to be discharged makes the assumption that someone or something, formal or informal, has a responsibility to ensure these rights.[5] These questions are becoming more pertinent in the 21st century, as some social institutions, enterprises and corporations are surpassing nation-states as some of the post powerful and oppressive bodies.

The sheer capability of such institutions alone leads to notions of human rights violations responses, especially if the violation is a consequence of or connected to the organization.[6]

Laura Valentini made a strong case for including transnational corporations as qualifying for human rights duty bearers, while holding to what may be seen as characteristic of political approaches according to which the duties always fall on political agents. In doing so she examined a political approach which confines the allocation of the duties correlative to human rights, not to states alone, but, more generally to those political agents who have 'an authority-plus-sovereignty package' and 'have the capacity to discharge them [the duties]'. She highlights the distinction between primary duty bearers (those who have '*stringent obligations* to *secure . . . respect, protect, and fulfill* human rights'), and secondary duty bearers (those who have 'remedial' responsibilities in the instance were the primary duty bearer is unable or unwilling to discharge their responsibilities). Identifying human rights duty bearers (which satisfy certain criteria) beyond the conventional state is a crucial and timely pursuit for those occupied with human rights conversations and practice, especially in our globalized and interconnected world. To do so is paramount to appropriately shaping not only allocations of blame and praise, but also to articulating who or what we can turn to with the expectations of response or restraint.

In a similar vein, we are prompted to consider whether individuals or small groups of individuals – not just large official organizations – can be discharged with human rights responsibilities. Holding an individual account for the violation of another's human rights has a profound impact on the way in which we consider notions of blame and responsibility. One such case is made compellingly by Sonu Bedi, who argued that individuals can be bearers of human rights responsibilities, citing what he calls the 'horizontal effect' in the example of domestic violence. Although human rights law does not consider perpetrators of domestic violence as violating the human rights of their victims, individuals as recipients of rights duties not to violate human rights means human rights responsibilities can be placed directly on individuals. Bedi therein tears down the private and intimate sphere that shrouds domestic violence, a violation of human rights that is shielded from legal counter measures by the assumption of the principle of privacy in intimate relationships. Extant human rights literature can further consider such sentiments concluded by looking to the cosmopolitanism approach to human security (both in terms of freedom from want and freedom from fear), wherein each individual can be considered responsible to an extent for the security of others simply by refraining from compromising that security in an unacceptable way.[7] As in many cases where it is the individually perpetrated act that strips another of their fundamental human rights – as well as the complicit failing of the state not to obstruct or punish such an act – this is an important consideration to be made in regard to human rights practice. Seumas Miller in his chapter on the human right to self-defence as a natural, legal, and political right further forces the individual into the spotlight of rights realizations, the necessary conditions of these moral rights and considerations of concomitant moral obligations.

Another interesting point to come out of these discussions is the idea of institutions having the duty to pre-emptively prepare for human rights catastrophes, rather than simply responding in the face of adversary. According to Kylie Bourne's account, Beitz's assertion that the international community acts as a 'guarantor' for human rights is inaccurate; rather, the international community guarantees the effective access to the state as the primary duty bearer of human rights. By re-casting the reality of stateless peoples as a 'predictable threat' to international peace and stability, Bourne moves beyond simply ascribing states as institutions of discharging and protecting human rights. Instead, she advocates for the international community to act co-operatively and pre-emptively prior to wide-scale statelessness.

Such calls to the international community 'and those acting as its agents'[8] as guarantors for access to human rights prompt questions regarding the elusive but liberally used term 'international community'. Here we return to the need for clearly defining correlative duties and, in doing so, determining which constituent bodies can be coherently expected to discharge such human rights responsibilities. The 'international community' has been used to refer to international organizations (such as the United Nations), as well as the general constellation of all states working individually, collaboratively or collectively. Are the in-vogue 'coalitions of the willing', as a group of states, representative of the international community?[9] Or by exclaiming that the international community must 'do something' we really mean certain states with greater capacity and opportunity to intervene? With the changing face of war-wagers often called upon to act in the face of grave human rights violations and depravity, private military contractors could also be considered duty bearers. The phrase 'international community', while often incited with a degree of gravity and immediacy, lacks clarity and it is in this opacity that pointed accountability is lost.

Perhaps what is needed is a clear account of moral agents of human rights responsibilities conceived of in three, inter-locking ways. The first as those who/what are responsible for discharging or awarding such human rights – the positive act of providing the opportunity of rights for individuals. The second could be those who/what are responsible for merely refraining from human rights abuses. The third are those who/which can be reasonably expected to respond to human rights violations. In each of these cases it is paramount to hold each accountable for failing to perform their responsibilities; in each case a moral agent can be coherently regarded as having one, two or three of these responsibilities. Establishing correlative responsibilities for human rights is fundamental to further elucidating a political philosophy of human rights. In tandem is settling upon who decides the form of human rights which should be taken in its various situations (and how), and balancing human rights' inherently democratic core with the majoritarian decision-making processes attached to democracy.

4 The democratic core and enabling human rights

There are two core themes that arise from the volume that is discussed in this section. The first concerns the democratic core of human rights. Taking up issues relating to deciding who decides when it comes to determining the form and content of the human rights that are to be applied in different contexts, this volume considers the need for the essentially fundamental role of democratic decision-making, but of a type quite different from the caricature of 'majoritarian democracy' set up as the target of those who favour juristocracy. What must be emphasized is not the greatest-number-rules process of democracy but the very moral-rich foundations distinct to democracy itself. A rejection of the version of democracy that takes both the process of majoritarian decision-making with the embellished morally virtuous sentiments is canvassed in a way by James Allan. One of the most profound contributions for this chapter is Allan's position that extant human rights practices undermine the extent of democratic decision-making in the firmly established democracies today. Allan toys with the idea of keeping a country's decision-making processes separate from whether those decisions are respectful of human rights or morally acceptable. Although getting at the democratic heart of human rights' morally normative weight, such a position invariably raises concerns regarding how these two are to be kept detached, and one favoured over the other, and how this should be pursued.

The second major theme that articulates this volume's value is the focus on the enabling (yet, if denied, simultaneously disabling) factors of human rights as the true normative focus of rights themselves. Whether we think of it as digits on a bank screen or the sheer ability to secure food each day, finance must persist being a focus in the human rights rhetoric. Put perfectly by David Kinley, economics and human rights are intimately bound to one another. The sheer existential fact is that their relationship is parasitical: 'Neither exists, nor can flourish, in the absence of the other'.[10] To casually put aside economic human rights as peripheral or luxury rides roughshod over the true rudimental condition for humans to exist: subsistence. The very dismissal of economic human rights in dominating human rights discourses is a signpost of privilege.

Many have conceded the unequal attention afforded to (and, indeed, the neglect of) economic and social human rights over that of civil and political. Octavio Ferraz supposes that this phenomena in human rights is due to the inadequacy of social human rights conceptions – notably, their lack of a stable consensus concerning their justification and content, or what he terms 'indeterminacy'. Moving away from the basic needs conception, Ferraz proposes an equality conception: an equal opportunity to meet basic needs. This sentiment sets the benchmark for human rights practice. Rather than pursuing the minimal standards of needs as rights themselves, a more legitimate approach is to think of social and economic rights as rights to equal opportunity that empower individuals. Atop Ferraz's convincing framework that draws on extant empirical data toward specification of the minimum thresholds, how might a complete equal opportunity complex look in the 21st century, taking stock of the tapestry of socio-economic inequalities, systemic violences, gendered divides, cultural prejudices, prerogatives, traditions and histories within each state, let alone globally? Harking back to the overtones of the democratic core, how is an 'equal opportunity' complex to be decided on, and by whom?

Democracy and human rights are largely considered part and parcel of one another. Demands for fulfilling notions of dignity and worth are thought to be antidotes to undemocratic, oppressive regimes, collectivities and ideologies. But to agree with the central tenets of such a political disposition does not mean we are excused from critically examining democracies' ever-changing façade to serve itself at the cost or dismissal of human rights. Political correctness, for instance, is as rife as it is held to ransom by both sides of the political spectrum in states thought to be the mantelpieces of democracy. In an age of President Donald Trump, Senator Pauline Hanson, recent Presidential Candidate Marine Le Pen, and Brexit, political correctness in democratic nations is debated as the very contagion causing segregation and enmity rather than championing or protecting the rights of all (but especially those thought to lack them most). Identified marginalities and feared majorities are ever increasingly fiercely vilified and rejected in those democratic nations that have long espoused best-practice and speaking political correctness, dealing in stereotypes. Appraising current democracy – economics, history, social and politics – and its convergence with rights philosophy and practice is paramount to conversations in human rights and diversity (apparently) cherished by democracy.

5 The need for the future of human rights

The future of human rights studies is facing a divide. For too long, disparate approaches have engaged in acontextual conceptual battles that gravely threaten human rights' coherence and relevance. In an era where there is a growing alienating disconnect between the 'haves and have nots' in both developed and developing nations, wrangling anti-foundationalist and political human rights ontologies into futile obscurity inadvertently further cements this gulf and detracts from its content, normativity and pursuit. This volume is a step back from the cliff-face. But it is only one step.

The choice to reject prevailing jargoned stalemates in the pursuit of something more philosophically and practically plausible is the triumph of the emerging conversations in human rights. The need is to continue such efforts, to seek to be critical, and to work toward a coherent political philosophy of human rights that is flexible, inclusive and truly universal.

Notes

1 James Griffin, *On Human Rights* (Oxford: Oxford University Press, 2008), p. 192.

2 Charles Beitz, *The Idea of Human Rights* (Oxford: Oxford University Press, 2009), p. 13.

3 Despite advocating for a distinct approach to what is laid here, Beitz alludes to a similar sentiment in the final pages of his *The Idea of Human Rights:* it would be a mistake to conceive of human rights 'in one or a few clear moral ideas, to formulate a canonical list of rights, or to devise a single authoritative means for bringing them to bear on practical choices.' See Beitz, *The Idea of Human Rights,* p. 212.

4 David Miller, 'Joseph Raz on Human Rights', in *Philosophical Foundations of Human Rights,* edited by Rowan Cruft, S. Matthew Liao, and Massimo Renzo (Oxford: Oxford University Press, 2015), p. 241.

5 According to Onora O'Neill, human rights and obligations are presented as 'corollary normative claims', yet the matter stands that there are some right-claims that go unanswered and unaccounted for; we cannot coherently speak of there being 'some universal rights' unless we identify 'counterpart obligations'. See Onora O'Neill, 'The Dark Side of Human Rights', *International Affairs* 81 (2005): p. 433.

6 For an account grounded in moral theory, see Jilles L.J. Hazenberg, 'Transnational Corporations and Human Rights Duties: Perfect and Imperfect', *Human Rights Review* 17, no. 4 (2016): pp. 479–500. See also David Karp, *Responsibility for Human Rights: Transnational Corporations for Imperfect States* (Cambridge: Cambridge University Press, 2014), especially ch. 4; Ivar Kolstad, 'Human Rights and Assigned Duies: Implications for Corporations', *Human Rights Review* 10, no. 4 (2009): pp. 569–582.

7 On security cosmopolitanism, see Anthony Burke, 'Security Cosmopolitanism', Critical Studies on Security 1, no. 1 (2013): pp. 13–28.

8 Beitz, The Idea of Human Rights, p. 108.

9 See, for example, Toni Erskine, 'Coalitions of the Willing and Responsibilities to Protect: Informal Associations, Enhanced Capacities and Shared Moral Burdens', *Ethics and International Affairs* 28, no. 1 (2014): pp. 115–145.

10 Kinley chapter page number for the quote

Index

For Product Safety Concerns and Information please contact our EU representative GPSR@taylorandfrancis.com Taylor & Francis Verlag GmbH, Kaufingerstraße 24, 80331 München, Germany

Batch number: 10726294

Printed by Printforce, the Netherlands